BIG BROTHER
THE OFFICIAL UNSEEN STORY

BIG BROTHER
THE OFFICIAL UNSEEN STORY

JEAN RITCHIE

First published 2000 by Channel 4 Books
an imprint of Macmillan Publishers Ltd
25 Eccleston Place, London SW1W 9NF
Basingstoke and Oxford

www.macmillan.com

Associated companies throughout the world

ISBN 0 7522 1912 X

A CIP catalogue record for this book is available from the British Library.

Designed and typset by Blackjacks
Printed and bound by Mackays of Chatham plc

This book accompanies the television series *Big Brother*, made by Bazal for Channel 4.
Executive Producer: Ruth Wrigley
Series Editor: Conrad Green

Picture Acknowledgements
Contestant photographs by Amanda Searle except the following: Peter Aitchison: 8 (*br*),
13 (*tl and b*), 14 (*tl and br*), 16 (*all*); Grenville Herrald and Craig Watson: 1 (*b*);
Chris Ridley: 15 (*b*); Michelle Sadgrove: 9 (*t*), 10 (*t*).

Acknowledgements
The author would like to thank the Big Brother production team and all the contestants
for their help. Particular thanks to (in alphabetical order, like the nominations): Toni
Cox, Sandy Fone, Jonathan Francis, Helen Hawken, Roger Houghton, Colin Pigott,
Gemma Wickes, Verity Willcocks, Keith Woodhams, Ruth Wrigley.

CONTENTS

10 CONTESTANTS

9 WEEKS

1 HOUSE

On half an acre of derelict land next to the River Lea in East London, encircled by high, metal security fences topped with razor wire, stands a strange-looking building – a space-age bungalow made from what appears to be silver foil. There are no external windows, a plain blue door, and the scrubland surrounding the building is covered with weeds threaded with duckboards. To get to the building, you have to cross a bridge over Bow Creek, part of the lock system of the river. Over the summer months of the year 2000, security men policed the gate and two guards with dogs were on constant patrol.

High security was paramount because *everybody* in the UK wanted to know what was going on inside the walls of this particular building. The surreal structure was home for sixty-four days to the contestants of *Big Brother*, the Channel 4 television show that became compulsive viewing for millions of people. Six evenings a week, viewers tuned in to watch the inhabitants going about their lives inside the house. Millions more watched live pictures of them on the show's website. All their movements were tracked by cameras; all their conversations were recorded by microphones. The result was part documentary, part soap opera, part game show and part nature programme. Altogether, these elements combined to make *Big Brother* the most fascinating, compelling and ground-breaking series to hit British television for years.

Essentially, *Big Brother* was a game show, but a game show like no other. Ten contestants were carefully selected to live in a controlled environment with no contact with the outside world: no radio, television, telephone, post, or even music. Due to the constant presence of the cameras and microphones, they were never out of the spotlight; there was no half-time in this game, no chance to recuperate. Everything they said and did twenty-four hours a day was exposed. To survive, they all had to co-operate with one another but, at the same time, they were in competition with each other.

Once a week, each of the players in the house chose two of their fellow contestants to be evicted. Their nominations were added up, and those with the two highest number of votes were announced as candidates for eviction. Voting then took place outside the house, with viewers telephoning in their choice, and with the candidates facing an agonizing four-day wait for the verdict. Every Friday evening, for eight weeks, one of the contestants had to pack his or her bags and leave the *Big Brother* house behind, forfeiting the chance of picking up £70,000 in prize money. When the number was reduced to three, the vote was to find the overall winner.

Specially built for the show, the house had two bedrooms, each with five beds, all single except for one double. There was a spacious open-plan living, dining and kitchen area, and a toilet, washroom and shower room. There were two other important rooms: the Store Room and the Diary Room. The Store Room, which was unlocked for the contestants for only one hour a day, is where their food and supplies were kept. The Diary Room was small with a large purple chair facing a camera: it is in here that the contestants could talk to Big Brother, the unseen presence who ruled their lives in the house. They could choose to talk, or they could be summoned to the Diary Room by a disembodied voice. They could also, at any time, ask for a private conversation with a counsellor, and this was the only time in the whole *Big Brother* experience that they could talk without any risk of what they said being broadcast to the nation.

Watching how people react to extreme circumstances has been done on television before, but *Big Brother* was the first time in Britain that ordinary people had been observed right around the clock, with cameras filming even while they slept, and for a long period of time, nine weeks in all. Before the programme launched it was accused of being voyeuristic, even pornographic. In fact, its main fascination for viewers had nothing to do with occasional glimpses of nudity. What held the nation enthralled was observing the interplay between the contestants, eavesdropping on their private conversations, participating in their plotting and planning for survival, speculating about their romantic feelings for each other. The ten contestants, and particularly those who survived to the last rounds, became as familiar as close friends and family to a television audience that had become addicted to them. Their lives became as compulsive viewing as any soap, with the added frisson that it was all happening for real, and nobody was writing the script.

The continuous presence of cameras meant that *Big Brother*, a phrase that originates from George Orwell's novel *1984*, was the obvious name for the show. Orwell envisaged a futuristic society in which the state, or Big Brother, could watch everybody's movements at all times. The year 1984 has come and gone and, fortunately, the world bears no resemblance to his nightmarish vision of life under the microscope. However, one part of his prediction has come true: we do now have the technology to keep a permanent eye on any part of our environment that we choose (we are already doing so with CCTV cameras). So when the idea for a television show which observed people for twenty-four hours a day, seven days a week, first came up, it was natural to dub it *Big Brother*. By coincidence, the show was broadcast in the year of the fiftieth anniversary of Orwell's death.

The first *Big Brother* television show was not British. The idea came from Holland, where the format was mulled over and refined for three and a half years before it hit Dutch screens in the autumn of 1999. Nobody predicted how big a hit it would be; it averaged a million viewers per show, out of a total population of fifteen million. By the final programme, when the winner was declared, more than 70 per cent of television viewers in Holland were tuned in to *Big Brother*. It had the second highest ratings of any programme for the whole year – the highest was a news programme covering the declaration of war in Kosovo.

Inevitably, other countries were interested in emulating the Dutch success. Germany was the second country to run *Big Brother*. Then came Spain, where viewers were treated to three daily episodes from the house. The Americans also ran it on CBS, starting just a few weeks ahead of the British show, and clocking up a healthy twenty-two million viewers for the first episode. Interestingly, only the Spaniards translated the name, calling it *Gran Hermano*. Both the Dutch and German programmes used the English name. Other countries, including New Zealand, Australia, South Africa, Sweden and Portugal, are producing their own *Big Brother*s, while in Holland and in Germany they are running a second series.

In Britain, Bazal, being linked to the Dutch company which invented *Big Brother*, had the first option on using the format. After an initial trip to Holland by the managing director, Nikki Cheetham, and the creative director, Peter Bazalgette, it was decided to go ahead with the British show. The project was handed over to Sandy Fone, who became the production executive, and Helen Hawken, who was working in the project development department of Bazal. Helen Hawken subsequently became senior producer on-line and omnibus producer on *Big Brother*. Bazal was a natural home for an innovative and experimental series, having pioneered shows like *Changing Rooms, Ground Force* and *Ready, Steady, Cook*, all of which have an element of unpredictability and participation by ordinary viewers. However, everyone agrees that nothing prepared them for the scale of the *Big Brother* production.

Eight months after Sandy and Helen started work on the project in November 1999, the programme was going out six days a week, including two live half-hour shows, a one-hour documentary, a one-hour omnibus and three half-hour shows. Only television news had a bigger weekly output. Like the news, nothing on the *Big Brother* programmes could be prepared and edited more than a few hours in advance, and the content of the programmes, like the news, could not be predicted or orchestrated. Everything was dependent on what happened in the house and the production staff had no influence over this. While going about their everyday lives in the strange environment of the *Big Brother* abode, the contestants were calling the shots and dictating the stories.

Events in the house were also being broadcast live on the internet, twenty-four hours a day. Viewers could see four different live pictures of what was happening at any one time and could hear the contestants talking to each other. There have been other live twenty-four-hour net broadcasts in Britain (Netaid, for example) but never any which had run for so long or included so many streams of pictures.

Sandy and Helen spent two days in Holland, during that time they had to absorb the complex logistics of making the programme. When they returned to Britain, they beavered away, frantically writing reports – Sandy working on the budget and Helen on the schedule of finding a site, recruiting staff, starting the building of the house and, vitally, choosing contestants.

'Remarkably, it more or less went according to that first master plan, although with lots of minor modifications along the way,' says Helen.

By January, it was agreed that the programme would go out on Channel 4 and that the winning contestant would walk away with £70,000. It had to be a reasonable amount; people were being asked to give up as much as nine weeks to live in the house, which in many cases would mean handing in their notices at work. It was also stipulated that the programme should not just show what went on in the house, but should explore human relationships with the help of top psychologists.

The *Big Brother* production team grew rapidly. By February, executive producer Ruth Wrigley was in place and one of her first jobs was to build up a core of staff. By the time the show was up and running, 200 people were working on *Big Brother*, including a pool of fifty cameramen and thirteen producers.

Ruth, who started her career as a journalist and worked for London Weekend Television for ten years, was not fazed by the formidable task. She had been involved in setting up *The Big Breakfast* with Chris Evans and Gaby Roslin and had rejoined it for the relaunch with Johnny Vaughan and Denise van Outen. She then moved to Bazal to produce *The National Lottery Show* with Brian Conley.

She was excited by the *Big Brother* project, but felt the format that had been used in Holland and Germany needed some modification for the British audience.

'We were planning to put it out late in the evening, whereas it had been on at 8 p.m., in a family viewing slot, over there. It was a bit too slow. We needed it to be pacier and more sophisticated. The audience at that time of the evening is young, used to watching movies, videos, lots of television. In Holland and Germany, they evicted someone from the house every two weeks – we stepped it up to every week. So our show ran for sixty-four days instead of a hundred, and it had a younger, sharper audience,' she says. 'Staffing it was like staffing a mini-channel. I needed to find twenty-two directors, thirteen producers, endless editors, researchers and runners. Luckily, I knew a big pool of people, many of whom had worked on *The Big Breakfast* and were used to the pressures of live television. We were producing a phenomenal amount of television. Every Monday evening we put on a one-hour documentary; it normally takes six to eight weeks to turn round a documentary, and we were doing it in twenty-four hours.

'Producers were working through the night, on twenty-four-hour shifts, to do the half-hour programmes that went out on Tuesday, Wednesday and Thursday evenings, and then we had two live shows on Friday plus the omnibus. For all of us, it was unlike anything we had done before. Normally, with a TV show, you produce it – you decide what shape it will take. With this, every twist and turn was down to the behaviour and personalities of the people in the house, and it was our job to craft what they gave us and turn it into digestible programmes.'

The team did not want to impose their own perspective on the show – they wanted it to be as truthful as possible. For this reason, the voice-over commentary was kept to a minimum, and only reported facts without editorial comment.

'One of the greatest moments for me was when Sada left the house and watched the videos and, in an interview, said that she felt that what we presented was very truthful. She'd been expecting it to have a slant, but it didn't,' says Ruth. 'We all had to learn new skills. Sitting in the gallery with thirty cameras showing the inside of the house, and not knowing where anyone would go next or what they would do, was a strange feeling. We had to cover the action, but we had no control over it. It wasn't a gradual learning curve, it was a vertical ascent. Programmes had to be made so fast there was no time to spend agonizing over the rushes. Having done *Big Brother*, I'll never be scared of anything again.'

Ruth was determined that the British *Big Brother* would live up to expectations: 'I made up a system of working that involved the producers doing a twenty-four-hour shift when it was their turn to produce one of the week-night shows. They had a whole day's material to select from. As the contestants did not often go to bed early, this could stretch well on into the night. Then they had to cut a package during the rest of the night so that a rough version of the programme was ready the next morning for me to see. They would then spend that day refining it, ready for transmission that evening. They then had two days off, worked normal shifts for four days, and then hit the big twenty-four-hour marathon again. It was the only way to get the continuity we needed.'

Ruth also wanted the live Friday evening shows to have a feeling of excitement and urgency about them. It didn't matter if cameras came into shot, or if the set looked like what it essentially is – a huge hangar, with the control room attached.

'The audience we attracted understand television, they've grown up with it, they know its grammar. The crew was used to working in light entertainment, and they assumed we'd have the sort of set where a presenter like Cilla Black would walk on and everything would happen smoothly and seamlessly around her. But that's not what I wanted. I wanted it to look live and exciting, I wanted viewers – and the contestants who were evicted – to see the control room, to get an idea of all the behind-the-scenes work.

'After all, this was not meant to be a piece of polished drama. We were filming it for real, and it was a virtue of the programme that viewers understood that.'

Before all this, one of the main problems the team faced was finding a site. *Big Brother* could not be made in any television studio; adequate space was needed so that a whole house could be built. Sandy Fone spent two months seeing lots of different places, including sites at Shepperton, Radlett and Bushey, before the Three Mills Studio site at Bromley-by-Bow in East London was eventually chosen. It was decided early on that there should be a short distance between the house and the studio, so that the contestant who was evicted could be filmed making what was dubbed on set as 'the walk of doom'. This meant that the site had to include premises for a studio plus a nearby plot for the building of the house. There were always problems: on one site the house would be so far from the studio that the evicted contestant would have to travel in a buggy; on another there was a planning restriction that said nobody was allowed to sleep there overnight. In the end, the Three Mills site was the best.

'The site was nicely isolated, and there was the attraction of going across a bridge over the river,' says Sandy.

Three Mills Studio is a complex of old brewery, distillery and mill buildings. There has been a mill on the site since the *Domesday Book* records and its claim to fame is that it is the oldest tidal mill in Britain. It has not been used as a mill since the Second World War and the spacious old buildings have been converted into studios for the film, television and music industries. Mike Leigh used them to prepare the cast for his Oscar-winning *Topsy-Turvy*, and other recent British films that have been shot there include the All Saints' movie, *Honest*, *The Guv'nor*, and *Love is the Devil*. The TV series *London's Burning* and *Bad Girls* are filmed there also.

The land across the river, where the house stands, had lain derelict for years. Temporary planning permission was obtained from Newham Council to put up the house, and work started on clearing the area and gutting the studio. *Big Brother* took over the furthest studio in the complex, closest to the house site, and Sandy's first job was to have a load of rusting machinery removed from the adjacent yard. The studio was gutted to prepare it for the Friday evening live shows, and the control room was set up. This room, the nerve centre of the whole production, looked like the flight deck of the Starship *Enterprise*, with two banks of desks, twelve in all, facing thirty-nine wall-mounted screens feeding pictures to ten different video recorders. At all times, day and night, two loggers recorded everything that was going on in the house on special computer software.

Outside, in the cleared yard, fourteen temporary prefabricated cabins were erected, seven on the ground with another seven stacked on top. These became home to the editorial and production staff for the whole of the summer of 2000. The accommodation included some makeshift sleeping quarters for the producers who worked twenty-four-hour shifts every few days. For the staff who arrived on site during the very heavy rain in May, wellington boots became a necessary fashion choice.

'We woke up every morning hoping the weather had got better, but it never seemed to,' says Sandy. 'Every day was a matter of crisis management – there was always another problem, mostly caused by the non-stop rain.'

Running the cable from the cameras in the house to the control room was a major headache for Sandy Fone. It was a 200-metre run, and with any long run there is a risk of the signal deteriorating. Although longer runs have been done for outside broadcasts, these have been for short slots. This run had to last for the duration of the show. A trench – known as 'Sandy's trench' – was dug across the yard to the bridge leading to the house, and a decking floor was added to the bridge so that the cable could run beneath it. The trench then continued across the ground around the house. In total, more than 160 kilometres of cable was used on the *Big Brother* site. For the two live Friday night programmes, a master control-room truck was parked round the back of the studio to broadcast the shows, and there was more than seven kilometres of audio cable inside the truck alone. Director of engineering Peter Webber regularly doubled his estimate of how much he needed – and then found it was still not enough.

A completely new post-production and logging system had to be devised and set up. The logging system meant that any sequence from the thousands of hours of tape that were recorded could be found instantly. For example, if a producer was trying to put together a film package on two of the contestants, he or she put their names into the computer and it would deliver every instance when they were filmed together. By adding the keyword 'touching' this would be refined to any sequence of them making bodily contact with each other. It was an invaluable system, but hard work to set up. Dr Peter Collett, an experimental psychologist from Oxford University and one of the experts whose theories about the contestants' behaviour was used throughout the series, was involved with planning the logging system, helping to compile the list of keywords. He wanted the log to include body language, instances of isolation, and both negative and positive gossiping, which translated into the keywords 'bitching' and 'gossip'.

The goings-on in the house were recorded twenty-four hours a day and seven days a week by thirty-one cameras, five of them manned, eight of them 'hotheads' which could be controlled remotely and turned to follow any action within their range, and the rest of them fixed security cameras. There were twenty-six microphones fixed around the house and all the contestants wore radio microphones at all times except when asleep or in the shower.

The manned cameras operated in a moat-like dark passageway around the perimeter of the house. Large windows in the walls of the house and the garden, which appeared to be mirrors to those inside, allowed the cameras to film. These cameras were manned at all times, ten cameramen splitting the day shifts and two more taking over for the night. Infrared lights allowed them to film in the darkened bedrooms, and the main lights stayed on in the rest of the house. To lessen the possibility of a reflection from a camera being seen through the mirrored glass, the cameramen wore black and the cameras were enveloped in black cloth. The backs of the windows were hung with black gauze, so that only the camera lens poked through. The men had to work in absolute silence. The blacked-out camera runs, with their shrouded cameras and black-clad operatives, were one of the strangest parts of the *Big Brother* project. Less than a metre away, through the glass, the housemates carried on their lives, oblivious most of the time to the presence of the ever-watchful electronic eyes. Occasionally, if the contestants were quiet, they would hear the whirr of a camera or the sound of movement in the camera run, but that was the only reminder of the outside world.

'It was a new discipline for the cameramen,' says Sandy Fone. 'They had to know exactly where to go to silently relieve the cameraman on the shift before theirs, and when they took over they had no idea what they would be filming. There were no breaks – what was happening in the house was continuous.'

Sandy's television background includes working on news, drama, sport and light entertainment programmes and doing outside broadcasts. It was the outside broadcast experience that she valued most highly on the *Big Brother* project. She echoes what everybody else involved with the show says: 'It was not like anything I had ever worked on before. We could plan for different things that might happen, but we had no idea what would happen. For me the strangest part of it all was the contestants. Because I was completely immersed in the technical problems, I didn't have any part in the contestant selection procedure. When they walked into the house they were as new to me as they were to the viewer, and I found myself instantly drawn in to watching them. They were a huge surprise to me. I'd spent so long preparing for them, but I'd got no idea who they would be or what they would be like.'

They turned out to be an energetic bunch and Sandy found herself having to constantly replace their radio mikes. 'They broke loads of them, mainly through doing their aerobics, and wrestling around together. It was things like that which made me aware how little control we had; they could do anything they liked in there, and we had to react to it. Unlike other television programmes, we had no part in creating it. It was bizarre. By the time it went on air, I was almost too tired to be excited, but there was a very big buzz about it. We had to remain calm, keep a lid on it, but there was a feeling of achievement.'

The house was designed by Colin Pigott, who has a long track-record of producing sets for television programmes. He's worked on some of the most famous British series ever made: *Rising Damp, Steptoe and Son*, the *Black and White Minstrel Show, Z Cars*. However, he had never designed a whole house before, let alone one as bizarre as *Big Brother*'s.

Colin was in the middle of a revamp of Channel 5 *News* when Sandy Fone contacted him towards the end of 1999. She had worked with him before and was very keen to have him involved from the beginning. Colin initially said no, because he was too busy, but Sandy badgered him and he gave in. Now, he is extremely glad that he did, ranking *Big Brother* as one of the most exciting projects he has ever been involved in.

'I didn't really understand what Sandy was on about at first. The whole concept was new, and I had no idea I'd have to design a whole house. But there's no great mystery to building a house, lots of people plan their own and build it. It was just great fun, although there were plenty of problems.'

His first move was to spend a damp day in Holland looking at the Dutch house. He went with Michael Lingard, the lighting director. The *Big Brother* series had just finished in Holland and the furniture and fittings from the house had been auctioned off. However, even making allowances for the fact that it was stark and empty, it was quickly clear to Colin and the Channel 4 executives who were there at the same time, that the British house was going to have to be very different. The Dutch house was small; it abutted directly on to the control room and was made up of a series of linked prefabricated cabins.

'They'd started from scratch and had to make it up as they went along, but we had the advantage of being able to learn from their experiences,' says Colin.

It was decided that the British house would be a stylish, purpose-built structure with plenty of room inside. There was a brief concern that planning permission for the house would be opposed by environmental groups anxious about wildlife being disturbed. The *Big Brother* team allayed their fears. One dedicated birdwatcher was even given a *Big Brother* crew pass, which allowed him to come and go around the site while the programmes were being made.

The land, which was knee-deep in brambles and rubble, had to be cleared and, before anything else happened, the fence was erected. A concrete slab was laid and drains and a cesspit were installed – waste material from the house flushed into a 9,000 litre tank (which was emptied twice a week by contractors until the numbers in the house dropped below six, when it was emptied just once a week).

The building is steel-framed and the frame was made by contractors in Hounslow and then assembled on site, so that it could be taken down again and stored. Unfortunately, the month when most of the building work should have been done turned out to be the wettest May in more than fifty years. The whole area where the house was to stand became a quagmire and lorries delivering materials sank into the mud. Eventually, the track leading to the site had to be relaid with rubble to allow them to get close. The ground beneath the house is clay, and the men working on the construction found their boots weighed down with it.

The steel structure was infilled and then covered on top with the shiny metallic material – foil-clad bubble wrap – that gave it its space-age look. This material is used in conventional buildings for damp-proofing in between layers of brick but has never before been used on the outside of a building. Neil Dowsing, the project manager, came up with the idea of using it because not only is it waterproof but it is also 90 per cent reflective, therefore keeping the interior of the building cool. Prefabricated buildings can be notoriously hot in summer. The *Big Brother* house, which has no heating, was so cool that for the first few days when the contestants were inside, and when it was unseasonably cold, they requested more bedding. However, when the summer warmed up the house came into its own, staying cool and pleasant even when the sun was beating down.

One unexpected consequence of the shiny colour was that the building came in for a lot of attention from jays and magpies, birds notoriously attracted to anything glittery. Their pecking caused problems. When Neil Dowsing made his weekly check on the roof he found dozens of tiny holes, some of them penetrating the waterproof lining. In heavy rain, the contestants sometimes had to use buckets to catch the drips while running repairs were carried out.

Another worry during the construction of the house was the wind. The site is exposed and windy, and, at one point, there was a real fear that the structure might blow away or be severely damaged if a gale blew up. Extra attention was given to fixing it to the ground.

Colin Pigott's main constraint when designing the house was to come up with accommodation that could be observed at all times from the camera runs, the dark passageways around the house along which the five manned cameras trundle, filming through the two-way mirrors.

Inside the house Colin had a free rein and came up with a plan which curved the walls around the sitting area, giving it a stylish, modern look. The colour scheme is predominantly pale blue; the walls in the kitchen and living area are blue, and so is the exterior of the house which faces the garden. 'Blue is a good colour for enhancing flesh tones – in the old days of black-and-white television everything was painted blue. We also thought it was a restful colour,' explains Colin. The two bedrooms were painted green and lilac and, predictably, the girls colonized the lilac one and the boys the green one.

Some of the furnishings and fittings were donated. The stainless-steel fittings for the shower room, lavatory and washroom came from a company specializing in sanitary fittings for prisons and hospitals.

'In a way, we didn't want it to be too much like home. I wanted it to feel comfortable, but a little bit like an institution. It had to be a bit clinical, and it also had to be a bit of a blank canvas for them to stamp their identity on,' says Colin.

The nicknames for Colin's style among the *Big Brother* team were Penal Chic and Jailhouse Mock.

The sofas and dining table were screwed to the floor and, originally, it had been planned to screw the beds down too.

'We wanted to keep all the major items of furniture in good positions for the cameras,' says Colin. 'In fact, the beds were not screwed down and nobody tried to move them. One of our obsessions when designing the house was for there to be nowhere that the people inside could hide, so we even had secret cameras that would pick them up if they went under the beds or into the lockers. We spent days working out the angles. But nobody seemed to want to hide.

'We completely got that wrong. They seemed to be delighted to live on camera, acting out their lives for our benefit. They could have hidden – they could have put a couple of sheets over the dining-room table and gone underneath, like children do to make dens. But they were not at all secretive, or that desperate to escape being watched.'

Another problem that Colin predicted, but which never happened, was queuing for the lavatory. With ten people in the house, and only one lavatory and one shower, he thought that the corridor outside these rooms would be the scene of confrontations as they all tried to use them at once, particularly during the one hour of hot water per day. However, there was no friction over it, and the only minor sign that the washing facilities were inadequate came when Sada cleaned her teeth at the kitchen sink in the first week.

Like the producers and directors, it was a strange experience for Colin Pigott and Michael Lingard to have to hand their work over to the contestants and relinquish control of it.

'Much of the lighting was fixed but they could move some of it around. They could shift a lot of my stuff around,' says Colin. 'I'd switch on the television and think "Why have they moved that? It shouldn't be there." At one stage they put all the plants out on the patio and it looked odd. But from the moment they went in, it was their set, not mine, and I had to get used to that.

'I was in the house until ten minutes before they arrived. There were so many last-minute things. For instance, Conrad Green, the series editor, thought it would be a good idea to have a bell outside the Diary Room, so that they could ring to signal that they wanted to go in. They were arriving at 11 a.m., and at 9 a.m. one of the team was waiting outside Homebase for the store to open, so we could buy the bell. It had to be cordless because there was no time to wire it up.

'Sandy was yelling at me to get out as it got nearer and nearer to the time of arrival. I kept saying "Can't I just..." and she'd scream "No!" It was a weird sensation handing the house over to them. My team had been in it seven days a week for three months and it felt like our home not the contestants'.'

Sandy felt something similar: 'I almost resented them being there, I felt they didn't belong in Colin's house. Most of the rest of the *Big Brother* team had met them all and been involved in the selection process, but I didn't relate to them until I started watching the programmes.'

Despite his initial feeling that these strangers did not belong in the house, Colin had no problem with Nichola deciding, very early on, to put her imprint on the house – literally – by daubing her body with clay and pressing it against the wall. Several of the others joined in.

'I loved the fact that she was being creative with the space. She did quite a lot to decorate it – she's the only one who did. In the Dutch house, they carved their names on the wall, they ticked off the days, and they wrote cryptic lines from pop songs – much more the sort of stuff that prisoners do in their cells. I think because ours was so much more spacious they didn't feel quite so incarcerated.

'But apart from Nicky, they didn't really colonize the space. The Dutch and German contestants all unpacked their suitcases and put them tidily away under the beds. Our lot seemed to live out of them – and the girls were untidier than the boys.'

Outside, the garden was planned and planted by Chrissy Robinson, the art director. The vegetables were all started in polytunnels in April, ready to be transplanted out at the beginning of July. Courgettes, onions, beans, beetroot, peas, lettuce, aubergines, peppers and potatoes were planted, with tomatoes in the greenhouse and a herb garden. The decision to have chickens was taken as a direct result of the experience of the other *Big Brother*s abroad. They gave the contestants something to do and, at the same time, provided them with fresh eggs – an average of five per day.

There were no major problems with the design and building of the house, although there were plenty of minor hiccups. On Dutch advice, the two-way windows were double-glazed which had been necessary to avoid condensation in a Dutch winter. However, this was a British summer and the double panes caused a reflection.

'So we had to have them all taken out and single panes put in,' says Sandy Fone. 'We'd even had Dutch experts over to do the silvering of the mirrors, then we discovered we could get it done locally anyway.'

Another last-minute adjustment came when a window was cut into the wall of the Diary Room, so that a camera could film the door of the house.

'We noticed from the Dutch experience that on the night of an eviction, as the others crowded round the door to wave goodbye, all the camera had was a back view of them. So we made the extra window to allow us to film that moment,' says Colin.

The Diary Room and the Store Room were part of the camera run, but the manned cameras were removed when the rooms were being used by the contestants.

'If I could go back and change anything, I'd have a camera run all the way round the building and not going through any of the rooms,' says Colin. 'But on the whole it worked very well, and didn't cause any problems.'

All the contractors who work different parts of the house returned to see it when it was completed – and they all became *Big Brother* addicts. As did Colin. 'None of us will ever do anything like it again. Even if there is another series, or other ideas which are similar, this was the first.'

Presenter Davina McCall, who fronted the two live shows each week, came on board early in the planning stages and Ruth Wrigley was delighted about this.

'Davina's bright, flexible, and has a real empathy with people without being sickly sweet. It was a tough job; presenters are used to having everything given to them on an autocue. Davina is able to function in a live situation perfectly. The great thing about her was that she was really into the programme. She would ring me during the week to discuss the goings-on in the house, gossiping about what they were all getting up to. I could have had a presenter who didn't know or care who the characters were.

'At the very beginning, when we were doing run-throughs, she was a bit too polished. Off-camera she was chatty and really into the programme. I told her that the feel I wanted for the viewers was what she was doing off-camera. My motto all the way through has been "Keep it Real". That's why I didn't want a phoney studio, polished links; I wanted it to look live and real.'

Designer Colin Pigott was not the only one working until the very last minute. The website team were struggling with the web video streams until three minutes to 11 a.m. – the hour that the contestants went inside. The evening before the programme was due to start, two of the six streams were working and the other four came on-line the next morning, the last one with only three minutes to go. A cheer went up when the problem was solved and the final stream of pictures came on screen.

Altogether around fifty people worked on the website. By the second week of the show, it was fast becoming one of the most-visited websites in Britain – and that was before it got really busy. A constant stream of news about life in the *Big Brother* house was compiled by nineteen journalists who monitored the house in shifts. Between 900 and 1,500 e-mails were received every day and all were read. Some of the tasks given to the contestants were suggested by the web readers including the portrait painting, putting on a play and writing poems. Even some of the questions Davina McCall asked the evictees on Friday nights came from suggestions to the website. Readers could use the web to order special *Big Brother* gear, and could vote on the most appropriate holiday for each of the contestants to go on.

One problem faced by the website team, under Helen Hawken and Chris Short, content manager for *Big Brother* Online was the risk of one of the contestants saying something that could land *Big Brother* in legal problems. There was no built-in delay between what happened in the house and what went out on the web. It was all live, happening in real time, and the only slight delay was because of the internet system. What the contestants said was being monitored twenty-four hours a day and the audio feed had to be switched off several times.

'It is natural that when a group of young people get together chatting that they gossip about famous people, film stars, pop stars. They speculate about the stars' love lives and their sexuality. Channel 4 wanted to avoid that going out in case it was defamatory. So we pulled the plug a few times,' says Helen. 'Although you can get away with a lot more on the web than you can on television, we were aware that until 9 p.m. our website had to be regarded as family viewing. Obviously, we couldn't avoid the odd swear word, but if there was a barrage of swear words we shut off the audio feed. Our loggers were literally listening with their fingers on the button, ready to close down anything inappropriate.

'But we didn't compromise the honesty of what was going out. It was still an accurate record of what was happening in the house. Any censorship we did was simply to protect ourselves from legal action and the family-age-group viewers from nudity and obscenity.'

Unsurprisingly, the British *Big Brother* has worked out very differently from the series that have run in other countries. Any mix of people will obviously produce different results, compounded by national characteristics and expectations. A major part of the appeal of the first Dutch series was a love affair that developed between two of the players, Bart and Sabine. It was a tender liaison that culminated in them making love under a duvet in the week when they both faced eviction and knew that they would be parting. Bart, a twenty-three-year-old ex-soldier, went on to win the whole Dutch contest. Despite being nominated by the others in the house almost every week, he proved immensely popular with the audience. When the show ended, his affair with Sabine, who was a year older and a fashion stylist, did not survive the outside world. Within two months, it was over. But they both benefited from their *Big Brother* television exposure. Sabine went on to become a TV presenter and was signed up for a spread in *Playboy*. Bart became a national heart-throb, landed a modelling contract, guest-presented a radio show and started his own clothing company, Big Bart. He has a website, opens supermarkets and for weeks after the programme ended had to fight his way through fans to get into his home.

Another Dutch contestant, Ruud, became famous with the audience for his habit of hugging everyone. On being evicted, he published a best-selling book called *Let's Hug*. While the contestants were still inside the house they recorded a CD single which went straight to the top of the Dutch pop chart.

In Germany the winner, John, has also launched a career as a pop star with a hit single called, predictably, 'Winner'. Another German contestant, Zlatko, has been even more successful despite not winning. He has his own prime-time TV chat show; has had a beer named after him; and has released a chart-topping record, a duet with yet another of the contestants. The German show contained a lot more sex than the Dutch version, with three couples regularly getting it together and partners changing when individuals were evicted. However, it failed to achieve the erotic tension of the Dutch love affair. Nonetheless, the German programme was a sensational ratings hit, with over twenty million viewers. Of those viewers aged fourteen to twenty-nine – the target *Big Brother* audience – a massive 40 per cent were watching whenever it was on.

In Spain, the programme was an even more dramatic success, with the streets of the country emptying for the live broadcasts on Wednesday and Saturday evenings, and even King Juan Carlos going on record to say that he was hooked on the antics in the house. Passions ran extremely high and the first person to be evicted, a willowy blonde called Maria José, took her newly acquired lover with her when she had to leave. They are now planning to marry and have a busy media career, appearing on chat shows and in magazines. Another of the women to be booted out, Monica, also took her man with her. Monica now presents a radio programme.

The antics of the volatile Spanish contestants were so compelling that the show even clocked up bigger viewing figures than the Real Madrid–Bayern Munich Champions League semi-final, an astonishing victory in football-mad Spain. The most exciting moments of the Spanish show came at the end when a mob of 2,000 stormed the house to try to meet the overall winner, Ismael. He had to be airlifted away by helicopter, while security guards rounded up the hens and the show's pet spaniel.

The level of feeling was the same for the British show within days of it going on air, as the ten contestants became as much a part of viewers' lives as their own family and friends. Ruth Wrigley sums up its fascination: 'What it does is hold up a mirror to the people in there, who are forced to look at themselves more closely than ever before, and it holds up a mirror to us, as a society. We can all see elements of our own lives in there, of the worlds we live in. We watch people behaving in different ways towards each other, and we know that in our own lives, in the places we work, there are people behaving like that – but we never see it from outside, like we do with *Big Brother*.'

BIG BROTHER TRIVIA

- 23.8 kilometres worth of paper was used for *Big Brother* application forms.

- Over 160 kilometres of cable and wiring were used on the whole production, most of it linking the studio to the house.

- 32,208 metres worth of videotape was recorded every day. By the end of the series it would have filled all six lanes of the M1 from London to Leeds.

- Pictures and sound were stored in the programme archive on a server capable of storing 1,500,000,000,000 bytes of information, roughly equivalent to 2,200 compact discs.

- The amount of information passing through the five *Big Brother* edit suites was double the whole internet capacity of the UK just three years earlier.

- The *Big Brother* chickens laid approximately 320 eggs, an average of five a day, throughout the show.

THE SELECTION PROCESS

When the ten contestants walked through the blue door into the house that was to become their home, they found a terse note which said 'Welcome to *Big Brother*. We look forward to watching you.' It was a timely reminder that they had surrendered their independence, and that their new world was controlled by an unseen presence. They may have had the freedom to do what they wanted in the house but they were always under the watchful eye of Big Brother.

The ten had accepted that they were leaving behind their families, friends and lovers, and that they would have no contact with the outside world for a minimum of two weeks but possibly for as long as sixty-four days. There were also strict rules about what they could take in and how they would live when they were inside.

Each of them had been issued with two special suitcases, a big one and a little one. They were allowed to fill the big one with clothes and the smaller one with personal belongings, with a strict list of what could be included.

They were allowed two bottles of wine or six cans of beer; two books and two magazines; and games that did not require batteries. The toiletries they could take in included toothpaste, moisturizing cream, shaving foam, shampoo, conditioner, hair gel and suntan lotion, but they were limited to one of each. If they needed any more toiletries during their stay these would have to come out of the weekly shopping allowance. They could take in cigarettes, photographs, and a musical instrument as long as it did not require amplification.

They were not allowed a mobile phone; a radio; a personal stereo or CD player; any kind of computer or electronic diary; a television; any electronic equipment or any items needing batteries; a calendar; an alarm clock; watches; any drugs or narcotics; any personal medication unless agreed with Big Brother; any weapons; pens, paper or writing equipment; diaries; clothes with prominent logos; any alcohol other than the wine or beer. Their suitcases were carefully searched before they went in.

They were provided with certain basic supplies: dried beans, lentils, dried peas, wholemeal and white flour (enough to bake three to four loaves of bread a day), potatoes, dried pasta and rice. There was also a limited supply of meat, fish and poultry in a freezer that was restocked every fortnight. On the first day they entered the house there was enough food to keep them going to the next day; after that they had to order their shopping each week. They were allowed £1.50 per day per person to supplement their basic supplies, but they could wager between 20 per cent and 50 per cent of the total against their ability to complete tasks set for them by Big Brother. In other words, if they managed to complete the task, the amount of money available went up by the percentage they chose to wager. If they failed the task, it went down by the same amount.

To order the shopping they were given a price list, and a blackboard and chalk – no other writing materials were allowed in the house, and the chalk had to be handed back in when the list was completed. Special requests for food not on the shopping list could be made in the Diary Room, but only at the time of making the main shopping list – the contestants had to cope without anything they forgot to order for a whole week. The shopping list had to be compiled on Saturdays and the food, drink, cigarettes and other luxuries were delivered on Sundays.

Every week the group were given a task, set at 10 a.m. on Saturday morning. It had to be completed by Wednesday, and the group were given half an hour to decide how much of their shopping money to wager on completing it. The shorter tasks varied – some were mental and some were physical – but they were all designed to make the contestants pull together as a team. Everyone had to take part, and if they didn't they could be evicted from the house by Big Brother and replaced by one of the reserves. Other tasks could also be set – some compulsory and some voluntary – by Big Brother, and for completing these the contestants would get treats and prizes.

There was a daily rhythm to life in the house. One of the main deprivations the contestants suffered was lack of hot water. The hot-water system was switched on for only one hour a day, between 9.30 a.m. and 10.30 a.m. Any showers taken outside this time were cold! Clothes had to be washed by hand, although there was a wringer to squeeze water out of them.

The Store Room, where food supplies were kept, was open from 10 a.m. to 11 a.m. If the contestants slept through (as they did on more than one occasion), they could not get access to the day's food unless Big Brother took pity on them and set them a task which was rewarded by the Store Room door being opened.

Contestants could be called to the Diary Room at any time. In the purple chair, facing the camera, they would hear different Big Brother voices throughout their stay in the house – all members of the production team. But even if a contestant recognized, or thought they recognized, a voice, they were not allowed to use any name other than Big Brother (although this was soon affectionately shortened to 'BB'). They could ask Big Brother questions, but the standard reply was 'Big Brother will get back to you on that', and the reply would be given later when the editorial team had discussed it. Twice a day, at 10.30 a.m. and 8 p.m., new batteries for the radio microphones which the contestants had to wear all the time were left in the Diary Room, and had to be changed. If any of the housemates had tried to communicate with each other without microphones, or had tampered with any of the recording equipment, they could have been expelled. Some of them did have to be reminded of this rule.

Weekly events included making nominations for eviction every Monday. One hour after all the contestants had privately confided who they wanted to see out to Big Brother, the disembodied voice on the PA system (known to the crew as the 'voice of God') announced the names on the hit list. The result of the telephone poll of viewers, to decide who would go, was given on Friday evening on the live television show between 8.30 p.m. and 9 p.m. After the announcement the chosen one had two hours to say goodbye to their friends in the house and pack, before leaving during the second live show at 11 p.m. When people were evicted they were not replaced so the number inside dwindled each week.

Staying in the house was not compulsory. The contestants were all free to leave at any time. If one of them left, a replacement could be drafted in immediately.

Before they came face to face with the rules and regulations of the house, the contestants had already been through an ordeal almost as great: the selection process. Choosing the contestants was the trickiest part of the whole *Big Brother* operation. Everyone knew that the ten strangers who walked into the house at 11 a.m. on Friday, 14 July, would make or break the programme. If they were too boring, viewers would switch off; if they were too over-the-top, they would not be able to stay the course. Also, it was not just a matter of them making good television. The *Big Brother* team knew that it was asking a lot from the participants, and they wanted to be sure they would be able to survive a very strange and destabilising experience.

The selection procedure began in March. A thirty-minute programme about the project, using material from the Dutch show, was broadcast on Channel 4 on Friday, 24 March, and at the end viewers were invited to phone a hotline for an application form. They were also given an internet address to download a copy of the form. The response was astonishing: there were 25,000 telephone requests for forms, and another 20,000 were printed off from the web. Sacks of mail arrived at the *Big Brother* office, and the small production team, who were being recruited by the day, spent their first few weeks photostatting forms and stuffing them into envelopes. All applicants were asked to send in photographs and, if they could, a video of themselves.

'The replies were overwhelming, and it soon became clear that we needed the video – it was a really useful way of sorting out the candidates who would have a good chance. If you see people you get a real sense of what they are like, which doesn't necessarily come over in a letter or an application form,' says executive producer Ruth Wrigley. 'So we had to contact lots of them by phone or e-mail and ask them to send one.'

About 5,000 promising applicants were sent a second sixteen-page form to fill in. It was specifically designed to be long and exhaustive. Brett Kahr, a senior lecturer in psychotherapy at Regent's College, London, was an early and invaluable recruit to the *Big Brother* team. He was initially invited to take part in the launch programme, talking about the type of people who would want to take part in the *Big Brother* experience. His involvement grew organically as the team realized they needed professional help with the selection procedure. It was Brett who advised the production team on the design of the second form.

'The form was just the first stage of a long application procedure, and I felt it was important that it was long and almost daunting,' he says. 'I realized a lot of applicants would be put off by the form and would not fill it in. As *Big Brother* was going to be a long, drawn-out procedure that would need commitment and staying power from the contestants, the form was a first hurdle. We were all aware of what a big piece of work the programme would require psychologically from the participants, and just filling in sixteen pages was a first guide to how committed they would be.'

As well as asking for lots of background details about the applicants' lives, the form gave them the chance to describe their own personalities, and to write about their good habits and their bad (they were encouraged to ask friends). They were asked what they expected from the future; where they thought they would be in ten years' time; and what they would change in their lives if they could start again. They were even asked to consider how they would react if they were selected to go into the house and found that ex-girlfriends and boyfriends sold unpleasant stories about them to newspapers. Despite the fact that the form was designed to be off-putting, most of those given out were returned.

Initially, the production team stipulated that nobody under eighteen could apply to the programme. The minimum age was soon changed to twenty-one.

'We realized that people under this age did not have very much life experience to bring with them to the house,' says Ruth Wrigley. 'At eighteen, they have been at school, college and lived at home, and that's about all that has happened.

SAMPLE QUESTIONS FROM APPLICATION FORM

- What qualities/habits about you annoy other people most?

- What habits and behaviour do you find most annoying in others?

- What three things frustrate you most about everyday life?

- If you were a contestant on *Mastermind*, what would your specialist subject be and why?

- In your quietest moments what do you think/dream about?

- If someone was making a film about your life, who would play the lead role?

- How do you really feel about cameras in the loo and shower?

- How do you really feel about everything you do (sex/farting/picking your nose) being seen by millions (and your Mum and Nan!)?

- What would make you leave the Big Brother house?

- Have you ever been rejected/turned down for anything? How did you feel?

- Who in your family do you not get on with? Why?

- Are you usually the dumper or the dumpee? What happens – why do you think that is?

- If you could start all over, what would you like to change in your life?

- What is your biggest fear?

They haven't really been through the emotional mill. We wanted people who would have stories to tell the others; people who had done a few things.'

The oldest applicant who was considered was a woman of fifty-four.

'Brett advised us to look very carefully at anyone over the age of forty-five who was applying,' says Helen Hawken, who was closely involved in the selection procedure. 'They weren't ruled out, but we had to examine their motives with particular care.'

The vast majority who applied were in the eighteen-to-forty age range, with more men applying than women. A very large number of applicants saw *Big Brother* as a stepping stone to a career in television or show business.

'We had loads of wannabes, people trying to break into media or showbiz careers. It's an inbuilt problem with *Big Brother*. The contestants from other countries have become famous, and some have gone on to have careers in television presenting, so naturally a lot of those who apply think it's going to be their big break. They want to be superstars,' says Ruth Wrigley.

Wanting a career-opening from the show was not an automatic barrier to being chosen, but it did mean even closer scrutiny of candidates who hoped this would happen.

For the second round of the selection procedure applicants were invited to attend mass auditions held in hotel conference rooms and church halls across the country. The first one was held on Saturday, 1 April, in London, in the boardroom of the television company. This was a large audition for about 200 people and its aim was to weed out many of the wannabes. Ruth Wrigley described it as being like an audition for *Oliver*, with everyone desperate to grab the attention of the production team. They were each given five minutes to talk about themselves and say why they should be chosen for the house.

'You know within that space of time whether someone holds your attention. On that very first day, for instance, we spotted Andrew. He had this great smile and he was articulate and confident. We all marked him down as a possible,' says Helen Hawken.

After the first London audition, more were held in Bristol, Birmingham, Manchester, Edinburgh and Belfast, and another six sessions were held in London. Altogether 278 people attended this second round of screenings, 115 women and 163 men. The mean age was twenty-six. There were fourteen in their forties, and just one over fifty.

As well as talking individually about themselves in a filmed interview, would-be contestants were also asked to take part in group activities to see how well they functioned as part of a team. It was exactly the sort of role-playing and game-playing that goes on at management courses and was used to establish who came forward as leaders, who was articulate, who was funny.

There were problem-solving exercises and also some that were fun but nonetheless revealing, like threading necklaces of popcorn and playing Twister. The whole procedure was filmed. Brett Kahr was involved with the production team in choosing which games to try on the applicants.

The auditions generated a great buzz of excitement in the production team, who split up to attend different ones. They were ringing each other saying, 'We've found the most amazing person...' and 'So have we...'

'*Big Brother* only began to seem real when we came face to face with real people who wanted to go into the house,' says Helen Hawken. 'That was when we began to see just how different it was from anything else, and we started to appreciate the enormity of the decision about who went in.'

As well as Helen, the team for these preliminary selections was Simon Welton, Tess Cuming, Kate Brown, Aidan Hansell, all producers; Amanda Murphy, senior producer; Jonathan Francis and Toni Cox, researchers; and, Zoe Page, Mark Charman and Emma Curtis, runners. The opinions of all of them were canvassed.

The production team used a code of A to D to assess everyone, with D standing for 'dull'. Anyone above a C was given serious consideration, and a shortlist of forty was drawn up. The filmed interviews were shown to Brett Kahr, Ruth Wrigley and Conrad Green, the series editor, all three of whom then interviewed the applicants.

'Whittling them down was not an easy process,' says Brett. 'I made it clear from the very beginning that I would not be making the final choice: that was for the television team. But we all agreed that whoever went into the house had to demonstrate reasonable evidence of psychological stability. My reservations and hesitations were listened to very respectfully by Ruth and Conrad. However bubbly and televisual the person was, if they were psychologically unsuitable it would not work.

'I discovered that the production team who met them at the auditions were very good at flagging up any cause for concern. They developed a good feel for anyone who was too manic, too depressed, or too frightened by the project. The applicants had already shown considerable resilience and longevity just getting through to this stage of the selection process, and from their films and their detailed forms I was armed with quite a lot of information when I met them.

'They all came to London to meet me,' says Brett. The interviews were totally confidential, and designed not just to help the producers decide which candidates to use, but also for the private well-being of the applicants. For the vast majority of them, it was the first time in their lives they had had a detailed session with a mental health care professional, and many of them thanked me afterwards and said how impressed they were that a television show was taking such care of them.

'I structured the interview entirely for their benefit, to make sure they realized that, although they had got a long way through the selection procedure, they could pull out at any time if they wanted to. I wanted them to realize that they would not be letting the production team down if they changed their minds and that going forward was entirely up to them. I wanted to be sure they understood the ramifications of the situation they were putting themselves in. I wanted them to be able to have a sense of participating with informed consent.

'Although I was there to help the *Big Brother* team, I felt my main duty was to the contestants. I needed to feel confident that they would be able to cope with isolation from friends, family and normal support networks, and also that they could cope with rejection in the house. The procedure involves rejection by teammates; to be nominated you have to be chosen for eviction by people you perhaps think of as close friends. You also have to accept the rejection by the audience, who vote on who is to leave. These are difficult things to handle, however much they took the attitude of it only being a game show. Because it was a twenty-four-hour-a-day commitment it was much more than the average game show where participants are in the spotlight for only a few minutes, and where there may be a sense of failure for not answering questions right or fast enough but there is no sense of being personally rejected by your peers.

'What I was looking for was any sign in their past of destructive behaviour towards themselves or others, any depressive illnesses, any suicidal tendencies, and any indication that they were not telling the truth either in their forms or their television interviews. I was also looking for as contra-indications, severe psychological trauma or abuse – physical, emotional or sexual abuse – in their childhoods, which they were perhaps trying to resolve by putting themselves in another potentially traumatic situation. People who have experienced abuse could have had the wrong reasons for wanting to be there although not aware of it themselves.

'Early abuse can leave people with the experience that their bodies do not belong to them, and I felt the show might attract people who unconsciously wanted to be exploited by the cameras as a way of re-evoking and resolving their childhood abuse. My role at this point was to protect them from themselves, from things that they did not appreciate in their rational, conscious minds.

'I was also very keen to explore the motivation of those who had children. The effect on their children was something they had to think about, and also the effect on them of being parted from their children. I wanted them to consider seriously how they would prepare their children, particularly if the children were old enough to understand that so many people would be watching the programmes and making judgements, not necessarily favourable, about their mother or father.'

Brett also insisted that the applicants look at the impact going into the house would have on their lives – the impact that seeing them live on television would have on friends and family and the impact on their jobs.

'I felt it was impossible to overstress the impact this was going to have on their lives. Some of them did decide after talking to me that they wanted to pull out. After seeing them all, I gave the thumbs up to about twenty-five of them, who I felt were relatively secure within themselves, reasonably stable and well aware of the possible downside of taking part.'

Brett Kahr was not the only one stressing the downside. Ruth Wrigley and Conrad Green saw all the shortlisted contestants.

'I did something you never normally do – I spent a lot of time telling them why they should not do the programme,' says Ruth. 'We outlined four big issues that they all needed to think about: 1. The back-to-basics nature of the house. They had to realize they wouldn't be able to have a Coke or a cup of coffee or a packet of crisps whenever they wanted to. They couldn't pop out to the shops to get anything they needed. 2. They would have no privacy. Ten people in an enclosed space, as well as cameras everywhere, means that there's no way of ever being alone. It's all very well choosing to run around naked when it suits you, but what about those private moments when you just want to change your pants? Also, by being so much in the public eye, when they came out of the house they'd find all sorts of people had an opinion about them. 3. They'd have to accept that Big Brother was in control and that they had no control over what we would show on the screen. Both Nick and Sada went into the Diary Room quite early on in the show and asked us not to screen particular bits when they thought their actions or conversation might be misconstrued. But we had stressed to them at this interview stage that it was out of their hands. Nobody can keep up an act all the time in front of the cameras – the world was going to see them as they really were. When it was over people in the street would have an opinion of them, and would express it and it might not be nice. To have made it to the shortlist they were invariably strong people, in control of their lives, and they had to understand they were losing some of that control. 4. Coping with rejection was a major thread in what we wanted them to think about. They had to accept that they would be nominating others to be evicted, and that they in turn would probably be nominated. If they were nominated, they would have to live in the house for four days knowing that some of the people around them wanted them out.'

Ruth and Conrad also went into the knock-on effects of the programme. They told the contestants that while they were in the house ex-boyfriends and girlfriends might talk about them, in an unflattering way, to tabloid newspapers. They stressed that if any of the applicants had skeletons in their cupboards they did not have to reveal them, but that they should be prepared for them coming out in the press, and their friends and family finding out. If they were not comfortable with that, they should think again about taking part.

Ruth and Conrad were looking for many of the same things as psychotherapist Brett Kahr. 'We didn't want people who saw *Big Brother* as a good way to complete their nervous breakdown. A lot of our choosing was done on good old-fashioned instinct, and it turned out to be sound – there was nobody Brett questioned about whom we didn't already have reservations.

'We didn't treat it like casting a play. We weren't consciously looking for types – for instance, a mother figure. We simply went for people we liked, people who were charismatic, interesting, and whom we thought generally would get on with each other. It would have been easy to throw in people who would obviously disagree, like putting a racist and a black guy in together. But we knew opposites like that would have a big fight and then stop communicating, and in the house they had to keep communicating for a long time. So, we were looking for people who were all different, but whom we felt would relate to one another.

'Despite the rumours that flew around, nobody was planted and nobody was chosen deliberately because we thought they would stir things up. Nick was not cast as a villain. He was the last one chosen, and we went for him because he was an intelligent older man, well-educated and articulate. If we'd deliberately cast a villain it just would not have worked.'

Although more men applied, it was easier for the team to decide on the women. Even at the interview stage, it was clear that women applied for *Big Brother* for different reasons and in a different way from the men. The men saw it as a competition, a game show, something that they were entering in order to win. The women saw it as a different kind of challenge – they were interested in the emotional impact of it. They saw it as a life-enhancing experience, and were a lot less concerned with walking away with the prize money.

'It was a bit like life, really. The men were gung-ho and wanted to get on with it; the women were fascinated by the implications of it,' says Ruth.

As well as these detailed interviewing sessions, the applicants had to agree to have health checks and police criminal records checks carried out.

'We weren't worried about minor driving convictions; we were looking for any convictions involving violence. When all that was cleared, the producers spent two or three days just hanging out with them, to get to know them really well,' says Ruth. 'At the back of my mind all the time was the knowledge that they were real people, not actors or show-business professionals giving a performance. I felt responsible for their safety. I wanted to be sure the experience would not harm them, and that there was no risk of them harming any of the others in the house.'

With twenty to thirty people cleared and selected, the real arguing began. Only ten could go into the house, and there were lots of discussions about the pros and cons of the candidates. More films had been made of them and these were played endlessly. Everyone who had met them, runners as well as senior producers, gave their opinions.

'It was a matter of trying to balance the group,' says Helen Hawken. 'We had a lot of fantastic women in their late twenties, lots of geezer men in their early twenties. There was never a problem with ethnic diversity; we didn't have to look for black contestants. Mel and Darren both came through the selection process because they were fab.

'We argued for hours. We had their photographs pasted on pieces of paper and we shuffled them about, putting them in different combinations and trying to work out how they would react with each other. Everyone had their favourites and we were all fighting for them. It was a very difficult process. We would have been delighted with any of those last twenty-five or so going in.'

At this final stage executives from Channel 4 also joined in, poring over the films and the detailed files that had been built up on the applicants.

'We all agreed on six we definitely wanted,' says Helen, 'but finding the right final four to go with them was tough. The final decisions were not made until two weeks before they went into the house, although a couple of them were told earlier because we knew they had to give notice to their jobs.'

When the selection was made, the others were put on standby. They were the reserves who had to be ready at a moment's notice to be drafted in.

Those who were going in were paid a flat rate of £30 per day for the duration of their stay in the house – a basic payment calculated to be in line with payments for jury service – to enable them to keep up whatever financial commitments they had outside. All the contestants were free to walk out of the house whenever they wanted to, and the rules said they would be replaced by someone if they went. Experience with the shows abroad had shown that women were the most likely to walk out, so Ruth Wrigley had more women than men on her standby list.

Before the ten finally moved in, some of the other applicants were asked to test out the house. Six of them moved in from Monday to Friday to allow the camera crews and everybody else to get the hang of the systems.

The following week, for one night only, ten people slept in the house, again just to try the place out with the full quotient of people. One of this last group described her experiences to the *Sunday Mirror*, where the story was splashed across two pages. Despite the headline, BIG PORN, she said nothing more about the house than was already public knowledge. The press had been given a tour inside it before the show started and there was no secret about the cameras in the shower, the lavatory and the bedrooms. Her name was taken off the standby list, of course. She had broken one of the main rules that the contestants and stand-bys had to observe. They had all been told that if any word of their involvement reached the press before the first day they would be excluded.

'It was a difficult time for them because they had had to confide in close family and friends, and perhaps even employers,' says Ruth, 'so they were all desperately worried that someone else would spill the beans and ruin their chances.'

Nobody did. The night before they went into the *Big Brother* house, all ten contestants were brought to London and put up in a hotel. They did not realize it at the time but they were all in the same hotel, each of them chaperoned by one of the production team. The following morning they were taken to the house, with the two special suitcases they were each allowed to fill with clothes, toiletries and luxuries, in separate cars. They first set eyes on each other, a clutch of complete strangers, at the entry to the bridge that would take them across the river and into the house. It was a strange moment for all of them, but there were many much stranger moments to come in the weeks ahead.

THE CONTESTANTS

The lucky ten contestants who walked excitedly through the blue door of the *Big Brother* house became as familiar as our friends and family. They were:

ANDREW

FULL NAME	Andrew Davidson
AGE	23 (24 when he came out of the house)
DATE OF BIRTH	24.7.76
STAR SIGN	Leo (on the cusp of Cancer)
HEIGHT	5 feet 10 inches
WEIGHT	10 stone 7 lb
PIERCINGS AND TATTOOS	None
FAVOURITE SONG	'All I Need' (Air)
BOOK	*Dead Babies* by Martin Amis
FILM	*Happy Gilmore*
AMBITION	To run an adventure holiday company for Europeans and Americans visiting the Philippines
WHAT'S IN HIS SUITCASE?	Sewing kit, Jenga, tongue scraper

Andrew is a real lad – a boy's boy – who loves motor racing, going out with his mates, and sex. He was honest from day one in the house about his need for sex. Sometimes perhaps too honest, because not all of his comments about prostitutes and threesomes went down well with the other members of the *Big Brother* household (particularly Sada).

Originally from Hemel Hempstead, Hertfordshire, Andrew now lives in London. His father is a commercial artist and his mother works as a florist. The oldest of three sons, he is very close to both of them and says that his father has been the main influence in his life.

With his wit and charm he is a popular, confident young man and has a lot of really good friends who make him laugh, and who he makes laugh. He's easy to talk to, and has a genuine interest in other people.

The whole family is mad keen on go-karting and motor racing. Andrew was a promising go-kart racer until he had an accident when he was eleven, breaking his ankle badly. He switched his attention to the mechanical side of the sport, becoming his brother's mechanic. Anthony is two years younger than Andrew and has won a whole series of international prizes since he went professional in 1997. Andrew flies the world with him to maintain his kart. Anthony has his sights set on becoming a Formula One racing driver. He is now racing Formula Ford, and Andrew predicts that in two years time his brother will be in the big league, lining up on the starting grid against the likes of Michael Schumacher and Eddie Irvine. When Andrew left the house, he was thrilled to learn that while he had been in there Anthony had won his latest race.

Andrew says he is not envious of his brother's success. 'It's everything our family have worked for for fourteen years,' he says. 'If I had to choose between winning *Big Brother* and Anthony becoming a top racing driver, there would be no contest – I'd choose Anthony's career.'

Andrew's sporting activities include cycling and he regularly takes part in the London to Brighton cycle race.

At school, Andrew was a hard worker, and left with very good grades in his four A levels. He then went to Sussex University (as Mel did, but the two had never met before *Big Brother* although when they compared notes they discovered they knew some of the same people). Andrew read Culture and Community Studies, which involved many different elements, including anthropology, sociology, and media studies.

After leaving university Andrew took a job as a marketing product manager for a company in London. It is not, he admits, his dream job and he's hoping that his *Big Brother* exposure will lead to something new. He'd love to work either behind or in front of the cameras in television. He enjoys performing and was good at drama at school, taking lead roles in shows. His long-term goal is to run an adventure holiday company for Europeans and Americans visiting the Philippines. He has a longstanding love affair with the Philippines, which he first visited when his brother was racing there. He has a friend who lives there, and it is now his ideal holiday destination. One of the reasons for this is that he loves the Filipino bar girls, the semi-professional prostitutes who work in the bars in Manila.

'They have a lovely, open attitude to sex. They are not doing it for money; they genuinely enjoy your company. I have become good friends with some of the girls – they write to me and have had holidays with me. It is not the seedy, exploitative thing that people seem to think it is.'

He failed to convince Sada, who accused him of being a 'sex tourist' and taking advantage of girls who were forced into prostitution by poverty.

Andy's revelations to the rest of the house – including having taken part in a threesome on his twenty-third birthday – shocked his parents.

'I think they had a good idea what I was like. My dad definitely knew I'd been with prostitutes. I think they were shocked to hear it on television, especially as there were only snippets of it used and I didn't get chance to explain it properly.'

He stresses that the threesome did not involve him sharing a bed with two other people. It was a husband and wife couple who picked him up in a bar in London, and the husband watched while Andy had sex back at their place with the wife.

'I've taken my clothes off and had simulated sex in a live sex show, and I don't see anything shameful in that. I wish we could take all the guilt out of sex, and be honest about enjoying it.'

His open attitude to sex, and especially to performing in public, means that he was always favourite to be the first to have sex in the *Big Brother* house – and he says he would have done, happily, if the chance had arisen.

'The cameras would not have bothered me. Me and my mates used to wish we'd caught on camera some of our moments hanging out together arguing, shagging and having fun.'

In the light of this, his answer when asked what he could not live without is unsurprising: his penis. He reckons he would have 'brothel cultures of the world' as his specialist subject on *Mastermind* as he's well on with the research!

Despite what seems like a preoccupation with sleazy sex, Andrew admits that what he wants in life is to meet the right partner and have a family. He has had a few long-term relationships, which meant a lot to him, but the latest was over by the time he joined the *Big Brother* team, and he was enjoying being single. He has almost always managed to stay on friendly terms with his exes.

His ideal relationship, he says, would be 'fun, honest, respectful, sexually open-minded, two separate lives enriched by being together, not dependent on each other'.

His favourite possession is his car, a silver Honda CRX.

His favourite book is *Dead Babies* by Martin Amis, which he describes as hilarious. However, he also has a serious intellectual interest in the links between quantum physics and Eastern mysticism, and the book he took into the house with him was by the physicist turned philosopher, Fritjof Capra.

His favourite film is *Happy Gilmore*, starring Adam Sandler. He managed to convert some of the other contestants when they watched it when they were allowed to choose a video.

His favourite song is 'All I Need', by Air, because, he says, it is a 'pure love song, very atmospheric'.

The famous person he most admires is the racing driver Michael Schumacher, whom he has met and says is not at all arrogant, even though that is how he appears to the general public. (Interestingly, that is also how Andrew appeared on screen in *Big Brother*, though in real life he comes across only as confident.)

His hero is Homer Simpson, because he says and does exactly what most men would like to do, but without any conscience.

If Andrew had won the £70,000 prize he would have jetted his friends off for a sensational holiday somewhere hot to 'have the best party ever'.

Andrew took Armani perfume; photos of his friends and family; Radox shower gel; his glasses, contact lenses and sunglasses; a Disney toothbrush; a sewing kit (taken from a hotel room); a pack of cards and a game, Jenga; two bottles of red wine, four packets of chewing gum and a tongue scraper. He also took thirteen condoms 'because I believe in safe sex'. Unfortunately for him, the same number came out with him.

Although he doesn't smoke, Andrew took in 400 cigarettes because he felt it would help out the smokers in the group, and mean that the household budget need not be wasted on cigarettes.

ANNA

FULL NAME	Anna Nolan
AGE	29
DATE OF BIRTH	16.10.70
STAR SIGN	Libra
HEIGHT	5 feet 8 inches
WEIGHT	9 stone 8 lb
DRESS SIZE	12
PIERCINGS AND TATTOOS	None
FAVOURITE SONG	'Loving You Is Easy Because You're Beautiful' (Minnie Riverton)
BOOK	*Wuthering Heights* by Emily Brontë
FILM	*Cinema Paradiso*
AMBITION	To tour China
WHAT'S IN HER SUITCASE?	Large Galaxy bar, chewing gum

Tall, slim, with dark hair and a creamy complexion, Anna has a soft, beguiling Irish accent. She comes from Dublin, but now lives in London with her partner and is open about being gay. She has a gentle personality and fits in with everyone, but there's real strength underneath her quiet calm. Unlike most of the other contestants, Anna thought it unlikely that she would win – and her friends were of the same opinion. She (and they) felt she was not dynamic enough, was too normal, lacked flamboyance and excitement. However, it was clear from the very early days that Anna was an important, calming influence on the group. She's friendly and chatty, but steady and sorted.

She has done a variety of jobs, most notably spending a year as a novice nun before deciding that taking the veil was not for her. She says she got out when she started to fancy the other postulants! However, this is probably a mischievous explanation for something that she thought about very deeply. Having to go on silent retreats during her novice year was good preparation, she says, for being cut off from the world in the *Big Brother* house. She has also worked in a bank, as a basketball coach, as one of the ancillary staff in a maternity hospital, and in a female prison. At the time she went into the *Big Brother* house she was the office manager for a skateboard company.

Anna comes from a large family, with five sisters and one brother, all of whom still live in Dublin. Her mum and dad split up some years ago and her mother completed her degree in classical mythology while Anna was in the house. Anna chooses her mum as her hero for bringing up seven children and then having the guts to go back into full-time education. Even as a child, Anna is remembered as being sweet and conciliatory, trying to stop her sisters squabbling. These natural traits of her personality were strengthened by the counselling and psychology courses she did as part of her convent training. However, she's also quite assertive and can stand up for herself.

She loves going back to Dublin to see her family. She left the city when her first girlfriend dumped her, moving first to Edinburgh and then to London where she did a degree in musical-instrument technology at the Guildhall University. She would love to find a job where she could use her musical skills, either playing instruments (she plays the violin and the guitar) or working with them, but she hasn't managed this so far. She reckons it's impossible to get in unless you know someone.

Anna likes a good time and admits that when she gets pissed she can be noisy and annoy others by trying to get them to join in a sing-song. However, most of the time she and her partner live a quiet life in a flat they love. In ten years' time she would like to be with the same partner, with some children and a house of their own, all of them healthy and contented.

She's very happy about her sexuality, although she told her housemates that up to the age of twenty-two, she tried to go out with boys. Now, she says, she's 'an easy-going, gay, game-for-a-laugh, ex-novice nun; sweet, kinky, devilish and dirty deep-down, gentle and kind to boot.'

She describes her own personality as 'chatty, bright, funny, eccentric, an organizer who can take a back seat too, unpredictable, a true performer, open about her sexuality, likes a drink, chilled, good listener, cracking sense of humour, always buys a round, down to earth, resourceful, sociable, gregarious, calm, caring'.

What she doesn't like in other people are 'big egos, selfishness, superficiality and bigotry'. What other people don't like in her are her untidiness, her habit of picking her toenails, and her noisiness when drunk.

Although Anna had given up smoking before going into the *Big Brother* house, the tensions in there meant that by the time she left she was desperate for a nicotine fix.

She keeps fit at home by jogging three times a week, and tries to go to the gym whenever she can. However, she admits that meeting friends for a drink will always win out over the gym. She lost a noticeable amount of weight in the house because she was eating and drinking less than normal, and doing more regular exercise. She is naturally sporty; she played basketball at international level, representing Ireland in a junior competition in Canada and the USA. This gave her a love of travelling and her ambition is to tour China.

Her favourite song is 'Loving You Is Easy Because You're Beautiful' by Minnie Riverton; her favourite film is *Cinema Paradiso;* and her favourite book is *Wuthering Heights* by Emily Brontë. One of the books she took into the house was *To Kill a Mocking Bird* by Harper Lee, which Nicholas chose as one of his top reads of all time. She also took in two bottles of white wine, lots of chewing gum and a large Galaxy bar – she and Caroline share a passion for Galaxy.

CAROLINE

FULL NAME	Caroline O'Shea
AGE	37
DATE OF BIRTH	1.4.63
STAR SIGN	Aries
HEIGHT	5 feet 2 inches
WEIGHT	8 stone
DRESS SIZE	8
PIERCINGS AND TATTOOS	Ears, both nostrils and belly button
FAVOURITE SONG	'High Hopes' (Frank Sinatra)
BOOK	*Heal Your Life* by Louise Hay
FILM	*The Wizard of Oz*
AMBITION	To have her singing and songwriting talent recognized by the public
WHAT'S IN HER SUITCASE?	Lipliner, Galaxy bar, nine packets of Rolos

The oldest member of the *Big Brother* household, the blonde bombshell was also the noisiest. Known to her friends outside – and the ones she made inside – as 'Cag' or 'Caggie', she has a raucous laugh, a fondness for four-letter words and a habit of speaking her mind, loudly. As the middle one of a family of seven children (she calls them 'The Magnificent Seven'), she always knew she had to speak up to be heard, and she certainly made sure the other contestants in the house never missed her point of view. Her saxophone practice also contributed greatly to the noise level although she mainly practised in the garden. She took up the instrument only ten months before the show.

She became famous across the land for her trademark pink lips – outlined in darker lipliner – and her mop of blonde hair. She was nicknamed 'Nylon Head' at her last job because of the amount of time, energy and money she spent on her hair. It's not surprising then that the things she missed most while in the house were her hairdryer and straightening irons.

Caroline comes from Birmingham and left school as soon as she could with no qualifications. Since then, she's taken an open access course in drama and theatre studies. She's had lots of different jobs including working as a mortgage consultant, a telephonist, a special constable for the West Midlands Police, a cleaner in a gay bar and, most memorably, a seller of marital aids. All the time, her real hope has been to get a break in show business. She's been writing songs for as long as she can remember – she started writing poetry at the age of seven or eight, and has never stopped. She now writes and performs songs with a partner, an ex-boyfriend. At the time she went into the *Big Brother* house she was unemployed and quite honest about hoping that the television exposure would make her famous and open up career opportunities for her.

She's unmarried, and has been hurt and let down by men in the past because, she says, she 'falls in love too easily, gives too much and receives little in return'. She'd love to find a relationship based on 'love, laughter and loyalty'. She's had two really significant relationships when she was, she says, 'head over heels in love'. The latest ended just three months before she went into the house.

'I fell in love really passionately when I was twenty-seven, I'd never felt anything like it, I thought it was for ever. It was mind, body and soul. Everyone thought we would marry. But when the good times were over I discovered that I was the only one trying, and when I stopped trying it was over. It was over not because I didn't love him, I loved him madly, but he was breaking my heart. I let go before he drove me insane.'

Later she started a relationship with his brother, which was every bit as passionate and is the one that has recently ended.

'We split up before we fell out seriously. We tended to get on each other's nerves, then there would be a big explosion and then we would get back together. As he's my songwriting partner, we decided it was more important to be able to work together than to stay lovers. So far it's working out – we have a really good laugh now.'

She lives on her own in a very feminine flat, decorated in pink and purple, and covered with frilly cushions, cuddly toys and other girlie bits-and-bobs. Caroline really does enjoy being a girl. She has loads of nieces and nephews, who she adores. She also loves animals, although she can only keep fish in her flat. One of her two goldfish, Hannibal the Cannibal, died shortly before she went into the house but the other one, Hoover, was waiting for her when she came out. She loves the flat, but ideally wants to live somewhere with a garden. She would also love to have a car.

She has lots of friends, including her brothers and sisters who all adore her, and she is particularly close to her mother. The main compensation for being nominated so often for Caroline was that her mum and family were at the *Big Brother* studio on eviction nights, and she was able to catch a glimpse of them before she was sealed back into the house. When asked what the worst thing she could ever imagine happening was, she said, 'Losing my mum.' She also chose her mother as her hero, 'for her strength and courage'.

She describes her own personality as 'Energetic, open, truthful, and with a great sense of humour. Perceptive, tolerant until really pushed, then, apparently, I'm scary.' Her best qualities, she believes, are her optimism, her ability to bounce back, and being a good listener and a good conversationalist. She believes her determination not to conform is the quality she believes that most irritates others, but she also owns up to being unpunctual, untidy, scatty and disorganized.

She has been a real party animal – staying up all night drinking and dancing – but she reckons that she's starting to calm down. Her sense of fun has landed her in trouble from time to time. On a holiday to Ibiza she was forced to fly home a week early when the hotel manager objected to her squirting the reception area, and some of the guests, with water. Her dream holiday would be to travel to Egypt or South America to explore their ancient civilisations.

Before she went into the house, she was smoking five cigarettes a day, but like all the smokers she found her habit increased while she was there. That might not have been healthy for her, but in one important way she made a great contribution to the health of the whole community by running daily aerobics sessions, that were participated in by everyone who was awake at the time.

She's very into holistic and alternative healing – it would be her specialist subject on *Mastermind* – and she reads a lot of self-improvement books. She took a book about healing and a book by the ex-sports-commentator-turned-evangelist David Icke into the *Big Brother* house.

Her description of herself as an optimist is borne out by her choice of favourite songs and films: her top-rated song is 'High Hopes' by Frank Sinatra ('it made me happy and inspired') and her number one film is *The Wizard of Oz* ('for the music and the message'). Her favourite book is *Heal Your Life* by Louise Hay ('It has helped me to see we are responsible for everything.').

Among her favourite foods she lists broccoli – and it's a top favourite, because it is also the one thing she reckons she could not live without.

She hopes that in ten years' time she will have fulfilled her ambition to have her singing and songwriting talent recognized by the public, be financially stable, and be sharing her life with 'Prince Charming', which is also the title of the record she released after coming out of the house.

Among the things she packed into her small suitcase of luxuries and personal items were Persil washing tablets, Galaxy chocolate and nine packets of Rolos (she's a real chocoholic), a large supply of cigarettes and four cans of Stella lager. The rest of the case was filled with toiletries and make-up, including her trademark pink lipstick. She managed to bend the rules by smuggling in an extra lipstick and lipliner, concealed in the turn-up of her jeans.

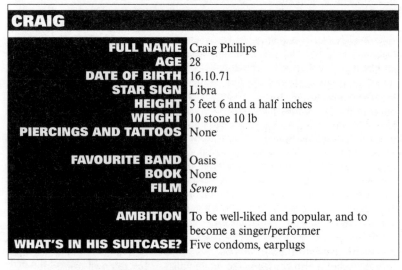

CRAIG

FULL NAME	Craig Phillips
AGE	28
DATE OF BIRTH	16.10.71
STAR SIGN	Libra
HEIGHT	5 feet 6 and a half inches
WEIGHT	10 stone 10 lb
PIERCINGS AND TATTOOS	None
FAVOURITE BAND	Oasis
BOOK	None
FILM	*Seven*
AMBITION	To be well-liked and popular, and to become a singer/performer
WHAT'S IN HIS SUITCASE?	Five condoms, earplugs

Craig is the scally Likely Lad. He has a strong Liverpool accent, although for the past ten years he's lived in Newport, Shropshire. He spends a lot of time in the gym and so he has a super-fit muscular body. He also reckons it's a great place to meet girls. As well as the gym, he enjoys Thai boxing and bird-watching, feathered as well as female! He has a cheeky smile, a lot of enthusiasm, and he's a hard worker – although, as his housemates noticed, he's also capable of spending a great deal of time asleep.

Tragically, Craig's dad was killed by a drunk driver when Craig was only thirteen, a traumatic experience made worse by the fact that the driver lived in the same neighbourhood. To help out at home, where he lived with his mum and sister, Craig got a job in a local butcher's shop, working every night after school. Not surprisingly, schoolwork was not high on his agenda and he left at fifteen with no qualifications. If Craig could change anything about his life it would be his time at school, as he knows he did not work very hard. He worked full-time for the butcher and by the time he was eighteen he was manager of the shop. He also moonlighted delivering strippergrams.

When his mum married his stepdad, and went to live in Newport, Craig, who was sixteen at the time, and his sister stayed on in Liverpool. His sister, who now has two little girls, is very fond of Craig and he dotes on her daughters. Two years after his mum and stepdad moved, he followed them to Newport, setting up his own building company soon after arriving there. He's made a success of it, and has thirteen people working for him. The men who work for Craig are all older than him, and take the mickey out of him. It rolls off his back, and he laughs with them. He's very proud of his business success, even though he worries about the future. Two years before *Big Brother,* he set up another company, hiring out marquees. He has not lost touch with Liverpool – about once a month he goes clubbing with a gang of mates, either there or Manchester. He lives with his three dogs (two boxers called Esso and Narly, and a bull mastiff called Ratheky) in a rambling cottage which he is doing up. Of all the things he expected to miss while in the house, walking in the woods with his dogs came top. He spoils them rotten, cooking special meals of pasta and tuna for them, and has built them a home of their own in the garden.

The most important relationship he's had was with one of his ex-girlfriends, whom he went out with from the age of eighteen to twenty-three. *Big Brother* viewers heard him confess that he would like to marry her. He says they always reckoned they would marry one day. However, before he joined the house he admitted that part of his reason for being there was to find love.

'I am single, and I'm human,' he said, adding that the one thing he could not live without is sex. He proved himself wrong because he went sixty-four days without it in the *Big Brother* house. He's very keen to have his own family, and hopes he will be settled and having babies within the next five years. In ten years' time, he wants to have a large family and have made enough money to be semi-retired. He's never had his heart broken, although he admits to 'a couple of cracks here and there, which weren't a problem to mend'. He has a great track-record for picking up women, and admits he'll try it on with any woman as long as she's not fat.

He quotes his favourite band as Oasis – he likes most of their songs – and his favourite film is *Seven.* He is refreshingly honest about his favourite book: he doesn't read. The only book he can remember reading is Sylvester Stallone's autobiography, which he read when he was at school. However, he did take a book with him into the *Big Brother* house – Richard Branson's autobiography (which Nicholas also chose to take in) and also knuckled down to read it.

Most members of the *Big Brother* household were a bit apprehensive about being filmed while on the loo or in the shower, but Craig's attitude was very positive.

'If there's a sexy girl in the house and I don't get to have sex with her and share the shower, my family will video all the episodes and at least I'll get a glimpse.'

Craig describes himself as 'lively, friendly, talkative, natural, courteous, confident, prefers to be a leader but knows when to take a back seat, and can be argumentative'. He could see in advance that ten strong-minded individuals living in a strange environment was going to cause major problems, but felt that he would be able to help the team 'keep a fine balance and focus their minds'.

Transparently straightforward himself, Craig lists the qualities he most dislikes in others as 'people telling lies, trying to hide things, twisting things and trying to blame others'.

Among the things he packed into his small suitcase were two magazines, *Men's Health* and *FHM,* two bottles of white wine, five condoms and a set of earplugs.

DARREN

FULL NAME	Darren Ramsay
AGE	23
DATE OF BIRTH	7.7.77
STAR SIGN	Cancer
HEIGHT	6 feet 3 inches
WEIGHT	14 stone
PIERCINGS AND TATTOOS	None
FAVOURITE POSSESSION	£200 Prada shoes
SONG	'Thong Song' (Sisqo)
FILM	*Liar, Liar*
AMBITION	To become a TV presenter
WHAT'S IN HIS SUITCASE?	Designer clothes, Golden Virginia tobacco

The only member of the household with children, Darren is also the youngest and the tallest. His physical size gave him one immediate advantage when the contestants walked into the house – he got the double bed! He's handsome and hunky and cares a lot about his appearance. He works out with weights, but reckons he gets a lot of exercise from dancing. Although he is drop-dead gorgeous, he's not impressed easily by women who target him only for his looks.

He has three children: a daughter who is five, a son who is four and another daughter who is one. The birthday party of his youngest child was filmed and shown to Darren and the others inside the house. It was a moving and tearful moment, not just for him but for his housemates and many viewers too. He has known the mother of his children, who is two years older than him, since junior school days. They started going out together when he was fifteen, but split up six months before *Big Brother*. They have stayed friends, and Darren still lives in the same South London flat as his family whom he adores. It was his ex who made Darren fill in the *Big Brother* application form.

He comes from a large family, and is very close to his mother, his three brothers and one sister. After leaving school, he went to Lewisham College, where he achieved a BTEC in business and finance. Before *Big Brother* he was working at the Millennium Dome as a senior host, meeting and greeting up to 20,000 visitors a day and also supervising a team of ninety hosts. He was known to the rest of the staff at the Dome as 'Mr Motivator'. Previously, he has worked as a delivery driver, a chef, a builder and a sales assistant in a clothes shop. Darren loves clothes and shoes, and spends a fortune on designer labels. When he compared notes with his housemates on the possession they would save if they could take only one out of the house with them, Darren's choice was his £200 Prada shoes. He uses lots of toiletries, and used to be particularly fussy about his hair. He admits that when he was having a bad hair day he wears a hat. He's solved the problem now by shaving his head.

According to Darren, his friends all accuse him of being a flirt, a ladies' man and a big overgrown girl 'because I change my hairstyle frequently and carry a backpack wherever I go'.

Describing his personality he says: 'I have always believed I am shy but have always been told that I am the opposite. I am a self-conscious, caring, respectful, kind individual, obsessed with cleanliness and the way I look.'

He worries that his personality attracts other people to share their problems with him, and he always ends up supporting and advising them. He describes himself as an 'agony uncle' and even though he does not mind helping others he would like to be able to say no sometimes.

His bad habits are burping and picking his nose. In other people, he is most annoyed by bad jokes and 'hard nut' behaviour. Unlike the girls in the house, he really dislikes body piercings and tattoos.

Having three children has forced Darren to be more domesticated than some of the other men in the house. He enjoys cooking, and because he worked as a chef he knows quite a lot about it. If he had to choose a specialist subject for *Mastermind* he says it would be food. He can't stand mess – he says he won't even sit down in a dirty house. So it was no surprise to find him nagging the other contestants about the state of the kitchen area in the *Big Brother* house.

His favourite song is 'Thong Song', and his favourite film is *Liar, Liar* starring Jim Carrey. Like Craig, he is honest enough to admit that he doesn't have a favourite book because he never reads books. While he was living in the house, he borrowed *Wild Swans* by Jung Chang from Melanie, and read it. He also took an anatomy book in with him.

Darren's ambition is to either become a presenter for MTV or a children's programme, or to run a major tourist attraction in America, preferably one with animals. His dream holiday would be to spend six months in Florida. 'I'm young at heart, and I love America even though I've never been there.'

As *Big Brother* viewers know, he had a fear of chickens although, with the help of Mel, he managed to overcome this when he made friends with the chickens in the *Big Brother* garden, especially Marjorie, who became the most famous chicken in Britain. Another of his great fears is mice.

His hero, and the person he most admires, is paralysed film star Christopher Reeve. Darren met him when he visited the Dome. 'His courage and bravery brought tears to my eyes.'

Before he went into the *Big Brother* house Darren was smoking just ten cigarettes a day but like everybody else, his habit grew as the days went by. As well as Golden Virginia hand-rolling tobacco, he took in *FHM* and *Loaded* magazines, a supply of chewing gum and lots of designer-label clothes.

MEL

FULL NAME	Melanie Hill
AGE	26
DATE OF BIRTH	18.1.74
STAR SIGN	Capricorn
HEIGHT	5 feet 6 inches
WEIGHT	8 stone 5 lb
DRESS SIZE	8/10
PIERCINGS AND TATTOOS	Two piercings in each ear; tongue and clitoris pierced; tattoos around her navel
FAVOURITE SONG	'As' (Stevie Wonder)
BOOK	*Slaughterhouse 5* by Kurt Vonnegut
FILM	*Clerks*
AMBITION	To be a travel writer or TV presenter
WHAT'S IN HER SUITCASE?	Feather boa, teddy bear, lipstick

The word everyone uses to describe Mel is 'feisty' – a stunningly beautiful girl with a very upfront, no-nonsense personality. She's naturally flirtatious and had a lot of attention from the men in the house. She seemed at first to find it easier to form friendships with the men than with the women in the house, but outside Mel has plenty of female friends.

She's an only child and lives with her mum, in North London. Her parents separated when she was young, and her mother and grandmother brought her up. Her mother is from Trinidad and Tobago, and works as a midwife. Mel and her mum adore each other, and are very close friends. They spend a lot of time together renovating their house. Mel's favourite foods are the traditional Caribbean meals that her mum and her grandmother make: plantains, sweet potato soup, and rice and peas. She hasn't seen her father for over ten years and thinks that one day she will meet him to talk about why he didn't play a part in her life after the marriage broke up.

Mel works in computer systems sales, selling a system to banks all over the world. She spends her working days on the phone, persuading and cajoling customers into having the system. Each sale takes a long time, but Mel is good at it and the job pays her well. She got ten GCSEs and three A levels, and went to Sussex University where she did a degree in psychology and cognitive science. She started studying philosophy, but switched to psychology when she realized that she was more interested in people than abstract concepts. One of her main reasons for wanting to go into the house was because she finds watching people react to different circumstances fascinating. She also felt she would learn about her own strengths and weaknesses. Before she landed her present job, she worked in the civil service and as a jewellery buyer.

She hates being described as a Scary Spice lookalike, but even her name makes comparisons with Mel B inevitable. And according to her friends Mel really can be scary when she loses her temper, which doesn't happen very often. There are lots of other things she hates: people who stand on the wrong side of escalators, newsprint on her fingers, bad mobile-phone reception, American tourists in London, hairy backs, Thatcherites, Jim Davidson, Dale Winton, meat, and English tomatoes. On the other hand, she loves Elvis, Stevie Wonder, computers and numbers, shoes and Seventies soul and funk.

Like Nichola, Mel has had lesbian experiences but she is predominantly heterosexual. She finished a four-year relationship with a boyfriend shortly before going into the *Big Brother* house because, she says, 'there were too many issues going on'. They were reunited shortly before she went into the house, but she's not sure whether they will stay together.

She describes herself as 'honest, intelligent, sexy, engaging, charming, interesting, a good listener, very interested in people, loyal, good at coping with pressure, reliable'. She's also very organized, with everything neatly kept in place. She recognizes that other people may find her 'bossy, brash, blunt, abrasive, fidgety, restless, and with too much nervous energy'. She says her bad habits are forgetting birthdays, never brushing her teeth or taking her make-up off before bed, having no shame, and always questioning everything. She dislikes 'incompetence, inconsistency and vagueness' in others.

Her family describe her as 'assertive, logical, practical, selfish, someone who pays great attention to detail and is considerate to others.' Her friends say she is 'dependable, a poor timekeeper, stylish, courteous, polite, tactless, opinionated, easygoing, flexible, kind, adaptable, with a lust for life and learning, tactile, eclectic.'

Happiness for Mel would be 'complete understanding and contentment, which I will find incredibly difficult to achieve. Ultimately, happiness would be fulfilment in helping others and reconciling the feeling that we have no purpose.' Her ambitions are to have five children, to travel through South America and Africa, to meet the Dalai Lama and have a one-to-one talk with him, and to end up in ten years' time 'surrounded by people I love and who love me'. By then, she hopes, she will be in her ideal job, which would be travel writing or television presenting. Her hero is Stevie Wonder, and the men she most admires are Oliver Tambo, for his work in dismantling apartheid in South Africa, and Ken Livingstone, for speaking his mind – even though she does not always agree with him.

She cares about how she looks – she wanted to take seventeen lipsticks into the *Big Brother* house with her, but was told she could only have one. She works hard at keeping fit, going to the gym three or four times a week, but is still obsessed with the size of her bottom although she says she's grown to like it because men have told her it's attractive. Her genital piercing caused a lot of comment in the house. 'I've never really talked about it before, because it's private and personal. But now everybody knows about it. I thought about it a long time before I had it done. It is functional: it improves things sexually, enhances a lot of things and I now love the way it looks, too. I had it done in Brighton, but I didn't rush into it. I'm really glad I had it done. I had my tongue pierced because I was bored, doing my university finals. It's really far back, so you don't see it unless I open wide.'

Mel's mother does not approve of her piercings. Mel had to confess to her about the clitoral piercing before going into the house, because she knew it would be a shock if it was revealed on television. 'She minds about it, she thinks it's body mutilation and she can't understand why I wanted it done. But she's very accepting.'

Mel works long hours at her job, but when she does get leisure time she likes to spend it with friends, meeting new people, and listening to funk, disco, garage or Seventies soul music. She loves travelling, and at nineteen went on her own around Asia.

NICHOLA

FULL NAME	Nichola Holt
AGE	29
DATE OF BIRTH	12.8.71
STAR SIGN	Leo
HEIGHT	5 feet 5 inches
WEIGHT	8 stone
DRESS SIZE	8/10
PIERCINGS AND TATTOOS	Piercings in her nose, ears, lip, belly button and tongue. Tattoos around her belly button, at the bottom of her spine, and between her shoulder blades.
FAVOURITE SONG	'Forbidden Colours' (David Sylvian and Ryuichi Sakamoto)
BOOK	Anything by Carlos Castaneda
FILM	*The Cook, The Thief, His Wife And Her Lover*
AMBITION	To be a circus performer
WHAT'S IN HER SUITCASE?	Spiritual stones, scientific wire, screwdriver, teddy bear

With her shaven head and her penchant for walking around wearing very little, Nichola is the wackiest looking of all the *Big Brother* contestants. She's loud, chatty, a bundle of energy, and just as free with the f-word as Caroline, her mate in the house.

She has a degree in textile design from Winchester School of Art and Textile Design, and is very into her art. There are two recurring themes in it: reincarnation and the female form. She creates sculptures of human hands emerging from eggs, and she makes dresses that have her body print on the front and back. It was Nichola's idea to make body prints on the wall of the *Big Brother* house, which certainly broke the ice for the contestants.

She comes from Bolton but may have a frosty reception when she goes back there, because when introducing herself on camera at the start of *Big Brother* she claimed that she was different from the women of her home town, who, she said, wear shell suits, white socks and stilettos. There was, predictably, a cry of outrage from the fashion-conscious women of the town, who claimed that shell suits have not been seen in Bolton for five years.

Nichola works as an art teacher, teaching youth groups, and as a barmaid to fund her art work, which is the main love of her life. She was the one member of the *Big Brother* household who worked while in the house, having various art projects on the go all the time. In the past she has earned a living by working as a tax officer, a life model and a waitress. She once had a job supervising children's rides on a roundabout on Brighton pier, but it did her head in listening to nursery-rhyme music all day.

She's bisexual and has had two or three relationships with women as well as several long-term ones with men. Before she went into the *Big Brother* house, she ended a long-distance affair with an Englishman, a new-age traveller, who lives in a caravan in Spain. They met when she went to Hungary for the solar eclipse in the summer of 1999.

Her dream is to be a circus performer, and she's taking lessons with a street performance group called Artisani in being a trapeze artist and a stilt walker. She and another artist were given a small grant by Bolton Council to get involved in Artisani's work and in return they are teaching her circus skills. She says that when she first climbed on to a trapeze it felt like she was going home. 'I was like a bird, up on a perch, and my whole body became part of my art – on the trapeze the human body is a moving piece of art. I loved being so high, swinging over everyone's heads.' She wants to do a degree in circus training, and defines happiness as 'swinging from a trapeze'.

She is very into spiritualism. She likes to meditate, believes in angels and fairies, and took her parrot-feather wand, which she claims has healing powers, in with her. She also took in two books – one on Chinese healing and another entitled *Ask Your Angels*, which is about meditation and relaxation.

Nichola has a good singing voice. She used to sing soprano in the church choir and the Bolton Youth Choir. Her favourite song is 'Forbidden Colours' by David Sylvian and Ryuichi Sakamoto (from the film *Merry Christmas, Mr Lawrence*) because it reminds her of making love to a very special person. Her favourite film is *The Cook, The Thief, His Wife And Her Lover*. Her favourite author is Carlos Castaneda, who writes about sorcery and magic. If she found herself on *Mastermind*, her specialist subject would be spirituality and religion. The famous person she most admires is Picasso and her hero is dress designer Vivienne Westwood because 'she's done what I want to do and I love her extrovert personality'.

For several months before *Big Brother* she was living at home with her parents, but hopes to move to London soon. She first left home at seventeen to live with a boyfriend. She admits that her mother, a regular churchgoer, finds it hard to cope with her eccentric looks and her extrovert behaviour, but they get on well and are close. Her past problems with drugs have caused family rifts, but she believes all that is behind them. She admits her mum and dad would love a conventional daughter like her sister but says they've come to terms with her.

She says she is a natural exhibitionist, and one of her main reasons for volunteering to go into the house was to get recognition 'as a multi-talented person'. She describes herself as 'friendly, playful, creative, generous, focused, energetic, open, a leader, good for a laugh, reliable and caring'. But she also owns up to 'having a big gob', getting too drunk and taking her clothes off in public, and swearing too much. She knows that people get irritated by her habit of playing with her piercings and her talk about fairies and spiritualism.

What she most hates in others are 'talking over someone else, men talking at your tits, drunk beer monsters, women screaming at or hitting children'.

The one thing shaven-headed Nichola says she could not live without is her clippers. Her twin obsessions are cutting her hair and making sure she does not get fat. She suffered from bulimia for ten years and, although she is over it, she says she still has a body image of herself as fat.

In ten years' time she would like to be travelling around the world, making costumes, having a ball and to be 'hopefully the best trapeze artist in the world'. She would also like to be in love.

Among the things Nichola packed in her small suitcase, were a collection of stones, some scientific wire (she knits with it and made her eviction day dress from it), a screwdriver and a bottle of Rioja. She also took five packs of hand-rolling tobacco and five packets of cigarette papers. And her teddy bear.

NICK

FULL NAME	Nicholas Bateman
AGE	32
DATE OF BIRTH	3.11.67
STAR SIGN	Scorpio
HEIGHT	6 feet 1 inch
WEIGHT	13 stone
PIERCINGS AND TATTOOS	Tattoo of scorpion, his zodiac sign, on his right arm
FAVOURITE SONG	'American Pie' (Don McLean)
BOOK	*The Unbearable Lightness of Being* by Milan Kundera
FILM	*Kind Hearts and Coronets*
AMBITION	To become a TV presenter
WHAT'S IN HIS SUITCASE?	Football, Kangaroo cuddly toy, book on Indian head massage

A good-looking, suave, public-school-educated City gent who quickly found himself in the role of most hated man in Britain, Nick has a phobia about being trapped in a room full of rats and snakes, but that's nothing compared to what the tabloid press wanted to do to him!

One of a large family, his father died when he was young and his mother remarried. He grew up with four sisters (three of them triplets), but also has two half-brothers and two half-sisters from his father's first marriage but 'they were not predominant in my childhood.' The family home is in a quiet village in Hampshire, but Nick owns a house in Southwest London which he shares with two other blokes. He was educated at Gordonstoun, the boarding school Prince Charles, Prince Andrew and Prince Edward attended. Edward, four years older than Nick, was his house captain.

Nick left school with seven GCSEs and then travelled and worked in Australia for three and a half years. He worked as a fruit picker, in a nursing home and for a television company. During this time he grew his hair long and was a hippie; as a result, when he returned to London the only job he could get was in a canteen. He then cut his hair and found himself a job working as a broker in the City. Although the job and his clothes may at first sight make him seem ultra-conventional, the hippie streak is still there. Nick is into Indian head massage and reiki healing. (Reiki is a form of healing in which the practitioner holds his hands above the patient's body and generates heat by 'channelling universal energy' and 'making [the patient] whole'.) Darren was the only housemate who seemed reluctant to have a healing session with Nick, but not all of them enjoyed it. Sada said she felt a very strong 'sexual energy' coming from Nick during the session. But Andrew, who claims to be the arch-sceptic about alternative healing, found that his session worked, generating heat in the ankle he broke badly when he was eleven, and in the knee of the same leg, which he had been warned he might have problems with. Thomas felt himself 'drifting away' during the treatment.

Nick describes his own personality as 'outgoing, reliable, even-tempered, excitable, bullish and trustworthy'. The last is not quite the word that would spring to mind for many people after his performance on the show. His best qualities, he said, are being 'fair, honest, speaking my mind and always on time'. Punctuality is one of Nick's mild obsessions, and he missed having his watch in the house. He admits that other people get annoyed by his excessive tidiness, as well as by his habit of taking the high moral ground on some issues, leaving the cap off the toothpaste, leaving lights on and singing in the shower. (That wasn't all he did in the *Big Brother* shower!) His nickname among his friends, he says, is Crazy Horse.

His biggest fear is to die young, leaving a wife and young children behind. He has happy memories of his childhood, especially traditional celebrations like Christmas and Bonfire Night but remembers being embarrassed by having an older father (he was fifty-eight when Nick was born).

He keeps fit by swimming every morning, has two kung fu lessons a week, and plays tennis at weekends. He is a vice president of Fulham Football Club and a member of the Hurlingham Club. He is having flying lessons and likes playing bridge, which he knows is unusual for somebody of his generation.

His ambition is to become a television presenter, preferably for a travel or sports programme. In ten years' time, he would like to be married with five children, but he does not crave security: 'A boat in harbour is secure, but eventually the bottom drops out,' he says.

He claims to have had a string of short relationships up to the age of twenty-four, and since then to have had three major relationships. He says he would still marry two of those girls if he could, but reckons that he is enjoying being single, because he can please himself as to what he does. One day he wants to meet a woman and fall in love 'until we both died'. It need not be a claustrophobic relationship because he feels both partners should have space to pursue their own goals. The theme of meeting the right person comes up again, in his dreams and in his definition of happiness: 'Being content with one's life. Being the right person with the right person, having enough money not to worry, doing things for people that they will never find out about. Also, to see old people still very much in love makes me happy.' He dreams, he says, 'of finding the right person, like my parents, and being with them for ever'.

He wanted to join *Big Brother* because he saw it as a challenge 'and to see if I am still as tolerant as I was at school'. He knew he would miss swimming, football games, his friends and the radio but felt he would cope because he enjoys being alone, as long as it is not for too long.

His favourite song is 'American Pie' by Don McLean, his favourite film is *Kind Hearts and Coronets*, and his favourite book is *The Unbearable Lightness of Being*. He took two books (one was Richard Branson's autobiography and the other was a book on Indian head massage) into the house with him. He also took two bottles of red wine, a football and some tennis balls, as well as the cuddly kangaroo which goes everywhere with him.

He didn't take any cigarettes or tobacco because, before *Big Brother*, he classified himself as a non-smoker. This will come as a surprise to viewers who saw him surreptitiously smoking his way through Andrew's cigarettes while the rest of the house was suffering nicotine-withdrawal symptoms.

He had one great advantage over the others when it came to sharing the dormitory and the restricted washing facilities. He was the only member of the group who had been to boarding school. Gordonstoun, where he went, is noted for its spartan regime and was, he thinks, a good training ground for *Big Brother*.

SADA

FULL NAME	Sada Walkington
AGE	28
DATE OF BIRTH	10.5.72
STAR SIGN	Taurus
HEIGHT	5 feet 8 inches
WEIGHT	8 and a half stone
DRESS SIZE	10
PIERCINGS AND TATTOOS	Both ears; used to have nose pierced
FAVOURITE SONG	'If I Don't Have You' (Gregory Isaacs)
BOOK	*Breaking from Truth, Quotations from Rumi*
FILM	*Blade Runner*
AMBITION	To teach yoga
WHAT'S IN HER SUITCASE?	Yoga mat, juggling balls, recipe book

Big Brother's beautiful hippie chick, a natural blonde with lots of interesting ways of wearing her long hair, Sada's into yoga, holistic healing and tarot cards – reading the cards for other contestants provided some early fun.

She lives with her boyfriend in a small minimalist flat in London. They have a Bohemian lifestyle: no televisions, radios, mobile phones or computers. She probably felt less deprived than the others when she moved in to the *Big Brother* house with its lack of modern technology. She's also lived in a commune in India, which should have prepared her for sharing with nine other people.

Sada, who changed her name by deed poll from Alison when she was twenty-one, has a master's degree in art and archaeology from the School of Oriental and African Studies in London. She's worked as a waitress, an actress, a model, an apprentice gardener and an art researcher, but immediately before going into the *Big Brother* house she had been busily writing her first book, *The Babe's Bible*, co-written with a psychologist friend, Elizabeth Hearn. It's about different types of men, and how women can spot them and treat them.

Her ambition is to be a yoga teacher. She's been studying yoga for four years. She's close to her family, although her brother and sister have both at times disapproved of her alternative lifestyle. She gets on well with her mother, a health visitor, whom she rings all the time to ask for recipes, and especially well with her grandmother, who has a similar personality to hers. Her happiest childhood memories are of Edinburgh where she lived before moving to Wakefield.

When she left school (with four A levels and eight GCSEs), she wanted to be an actress. She'd been a member of the National Youth Theatre and was short-listed for Bristol Old Vic. She spent six months studying mime and did a course on Shakespeare before becoming a model.

She's always wanted to be different and has been independent from an early age. Her mother remembers her taking herself off around France on her own when she was seventeen. At her eighteenth birthday party, when all the other girls were wearing Laura Ashley dresses, Sada wore an outfit from the trendy store Hyper Hyper, with two differently coloured shoes. When she walked into the *Big Brother* house, she was sporting £250 worth of hair extensions.

She met her boyfriend, a tall, elegant man, a year before *Big Brother* and moved into his flat six months before the programme started, so she joined her house-mates with, in her words, 'my heart space taken'. She missed him a great deal while she was in the house. When asked before she went in what she would miss most she said: 'Bicycling around town on a summer's evening, long walks in the park, my lover, my best friends, and long phone calls with my mum about cooking.'

She's a vegetarian, although she eats fish, and her insistence on having tofu on the shopping list caused problems with the other contestants.

She says there's nothing about her life she would change 'because I believe that everything happens the way it is meant to happen. I also believe that change is a prerequisite to happiness. We steer our own destiny.'

In ten years' time, Sada hopes she will still be working for herself 'and I would like to think I will still be interesting and interested'.

Her definition of happiness is: 'The ability to see and experience joy. Seeing other people give to one another and to me makes me happy. I feel happy when I realize I can do anything in life if I put my mind to it. I feel happy when involved with people who like me as much as I like them. Also, I love to relax.'

If she'd won the £70,000, Sada would have used it to improve, but not change, her hippie lifestyle. She wanted to buy a teepee, an old VW Beetle, and put a down payment on a cottage in Cornwall.

She describes herself as 'honest, outgoing, fun-loving, patient, dedicated, kind, determined, laid-back, witty, considerate, relaxed, social, interested, insight-ful, sensitive, optimistic, forgiving, inclusive, beatnik, practical, a dreamer, sane, informed and natural'. However, she acknowledges that she can irritate those around her by being very organized, by thinking aloud, and by being too open.

'I can be gullible, and at times I'm too caught up in my own head-space,' she says.

The traits she most dislikes in other people are sarcasm, being judgemental and not looking her in the eye when talking to her.

Her favourite song is 'If I Don't Have You', by Gregory Isaacs, which she describes as the best love song ever written. Her favourite film is *Blade Runner*, because it is 'speedy, futuristic, spiritual'. Her favourite book is *Breaking from Truth, Quotations from Rumi*. Going into the house one of her allowance of two books was spiritual, but for her second choice she showed her practical streak by taking a recipe book. She also took her yoga mat, juggling balls, and some tennis balls. The boys, she claimed, soon commandeered the balls for their games.

Before she went into the house she said, 'If I was voted out first I'd definitely be a bit upset.'

TOM

FULL NAME	Thomas McDermott
AGE	31
DATE OF BIRTH	29.5.69
STAR SIGN	Gemini
HEIGHT	5 feet 10 inches
WEIGHT	11 and a half stone
PIERCINGS AND TATTOOS	A tattoo of the devil on his left shoulder blade which has been done with henna so that it will fade naturally in a few years
FAVOURITE SONG	'Ironic' (Alanis Morrisette)
BOOK	*To Catch a Thief* by Jeffrey Archer
FILM	*Blade Runner*
AMBITION	To open a guest house
WHAT'S IN HIS SUITCASE?	Jenga, skipping rope

Naturally shy, the quiet Irishman seemed out of place in the first raucous days of the *Big Brother* household. While others were pressing their naked bodies against the wall, Tom took refuge in the garden. But it only took a few days for him to warm up and join in, although he never became one of the loud-mouthed, high-profile members of the gang.

He's the youngest of eight children and the only boy. With seven older sisters, he admits he was spoiled as a child. He lives at home with his parents on a farm in the small town of Greencastle in Omagh, Co. Tyrone. The farm has been handed down, father to son, for generations. The first records were kept in 1840, but the McDermotts were probably there long before that. The name Thomas has also been handed down to the eldest son. Farming is a difficult life and the farm is now a lot smaller than it was, and no longer has dairy cattle. There are twenty cows with ten calves, and it's Tom's job to check on them every morning before he sets off to his other job, working as a computer systems software engineer. It's his sister's company and it's based fifteen miles from the farm, at Dungannon. If Tom works late, he often stays over at his sister's house. He likes the job because sometimes he has to travel to places where the software has been installed, and he therefore meets a variety of people.

Three times a week he goes to Gaelic football practice and he plays for his local team. One of the wits in the *Big Brother* house asked him if Gaelic football was just like normal football but you got pissed on Guinness first! In fact, it's a tough contact sport, and Tom has had a few minor injuries. He also coaches the ladies' team and he is very popular with them. After training, there's usually a session in the local pub. He also plays racquetball and handball four or five times a week.

Five of his sisters live in England, and Thomas himself was born there. His family moved back to Omagh when he was a child, and his parents kept a newsagent's shop before taking over the farm when Thomas was eleven.

The big decision that Thomas faces, and which the *Big Brother* experience may have helped him make up his mind about, is whether he should follow in the family tradition and take over the farm. He's got loads of nieces and nephews, and is very popular with them all, particularly his teenage nieces who regard him as an older brother. He's known in the family and the local community as a bit of a Romeo – his sisters joke that he spends more time in the bathroom getting ready to go out than they do. When he confessed on *Big Brother* that he had slept with a different girl on average once a fortnight since he was eighteen, it was worked out that he must have totted up a total of more than 300. Even if that's an over-the-top estimate, there's no doubt that Tom is a charmer. The local community threw themselves behind the *Big Brother* effort, and held several charity concerts in his name while he was in the house.

He was not academic at school, and left to take bricklaying and joinery qualifications at college. He's worked as a bricklayer, a painter, an electrician, a joiner and a heavy-plant driver at a quarry, where he was technically an assistant shovel operator – shovel being the name for the heavy machine he drove. He remembers with glee the look on the face of a young soldier who stopped him and a mate at one of the security blocks in Northern Ireland. The soldier asked what they did for a living. Thomas's mate said 'Shovel operator' and Thomas said 'And I'm his assistant.'

'I imagine he's still telling the story of the Irish who need two men to handle a shovel,' he says.

He wanted to do *Big Brother* because he thought he would enjoy the challenge of being in a closed space with strangers and he wanted to learn about himself. He describes himself as chatty, opinionated, witty and lazy – when he can get away with it!

His favourite song is 'Ironic' by Alanis Morisette, because it sums up all the things that can go wrong. Like Sada, his favourite film is *Blade Runner*, and he particularly likes its haunting soundtrack. His favourite book is a Jeffrey Archer blockbuster, *To Catch a Thief*. However, he took two practical choices into the house: a book on astronomy and a recipe book.

One of his dreams is to open his own guest house one day, because he believes that peace in Northern Ireland will bring tourists flooding into the country. Realistically, he thinks that in ten years' time he will be living on the farm with a wife and family in a house he has built himself, on a hill, with views all around.

Tom has a girlfriend, but so far it's not a very serious relationship. His ideal relationship, he says, will be with someone who is happy to let him keep up his friendships, and who is willing to try new hobbies and sports because he reckons he gets bored easily.

Among the things he took into the house was Jenga. (Melanie and Andrew had the same idea, and the *Big Brother* house ended up with three sets of the game.) He also took a skipping rope, a football magazine, some chocolate and two bottles of red wine.

WEEK ONE

'I'm not bisexual but I am bicurious.'

SADA

14 TO 21 JULY

They scream, hug, tell each other their names and rush around exploring their new home. It is just after 11 o'clock on Friday, 14 July and ten strangers have walked across the bridge and through the blue door into the house which will be home to them for weeks to come.

Three of them will stay for nine weeks, the others will drop out one by one after the end of the second week. But the cruel business of nominations and evictions is a long way from their minds as they begin to establish themselves in their new surroundings. Their first thought is: who are these other people? They have been given no information about the others – they have little idea of what to expect, and there is a lot of ice to be broken and ground to be covered. The excitement of the whole project carries them through the first awkward moments: just being there has given them all a tremendous bond.

They arrived at the *Big Brother* site in a fleet of limos with **BIG BRO** number plates, all travelling from the hotel where they had spent the previous evening chaperoned by members of the production team. They had believed the others were in different hotels but, in fact, they were all in the same one and their chaperones had had to walk past colleagues with blank faces.

There had been last-minute nerves. Nick promised to have an early night, going to his room at 10 p.m., but was later found in the bar with a bottle of wine. Anna had a dream that she would find two of her friends also in the house. She cried before breakfast, unsure whether she wanted to go through with the adventure.

As they left the cars and carried their suitcases across the bridge there had been a final chance to say goodbye to friends and family who turned up to wish them luck, as well as a barrage of press photographers to face. Then they were inside, the door was closed behind them, and they faced each other, the people who would be their comrades and their competitors in the weeks ahead.

Exploring the house is the first priority, getting to know the unfamiliar space which is about to become their home. They are all pleased because it is roomier, more modern and more comfortable than they had imagined. There is no argument about the dormitories – the only differences between the two rooms are the colour of the walls and the fact that one of them has a double bed among the singles. Without discussion or demur, the girls opt for the one with the more feminine colour scheme, with the lilac walls. In the boys' mint-green room Darren appropriates the double bed. Nobody minds – at six feet three inches, he is the tallest.

Chosen partly because they are strong, independent people, they cope with the difficulties of meeting a bunch of strangers very well. There is no shyness or awkwardness, except from Tom, who goes out into the garden with Sada and discovers the chickens while the others rush around like children.

Even amid the initial excitement, the characters of the individuals begin to assert themselves. Sada talks to the chickens; Craig, the cheeky scally, sees them and quips, 'Kentucky for tea, then?' Caroline starts as she goes on, with a cigarette and then a cup of tea. She managed to smuggle something into the house under the watchful eye of Big Brother: she put an extra lipstick and lipliner in the turn-up of her jeans. Andrew susses her, but assumes that her contraband is something more exciting – like drugs. He will come to realize, as will the whole nation, that for Caroline lipliner is an addiction and the thought of having to go without if she runs out would be akin to having her right arm cut off.

Nichola, the artist, colonizes her own space in the bedroom, sticking pictures on the wall, and presents her housemates with a 'Home Sweet Home' sign, which they hang in the living area. A monologue from Sada about her boyfriend, her book and herself soon bores Anna, who wanders away, saying nothing.

Already there are signs that Mel and Andy get on well. Having been to the same university, they discover they have friends in common, and plenty to talk about. But the most revealing conversation of the first day is between Andy and Nichola. Sitting in the garden with her, he discusses how he has used prostitutes in Amsterdam and Thailand. He explains that, in his eyes, what the prostitutes were doing was no different from him prostituting himself for money in his office job. Nichola tells him she wouldn't rule out working as a prostitute, although she never has.

'I've been a life model and I've sat nude for people, but I've never sold my body. But I mean, as I said to my dad the other day, if I'm really short of cash and I'm like fifty years old, I'll get my bits out and walk the street.'

The first game that the group plays is very revealing. It is not set for them by Big Brother, but is Nichola's idea. They all make three statements about themselves, two true and one a lie. The others have to guess the lie. But it is the truths that are more interesting. Andy has taken part in a live sex show in the Philippines and has played Nintendo with Princes William and Harry; Nick was at school with Prince Edward; Anna has been a novice nun; and Caroline has worked as a special constable. Craig manages to convince the group that he lied to Big Brother about being a builder, and that he's really a Pick'n'Mix and Slush Puppy vendor. Despite the rigorous selection procedure they have all been through, they gullibly accept that Craig has pulled the wool over the production team's eyes.

When darkness falls, they sit around chatting until two of the girls, Sada and Caroline, decide to go to bed. Both are surprisingly prudish. Sada tries to erect a screen to strip behind, away from the prying eyes of the cameras. When she is told by Big Brother that they must not do this, Caroline goes under the duvet to get changed. In the boys' room, Darren has also retired to bed early, wearing a fresh pair of designer pants. His fastidious personal habits will make him the butt of good-natured ribbing from the other lads in the days to come.

Out in the living room, everyone is very relaxed. Even Nicholas, who has been like a coiled spring all day, stops chain-smoking and tells his housemates about his skills as a reiki healer. It is only twelve hours since they met, but already they are getting to know a great deal about each other. Andy admits he fancies Mel, and she handles the admission with only a little embarrassment, saying 'I'm going to hide in the corner.'

Back in the girls' room Nichola produces a large white rock, which she has brought in as one of her luxuries. It is, she says, her skull from a former life as an Aztec. She says the universe has returned the skull to her, and now she uses it as a weight when she does weight-training exercises. In response to Caroline's suggestion that she lay off the acid, Nicky tells Caroline about the drugs she has taken in the past.

In the girls' dormitory there's a touching round of 'Goodnight and God bless' before the room finally goes quiet for the first night in the *Big Brother* house.

The boys stay up much later, and Craig sets the tone for their laddish discussion by farting loudly and then commenting that it will only be a matter of time before the girls fart, too. Then talk moves on to masturbation (Craig reckons he's found a place to do it where the cameras can't see him) and other all-boys-together trivia. Again, it's Craig who has the most to say, revealing that he's already made love on television – literally, on top of a set. He's also peed behind one at a friend's wedding.

The next day is their first true day in the house, they are about to experience the first complete cycle of *Big Brother*'s rhythm. Caroline, whose nickname Caggie is fast being adopted, particularly by Sada and Nichola, is still unhappy about being filmed without her clothes, and wears a pair of knickers in the shower. Darren beats her to the one-hour supply of hot water. The housemates soon realize that Darren is a man who likes to spend a lot of time on his personal grooming. Another thing they are beginning to find out about him is that he is an inspired cook; they will have plenty of time to appreciate his skills in the kitchen over the coming weeks.

Sada complains that she is not allowed a hairdryer, even though the *Big Brother* rules banning all electrical equipment were clearly laid down before they entered the house. After just over twenty-four hours, it's clear some of the others are already irritated by the glamorous hippie chick. Nichola has been heard to mutter that Sada needs her stylist; Caroline has been left in no doubt that Sada disapproves of her smoking in the bedroom (Sada didn't actually say anything, but the look on her face spoke volumes); and the boys have labelled her a 'wannabe'. They're bored by her constant talk of her boyfriend – Andy reckons she mentioned him 100 times in the first twelve hours. Nick, too, has joined the anti-Sada movement, telling the other lads that she plays up to the cameras.

There is one grievance she shares with the others, though, and Big Brother takes pity on them. There is no heating in the house, and it is colder than usual for the time of year, so sleeping bags are placed in the Store Room.

They also find the materials for their weekly task in the Store Room. They have been ordered by Big Brother to make their own crockery. They must each make a cup and a bowl by Tuesday morning. They've been given a potter's wheel and a generous supply of clay. Andy, competitive and determined to do well, makes a start. To his delight, Mel gravitates towards him and they work together, slippery hands brushing each other, like the famous seduction scene in the movie *Ghost*. However, Mel and Andy don't actually get beyond a few glances and touches. They find plenty to talk about though, and they have a shared sense of humour. When they spot Nichola and Sada talking quietly together Andrew suggests that they are 'comparing souls' which makes Mel giggle.

Nick gets the chance to demonstrate his healing powers by giving Caroline a reiki session. Without his hands touching her, she can feel heat from them and says she sees the colour purple throughout the session. There's more excitement for all of them when they hear a quick blast of music from over the garden fence. The PA system for a pop concert is being tested, and it's the first music they have heard in forty-eight hours. For several of them music deprivation is one of the hardest things to take in the *Big Brother* house, and they rush into the garden to make the most of it. Mel is hoisted up on to Darren's shoulders, but still cannot see out of the compound. Darren spins her round before lowering her to the ground. Later in the evening, inspired by the music wafting through the night, they decide to write their own pop song. Without pen or paper, the only way they can think of doing this is by cutting letters out of magazines and pasting them on to the wall. They plan to keep writing the song throughout their stay in the house – they even fantasize about the video they'll star in to promote it, which will, they hope, feature the house and the chickens.

Thomas has still not made much contact with anyone within the group, and seems happiest mooching around with the chickens. He answers questions, but never seems to initiate conversations. He doesn't even join in with a kick around in the garden, saying that he only plays Gaelic football (Nichola reckons that's the same as ordinary football 'but you get pissed first'.) Is Tom very unhappy? Called to the Diary Room to discuss how he's getting on, he explains that he is a late starter and he finds it hard to relate to a large group, but he is gradually relaxing. There are real fears among the production team that the shy Irishman is finding it too hard to take and will be packing his suitcase and walking out soon.

When Mel goes into the Diary Room, there are no such fears. 'It's fantastic, they're a fantastic bunch of people, a great group, and we're all getting on splendidly,' she tells Big Brother.

By late evening, it's time for more revelations. Anna tells the group she is gay. Sada, who is wearing the strange and wonderful 'ostrich' jacket, which Nicky designed and made herself, congratulates her and tells how she has kissed a woman.

Later, in the boys' bedroom, Andrew comments that Anna is the most attractive lesbian he has ever seen. However, he soon turns to the subject of his real interest, Mel. He announces that he loves her nipples, describing them as 'looking like she's smuggling peanuts'. The girls are also talking about Mel; they tell her that they reckon both Darren and Andy fancy her. Mel says she finds Nick the most interesting of the men, and Caroline coos about his lovely blue eyes.

Sex is obviously on everybody's mind. Darren leaps out of bed and announces that he's going to make a large clay penis to leave outside the girls' room. With much giggling the model is made and put in position. There is even more giggling when Sada finds it and calls the others. They want to know who the model was.

Sunday dawns quietly enough, but quickly turns into one of the most exciting days in the house as Nicky decides to use the clay to decorate the walls. She starts with a few handprints and is then inspired to remove all her clothes and thrust her clay-covered body against the wall. Others join in with Mel and Andy doing bottom prints side by side, and Craig stripping naked to put a full-length print of his body on the wall. When he complains it doesn't do justice to his manhood, Nichola makes the appropriate part of the print bigger – much bigger. It's fun and silly but interesting to see how the others react. Darren thinks they're mad, but happily adds his handprints. Nick watches. Anna helps Mel get her trousers off. Sada joins in, but wears her bikini. Only Tom and Caroline remain outside the group – Caroline practising her saxophone and Tom sitting in the garden.

After the 'decorating' is over, Craig carries Nicky to the shower and they wash the clay off each other. Why have they behaved so outrageously?

Living in such close proximity with one another, sharing restricted washing facilities, they are all going to have to get used to each other's bodies, and Nicky's exuberant naked painting helps at least some of them to get over any initial worries about this in a fun and outrageous way. As there are cameras everywhere they have all accepted that their bodies are on show, and by making such a public statement of the fact they have laid any fears to rest and got the issue out of the way.

The day continues to be lively. Nicky has her head reshaved by Darren, and again she's the spark for another craze. Both Craig and Tom have their heads shaved by Caroline.

Nick is quietly talking to all the others, asking them questions and planting ideas in their minds. He's playing a long game. He's the only one who at this stage seems to be aware that in just over a week they will have to nominate candidates for eviction. No one will be evicted in the first week, to give the contestants a fortnight to get to know each other. Nick asks Darren about his character, and Darren at first answers cheerfully enough. However, when Nick suggests that, because of his designer gear, some people might think he is a drug dealer, Darren takes offence. He is also offended by Andy's question about how he can afford to have three children. But Darren shows himself to be basically equable and his annoyance evaporates rapidly. It's clear, though, that he is no pushover.

Mel has flirted with Darren and has flirted lots with Andy. Now she flirts with Nick as they openly discuss the rest of the residents, and who will be voted out first.

The shopping list is a major weekly ritual, one of the few areas of their lives they have any control over. Anna, slotting herself into a maternal role, takes charge of writing out the blackboard list of goods to be bought with £105, calculated on the basis of £1.50 each per day. Sada, who told everybody on the first day that her vegetarianism would not create any problems, wants tahini, tofu and more fresh fruit on the list, and already some of the others see this as a problem. With so little to spend, it's vital they all agree on what they are going to eat. They come up with a surprising list. They don't seem to have much idea about forward planning. They have spent two-thirds of their money on booze, ordering five bottles of white wine, four of red, eight bottles of cider and ten cans of lager. Therefore, there's not going to be much food to go round for the week. And there's no toilet paper! Big Brother tells them that it is their own fault, and they discuss other options, including ripping up towels or using their hands – 'the Asian way' as Mel describes it.

But they are not left to fend for themselves completely and Big Brother provides a couple of useful presents: a heater and a first-aid kit donated because Darren has cut his finger opening a tin.

While everyone sleeps the garden plays host to an uninvited guest. A fox has managed to scale the walls and patrols the lawn. It leaves without harming the chickens, perhaps scared off by the movement of the ever-present cameras, or perhaps it is so much of an urban fox that killing chickens is too much like hard work when there are rubbish bins on neighbouring housing estates to raid. The fox has been seen before in the studio yard and it has even wandered inside the studio building.

Nick surprises Mel and wins Andy's undying admiration by telling them that he worked as a male escort in a business he ran with two of his friends. He charged £130 to make love to the women clients, but only did it, he says, if he fancied them. Mel is fascinated while Andy is bowled over and envious. Nick says he made love to twenty-three women, and if they were particularly nice he would stay the night and leave at 6 a.m. He rejects Mel's description of this as prostitution.

Already, the effects of food rationing are kicking in. Darren is hungry and he confides to Big Brother that he normally spends £105 on his own food alone. He fantasizes to the others about bowling down to the shops to buy a juice drink and a KitKat. He may also be fantasizing about Mel. He sings a song to her, slips his arm around her waist, and even sits astride her feeding her slices of orange. However, it seems that Darren just loves the attention of women, any women. He gives Sada a hug and enjoys a head massage from Nicky. Mel, not to be neglected, carefully massages suncream into Andrew's face and neck. Caroline and some of the other girls believe that she's just stringing him along.

Caroline is very worried that Big Brother knows about her contraband and will take her lipstick and lipliner from her. She isn't sure she'll survive without her trademark pink lips. However, she rallies and persuades the troops to join her aerobics class. Only Tom stays inside, while the rest stretch and bend on the lawn. Sada and Nicky chant, 'We must, we must, we must improve our bust.'

Tom still seems to be detached from the group, but he assures Big Brother that things are getting easier for him. He blames his reticence on his accent – because people don't readily understand him, he hesitates to speak out. In a one-to-one situation, though, he shows he has plenty to say when he settles down to a long chat with Mel.

Mel is evasive in her latest chat with Big Brother and boasts afterwards of how she avoided answering questions about her relationships with the others. Her trip to the Diary Room has a beneficial outcome in that Big Brother announces that if the housemates clean all the windows they will be allowed four toilet rolls. They set to work willingly – well, apart from Nick, who tries to pretend he has done the windows in the boys' room when he hasn't. Mel catches him out in the lie, but he seems unabashed.

Five days into the *Big Brother* experience everyone is having a problem with sleep. Forbidden watches or clocks, they have to rely on two clocks in the living area. With lights on in the passageways and living areas all night, the house is never truly dark. They are gradually staying up later and sleeping in later, a pattern that's been observed in other *Big Brother* projects. The Dutch contestants ended up sleeping all day and being awake all night. Some of the housemates are missing out on the one hour of hot water for showers. Also, with the exception of Nick, they're all napping during the afternoons. Craig is napping so much that the others have nicknamed him 'The Incredible Sleeping Man'.

The girls are better at getting up than the boys and Tuesday morning finds Mel and Anna having a quiet tête-à-tête. Anna reveals that she lost her virginity to a man at the age of twenty-two. It was after she had decided to abandon her plans to be a nun, partly because she found herself fancying the sisters in the convent. She decided to make sure of her sexuality by 'double-checking' with a heterosexual encounter. Mel, normally fascinated by every detail of her fellow contestants' lives, can't get into the conversation and decides to go back to bed.

The hens have already been the focus of a great deal of interest within the house, and they're now coming into their own. Supplies are low – putting alcohol above food was a rash decision, and now that it is also running out the housemates are really regretting their foolishness. But the hens have done them proud, and there are eggs for breakfast – as well as the pan full of porridge that Nick makes every morning. There are even enough eggs for Andy and Mel to make pancakes for everyone, an exercise which gives Andy the chance to put his arms round Mel as he teaches her how to toss them. The Mel-and-Andy relationship is developing quickly, but he's making most of the running. When she complains about the effects of sunbathing on her skin, he tells her that she is 'the perfect colour', and she rewards him by taking him into the garden and painting his toenails gold. Earlier in the day, Mel had been flirting outrageously with Nick over a game of backgammon in the garden. Nick, for all his apparent suavity, is surprisingly clumsy when it comes to flirting.

In the Diary Room, Andy tells Big Brother that he, Mel and Nick are getting on well, perhaps because they have more in common than the others. He has noticed how Mel asks a lot of questions but deflects any that are put to her.

'I've enjoyed meeting cool, different people through being in the house, and it's completely different from working with boring papers in my day job... People aren't trying to encroach or take over things. I like watching people and feeding my observations back to them. I'm particularly interested in Mel, but there is a double standard operating there, because she asks questions about others but won't answer any about herself.'

He tells Big Brother that he is pleased to be the subject of the first real gossip in the house. Everyone is speculating whether he and Mel really fancy each other.

Sada continues to lament about the wonderful boyfriend she has left outside the house. The boys are not at all keen on Sada, and she has acquired the nicknames 'Skoda', 'Lada' and 'LaLa'. At first Darren seemed to really like her, but she's managed to alienate him by cross-questioning about the book of anatomy he brought into the house with him. She wants to know if he is doing a course in the human body, and if he isn't, why is he interested in the subject? The affable Darren becomes surly under her relentless probing, but neatly turns the tables by questioning the extent of her experience in yoga. Why, he wants to know, does she have to keep referring to her textbook if she's been doing it for four years? He looks distinctly unimpressed when she fails to hook her right leg behind her head. True to form, Andy speculates that because Sada is so thin, and into yoga, she must be able to get herself into amazing positions for sex.

Nicky, the art graduate, is the only one of the group who has brought her normal everyday working life with her – even if there is nothing very normal about Nicky's art work. She spends her time knitting with wire. Short of other materials, she is gradually using up the supply of magazines to make papier-mâché models. She makes a large, colourful heart which she fixes to the door of the girls' bedroom.

There's still a giggly schoolkids atmosphere in the house, with lots of talk about silly jokes that the two camps – the boys and the girls – can play on each other. Most of the jokes don't get past the planning stage and most seem to involve putting chickens into the dormitories. However, the boys do carry one out: while the girls linger over the dinner table they raid the girls' bedroom, pulling their clothes off and diving into their beds. Andrew leaps into Sada's bed, Craig plunges under Nicky's duvet, Darren goes into Anna's, Tom into Mel's and Nick, who only removes his shoes, goes into Caroline's. The girls are astonished and, despite all the horseplay that has been going on between the sexes, irritated. Caroline shouts out 'Don't leave your willies and your pubic hairs in our beds!' and there are cries of 'No wanking!' and 'No semen!'.

Later on, when the house has settled down to sleep, Andrew makes another trip to the Diary Room to talk quietly with Big Brother about the growing pressure of his relationship with Mel. He says he does not want to come on too strong and scare her off. Back in the dormitory, he says much the same thing to Nick and Tom, asserting that he's going to take the relationship down a couple of gears 'or something's got to break'.

He tries, he really does. The next day he even announces to his mate Nick that he'll nominate her for eviction if she doesn't stop bitching, and says he could never go out with a girl like her. However, later in the day he massages her back for more than half an hour, so it seems as though he's slipping the gears back up again.

He has a long chat with Nick as they wash their smalls together in a bucket on the patio and it is a full-scale bitching session about their housemates. They agree that Caroline is useless, although Andy admires her drive and focus when she is running the aerobics classes, that Craig lacks integrity and only enjoys stripping off because he is well endowed, and that Sada has partially redeemed herself by being 'sweet', although they still laugh about her 'everything is beautiful' approach to life. Andy does have a good word to say about one of the others – he rates Tom 'a solid bloke'. Nick simply says that Tom is very silent.

The food crisis is growing, and there is the horrible realization that they are running out of sugar which they need to activate the yeast to make their daily bread. Even worse, there's no booze left, apart from a stash that Andrew has put away for his birthday next week. Although they are supposed to go into the Diary Room one by one, they steam in there en masse and plead with Big Brother for more, because, they say, they are all alcoholics. The answer, when Big Brother gets back to them, is no – they've already spent £64 on alcohol this week.

In the Diary Room Mel asks for more tasks, anything to keep her busy. She says she has a volatile nature, and she thinks having more to do would help her control the moments when she feels very tense. She tells Big Brother that the girls felt very uncomfortable when the boys got into their beds. 'It was an invasion of what little privacy we have.' She says she thinks the youngest participants, particularly Darren, who is missing his kids, are having the toughest time.

'Yesterday was the first day when the severity of it all kicked in, and I realized how hard it would be. It's claustrophobic because of the lack of space, and the need to occupy time. People are thinking far ahead, and I feel it is a shame that they have to make judgements about each other with nominations.'

Mel says that she is getting on 'very, very well' with Andy, and is intrigued by Nick and wants to find out more about him. The girls had a good bonding session the previous night, and she really likes Anna and wants to hear about her experiences and life. She sees various roles in the house developing. Hers is making the bread, although on Andy's advice she's going to stop doing it so much. Andy is the team leader, but Mel feels he needs to make sure he doesn't aggravate other people. Darren is the baby of the house and the others are all concerned about him. Sada is the shoulder to cry on 'or at least, she thinks she is'. And Caroline is the maternal onlooker. Mel says she knows that people don't like her temper. She's very good at understanding other people but not good at understanding herself, she says.

Despite her plea to Big Brother to keep her busy, Mel doesn't get a task. However Sada distracts her, telling her how she had a nose job to improve her modelling prospects. Mel is fascinated, yelling out loud 'You've had a nose job?!' Sada explains that her nose was broken when she had an accident when she was fourteen, and that it looked flat in photographs. Having the op helped her win enough modelling work to finance her travels around Bali and Thailand.

Anna has rivalled Tom as the quietest member of the group, and apart from two medical emergencies – she had a problem with one of her teeth and also burned herself with hot soup – she hasn't commanded a lot of attention from the others or from Big Brother. However, unlike Tom, Anna's quietness is a measure of her self-containment. She's not shy or unsure of herself in the group, and today she comes more into her own. She chats at length with Nichola, who talks about her own bisexuality and her lesbian relationships, laughing over her first amorous encounter with a girl when she was at college. Later on, Anna's wicked sense of humour comes to the fore, when she devises a practical joke that they all play on Darren. Aware that he is afraid of the chickens, they hatch a plan while he is in the toilet to tell him that Big Brother has given him the individual task of cleaning out the chicken coop.

Darren falls for it, and even makes a valiant attempt at it, but retreats to the Diary Room to complain. When Big Brother tells him that no such task was set, he finds it hard to believe that the others have conned him so convincingly.

'You're joking me!' he says to the faceless voice of Big Brother, only to be told 'Big Brother doesn't joke.'

The joke with the chickens is a moment of light relief for Darren, who earlier in the day in the Diary Room movingly confessed how much he is missing his three children, which is making life in the house hard for him.

Caroline is finding it hard, too, but for a very different reason. She took twenty-nine packets of cigarettes in with her but she's getting through them at a frightening rate. All the housemates who smoke are puffing away like mad – even Nick, who had described himself as a non-smoker, is lighting up every few minutes, smoking his way through the supplies that Andy (who doesn't smoke) brought in with him.

The food crisis worsens over the next two days as the end of the first week looms. It has its funny moments as the girls fantasize about who among the housemates they would eat first if times got really desperate. They decide on Craig, who would be good with a BBQ sauce marinade. As if he knows they are discussing him, Craig ambles into the girls' bedroom and climbs into bed with Caroline, who cuddles up to him for a chat – causing not just her temperature to rise, but the excitement level in the production control room to shoot up. However, Craig's body language says he is definitely there for a friendly chat and no more.

There's a little much-needed relief from the preoccupation with food when Big Brother gives them a box of fruit. It's small compensation for the news that

MAKING BREAD THE BIG BROTHER WAY

BASIC WHITE BREAD

You will need
500g strong white flour
  (for wholemeal bread,
  substitute 250g strong
  wholemeal flour for
  half the white flour)
1 sachet fast-acting yeast
1 teaspoon of sugar
  to activate yeast
  (if necessary, depending
  on type of yeast)
1 teaspoon salt
1 tablespoon vegetable
  or olive oil
350mls lukewarm water

METHOD

1 Add the sugar to the yeast. Add yeast and salt to the flour and stir in thoroughly. Add water and oil and bring together to form a dough.
2 Sprinkle more flour on work surface and knead the dough for 8–10 minutes. Add more flour if the dough is too sticky. When the dough is fully kneaded, it should be smooth and spring back lightly if pressed gently with a finger.
3 Pre-heat the oven to 190°C (fan oven) or 220°C (non-fan). Lightly grease a 2 lb loaf tin and put in the dough. Cover with lightly greased cling film and leave in a warm place for about 45 minutes or until doubled in size.
4 Remove cling film and place bread in oven about halfway up to allow it to rise. Cook for 30–40 minutes, until golden brown on top.
5 Remove bread from the oven and take out of the tin. If the bread is cooked, it will sound hollow when tapped. Cool on a wire rack.

they have failed their pottery task – several of their efforts have cracked in the kiln, and only Thomas has managed to make two that survived. As a result, they're going to lose £20 from their next shopping budget – a depressing thought when they've managed so badly on the full amount. Mel gives them all a pep talk about how important it is that they pass the next test.

As the week draws to a close, nominations for eviction begin to prey on everyone's minds and become a regular topic for discussion. Nick begins the first of his campaigns to make sure the voting goes the way that suits him, by getting the rest of the boys to agree that Caroline and Sada should be nominated. The girls are also talking about who should go out, but there is no discussion of their votes, only a suggestion from Sada that it would be better if it was a boy than a girl.

The feeling of two separate camps developing – boys versus girls – has been slowly increasing all week. When the girls have a late-night chat about their sexuality, Anna, Mel and Nichola all admit they have had relationships with both sexes. Sada, who describes herself as 'bicurious', feels left out, although she admits to having sucked a woman's toes, kissed a woman and almost been part of a threesome. Caroline also admits she has been attracted to women, but has never done anything about it. She wishes there was a gay guy in the house to have a laugh with. Mel says she is not comfortable about being labelled bisexual but it's nothing to do with her mum finding out. She says her mum would prefer her to date women, as she thinks all men are unreliable scoundrels. It is also easier, Mel says, to sleep with women because they know more than men do about pleasing a woman in bed, adding that she thinks the female body is much sexier than the male. Andrew tries to come into their room to join in but Sada gives him his marching orders, telling him it is girlie talk. Taking pity on him, Mel follows him out to the living area and hugs him.

The next day, Sada regrets her frankness, and in the Diary Room asks Big Brother not to show her sex talk on television, in case it is misconstrued. She is worried that she is going to be evicted. She says she has nothing in common with any of the boys. Later, she says to Mel and the other girls: 'I think everyone seeing it on telly will be going: "What a stuck-up bitch."' She is slowly becoming more paranoid about her unpopularity in the house, especially with the boys, and she tries hard to make sure that the girls are all her friends.

The sniping between the two camps continues. The boys think the girls are hoarding precious toilet rolls. Craig, 'The Incredible Sleeping Man', irritates the girls. Mel has a theory that he is conserving his energy because he really wants to win the contest. Craig says all Caroline contributes are Jim Bowen impressions. Sada says the boys are immature, and at twenty-eight, she has grown beyond talking about masturbation.

There are more intimate revelations before the end of the week. Craig talks movingly to Sada about his father's death, when he was only thirteen. He tells her that when the police stopped the drunk driver responsible, he didn't even know he had hit someone. Although Craig did not attend the court case, he was upset that the driver lived only half a mile away from him, his mum and his sister. Sada, listening attentively, tells him that she has had an easy life. Craig says he wishes he had been more mature at the time of the death, so that he could have helped his mum more.

'I feel guilty about what my mum went through. I wasn't very helpful at the time,' he says. Sada is very touched, and tells him that one day he will make a great dad.

Tom tells Anna, Darren and Caroline that he may already be a dad. The quiet Irishman has been told by two different clairvoyants that he has a child and, despite visiting the mystics four years apart, they both assessed the age of the child consistently. If they are right, Tom's son or daughter is now nine years old and unaware of his or her dad's existence.

Given an innocuous late-night discussion topic by Big Brother about whether they prefer dogs or cats, once again the group manage to turn it very quickly into sex talk by taking the names of their first pets, and combining them with their mother's maiden names to give themselves a new, porn-star identity. Darren becomes Champion Lloyd, Craig becomes Rocky Everett, Nick becomes Ross Hunter, Andy becomes Buster Coen, Tom becomes Blackie McDonald, Mel becomes Lady Walcott, Anna becomes Chloe Reagan, Caroline becomes Charlie Kelly, and Nicky becomes Ginger Greenhouse. However, best of all in the porn-star stakes, is Sada with Miffy Duncan!

As their first week in the house draws to a close, the group are rewarded with ice cream and alcohol by Big Brother, which makes their Friday evening meal altogether more palatable than those in the past few days, and they toast their success in making it this far. When they retire to their own rooms, however, the pleasant dinner has done nothing to bring the two camps closer together. The girls stay awake bemoaning the lack of an intelligent, attractive, older man in the house. They chat until Nicky, who is trying to sleep, sits up and delivers a tirade of abuse at them. They have all become accustomed to her liberal use of four-letter words, but this stream is stronger and longer than most, and achieves her aim. They all settle down to sleep.

Most of them have been to the Diary Room during the course of the day, to record their comments on life after one week in the *Big Brother* experience.

Sada is unhappy. 'I've been blocking out missing Raff. Andrew was saying he'd had a few moments – a cry – which made me realize I shouldn't block... It's good for me to have a little cry. I was nervous about what was being shown on television, not for me but for what my boyfriend would construe from it – the nakedness, the scenes around the house. My nerves were centred around those kind of issues, and I've been worrying about losing Raff.'

Despite these fears, she says she has no regrets about coming into the house. 'A big thank you for an interesting project. It's quite overwhelming, unlike anything any of us have ever done.'

Tom tells Big Brother that he has consciously slowed down the speed of his speech, so that people can understand him despite his accent.

'The hardest thing is that I can't slip out of the door to get a bar of choco-late, or go to the fridge... there's no pressure here, no outside influence. It's strange not to interact with the news. The imagination runs wild. Will we be popular? Is anyone watching? I feel marooned. But it's pleasant not to have to worry about bills, about pleasing people, about work, and it's good passing your days in the company of friends.'

Caroline, who earlier in the week told Big Brother she was naturally a loner, says that things are getting better. She knows the boys object to the girl/boy divide, but she thinks it is natural. She's over her fear of the shower and the toilet, but she misses going to the park with her nephews and nieces. She finds it hard to talk to the boys, and she's not sure why some of them came as all they want to do is sleep.

Darren's talk in the Diary Room revolves around how much he is missing his children – he thinks about them more than he expected, and he wishes there were other people in the house who had children and could share his feelings. He's not happy about the food, which is far too bland, and he's going to make sure they think hard about the next shopping list. But he's happy to be in the house, and he doesn't worry about the nominations because he will be just as happy to go home.

For Anna, one of the great discoveries of the first week is that they can have a laugh without a drink. It's the laughter that's keeping her going, she tells Big Brother. She's missing roast dinners, cups of tea and KitKats. 'But it's not really about missing anything, it's about here being difficult... Everyone is really insecure, everyone is pushing their personalities, and then getting slagged off just for their personalities.'

Craig's trips to the Diary Room are less frequent than those of any other member of the household, and when he is summoned there he waits to be questioned by Big Brother, and answers briefly. At the end of this first week, he reports that he is missing his normally active life, but enjoying not having to work. He says Caroline annoys him by putting on funny voices, and that Andrew and Sada had a real argument yesterday. Asked by Big Brother how he has changed, Craig says: 'I've gone quiet. My plan is to sit back and not jump in like everyone else. I'm holding my fire.'

Andrew reports in the Diary Room that the tension in the house is mounting, and he would normally deal with this sort of tension by going for a drive or going into his own room. He says he will concentrate on physical tasks, like sweeping the porch, and yoga. He predicts that Sada and Mel will have the first argument, as they are both strong characters. It annoys him that Sada doesn't listen. He describes them both as 'unyielding and confident ladies who know what they want'.

Mel ends the week by reiterating that she is getting on well with Andy, but that she hates being asked questions about sex all the time. The girls have told her that the boys have a crush on her. 'I'm not comfortable with that. Why would people come into the house for sex?' she says.

Nick tells Big Brother that he is really enjoying being in the house. 'It's good fun, everyone is pulling together, there are pockets of friendship forming.' He talks about the looming nominations, but more than any of the others he seems concerned about the impact the programme is having on the outside world, saying that the first round of nominations will be the hardest 'as the public don't really know us yet'. He is wondering how popular *Big Brother* is proving.

The housemates have spent their first week completely oblivious to what is going on in the outside world, and unaware of the impact the *Big Brother* experiment is making out there. The media coverage has been enormous, ranging from heavyweight discussions of the implications of the experience, to betting on the likely winner. The critics label the show 'voyeur vision', 'excruciatingly intimate' and 'the greatest show on earth for peeping toms and nosey parkers'. It is described as a 'human zoo' and the 'ultimate fly-on-the-wall documentary'.

However, it's not the nature of the show that dominates the headlines, but the ten contestants themselves. Their pictures, and potted biographies, are splashed across double spreads in all the popular newspapers. On the first evening that the programme is broadcast, five days after they arrived at the house, four million viewers tune in to watch them. The internet site is being visited so often that it is struggling to keep up with demand. The biggest complaint in the first week is that it is difficult to get through to watch the house live on the net. The techies at *Big Brother* race to get more servers on-line, to keep up with the thousands of people who want to call up the inside of the house on their screens.

After only a day on air, both the *Sun* and the *Daily Star* are running headlines about Nick and his machinations. 'Naff off, Nick,' says the *Daily Star*, based on a bookie's odds on who will be kicked out first. 'Kick out Nick,' says the *Sun*, delivering a readers' verdict on who the most hated man in the show is.

Several of the popular papers are appealing for readers who know the contestants to contact them, and already there are features appearing about their private lives. Before they went into the house, the contestants were warned by the production team that ex-lovers and ex-friends might come forward to do kiss-'n'-tell articles about them, and it has started. While Nick is drip-feeding his views on the others to each housemate in turn, a colleague describes him as a 'Walter Mitty character', and says that in ten years of knowing Nick he never heard about his escort agency work. A school friend describes him as 'a sandwich short of a picnic'.

Andy's antics are also subject to early speculation, with the *News of the World* claiming he made a move on Mel as soon as they met, before they got inside the house.

For Craig, there is even bigger exposure when one of his ex-girlfriends tells the *Sunday People* that when she was with him he was no super-stud – he simply went to sleep. That will come as no surprise to his fellow contestants, who have already dubbed him 'The Incredible Sleeping Man'. His girlfriend conceded, however, that the reason he was so tired was that he worked hard all day.

Craig also made the day for an anonymous punter who put on a £20 bet that he and Caroline would be the first to get between the sheets. Although it was only an innocent cuddle and chat, when Craig climbed in with Caroline it was enough to net the punter £500. But he lost out on his other bets – he'd also staked £20 on Caroline being first in bed with two of the other boys.

Even before the show went on air, bookies were offering odds on who would win, with the skateboarding and lesbian ex-novice-nun Anna topping the list. By the end of the first week in the house, the tide of bets is increasing.

WEEK ONE FACT FILE

TASK **PASS ■ FAIL ☒**	To make their own crockery with clay and a potter's wheel.
BOOKIES' FAVOURITE **TO WIN**	Mel is 4/1 favourite. Anna and Craig are joint second at 5/1.
TO WALK	Caroline and Nick are favourites at 4/1, with Sada next at 5/1.

WHAT THE EXPERT SAYS

'Nudity and semi-nudity were set up as a group norm very early on. The clay painting is a turning point in the house. Nichola initiates it, and it is very innocent, primal, tactile. Then Melanie turns up the heat and is like a catalyst. She completely changes the atmosphere; it becomes highly sexualized. It has changed from innocence to adult sexuality. Where can we take it from here? Perhaps we are going to see more private moments between two people who have paired off, more private nudity than full public displays.'

Anjula Mutanda, Counselling Psychologist

WEEK TWO

*'I don't want to play this stupid game and I don't
want to be nice to people I think are prats.'*

SADA

21 TO 28 JULY

At the end of the first week Anna, one of the quietest and most perceptive of the housemates, sums up in the Diary Room what living in the *Big Brother* house involves. There are eight things, she says, which she has to remember every day:

'You wanna get on with everyone. You wanna keep some sense of independence. You wanna have time to yourself. There's £70,000 to be won at the end of the day. You don't want to get evicted. You don't want to evict anyone else. You want to contribute to the group. But you don't want to come across as OTT.'

The strain of all these different demands is beginning to show, not just on Anna but on all ten contestants, as they slip into their second week. With nominations looming, there is friction and tension in the air.

Fortunately, Big Brother hands their second task to them on Saturday morning, and it's a task designed to make sure they all co-operate and chat to one another. They are each asked to answer ten simple questions about themselves, including their star sign, which bit of their body they most hate, their favourite movie, and what one thing they would rescue if their home was on fire. They must then memorize the answers everybody else gives, and on Wednesday they will be tested. If more than one answer from the whole group is wrong, they will have failed the test. They decide, despite misgivings by some about how good their memories are, to gamble 40 per cent of their weekly shopping total on the challenge. They are given blackboards on which to write their lists, but have to hand these in after half an hour. From now on, they must talk to one another. They are all desperate to earn some extra money, so they set to learning with a will. The girls are astonished to hear the very slim Sada say she hates her bum because it is too big. Caroline tells them all she hates her feet so much she never walks around barefoot. Darren, described by Sada as 'the vainest man in the world', says the least favourite part of his body is his back, because he can't see it.

Three of the girls are feeling distinctly unwell this morning, with upset tummies. The boys had taken over the kitchen to prepare the evening meal last night, and Mel thinks it was definitely something to do with the Spanish omelettes they cooked that has given her, Nicky and Sada stomach cramps. The others are unaffected. Darren didn't eat the omelette – not only is he afraid of chickens, he doesn't eat eggs.

However, his fear of chickens is about to be overcome. With Mel's encouragement, he goes into the garden and picks up one of the hens. He's not exactly comfortable with the experience, but it's an improvement on running away whenever one of the feathered inhabitants of the *Big Brother* house strolls by.

There is something more important than chickens on Darren's mind. Tomorrow is the first birthday of his youngest daughter. He's going to miss the party, and he knows it may be weeks before he gets to see her and his other two children.

Mel visits the Diary Room, and pours out her feelings about Sada to Big Brother.

'I'm getting particularly frustrated with one person, and I recognize the reason why and feel bad about it. Sada and myself are very similar: very strong-willed, stubborn, bloody-minded and opinionated. She's blinkered, she doesn't listen to anything around her.'

She says she has not told Sada how she feels. 'I would bring it up if I thought it would be positive, but it would only increase the friction between us. I feel guilty for feeling like this about her.

'She's caring, giving, fascinating. But she's also bloody-minded, rigid in her views and her thought patterns.'

Big Brother gives the group a discussion topic: tattoos and piercings. It's a subject most of them know something about. Darren, who says he hates piercings, admits that in his teens he had several coloured studs in his nose. They are all very interested in Tom's little devil tattoo, because it has been done with henna and will fade naturally after three to five years. But it's Mel's clitoris piercing that causes the most interest. She says it keeps her in a permanent state of arousal, and that's enough to make Nicky, Sada and Caroline want one. They ask Big Brother if they can have a visit from a professional piercer. After hearing Nicky's description of having her tongue pierced by a friend who did it with a needle while holding the tongue with baking tongs, they definitely want a professional! Nicky's tongue swelled up and turned green. Big Brother gets back to them with the decision that there will be no body piercing inside the house.

For the second night running, Darren doesn't eat with the others. He does not like eggs, and he doesn't like lamb, so it is sausage and mash for him while the others eat roast lamb. Sada won't give him any of her vegetarian rations, and he becomes the second person that day to go to the Diary Room to vent his irritation with her. Andrew tells the other boys he thinks that she'll be dumped when she leaves the house by the boyfriend she talks about so much because he will have been embarrassed watching her on television.

Whatever bad feelings the boys have about Sada, the girls are almost unanimously feeling the same about Andy. They think he's arrogant, and worse. They reckon Craig would be the easiest of the men to live with, even though he sleeps such a lot. 'That's what would make it easy,' says Sada. Only Mel doesn't share the general dislike of Andy. The two of them are very close, and getting closer. The girls are beginning to distrust Mel, bitching that she's playing games to ensure her popularity and that she's too eager to please the boys.

On Sunday, the shopping list has to be compiled, and it's going to be tough because they lost the challenge and have only £84 to spend. Sada takes control, and forcefully insists that tofu is on the list. She also wants chocolate instead of oranges, and refuses to give any ground. Only after she has handed the list into Big Brother do the others mutiny and insist that tofu comes off and is replaced with instant coffee. Big Brother takes pity on her and when the shopping arrives there is an extra package of vegetarian food, including tofu. It's a more sensible shopping list this time, with more food and less alcohol. (The alcohol they have bought is cheap beer and cider, to the horror of some members of the household.)

Exercise is a constant preoccupation of the housemates who find the days long and boring. The aerobics and yoga classes continue. Also, there have been games of Gaelic football and ordinary football and Craig came up with the idea of playing rounders using a frying pan. Unfortunately, the balls kept disappearing over the wall and nobody threw them back. Sada, who brought juggling balls and tennis balls into the house with her, complained later that 'the boys just did not respect my balls'.

Anna, who occasionally rises before the others, has shown that she's good at basketball, bouncing the ball around the garden before putting it safely into the bucket the boys have hung up as a net. Nick is always up for any kind of game, although when they played 'piggy in the middle' he was frustrated to find himself trapped in the middle for twenty-five minutes, with the others throwing the ball at him instead of over him.

Sada continues to be a thorn in the boys' sides, especially Andrew's. He practically reduces her to tears when questioning her about why she doesn't want the dormitories to be mixed sex. Sada, who told the girls two days ago that she felt all the men found her attractive and she felt a sexual tension from them, says: 'Unless I was having a physical relationship with a man, I would have to have my own privacy. I just feel shy. I don't actually think it would be very healthy. I think there are sexual dimensions to the group and I think that would probably provoke them.'

Andrew tells her he thinks she is a confident person. Getting away from the bedroom theme, he then opens up about his opinion of her. He tells her she is so keen to put her own opinion across that she ignores what others are trying to say. 'And you can wind people up by doing that.'

Sada is hurt, but puts on a brave face, confessing later that she might cry in bed that night.

Soon afterwards Andy and Mel are in the greenhouse together, tending the tomatoes, and he tells her about his attack on Sada. Mel agrees that Sada is causing the big divide between boys and girls in the house, and says she finds it hard to deal with 'girlie bitchiness'. However, Andy doesn't dwell too long on Sada. With Mel trapped in a small space with him, he wants to talk about matters closer to his heart, like her pierced clitoris. He says her story about it 'gave me the horn' and he says he would have married his ex-girlfriend if she'd had a piercing like Mel's. Then he tells her how all but one of his exes have cheated on him – with the kind of details he's been revealing about his sex life since he joined the *Big Brother* house he should hardly be surprised. Only the day before he was telling them how, on his last birthday, he had sex with a husband-and-wife team. He also admits that he sometimes fakes orgasms to keep girls happy. He would have had to with one girl he told Mel about whom he claims had fifteen orgasms a day. When Mel asks what went wrong with the relationship, he says he had to stop having sex with her before he killed her.

Big Brother has a message for all of them: they must stop discussing the forthcoming nominations. It works for a time, and the subject of voting is temporarily dropped. Nick, unable to take part in his usual plotting, still needs to talk about the nominations and goes into the Diary Room to talk to Big Brother.

'Tomorrow is the day we have to make our minds up. Probably everybody has already made their minds up. It is going to be sad to see anybody go. Once you leave this house it will be incredibly emotional. I will shed a tear when I leave.'

Nichola is also worrying about the nominations. She tells Big Brother: 'I'll feel upset if someone picks me. I don't want to leave early.' She explains that she leaves the group to do her own thing because she finds it 'boring playing cards and sitting talking rubbish'. However, she admits, 'It'd be bloody annoying if everyone was like me and running around all day.' She asks for more needles and wire, which she is knitting into 'a dream coat'.

This is a difficult day for Darren, and he goes into the Diary Room to blow kisses to his daughter. Her birthday must be on his mind as by Darren's standards he's up really early. He, more than any of the others has switched night into day, occasionally only getting up in the evening. The others have nicknamed him the 'Prince of Darkness' and 'The Count'.

Big Brother has a wonderful surprise for him. All the housemates are assembled around the large television screen on the wall in the living room – Big Brother can send them pictures, but they cannot use it as a normal TV. The pictures it relays to them now bring tears to lots of eyes. It is a video of his daughter's birthday party, complete with pink iced birthday cake with one candle. All Darren's kids look so cute that tears run down his face, and all the rest of the gang are choked. Craig goes and finds a bottle of wine from his stash to give to Darren. After thanking Big Brother, Darren sobs in Mel's arms. Everyone else suddenly feels homesick too and Caroline locks herself in the bathroom for a twenty-minute cry. She tells Sada it's her sister's children she is missing.

It's been an interesting day for Tom. He has had a reiki session from Nick, and had his tarot cards read by Sada. It's all a bit alternative and holistic for the Irish farmer, but he tells Big Brother how much he enjoyed it. The reiki made him float away, and then afterwards feel happy to be alive. The tarot, which Sada told him showed he had a strong masculine side, chimed with lots of ideas and plans that he has been thinking about.

Nichola is also having an emotional day. She tells Caroline about her ten-year battle with the eating disorder bulimia. She'd been doing some modelling and began making herself sick four times a day to control her weight. When it slipped down as low at six and a half stone she realized she needed help, and joined a self-help group. After a few meetings seeing other people with worse problems than hers, she learned to accept her body. When Caroline congratulates her for doing so well Nicky has to fight back tears.

Monday is a very big day in the house: the day of the first round of nominations. Most of the contestants will never find it easy going into the Diary Room to name two of their mates for eviction but the first time is particularly strange for them. Staying up and partying the whole of the night before (yes, the fresh supplies of alcohol had arrived) was the way most of them chose to cope with the stress, and for Tom, Craig and Darren it meant they slept through until 2 p.m., an hour before the nominations take place.

The reason for the night-time celebration was Andy's birthday – he's twenty-four on nomination day. The partying started just after midnight – with Andy being stripped naked and thrown under a cold shower, and went on to the early hours, with some people not going to bed until 7 a.m. Caroline stayed up all night and was at the centre of the drunken antics, pummelling Darren with a cushion and jumping on top of him to the amusement of Craig and Andy. Andy seems to have found a reason to like her: 'She does make you realize you're still sane.' A broken light, overflowing ashtrays, a sink full of washing-up and empty cider bottles strewn around the floor greet Sada and Mel who are first up.

Nichola, the artistic one, makes the letters of HAPPY BIRTHDAY out of bread and mounts them among the growing number of decorations on the wall.

For the earlier risers, it's a fraught morning. Sada prepares herself for the worst, but she and Caggie share a bed and a chat. They agree that they don't want to be nominated.

Andy is confident he won't be among the nominees, and upsets the sensitive Sada by suggesting they use a pack of cards to randomly select their victims. However, when he is called to go first into the Diary Room to make his nominations, there is nothing random about Andy's choices. Like all the boys he votes for Sada and Caroline causing concern for Big Brother who feared that tactical voting was being planned. The girls, who have not been as devious, underline the gender divide by voting exclusively for boys – with the exception of Mel, who nominates Sada along with Craig. Craig escapes any other nominations because the other girls have decided they like him for getting in touch with his feminine side – he's been a regular attender at the aerobics and yoga classes.

WHO NOMINATES WHO

ANDREW	Caroline and Sada
ANNA	Andrew and Darren
CAROLINE	Andrew and Darren
CRAIG	Caroline and Sada
DARREN	Caroline and Sada
MELANIE	Craig and Sada
NICHOLA	Andrew and Thomas
NICHOLAS	Caroline and Sada
SADA	Andrew and Darren
THOMAS	Caroline and Sada

REASONS:

CRAIG *on* **SADA**	'She's very selfish and extremely boring.'
ANDREW *on* **CAROLINE**	'She's bloody annoying.'
MELANIE *on* **SADA**	'She's quite bloody minded and stubborn, pretty much into things going her own way. She's not much of a team player.'

Sada has six votes, Caroline five, Andrew four, Darren three, Craig one, Tom one, and there's none for Nicholas, Anna, Mel or Nichola. At six o'clock the news is broken to the housemates (in future weeks they will not be told until the following day). Caroline bursts into tears but Sada smiles and remains very calm. She said earlier in the day that she was preparing herself and she's done it well. 'It's completely cool with me. I've had a great time. I was expecting it,' she says.

In the girls' bedroom, though, she, Caroline and Nichola cry together. Nichola says she doesn't want to play the game any more. 'I've had enough. I don't like it,' she says between sobs.

Sada says, 'I can't be bothered with it anyway. I have a life. I would like to go. I don't want to play this stupid game and I don't want to be nice to people I think are prats. This is not my home and these are not my people. I know they think I am a snob and too up myself but I'm not going to get upset about it.'

In the boys' bedroom, there's the reverse of this unhappy scene. Nicholas, Andrew and Craig are dancing with pleasure at the results, punching the air and giving each other high fives, covering their mouths to stifle their exultant laughter.

Sada, who has initially seemed so calm, goes into the Diary Room and cries. 'I don't want to play any more. I can't relate. I miss my boyfriend. I don't want to let the group down and I will feel like I'm failing if I walk... I don't want to let everybody down but I need to be free. I'm a sophisticated person who's twenty-eight and I'm becoming someone I hate. I'm worried about how I am portrayed... I don't want the money.

'I've had the most wonderful and the worst times of my life in here...There are only two others I connect with. I can't be myself.'

Later, she tells the group that she may walk out before Friday. She wants to be first out of the house – or last, and she reckons her chances of being last are pretty slim. If she waits until Friday she may not be the one chosen. The others tease her at first with a quick burst of the Clash's 'Should I Stay Or Should I Go', but when they realize she is serious they talk to her about it. Craig and Darren work hard at persuading her to stay and before too long she raises a glass of champagne to the others and promises she will wait until Friday.

The champagne has been provided by Big Brother for Andrew's birthday party, along with a sweetcorn and ham pie specially baked for him by his mum. Big Brother also offers him a choice of three games for his birthday present: Twister, Buckaroo or Scalextric. Unanimously, and within seconds of him reading out the choice, all the boys yell 'Scalextric'. The racing track is not his only present. The girls come up with the idea of giving him something he will really appreciate – a pair of black knickers and a pink thong. He delightedly puts them on his head.

The partying then begins in earnest. The girls paint the boys' faces with make-up and help them dress up in drag, and Nichola creates a work of art out of her own face and shaven head. In the middle of all the fun Nicholas detaches himself from the group and talks to Big Brother in the Diary Room. He says he has heard that Sada may walk out.

'I am perhaps a person who will be able to talk her out of doing it. I think it is important she doesn't walk out for her own good at the end of the day. I will do my best to try to make her see the light.'

However, after this offer of help to Big Brother he reveals the real reason for his visit to the Diary Room. It has occurred to him that the celebration the boys had after the nominations will look incredibly malicious and bitchy if shown to the nation on television. So he tries to explain it away and asks Big Brother not to show it.

'It wasn't a celebration that they were going. It was more a celebration that we weren't chosen. But obviously if it was aired it could be misconstrued.'

Back at the party, Andy is indulging in one of his favourite pastimes: sex talk. He reveals that he has spent the two previous birthdays in situations almost as bizarre as the *Big Brother* house: in a wife-swapping club in Belgium, and in a threesome with a married couple in London.

Andy's party champagne has also persuaded Darren to confide in the others about three dreams he has had since being in the house, the worst of which was finding he had become a gay icon. Several of the housemates say they have had increased and more vivid dreams in the *Big Brother* house than in their normal lives. Nicky and Sada blame it on the electronic equipment that surrounds them. Sada dreams that Nicholas is her husband and is waiting for her in Sainsbury's; Mel dreams that she and Tom are both heroin addicts and are in a psychiatric hospital; Nicky dreams that she and Sada are witches and then are transformed into scorpions; Nicholas complains that it takes him a long time to get to sleep and then he sees funny shapes.

Nichola goes to talk to Big Brother, and says this is the hardest day for her, with her two best friends being nominated. 'They are the core of the group, to me. I feel like a little girl in the playground. I know it's ridiculous to be upset because it's only a game... Caroline is my joy... Caroline and Sada feed my spirit... Sada is very well-spoken, articulate. She's so there! I love listening to Sada.'

She says she didn't come to the house to get away from her life, she came to grow. She doesn't want to be stagnant. She wants new ideas, experiences, energies. Then she announces, 'I'll bugger off now and just get on with it.'

The alcohol gets to them all, and the boys pile into the Diary Room and do a strip for Big Brother. Then Nicky and Sada stagger drunkenly into the Diary Room together. Sada wants Big Brother to ring her boyfriend, to see how he's feeling. She says that if he has deserted her, she'll have an affair with Nicky. Nicky, in the meantime, tells Big Brother she's 'gagging for a shag' and quite fancies Tom, but only in the dress he was wearing for the cross-dressing party. Nicky even asks Big Brother if he 'fancies a bit'.

When there is no reply, Sada and Nicky turn to each other. 'Give us a snog,' Sada slurs, drunkenly, and the two have a full-on lips to lips kiss. But before they leave the Diary Room, Sada pleads with Big Brother to let her boyfriend know that she's not gay.

Nicky makes another trip to the Diary Room, this time to ask for a vibrator. As usual, Big Brother says he will get back to her – nobody really expects her request to be granted.

For the two nominees, it is a tough night. They both, separately and together, cry, and are comforted by Anna, Nichola and Nicholas. Finding Sada alone and upset in the garden, Nicholas gives her a bit of moral support. 'You're very lucky,' he tells her. 'You've got the opportunity to make this very positive. You've got the looks, the height, the verve, everything that girls watching this want. And don't forget, where a door closes another window opens.'

Sada is so touched by his speech that she tells him he is a very 'sensitive and supportive man, and I appreciate your care and humility'.

Then Nick leaves her, goes into the bedroom where Caggie is crying, and delivers almost the same script to her. 'People who have seen you will think you are good fun. Always remember, where a door closes another window opens...' he says.

In their unhappiness about the nominations, the girls agree that Nick is a bright spot in the gloom and could be the bridge between the two camps. Fortunately for him, they don't compare notes on what he said to them.

The day after the nominations, everyone is subdued. There are hangovers to cope with, and most of the housemates stay in bed until lunchtime. Tom goes into the Diary Room and expresses the feelings that several of them seem to be sharing: guilt about the two people nominated. 'It feels like a dirty job, but something we knew we were going to have to do,' he says.

Mel is unhappy because she feels the girls are critical of her. She goes into the Diary Room and tells Big Brother that Sada thinks she is flirting with all the boys and has told the others that this is inappropriate. Mel doesn't want to be seen like that. She didn't want to go to bed in the same room as the other girls last night.

'I didn't feel comfortable going back to the girls' room to sleep. I felt that they felt I was to blame [for the nominations]. I'm always quite solitary anyway, and it felt really uncomfortable. It felt awful this morning getting up when no one was talking. I felt if I wasn't there they would be talking.'

Nicholas does not share the guilt trip that many of them are on after the nominations. He outlines to Andy his plans for the next round of nominations, 'Sada goes this week, then Caroline goes, Nichola goes, then Craig, Anna – leaving me, you, Thomas and The Count.' He seems to have missed Mel out of his calculations. Although he and Andy agree the boys must stick together, they lapse into mimicking Craig's Scouse accent, and mock his far-fetched stories. Just three hours later,

Nick is chatting like best buddies to Craig and tells him his place in the house is secure. 'In five weeks there will be five men in here. We will fight them off.' Nick says.

In the Diary Room Andy looks relaxed and happy. He tells Big Brother he has had an excellent two days, although the nomination process made him more nervous than he thought it would. He says he always knew he would have to do it, and he is surprised by how upset some of the people in the house are.

Caroline is next to enter the Diary Room. She confesses that she feels stupid talking to the faceless Big Brother. She's still reeling from the nomination.

'This morning I thought it was all right, then I had another cry. I hate crying, and feel like an idiot for crying. It's not that I'm really down, but my bubble has been burst.' She thinks Sada is handling it better than her, because Sada wants to go home to her fella, and she wants to stay.

'I'm too emotional to talk to the others. I cry because I wanted something good to come out of this show, and I'm worried I've let down the people who didn't want me to come into this house.'

In the evening Big Brother sets the group a discussion on their first loves. The stories are very revealing. Anna met her first love at the age of twenty-two. 'I was so smitten with her. Madly in love with her.' Unfortunately, nine months later Anna was dumped and was 'absolutely gutted'. The break-up prompted her to give up her job and her home in Dublin, and move to Edinburgh.

Darren's first love was an even more touching story. 'We met when I was five years old and she was seven. She was the school bully and one day she beat me up and I went running home, crying.' In secondary school the pair met again, and the bully had matured into a very beautiful girl. They started going about together and, in Darren's own words, 'One day she pounced on me'. Three years later, they had their first baby together, and now they have three. Although they are no longer together, they are best friends.

Craig's first love, he told his housemates, looked a lot like Melanie. They met when he was eighteen, stayed together for five years without rowing, and only split up because they realized they both needed to do other things. One day, he says, he will marry Shelley when they are both ready to settle down.

Tom's first romance, at seventeen, was with a girl called Michelle, and he met her at a disco. When he said 'Can I walk you home?' he had no idea what he was letting himself in for – it was eighteen miles! He sang to her and recited poems, but the affair did not last long. They met again when he was twenty-one, but split when she left the area to find work.

Nicky met her first love on the dance floor, and when her mum did not approve she left home to live with him. It lasted two and a half years, until Nicky walked out.

Mel was fifteen when she fell in love – but she's not sure whether it was her boyfriend or his dog, a little mutt called Gismo, that she loved the most. The boyfriend worked in a sandwich shop near her school, and the relationship lasted for four years, until she left to go travelling.

Andy met his first love at the age of eleven, in the home economics class at school. He was paying so much attention to her that he never learned how to cook, he tells the group. He was fourteen by the time he and the girl, Sarah, became boyfriend and girlfriend. They spent a lot of time in Andy's room, and he realizes, looking back, that he was really rude to his parents at the time. The affair ended when Andy took another girl to a Valentine's ball.

Caroline's tale is about a musician who broke her heart. They were very happy, went everywhere together, dancing and singing and having 'great love and great sex'. However, when his record deal fell through she found she was holding him together, mentally, and doing all the trying. They split up, but her next serious boyfriend was his brother. Sada claims that although she has had other relationships, her current boyfriend is the only one she has truly loved.

However, it is Nick's story that makes everyone sit up and take notice. At school, he tells the others, he met a French girl called Veronique. When he was seventeen and a half he spent the summer in France, at her home just outside Paris. When he announces that they got married in secret the rest of the group shout out in admiration, and question him about it. She wore a ring, he says, but nobody realized it was a wedding ring. The marriage was in a register office. Then they went to Australia, and had a terrible car crash in the Northern Territories. His 'wife' was killed. He philosophises about the impact on him: 'Unfortunately, it just was not meant to be.'

Later, when talking to Andy in the bathroom, he admits that his story was not entirely true, that he changed names and locations.

The first-love stories prompt Craig to go to the Diary Room for the first time in eleven days without being summoned there. He has, he says, never felt the urge to chat with Big Brother before, but he's just realized it is the tenth anniversary of the day he first went out with Shelley. He's been thinking about proposing marriage to her on air, but decides he needs to talk to her first. 'We probably will get married one day, but not yet, until we've experienced everything else. She's just started a new career. But it's the most coincidental thing that's ever happened, timing-wise,' he says.

Nick's thoughts are still on the voting and the nominations, and he's looking forward to Friday when the first eviction will happen. He tells Andy: 'We can sit out in the garden and listen to the suitcase being dragged across, see all the flash-bulbs going off.' Andrew tells his mate that he already knows who will be nominated for the second round of evictions, a prophecy he will come to rue. Nick says he can guess: 'Same Christian name as me?' he asks, and Andy nods.

The next day they are all up earlier because the memory test is scheduled for 11 a.m. It is a tense time as they all desperately want more money to spend on food and booze, and if they get more than one question wrong they'll be docked £37.80. They've been testing each other, and they're all fairly confident – with the exception of Craig. In a mock run-through they have, he answers correctly, but Andy and Nick privately agree that he may let them down.

The test involves each of them going into the Diary Room to answer three random questions. Only this time the Diary Room chat is not private – it is relayed on the screen in the house for everyone to see. When Craig only manages to get two right out of three, tension runs high. Everyone else must get a perfect score. Fortunately, they make it, and in the wild jubilation that follows Craig's slip-up is forgotten.

The schism between the two camps is widening and Mel, who was once seen as a bridge, now definitely seems to belong to the boys' camp. After a bust-up with Nicky over washing the dishes, Mel tells the lads she's 'really pissed off. The atmosphere is doing my head in.' Anna tells her that Nicky's temper blows up but disappears as quickly. Nicholas suggests 'a chick fight' to clear the air. Mel is so excluded by the girls that Craig is concerned enough to suggest she moves into the boys' dormitory – he'll sleep on the floor and she can have his bed. But Nick tells him this will only make matters worse.

There are many points of friction. The incessant whizzing of the Scalextric cars around the track, which is near the girls' dormitory, irritates them. Darren, who likes his sleep, complains that the girls keep him awake at night by playing games until the early hours. Sada says she is so sensitive to the negative energies in the house that she has to stay up late. A suggestion from Craig that they should all go to bed at the same time is met with opposition from Melanie, who says she does not want to be treated like a child. Nichola's artwork, which is gradually colonizing all the available wall space in the house, is also causing problems became she appropriates all the magazines to make papier mâché. The boys object. Darren needs a magazine and a ciggie for his ritual visit to the loo each day. Craig agrees with Darren, to the annoyance of Nicky who says 'He can't read anyway. He's dyslexic.' But Craig pursues the point and accuses Nicky of being selfish.

Darren is increasingly unhappy, and the production team are afraid that he might be the first contestant to walk out.

'All we've got is one boring Thursday, an exciting Friday because someone's getting kicked out, a dull Saturday, Sunday food, and the rest is crap. I will be so pleased to get out of here,' he says. 'When I get out I will run and run.'

Caroline is also desperately miserable with the impending eviction hanging over her. She is the first of the crew to request a private session with a counsellor. This is the only time in the whole *Big Brother* experience that the participants are not filmed, and their talk is completely private. Caroline spends over an hour in the Diary Room, and emerges to tell Anna, Sada and Nicky that the therapist has advised her to talk about her problems with the rest of the group. She asks Andy if she can talk to him later. He thinks this formal request is ridiculous, as he hardly has a diary full of appointments.

In the Diary Room Sada talks about having to cope psychologically with the two possible outcomes of being nominated: being evicted or staying on. She describes the whole *Big Brother* experience as weird.

'Subconsciously, people are responding to the weirdness of the house in their dreams and eating patterns. Our bodies are out of sync with the environment, the time, and each other.'

Big Brother's evening game for the group is to pick celebrity names out of a hat, then describe the person to see if the rest can guess who it is. Nicky and Caggie don't want to join in, but are ordered to do so by Big Brother. They are sulky about it. Sada turns out to be the star of the show, manically covering more stars in a minute than any of her competitors.

On Wednesday night Nichola and Caggie decide to sleep in the garden. Sada joins them at first, but the chilly night air and the uncomfortable bed force her to retreat to the bedroom. The other two listen to Mel and Andy getting very close on the sofa. They are playing a game together, and Andy artfully drapes his arm along the back of the settee and then drops it on to Mel's shoulder. After he strokes her affectionately she gets up and goes to bed.

Nicky suggests to her two great pals, Caroline and Sada, that they leave a lasting memorial to their presence on the walls of the girls' dormitory. Sada creates a tree out of strips of paper with a big red heart in the middle for her boyfriend. Caroline paints her trademark pink lips, using nail polish because she does not want to use up her precious supplies of lipstick. While Nicky and Caroline are working, they talk about orgasms and discover they both have them in their sleep.

'When my body doesn't get sex it just goes into automatic mode and I wake up having an orgasm,' Caroline says.

Nicky replies, 'They're normally the best ones. Sometimes I can have multiples.'

Caroline says that if she had multiple orgasms in her sleep she'd never get out of bed, but she has had them while walking down the street. They then decide that the female orgasm is more intense than the male variety. 'It's magic, what God did,' says Nicky, appreciatively.

Thursday is a very tense day in the house. Each of the housemates is summoned individually to the Diary Room to be told by Big Brother that they must not discuss votes or nominations. It is another attempt by Big Brother to defuse the tension and bad feeling surrounding the eviction, and the scheming that is already going on over next week's nominations. Everyone takes the rebuke on the chin, although Nicholas, the main schemer, stares into the camera-lens face of Big Brother in silence for several seconds, almost as if he is trying to outstare Big Brother. He looks uncomfortable, as if he perhaps recognizes that he is at the centre of the plotting and therefore the main butt of the reprimand. Afterwards, he chain-smokes and mooches out, alone, into the garden. He tells Craig he is having a down day.

To clear the air they have a group discussion, and air their grievances. Andy tells Caroline that her silly voices irritate him, and that he is also irritated by the way she puts the saucepan on to boil without a lid and only half on the heat. She tells him she cannot stand his competitiveness. Thomas tells them all they have to start respecting each other, and Caroline suggests – and gets – a group hug.

In the Diary Room Andy says Caroline and Sada 'think people are ganging up against them. Tempers are high. It's hard to get any logical comment from any of them.

'I've tried to stop the boy/girl thing, never disappeared into my own space, tried to stay in a good mood, go into the girls' room and chat to them, understand what they're talking about, be civil to people... I try not to bitch or talk about the nominations. I have to put myself in their situation, but I can't take them seriously.'

To give them all something else to think about, Big Brother sets them a task. They must paint portraits of each other, and then mount them on the wall as if they were in an art gallery. They work in pairs and the results are striking. Nicky, the art graduate, produces a Lucien-Freud-style portrait of Nicholas. Darren insists that Mel's version of him makes him beautiful. And Tom paints Sada as a small figure in the centre of the *Big Brother* room, with her yoga mat and other Sada-symbols in the background. As she has been telling everybody she is not completely in the *Big Brother* house, and that part of her is still outside, Tom deliberately paints her with half a leg missing.

Thursday night is a poignant night for the girls. Sada and Caroline know that it is the last night they will spend together. One of them will be leaving the house the next day. They talk into the night. Nichola is just as sad. She will miss whichever of them goes. But they have all agreed to be in touch when the *Big Brother* experiment is over. Nicky and Caggie have planned a wild night of clubbing, and Caggie can't wait to introduce Nicky to her large family. They believe they are the only two in the house who are truly being themselves. As the most outlandishly dressed, they find they have a lot in common – they have both been on the receiving end of uninvited comments from strangers in the street. Caroline tells her friend that a couple of years ago she was scared to go out of the house because she was being followed.

Friday is a long day in the house, as the clock ticks slowly towards the hour when the eviction is announced live on television. Caroline alternates between manic happiness and depression. She jokingly threatens the boys in the house with her four brothers. 'You can't stay in here for ever,' she warns them. Sada washes her clothes, telling the others that she has to prepare herself for staying as well as for leaving. She's thought through all the angles, and has already broached with the group the fact that one of the two nominees will stay, and will need to feel welcome to stay. It's a subtle thought, and not one that has troubled Caggie who is simply desperate not to be ousted.

At half past one, Sada and Anna go into the Diary Room together, to plead with Big Brother for some wine to help them get through the afternoon. Sada says they have all slept well and because of that the whole group are getting on better. She's really excited about the prospect of the show. Anna says the hour before the results of the voting will be the hardest.

When the big moment eventually arrives, they are all grouped in the living area, and react with wild whoops and squeals when Davina calls them on a live intercom. The voting has gone against Sada: 58 per cent of the voters have chosen to have her ousted and Caroline left in the house. Sada takes the news very well, with a delighted smile. It's possible to believe that she really does want to leave. She's always said she wanted to be first or last out, and she's got her wish.

Caroline celebrates. 'Caggie cut loose from the noose,' she shrieks. Then she swoops on Sada and the two of them hug. They're an unlikely looking alliance, the brash blonde Birmingham bird and the elegant hippie but they have formed some real bonds, which they believe will outlive their time in the house.

Sada has two hours to say goodbye to the others. There is no hot water for her to have a shower so they boil water on the stove and fill a large washing bowl and ceremoniously bathe her in the garden. She says later that Mel stops the boys from joining in the bathing, which at first she thought was protective. However, when she is outside the house, and watches videos of the behaviour of her fellow contestants, she changes her mind and thinks that Mel was envious of her.

When she finally emerges from the house she looks fantastic, wearing a backless red and yellow sparkly top and tight yellow trousers, with her pink-streaked hair and perfect make-up. She breezes across the bridge, the walk of doom, with her head held high and a huge smile on her face. The others crowd round the doorway, anxious to get any glimpse of the outside world. Caroline, spotting her mum in the crowd, is wildly excited. Then the blue door closes on them again, for another week.

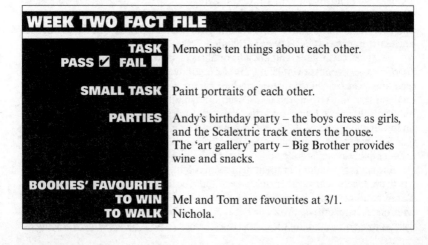

WEEK TWO FACT FILE

TASK **PASS ☑ FAIL ■**	Memorise ten things about each other.
SMALL TASK	Paint portraits of each other.
PARTIES	Andy's birthday party – the boys dress as girls, and the Scalextric track enters the house. The 'art gallery' party – Big Brother provides wine and snacks.
BOOKIES' FAVOURITE **TO WIN**	Mel and Tom are favourites at 3/1.
TO WALK	Nichola.

WHAT THE EXPERT SAYS

'Outside the house, Nick is seen as manipulative and fairly two-faced but he received no nominations from the house. Although he was instrumental in getting Sada and Caroline nominated and was very happy that they were, he takes time to pick them off individually and reassure them that he was not responsible. He uses the same stock phrase with both Sada and Caroline, 'When a door closes another window opens'. When he talks to Sada and Caroline he has enormous difficulty looking them in the face, particularly with Caroline where he wags his head from side to side and then does a huge eye-pop to persuade her that he really means what he is saying.'

Peter Collett, Experimental Psychologist, Oxford

SADA LOOKS BACK

In the live studio interview with Davina Sada is composed and gracious, surprising the presenter with her calm and very positive summary of life in the strange *Big Brother* environment. Shown clips from the programmes, she is amazed to see Nick's machinations. However, no matter how hard she is pressed, she refuses to say anything very critical about any of them.

Her mother shows no such reticence: 'The whole world has seen what he is like. He is a scheming rat,' she says.

Thirty per cent of the total television audience hears her say this. A massive 3.4 million are watching the show, and 387,000 people have telephoned their votes in – 150,000 during the live transmission earlier in the evening.

Sada has only been in the house for two weeks but, as she says, it felt like two years. Seeing the outside world is overwhelming, but she has no regrets about coming out. Her first night of freedom is spent in a hotel, reunited with her beloved boyfriend. The two of them spend the whole night talking. Sada, who has found sleeping difficult in the *Big Brother* house, is exhausted, and has had less than two hours sleep.

However, when she appears before twenty journalists at a press conference the next morning, she is smiling and positive. She describes living in the house as being in a cocoon, a very intense experience, and one that has ramifications for her relationship with her boyfriend.

'I've been letting him tell me his experiences of watching me on television... I had no idea what he was feeling. He's seen all different angles to me, it is a very broad experience and it is great to be with him and reconnect. We've tried to be very gentle with each other at a difficult time in our lives.'

She says she is grateful for the chance to have experienced the *Big Brother* environment.

'I take away friends, memories, a learning process on a personal level. I take away a chance to look at myself, and at other people.'

She says she does not regard being voted out as a personal rejection.

'There were ten of us, hand-picked, and we did a bloody good job of keeping it together. With me or without me, it's still a community. I appeal to people who relate to me for whatever reason: I'm not expecting to be loved or praised by everybody.

'We were a disparate group, thrown together. I learnt about dealing with people who come from other walks of life. I learnt I have to be more tolerant.

'I wasn't a guinea pig – I went for the project, it was a choice. It was a very ballsy thing to do; a personal challenge.'

She says she has promised her housemates to tell the world how difficult life in the house is.

'In the bedroom there are five large mirrors, and you know there are cameramen behind them. You hear small noises. You know that they are filming you even when you sleep. There is nowhere to run or hide. It makes it a very intense experience. You live in your feelings. I am very happy to be out. I have done my time in the *Big Brother* house, and I was ready to come out.

'The effects of sleep deprivation are very odd, your body loses track of time. I got up one morning and thought I'd have a shower, then found out it was 4 a.m. We all suffered.'

Like all the contestants who are evicted one by one, Sada has a long session with a psychotherapist after the press conference. She has already seen a counsellor immediately after the live programme on Friday evening, but this session gives her a chance to have more time going over the possible problems she may face. Afterwards, she talks about her experiences in the house. She says the videos of the television programmes have surprised her by their honesty. They really did capture the spirit of the house, without any editorial slant being imposed. She also says the *Big Brother* rules were so carefully worked out that everything ran very smoothly.

'Because there were rules there was no quibbling. We needed that to ground us, to give us personal boundaries.'

She says the atmosphere on nomination day was terrible, but it was a relief to her to find that she stood a good chance of going out.

'I really wanted to get chucked out, I'd had enough. I was honest myself, and I did not realize the extent to which some of the others were playing games. I knew the men were being very competitive, but I had no idea just how much.

'The women are very strong characters. I've always thought of myself as overpowering, but out of the five of us I would have come fourth – only Anna behind me – in the overpowering stakes. But they were great, and if I thought those girls were happy to have me out, I'd be upset. But only Mel nominated me from the girls, and I think she saw me as competition.

'The boys never respected me. When they found out I wasn't going to be interested in them sexually, a lot of those boys were quite downhearted because, believe me, they would have taken me to bed. They may not have been interested in me intellectually or any other way, but they fancied me and Mel.

'Andy got straight in there with Mel. Nicky and I believed it was genuine; Caggie said it was a load of bollocks. Later he told me that he really wanted to be with his girlfriend outside, and I realized it was a set-up. He talked about his sexual experiences all the time. He would love to have sex on *Big Brother* with the nation watching. All the boys would like to do it, except Nick – he's too shy. He never looks you in the eye.

'For the first four days Andrew and Mel were like my children, I looked after them. Then they teamed up against me. None of us girls were happy about them getting into our beds. I'm not anti-men, I'm very positive about men.'

She believes that ten years from now she will still be close to Nichola and Caroline.

'Nicky was my sister in there. Caroline was wonderful, she kept me up, she was my medicine in there. My heart goes out to her, because she has not had an easy life. I had a lovely connection with Anna, but she is very guarded. The five men were so different from the women. They would be happy spending the next seven weeks playing Scrabble and Jenga, talking about nothing, guarding each other and playing mind games and being strategic.

'Nicky, Caggie and I just didn't fit in with that, and we became separated from them. I took a day making a tree for my boyfriend, and I was criticized for being separate from the group. But the group did not want to do anything; they were so boring. The Scalextric drove me mad – I have a very sensitive vibration level, and it was right outside our bedroom.

'The only one of the men I thought was interesting was Nick, because he was holistic, but I felt a sexual energy coming from him when he was doing reiki. And now I believe he was a fraud.

'I never trusted Tom; he's got an eye on the side of his head. There was something about him I was never easy with. The men slept a lot. I wanted them to join in the yoga, but only Craig did.

'Mel was very provocative. She wanted me out, because I was a threat to her with the boys, she thought. She's got a few problems, I suspect. We all wanted to have clitoris piercing after she talked about it, but then she backed off and said we shouldn't have it done, it wasn't right for us, because she wanted to be the only one.

'If I had my time over, I would still do it. I know who I am, I know I can be self-obsessed and selfish. But I'm OK about not being a perfect person, and millions of viewers have seen me not being perfect. At least I was honest. I was myself. And if I can see what's wrong with me and learn from it, that will be great.

'It has brought up lots of things about myself that make me cringe, and I was worried while I was in there that I might have lost my boyfriend, because I love him more than ever.'

Sada's spookiest experience was going into the Store Room when the door was inadvertently left unlocked, and finding a cameraman in there.

'He didn't speak, just slid away very professionally, but he was hooded in black and it was a very spooky sight.'

The greatest physical discomfort she suffered, apart from sleep deprivation, was the mosquitoes. Because the site of the house is so close to the river, when the weather got warm the housemates were plagued by them, and Big Brother had to provide them with insect repellent.

'I'm a very weak Buddhist. I'm not supposed to kill living things but I'm there on film killing a mozzie, which is funny. They drove us all mad. We walked around with white blobs of calamine lotion all over us.'

Sada says she genuinely was not in it for the money, nor to promote the book she has written about men.

'I went for the challenge, and now it's over I have no regrets. I don't want to seem big-headed, but I'm blonde, slim, I've got my beautiful man and my beautiful life, and I'm glad to be back with them.'

In the two weeks she was in the house Sada received 1,304 e-mails to the *Big Brother* website. They are very uplifting: 'Hi, Sada, I think you are the bollocks. Marry me!'; 'I think you are really cool doing all that spiritual stuff.'; 'I may be only fifteen years old, but if I had £70,000 I'd give it to you.'; 'At the end of the day, walk away with your head held high. You had more style, grace and passion than any of those narrow-minded, sad, two-faced idiots. May the force be with you.'; 'Hi, hope you win, hippie chick.'

Sada admits that, as well as being a yoga teacher, she would love a career in television, and *Big Brother* gave her a big boost. In the week immediately after her eviction, she appeared on Steve Wright in the afternoon on Radio 2; Nicky Campbell's show on Radio 5 Live; *London Tonight*; Channel 5 *News*; Bullseye, a German TV programme; *Summer at the Top* on Scottish TV; and, was booked to do two magazine photo shoots. She also told her story exclusively to the *Daily Mail*, did a voice-over for a radio commercial and did a five-minute slot talking about *Big Brother* for *The Big Breakfast* every day for a week. She was given a Mitsubishi Shogun car to use for a year.

WEEK THREE

'It's a big political game in here,
and some of them are playing it really well.'

MELANIE

It is strange for the girls to settle down to sleep with an empty bed in their room. They do not go to bed until the early hours of the morning. The whole household is hyped up after Sada's eviction and their brief glimpse of the outside world from the doorway. For the first time in two weeks, they were able to listen to music. Big Brother pipes music into the house every Friday evening to drown out the shouts and chants of the crowds who turn up to watch one of the contestants walk across the bridge and out of the game.

Caroline, at first on an immediate high after the results of the voting were announced, begins to slump and needs a lot of comforting. She is not sure she can recover from the highs and lows of the past week, and get herself back on an even keel. The girls rally round and hug her. In the boys' dormitory, meanwhile, Nicholas asks Thomas which of the girls he least gets on with. Tom tells him that he is not happy talking about the others, so Nick turns his attention to the cameras, whose presence he never seems to forget. He wishes the internet viewers goodnight.

When she wakes the next day Anna tells the other girls she's had a weird dream about a sex romp with a priest, which she says was great. Caggie admits having her own erotic dream in the night but doesn't elaborate. Nichola is miffed. 'I haven't had one for ages,' she says.

The daily bread is made by Tom, who is always trying to make a loaf as good as his mother's. Not that his mother is ever likely to have made bread like this. The group have already tried banana bread, and Tom now takes the experiments further by adding baked beans to the dough. It looks horrible, but the others give it the thumbs up – especially Darren, who says it reminds him of taking his children on picnics.

The task system comes into its own on the days after evictions and nominations. If everyone is busy they don't have time to be down. This week they *are* going to be busy. Big Brother wants them to cycle the distance from Land's End to John o'Groats, on an exercise bike. However, there's a catch. They have to go via their own home towns, giving them a massive 1,800 kilometres to pedal before midnight on Wednesday! They have half an hour to decide how much they want to wager on success and eight of the group are agreed on the highest amount – 50 per cent of their shopping total. Darren does not take part in the vote because, true to form, he's asleep in bed.

Nicky tells her namesake, Nick, to wake Darren but Nick ignores her and goes into the Diary Room to place the wager. Big Brother reminds him that it has to be unanimous, and out he comes to check with Darren. Nicky feels vindicated, but so does Nick when Darren agrees to the full wager.

Determined that they will not fail another task, they decide to cycle day and night, on a rota of an hour's riding each. Andy, ever competitive, says they need to get into a strict dietary regime, with lots of pasta and potatoes and bananas for energy. Craig is unsure that they will be able to succeed, but Mel is up for it and rushes to put on her Lycra cycling shorts. Craig's worries seem to centre more on his own ability to perform the task than the group's. Since running in the garden a few days ago he has had a painful knee and is wearing a knee support. He asks for a doctor or physiotherapist to be called to the house. 'Obviously, I'm very concerned about my body and I want it to last me the rest of my life. I don't want you to feel I'm trying to get out of the task,' he tells the others.

The consultation with the doctor in the Diary Room ends with Craig being told to rest his knee for one day, and then join in the task. Big Brother benevolently gives the gang 300 kilometres towards their total.

The others get stuck in with a will. Nichola, out in the garden, keeps the spirit of Sada alive by having a yoga session. Before she left, Sada taught her some basic yoga exercises and she combines these with some breathing exercises given to her by a Buddhist she met while living in Brighton. Nichola encourages Caroline to try them, saying that they are good for stomach pains.

Darren tries a different way of relaxing after his bike session. He is the only member of the household who has not let Nick give him a reiki session, but he now succumbs. However, it is not for long. Darren calls off the session after a few minutes, but is unable to explain why he feels uncomfortable with it.

'I feel paranoid because everyone is on at me to have reiki. But I still want to learn how to be a reiki master myself so that I can heal my mum.'

Caroline and Mel accuse him of being closed off, unable to handle new experiences, and they want to know how he can ever become a reiki master if he cannot have it done to him. Darren explains that he was not relaxed, and therefore it would not work.

'I just wasn't ready. I wasn't scared, just paranoid.'

Andy, ever the pragmatist, suggests he should just lie back and let it happen. Later, Nick gives his verdict on Darren's reluctance: 'He bottled out.'

Darren is feeling generally irritable. His skin is sensitive, he tells the others, and life in the *Big Brother* house is not helping it. His bed squeaks, which stops him sleeping at night. Also he's becoming phobic about mirrors.

'I always wanted a room that's fully mirrored. Now, I look at the mirrors all the time and wonder if I look all right, then I think, "Shit, there's someone behind that".' He tells the others that once he saw a documentary about department stores where the fitting-room mirrors were two-way, with cameras behind them.

'When I come out of here, I want to know what it will be like to see a real mirror.'

Anna is called to the Diary Room and talks about the post-eviction feeling in the house.

'It's fine. It was eerie waking up in the morning without her there. Some of us, everyone probably, were a bit sad. It won't be so traumatic to be evicted next time. Last night made them feel more positive about eviction. Davina McCall being there was great. People are a lot more positive today. The group is quite close. Because it's smaller, there are less people to relate to so the group will get closer as the weeks go by. The staying behind will get harder.

'Some people just went hurrah when they heard it was Sada, but I'm sure they didn't mean it. It was really tough shutting the door. We all admitted we were envious of Sada going to join her mates.'

The cycling goes on all night. Melanie sleeps on the sofa, waiting for her next shift. Nichola worries that so much time in the saddle will give her piles. Caroline and Nichola cuddle up together under the duvet on the patio again and, before they drop off to sleep, compare notes on how lovely Nicholas is.

Mel, alone among the girls, is aware of Nick's plotting and planning. As she and Nick play backgammon, she asks him: 'How's she [Sada] going to feel about all the stuff you've been saying?'

'I doubt she's watched it,' he says.

'She'd have heard from her friends,' Mel persists.

Nick says, 'Mmmmm,' and changes the subject.

Mel and Andy's flirtation continues, to the irritation of other house members. As she kneads the dough for the day's bread, Andy comments on the way she is thumping it. 'I never have a problem with my dough rising," she says, provocatively. 'Show me your technique then.'

Andy replies, 'I just do it quite gently. I treat it as if it's a living thing.' As he demonstrates, he rests his hand on the back of her waist, and then pats her bum.

Caroline and Anna are watching. 'It's either Mel or Andy... there's no room for anybody else,' says Caggie. Anna nods.

The shopping list is the usual prominent feature of Sunday's activities. Anna takes charge, and they animatedly discuss what type of alcohol they should buy. The cheap cider that Nicky recommends is beginning to rot a few guts, and Andrew, Nicholas and Craig insist they should have lager, especially as they have more money in the kitty after meeting the memory challenge. Without Sada, Mel is the only vegetarian left and when Andrew complains about 4 kilos of cheese on the list she points out that one is for her, in place of meat. She is irritated when he suggests she should eat Sada's tofu supplies. They can afford a few luxuries, like chocolate, crisps and cola, but they also remember the sensible things like toilet rolls, disinfectant, scouring pads and washing powder.

Nichola is called to talk to Big Brother. She says she is unsure who to nominate.

'I will speak to the fairies and angels, because I have three names and I am trying to think who is best for the house. I don't want to do it on personal grounds, that's petty. I want it to be who is better for the group.'

She says she thinks the divide between the boys and girls is narrowing. 'We are communicating better. I was worried about Nicholas because I thought he was weird, but he has now opened up, and I'm more relaxed with him. I'm not connecting with Thomas because I don't do what he does. I'd really like to get to know him but he doesn't open up... Most of the time he is just blank and I think that I am giving more than him. We are just like chalk and cheese.'

She adds that Darren's cooking is 'wicked', but that if she had her way they would spend their money on alcohol and not worry about food.

When Andy goes into the Diary Room he says the opposite – he would rather have better food and do without alcohol. He talks about his feelings for Mel: 'We are too similar. We are strong-headed, stubborn. We sense that we should tiptoe round each other or we'll piss each other off. We can be more natural when we are alone together. I'm not very natural around her, I feel I have to compete with her. With her, if someone is better than her at something she refuses to take advice. Like with the racetrack, she doesn't listen and won't play with me because I beat her.'

It's a very hot day, and those who aren't cycling are sunbathing. Darren, however, is again slaving over a hot stove making banana fritters for everyone. He's in charge of tonight's meal, which will be one of his specialities – chicken and rice. He also promises a fish pie, and vegetable lasagne for Mel. She wants to know if he is now the official *Big Brother* cook.

Pedalling the bike goes on, all the time, as the background to every other activity. The housemates, some of whom are suffering bike fatigue, are not happy that Craig is not taking part. Andrew calls him 'a lazy bastard' to the others. Later in the day, Nick refers to him as a 'big girl's blouse'. Anna, Mel and Caroline are wearing knee supports. Nicky is complaining about her bruised bum and the fact that it is going to be 'sweaty and spotty'. Darren says his back is injured, as well as one of his legs. Big Brother provides a key to tighten the saddle of the bike, and the cyclists try using towels to pad it. Even when they are not on the bike, they find it hard to sleep because there is never a quiet time in the house.

Caroline feels particularly low. She complains that she is too tired to even put on her make-up. She's suffering a delayed reaction to the strain of being nominated last week, and losing her friend, Sada. Now the sleepless nights of bike riding are hitting her hard.

'It's this house, it's driving me nuts... I feel so foul. I don't feel like part of this group. I don't think I can make a recovery,' she tells Big Brother in the Diary Room.

When Tom is called to talk to Big Brother he speaks about his friendships in the group. His three closest friends are Nick, because they are similar in age, Andy, because he is so funny, and Mel, because she has a fascinating mind. Also, Anna has a similar background so they have shared interests. Craig he likes, but because they are both quiet they don't bring each other out.

'Darren is funny but he's a bit OTT. He's loud, has to be noticed. Caroline is also loud – it's all a performance. With Nicky it's not a two-way thing; I get nothing back from her.'

He tells Big Brother that he misses having hair, but it is much easier to look after now it has been shaved off. He has been trying to give up cigarettes, which was one of his goals when he came into the house. But he admits he's smoking – he's had three or four today.

Nicholas chooses to go to the Diary Room at half past nine in the evening, to talk about the nominations.

'It was easier last time because Sada didn't get on well as a whole with the team, and that was obviously reflected in the voting. Now everyone's being really nice to each other, but there's a lot of undertow beneath it all. My reasons for being nice in the house are because I think I'm a nice person. I haven't really changed my character... If you had a feeling that a few people were going for one person then it's a survival instinct to go along with that feeling. It's a question of being vulnerable. Yesterday, there were kids screaming the name of one of the guys, so it's hard to tell.

'Everyone is enjoying it more than we were last week, because we have worked out our task into a rota and everyone has flown into this task. Everyone is gelling. It was quite an acrid atmosphere last week. The boys certainly felt incriminated for whatever reason. It's hard for people knowing that they have to wait the whole week. Then again there is always the possibility of rejection, but I'm not worried. If my time is up, I would be disappointed, but you just have to get on with it... I set myself certain tasks. I would like to stay a minimum of four weeks, so now I'll just wait until tomorrow to know whether that task is achievable or not.'

Nick is the one who is most conscious of the cameras. The others forget they are there most of the time, although when Tom discovers one at a low level on the wall he bends down to give the viewers a wave. Nick, however, seems to be preoccupied by them. He and Darren go round the house naming them, and then

Darren tries to distract a camera by doing press-ups while Nick sneaks beneath it, out of camera range. They feel sure they have found a safe hiding place until Anna points to all the other cameras which are now focused on Nick. He gets Mel and Andy to join him in pretending that the camera link has broken. As they clean their teeth they all freeze. Big Brother is not fooled.

Nominations day dawns with Nichola creating a minor crisis. She somehow presses a button which resets the computer on the exercise bike to zero. There are horrified cries, from her and the others, as momentarily they confront the prospect of having to redo the 1,000 kilometres they have already clocked up. Luckily, Nicky presses twice more and the total comes up again. Anna has worked out that, despite the toll it is taking on everyone, they should finish by 5 a.m. the next morning, more than forty hours ahead of target.

Darren has pulled out of the rota, with his bad back and knee. This does not go down too well with the others, and the girls mutter about the boys in general being 'a lazy bunch of gits' and Darren in particular being 'a wuss' who should be confined to the kitchen. Predictably, the boys approach the bike riding very competitively, and compare notes about each other's hourly totals. Andy is proud of his record of 34 kilometres in an hour and jeers at Nick for achieving only 28. But then Nick and Tom join forces and do twenty-minute stints each, with twenty minutes off, over two hours, and Andy's record is broken. He's not happy and maintains it was an unfair way of achieving it. He's very keen for the house to complete the task, and offers to take over from anyone who gets too tired.

Mel rests from her exertions by lying on the sofa with her head in Andy's lap, while he runs his hand up and down her back slipping it underneath her top. They laugh about Nick and his problems with the bike, pointing out that he has been in Territorial Army and should be fit. Andrew tells Mel about Nick and his tactics, and she agrees that she is not impressed with his conniving. They have both noticed how irritable Nick gets when he lacks sleep, so they laugh about the consequences for the rest of the group tomorrow, after another night on the bike.

Out in the garden Nick asks Darren how he became scared of chickens. Darren tells him about being in Jamaica when he was nine and being asked to go to the chicken coop to get a chicken for dinner. He couldn't grab hold of the right one, and the others all came at him, pecking and scratching. His mother had to rescue him, and he has never been near a chicken since – not until he joined the *Big Brother* house. Now, he seems to care about them more than anyone else, and has even named his favourite one Marjorie. But there's bad news for the bloated chickens – their food rations are going to have to be cut down. The housemates failed to read the instructions about feeding them and they've run through ten weeks' supply of chicken food in just over two weeks. The note from Big Brother pointing this out also tells them to clean the chicken droppings every day. Nichola demands rubber gloves, saying, 'It's really unhygienic cleaning shit out with yer 'ands'.

In the afternoon, the housemates are called in one by one to give their nominations. They will not be told the result until the next day. Nick, who has nominated Craig, sits and chats with him in the garden, bitching about Tom and Andy. Craig says very little, but comments that the public may think Andy plays to the cameras too much. When Caroline joins them Nick talks about the horrible wait until the results, and she reassures him: 'Don't worry, reiki master, you will be here to the end.'

WHO NOMINATES WHO

ANDREW	Caroline and Nichola
ANNA	Andrew and Thomas
CAROLINE	Andrew and Thomas
CRAIG	Caroline and Nichola
DARREN	Andrew and Melanie
MELANIE	Caroline and Craig
NICHOLA	Andrew and Craig
NICHOLAS	Caroline and Craig
THOMAS	Caroline and Darren

REASONS:	
DARREN *on* **MELANIE**	'I think she is missing her mum and if she gets out she will see her.'
NICHOLA *on* **ANDREW**	'He's too competitive and self-centred, doing things for his gain.'
THOMAS *on* **DARREN**	'We can survive without his culinary skills, and in other areas he does not input enough.'

Over the course of the day the boys reveal their laddish sides, starting in the early morning, with a serious discussion in their bedroom about who farts the loudest. Then Tom tells how he and some friends went to help a man who was being attacked by about thirty guys outside a nightclub in Omagh. Unfortunately, the odds were against them and they ended up being kicked and punched. When they met in the pub the next night, they all had swollen jaws and black eyes and felt very sorry for themselves.

Craig also tells Darren and Mel that his muscly body sometimes attracts the wrong kind of attention, like when he was on holiday in Egypt and all the local likely lads kept asking to fight him. In the end, one insisted he went to his shop with him for a fight. Being slightly drunk, Craig agreed. He was shocked to find it was a china shop and that there was a crowd of people gathered to watch the 'fight'. However, it turned out to be an arm-wrestle. In the end, Craig took on all-comers, and won.

Nick initiates a late-night chat with Tom, Mel and Andy, asking them if they have ever been arrested. Andy says no, and Tom says yes, twice, but does not elaborate. Nick tells them he has been arrested three times. Once, while on a stag do to Florida, he was arrested in a bar after a woman accused him of taking her wallet. The police apparently took him into custody, not believing in his innocence because he was drunk at the time. Eventually, it transpired that he simply looked like someone else. The second time was in Australia, where he claims he was fined 200 dollars for trespassing on a railway line, after he was caught climbing Sydney Harbour Bridge. The third time was on St Patrick's night, when beer was going at 40p a pint, and he climbed into his car after having a few. He failed a roadside breath test but was under the legal limit when retested back at the police station.

Darren has used the vegetables from the garden to make a vegetable curry – they've all been very slow to wake up to the fact that there is food right under their noses out there. Anna reckons it's the nicest meal they have had since coming into the house.

In a game of Cheat, with Tom, Nick blatantly does cheat, fiddling the cards while Tom is distracted. He knows the cameras are on him so turns to the nearest one and raises a finger conspiratorially to his lips.

Anna sits with Andy during the night as he pedals on towards the final total, and they chat together happily.

When Nick tries to tell Andy later in the morning that Anna is dangerous within the game, Andy refuses to take the bait and replies that she is good company. He changes the subject to one of his favourites, telling Nick that he is gagging for a fuck, and that the next few weeks will be difficult without one. Nick presciently comments: 'Unless you are nominated.'

It is three minutes past eight in the morning when Mel finally cycles the last of their 1,796 kilometres. They are well ahead of schedule, but slightly later than their original prediction because of Darren's injuries. Nick capitalizes on the slight resentment the rest of the group feel towards Darren (after all, they've all got sore knees, backs and bums) by suggesting he should get fewer luxuries from the shopping list next week, which will now be up by 50 per cent to £126. He also suggests that Darren could prove to be a hindrance in future physical challenges. Melanie and Andrew advise him against suggesting Darren takes a smaller share of the goodies earned by the cycling marathon. They think he could explode with anger.

Andy sleeps on the settee and Mel goes over and sits on top of him. He strokes her legs, and his hand creeps up her side and then back to her leg again. Before they can take their love-in any further, Nick strolls over and talks to them.

The relief of completing the task is soon dissipated, as the tension of waiting for the nominations bites. The girls seem to feel it most. Nichola complains of an upset stomach. Caggie does what she always does under stress – reapplies her lipliner. Anna makes them all snakebites – a cider and lager cocktail. Darren is down in the dumps about his public image. He thinks that in the outside world there will be newspaper headlines condemning him for missing his daughter's birthday. Tom tells him that lots of fathers are at work on their children's birthdays.

Big Brother gives them a mini-task to fill the hours – they have to write, design and stage a play to be performed tomorrow evening. It's an idea that has come in from hundreds of viewers, who were asked for suggestions for tasks on the website. As a reward, they will be given a special video showing of any film of their choice. They have half an hour to decide. Tom's suggestion of *A Clockwork Orange* is rejected because it freaks Anna out. Her suggestion of *Stigmata*, a religious thriller, gets few votes. Darren comes up with *Porky*, a 1980s sex classic. But, in the end, it has to be light relief. Craig has never heard of Jim Carrey, and anyway the movie they want isn't out on video yet. So they settle for *Happy Gilmore*, which is Andy's favourite and which the others haven't seen. It's a slapstick comedy about a hockey player who discovers he has the most powerful golf drive in history.

It's appropriate that Andy gets his choice of video, because soon afterwards he and Caroline discover that they are the two housemates who have been nominated. He looks totally stunned by the news, but manages to smile and says, 'Blimey!'. Mel is even more devastated, unable to speak, and when she does she says, 'I feel sick'. Caroline yells at them all, 'You could have left me off the hook this week – you've made me into the most hated woman in the building.'

Later Nick, who nominated Caroline, chats to her, telling her that at the beginning of their time in the house he thought Andy would be the eventual winner. 'But as his character progressed it had to be win, win, win.' He says he is confident that Caroline will still be in the house on Saturday. 'You're genuine. You will be fine,' he says.

In the Diary Room Andrew talks about his feelings. 'It is pretty gutting. I can see what Sada and Caroline were going on about. I've been trying to figure out what I've done wrong, or what else could have come into play. You slog your guts out at any task, try to do your best, then get turned upon. The feeling is that everyone in the house is against you. It's hard to reconcile in your mind, but that's what's happened. I'd love to find out from people why, because I'd love to stay. It's a good experience.'

Mel, wearing a bikini top and tiny shorts, gives him a lingering hug, but doesn't allow it to develop as much as Andrew would like. She says she's sweaty from lying in the garden. It's a consolation hug, and she tells him how shocked she is by the news of his nomination.

She also tells Big Brother: 'I'm gobsmacked. Caroline told me all the girls voted for him, but I'm surprised. I'll be sad to see him go. I'm worried about Caroline, she'll get more drunk and take it personally. I get on well with Andy. I'll miss him. I think he's been nominated because he's too nice. It's tactical votes because they think he will win. I thought it would be Craig. You [Big Brother] are the only person I can be totally honest with. Craig contributes nothing; he never pulls his weight. Andy is feeling shit. He is taking it personally – and so am I. The minute it was announced I looked at people and thought "Which one of you did it?".'

Caroline goes to the Diary Room but she's been drinking since late morning and it's now mid-afternoon. She announces to Big Brother that she is pissed, and she looks it. 'I got used to it [being nominated] last week. I'm not as upset this week. I left my suitcase packed... I'm so happy about Andrew's nomination. He's that vile to me. He says he wants to be a pin-up and I hope he is, because I want to pin him up in my living room and throw darts at him for the rest of my life.' She apologizes to her friends and family who will be travelling from Birmingham again on Friday evening to see whether or not she is evicted.

Afterwards, she joins Darren on his bed and tussles affectionately with him. Darren takes it in good part, but rolls away from any real contact with her. Caroline's suggestion that they all spend the rest of the week bed-hopping is ignored by everyone, but they find it hard to ignore her loud singing. She's moved on from 'It's only a game show' to another of her own lyrics 'Reiki me, reiki me, who's gonna take me?'

Big Brother faces yet another of the tipsy girls. Anna, who has also had a lot of cider, goes into the Diary Room and talks about how horrible it is to do nominations.

'I felt extremely bad that one of the people I nominated got nominated. I kissed Caroline, and then I had to kiss Andrew. It was like Judas Iscariot who betrayed Jesus with a kiss – I know that Bible stuff. I felt awful. Then Andy says he's going to talk to people to ask why we nominated him. He's going to ask us and we are going to say "It's just you". He's a wee bit cocky and arrogant. Me and Nick and Nicky and Caroline and all of us were a little bit worried about the voting. Andrew was the only one who woke up this morning and didn't think that. He wound people up with his self-assurance, and that was why he was voted out.

'It seems to be the strong-willed lippy people who are not scared to say what they feel who are being voted out... People who voted for Caroline did it because she is gobby and doesn't try to get on with other people. In the morning she really annoys me with her singing... I don't feel I belong in any group in here. When I get up in the morning I sometimes sit with people who I know are quite in with each other. I don't feel close to anyone here. I do get lonely, and miss my flatmate loads... I can see when I get nominated I don't have enough ego to get upset. That's the thing with Andy and Caroline, they both have big egos and are devastated.'

Caroline is by now feeling so bad that Mel helps her to her bed and puts a bucket next to her in case she is sick. The talk among the rest is of the play, and they come up with ideas for a porn-style *Dracula*, with Darren as the Count, a comedy love scene between the two nominees, and for Nichola anything as long as she is tied to a bed. In the end, they half-heartedly agree on a Rocky-Horror-style plot about gypsies and transsexuals in Transylvania.

The contact between Mel and Andy resumes out in the garden. They talk about sexual longing, and Mel admits she gets it all the time, but tries to keep it 'in perspective'. She teases Andy with the information that when she was bored during the bike riding she leaned forward in the saddle to stimulate herself.

Nick is doing his rounds, talking to the different housemates individually. He tells Mel that he didn't nominate Andy (he didn't), and that the two people he most likes are her and Andy. Despite this, he still thinks Caroline will be the one who stays in the house on Friday because Andy may come over to the public as cocky. Then he says that Anna will win because she is unlikely to be nominated. He describes her as 'deadly like a snake'. Mel simply replies that he is cynical.

If Mel is beginning to question Nick's integrity, so is Darren, who late at night expresses his irritation at Nick's constant questioning. 'If I choose to tell you a story that's my choice. But you throw questions at me to try to analyse me, and sit and think "so Darren does this, I reckon he'll do that". You analyse so badly. You think you are smart and I don't buy it. I see it. Nobody else does, but I do, mister.' Nick dismisses him as paranoid.

In the early hours of the morning, the play discussion resumes and Caroline comes up with a good idea. The two nominees will murder the rest of the inhabitants of the house. Darren and Nick take up the idea and Caroline, who seems to be fully recovered from her drink-induced sickness, invents some good twists to the plot.

When the household finally sleeps, their night-time visitor, the fox, returns. He has not been around for a few days, probably because the bike riding kept the household active all night.

Not everyone was present at the play discussion, and the next morning Nicky is angry that the plot has been changed without consulting her. They call a group meeting to sort the matter out, and Nicky is soon won over. Her anger was mainly at Tom who told her peremptorily that the plot had been changed, rather than offering the new version for discussion. He apologizes, and they all start work on the details. It's a murder mystery set in the *Big Brother* house. Nick is cast in the role of a television news reporter who is covering the mysterious deaths of six people in the house. The two nominees, Andrew and Caroline, have gone on a killing spree and murdered all the other contestants in an appropriate way: Anna, the singing nun, is beaten with her guitar; Darren is killed in the chicken coop; Nichola is stabbed to death with one of her own knitting needles in the shower, like the scene from *Psycho*; Thomas is suffocated in the bread dough; Melanie's brain explodes when she can't work out $e=mc^2$; and Craig, The Incredible Sleeping Man, is suffocated in his bed with a pillow.

At noon, the group have a house meeting in which tempers become frayed. It starts sensibly enough with Nicky asking for a rota for keeping the kitchen clean. Caroline uses it as a platform to attack Craig for not pulling his weight. It's a blistering diatribe about him taking a day off from the cycling challenge, and about how little housework he does. Craig retaliates, but Caggie has the upper hand.

Mel has a long chat with Big Brother in the Diary Room about Andrew's nomination. She seems genuinely upset about it, sufficiently so for the other housemates and the production team to start wondering whether she will be able to stay on without him.

'It's very upsetting. I'm really pissed off that Andrew has been voted out. I'll be really upset to see him leave.' She believes some of the boys ganged up against him in the nominations because the three girls would not be enough.

'Caroline just said, "Has anybody told Andy the reason?" I said no because I don't know why he has been voted out. She just said, "Serves the bastard right." It's a big political game in here, and some of them are playing it really well.'

She cites Nick as the prime example, saying she has been watching him since the early days when he made efforts to befriend her.

'The first week he said things to me that were so obvious and in your face. He asked everyone who they had nominated. He's cleverly suggesting things to people. He's playing a political game.'

She says that he has been telling the others that 'Anna is someone to watch', and now they are looking at Anna in a different light.

'He has offered Caroline and Nicky a room in London because they want to move to London. Afterwards, he made it clear that what's said in here doesn't count in the outside world. That's very two-faced, quite a nasty unpleasant thing to do. Suddenly they're saying, "Isn't he sweet, isn't he lovely?" So it worked. I certainly don't trust him. If Andy gets voted out I just don't want to be here.'

Caroline tells the other girls she is disappointed that they did not support her attack on Craig, but Mel replies that in her opinion Caroline should not have done it. Caroline is unrepentant, and admits that she's looking forward to the scene in the play where she suffocates Craig.

Caroline repeats her disappointment to Big Brother. 'Everyone made complaints about Craig, not just me. Nobody backed me up, but it was something everyone had said. Craig told me I'm not a doctor, but all the girls were wearing bandages, and he never even broke a sweat.'

She says she's not as upset about the nominations as she was last week, as she was expecting to be back on the hit list. She thinks she'll be the one to leave on Friday, but hopes it won't be her.

Andy goes into the Diary Room when she leaves to puzzle more over why he has been nominated. He really wants to know who chose him, and their reasons.

'The majority of people say they are really surprised and shocked, so I think it must be a small number, which helps. Mel has been really nice, helped a lot, very supportive. Nick said he is sad. You don't know who to trust, they turn on you, but you still have to get on with them and achieve stuff. It's quite a head fuck. I'm going to ask again, but I wish people would be honest with me and if there's some good reasons, I've learnt something. I'd just like to know. I'll be pretty devastated if I'm voted out by the public... Maybe I'm too competitive, try to commandeer everything... I would hate to leave it the way it is now with Mel without anything being finalized or developing, that would be a shame. The way she was talking yesterday, maybe when we get out there may be something. But we may be two totally different people outside of these walls.'

The play performance goes very smoothly with no hitches, and they are rewarded not just with their video, but with ice cream, popcorn, corn chips and salsa dip, all served by Tom from a cinema usherette's tray. The boys love the film and laugh all the way through. The girls, particularly Nicky, are unimpressed.

'I'd rather be sucking me big toe with me thumb stuck up me anus than sat there,' she says later.

For the rest of the evening, everyone is quite prickly. Nicky and Andy have a silly altercation over an egg she says wasn't cooked properly. Craig tells Darren he is still upset by Caroline's attack. Cigarettes and alcohol are now in short supply, and it is beginning to get to the smokers. Nichola is talking about her favourite pizza topping and says she'd like one with extra tobacco. Darren, who tells the others he cannot go to the toilet without a ciggie, is fantasizing about next week's shopping. He suggests that they split the luxury money between them, and have £10 to spend each. Golden Virginia tobacco and Stella lager are top of his list.

At half past eleven at night, Nicky is the worse for drink and is in the Diary Room letting rip about Andy: 'He's a dickhead, he needs to be out on Friday. If he stays, I'll try my hardest to get him out. You're a fucking dickhead. Why did I try to believe you are a nice guy. He's so pissed off he was nominated, he thinks he's king dong and he can shag any woman in the world. He said he can't wait to go into a bar and see some fit-looking woman – what a nobhead. He's not good-looking. He can stick his head right up his arse. I didn't want to hate him, but he's taking everything personally... Apparently he's been slagging off Nicholas, being very vindictive to Nicholas and making sly comments.

'Craig's made an effort and been awake for most of the day. Today's been such a weird day. People get up in the morning and do their own food, don't make tea for everyone... Could you not have got us some proper men? Some real men who are a bit more spiritual. Nicholas is a nice guy. It's the others around him. If we had a few more like him – men who are in touch with more than their dicks. I'm sorry for any wives they get in the future; any woman who gets involved with them.'

Outside the Diary Room she joins her soulmate Caroline to slag off the men in the house, particularly Andy. Over the course of a fifteen-minute gossip they use an astonishing 140 swear words, the vast majority being the f-word. Caroline clocks up slightly more than Nicky. But Nicky is the angrier of the two, ranting about all the men. The only two she likes, she says, are Darren ('I could take him home') and Nicholas. She says she's not going to be part of the group any more, but will cook her own food and eat on her own.

Meanwhile, Mel goes to see Big Brother to discuss Nicky. 'She is drunk and will not react in a good way. She has this explosive way of dealing with things, difficult in this environment. People will start to be less tolerant. If she snaps at me I will lose my temper. I have done well to keep cool, my blood is boiling.'

However cross Mel feels about Nicky, she is soon diverted by a huge spider she spots. She asks for more lotion for the mosquito bites they are all suffering, and then asks Big Brother if he likes her with her hair in bunches.

On Thursday the row between Caroline and Craig erupts again, at the house meeting. This time Craig starts it, saying he wants to respond to her criticisms of him. They argue about who did a longer stint on the exercise bike and things start to get nasty. The others tell them that this is not a subject for a general meeting but something they must settle between themselves. Caroline agrees, but Craig wants to carry on. They are both angry. Craig says he has been wrongly accused.

Andrew says, 'You guys may have to live with each other for another seven weeks.'

Tom adds, 'And we have to live with you, too.'

Taking charge, Tom suggests they adjourn the house meeting for an hour. Still bickering, Craig and Caroline separate. She offers him an olive branch by asking if he wants a cup of tea. 'You know you love me really,' she says.

'I honestly don't,' Craig murmurs, but the nastiness has abated.

Andrew follows Mel into the girls' room and again they discuss not trusting Nick, and who may have nominated Andy. Mel tells him, 'If you go, I don't particularly want to stay. I hate everyone in here. Nick has been suggesting things to me, it makes me think, and then I take a step back and wonder why I'm thinking it, and it's because he suggested it.'

As she says she does not want to stay without him, Andrew leans forward and kisses her tenderly on her lips. 'You shouldn't have done that,' she says, gently pulling away. 'I don't think you could handle me out in the real world. I don't think you could. I'm very, very fiery.'

'I'm willing to give it a try,' Andy says, but before he can put in any more practice, Nick walks in to ask Mel if she has labelled her cheese. It is not the first time that he has interrupted them just when their flirtation is on the brink of turning into something more serious.

Later, after the short meeting, Mel is talking to Darren. These two share a distrust of Nick, and are discussing it openly for the first time. Mel says he will do anything to win and that 'pretty much everything that comes out of his mouth does so for a reason'. Darren agrees, and they are about to get further into comparing notes when Nick, who has been skulking outside the room, comes in. He asks Darren whether there is anything he does that annoys him, but Darren refuses to be drawn.

Although Andrew seems to be even closer to Mel, there is one harsh moment for him, when he watches her launch into a physical flirtation with Tom. The two of them play at stealing each other's microphone batteries, and tussle together on the double bed. 'Leave my breasts alone,' Mel is heard to exclaim, as Tom lunges for her microphone. Andy is just outside the room, playing with his Scalextric. Tom and Mel chase each other into the living area, both red-faced and giggling.

One thing that has been decided at the meeting is that the house is dirty, and everyone pitches in to do some cleaning. By the evening, morale in the group is better, and they play party games together. Late at night, Nick talks to Andy and Mel about Anna, describing her as 'very dangerous, very calculating, almost like a cold killer... She has more hidden agendas than a Pandora's box. She's a chameleon.' Andy says Anna has annoyed him, and when Caroline goes she'll be the one to watch. He's intent on stroking Mel's feet, but Mel takes in what is being said and challenges the conspiracy theory.

Before they settle to sleep, the boys discuss the size of their willies. Andrew is the one who has been making comparisons, and he reveals that Darren's is the biggest, even bigger than Craig's.

Friday is, as usual, a tense day as the two nominees wait to see who is going to be evicted. It's particularly difficult for Andrew. Not only is he under threat, but Mel appears to be getting into Tom in a big way. She accuses him of nicking some of her cheese and another play-fight breaks out. Tom lies on top of her and smacks her bottom, then runs into the garden with her in hot pursuit. They struggle together and eventually Mel kicks Tom, then strokes him to ease the pain. As the fight breaks up, they hold hands briefly.

The other girls watch from inside the house. 'She could at least have waited for Andrew to go,' says Caggie. The girls agree that they prefer the combination of Mel and Tom to Mel and Andy and then they speculate about who she will go after next. They reckon it won't be Nick, but it could be Darren or even Anna. Anna says Mel is not her type.

The cameras hidden behind mirrors are picking up lots of the strange beauty rituals of both sexes. Darren's are the most elaborate with lots of time spent cleaning and flossing his teeth, two different types of deodorant (first a roll-on, then a spray) and lotions for his body, face, hands and lips. Nichola deals with her facial hair by borrowing hair remover from Mel – outside the house she apparently waxes her upper lip. Mel spends ages every day squeezing her spots. Tom and Nick also have facial hair problems. Tom shaves right inside his nostrils, and Nick shaves his forehead.

Craig and Caroline are both prepared to make concessions to get over their fight and make friends, with Craig giving Caroline a relaxation session in the bedroom to help her cope with the stress of once again waiting for the voting results.

When they finally come, she has been reprieved for the second time. More than a million people have voted and 68 per cent want Andrew out. His face collapses at the news and he swears. The others hug him, even the jubilant Caroline, before she makes a lap of honour round the garden singing 'I Love You, Baby' at the top of her voice.

Andy is not as gracious in defeat as Sada was. With two hours to go before he must leave the house, he stares at his reflection in one of the bedroom mirrors, devastated. To Craig and Nick he describes Caroline: 'She's annoying, she's stupid, she makes a lot of noise, does fuck all and she's ugly!'

On his own for a few moments in the garden, he comments wryly that even the hens don't seem to want to talk to him. Then he finds Mel on her bed. She says she is being selfish, but she does not want him to leave. She says she cannot stand the thought of spending another week with any of the others, apart from Tom. Andy bitterly asks, 'What happens if she [Caroline] wins? What does that say about our country?'

The two of them are so close together that their radio microphones pick up each other's heartbeats as Andy hugs her towards him. She cries. They talk about Nick, with Andy reluctant to be as cynical about him as Mel is. They get up to rejoin the others, hug, and their mouths lock together for their most passionate kiss so far, only minutes before Andrew has to leave the house.

He may not want to leave, but Andy finds one instant compensation – he walks across the bridge to the studio with his arm firmly round Davina McCall's waist. The crowd lining the walk to the studio are chanting Andrew's name. Many of them are waving posters with Nick's face on them, and the words 'Out on Your Nichol-Arse'.

Andrew is shocked to discover the level of bad feeling aimed at Nick. He says that as he left the house he gave Nick a hug, and handed over the last of his supply of cigarettes. Davina tells him that Mel has asked the production team to pass her telephone number on to him, and he confirms he would definitely like to see her when she leaves the *Big Brother* house.

Back inside, both Tom and Nick go to the Diary Room to express their regret that Andy has gone – they both, individually, regarded him as a friend. But no sooner is his friend out than Nick's mind is on the next round of nominations, and he whispers about the choices to Darren and Mel, using initials instead of full names. Big Brother calls him to the Diary Room, where he is given another warning about plotting and rigging nominations.

WEEK THREE FACT FILE

MAIN TASK PASS ☑ FAIL ■	The cycling challenge.
SMALL TASK	To write, design and stage a play.
TREATS	For staging the play they get to watch a video and gorge themselves on ice cream and popcorn.
BOOKIES' FAVOURITE TO WIN	Anna is favourite at 2/1. Former favourite, Mel, has slipped to fourth position at 4/1. Tom and Darren move into second and third place, with odds of 3/1 and 7/2.
TO WALK	Caroline is the hottest tip for eviction next week.

WHAT THE EXPERT SAYS

'Since Andrew's nomination Melanie has become a lot more tender and caring towards him. Her behaviour towards him has not always been consistent. For example, in the first kiss she lies on the bed very open and receptive to the kiss, but as soon as he goes in for the plunge, she says that wasn't such a good idea. She always leaves that little bit of room for uncertainty. When he hugs her, she says she's sweaty. What she is trying to do is assert control over the relationship. There are two possible reasons for blowing hot and cold. The first is self-preservation. She doesn't want to have a full-blown relationship in front of millions of people. The second is more strategic. Mel is used to using her sexuality and femininity to attract men and keep them on her side. Now Andrew has gone she won't significantly change the way she relates to other people. When we feel anxious or under threat we revert back to our tried and tested strategies of relating to one another. What's Melanie's tried and tested strategy? Using her femininity and sexuality. So although Andrew has been the lucky one on the receiving end of this so far, I don't think he'll be the only one. There will be lots more flirting in the house, and it will be instigated by Melanie.'

Anjula Mutanda, Counselling Psychologist

ANDREW LOOKS BACK

Andrew's eviction is watched by 3.6 million viewers, making it the peak-rated programme, with 30 per cent of all viewers tuned into it, even beating the ITV *News* which has coverage of the Queen Mother's birthday celebrations. The voting figures are up 60 per cent on the first week, and even after the poll has closed viewers continue to try to register their votes.

The next morning Andy is still reeling from the discovery of Nick's duplicity and the level of bad feeling about him in the outside world. Starved of any information about how the show was going down with viewers, Andrew had imagined all sorts of interest. But he never dreamed that his mate Nick would be cast in the role of the nation's number one villain, with newspapers like the *Sun* running campaigns to have him ousted. Stories of his lies – for instance, the tale of his seventeen-year-old wife dying in a car crash – have been published, and he is universally known as 'Nasty Nick'.

Andrew faces a press conference of eighteen journalists and a television crew, who question him about Nick but also about his feelings for Mel and his hopes of seeing her again when she leaves the house. He tells them that he would definitely have liked the relationship with Mel to have gone further, and would prefer her not to get too close to anyone else, but he accepts that it may happen.

Afterwards, he says he has no regrets about how he behaved on the show, because he was honest and himself, and didn't pretend he was happy to leave, because he wasn't.

'I was enjoying it, I wasn't bored, I wanted to stay. The interplay between the people in there was fascinating, and I expect to find it even more fascinating when I can watch it and see it from all sides. But even just from my own point of view I kept thinking "God, this is brilliant." On one level it's interesting gossip, and on another it is as deep as a Chekhov play, with lots of undercurrents of feeling.

'The concept of eviction may be hard to get your head round, but we all face threats in our daily lives – we face the end of relationships, leaving home, changing jobs, and, ultimately, dying. It is just a microcosm of life. When people talk about walking out, they are giving up, committing suicide, and I think that's wrong. I hope Mel has the strength to stick it to the end.'

Andrew's enthusiasm and pragmatism meant that he stayed on a more even keel than many members of the household, whose emotions veered from ecstasy to deep depression.

'I felt a certain level of excitement the whole time I was there and I only had two really hard days. The first four days were an adventure, because there was so much to find out about, and I was excited to have met someone like Melanie whom I liked. But on the fifth and sixth days Melanie was very flirty and tactile with other people, and it started to annoy me.

'By that time, the sleep deprivation was kicking in. Although the lights go out in the bedrooms, the lights in the rest of the house are full on, very bright, and it messes up your brain. We all slept when we were exhausted, not on a regular pattern. At home, you wind down to sleep. You go to bed, have a soft reading light on, and the hard drive of your brain stops spinning. But in the house you are never on your own; there is always another human being very close to you. And because we were all new to each other, we hadn't reached the stage of comfortable companionship. I reckon I was only on my own for about 1 per cent of the time in there. You can switch off from the cameras – you have to do that, for the sake of your sanity. But you can't switch off from other people.

'So you stay up late, playing games, and then you make noise which disturbs those who are trying to sleep, and everyone gets ratty. Small things like the shopping list then become important. If someone has a fried egg, you all have to have a fried egg. Caroline makes tea because she's bored, and then acts surprised when we run out of tea bags.

'They surprised me by their lack of self-control. If there was chocolate or alcohol, they had to have it then, not budget it to last.

'I took a book in which I was looking forward to reading, but I never even started it. Reading is a solitary act, and concentrating on anything more demanding than a magazine was for me impossible. You are always slightly on edge, waiting for the next thing to happen. If someone starts a ball game, you want to be there.'

Andrew was irritated and upset by the boy/girl divide which developed. 'Some of the girls wanted private space, and when you come into a show like *Big Brother* you know that you are not going to be able to have it. The divide set up so many tensions, it was like going back to the junior-school playground. The women were all older than me and I couldn't believe they were behaving like that. If we had mixed the dormitories we would have forged some real bonds between people, not just on the basis of gender. Yet when I suggested it, some of them behaved as though I was a disgusting pervert who wanted to see girls naked. As if I haven't seen tits before.'

Andrew is surprised that some of the others seemed uncomfortable with the cameras.

'Caroline acted as though she didn't know beforehand that there were cameras in the bedroom. There was all this silly business of holding up towels to get changed. What did she think she was coming into? Caroline definitely had an issue about nakedness and so did Nick. I never saw Nick naked. I never saw him with his top off – he slept in a T-shirt and I never saw him changing. He didn't strip off to sunbathe.'

Andy wised up to Nick in the first few days – but then dismissed it. 'He was going to everyone, getting their opinions, amassing information for his own reasons. I thought he might be very cunning, and then I thought it was ridiculous, nobody could be treating it as seriously as that, and I went back to taking him at face value.

'When I had my first kiss with Mel, she warned me about Nick. She said he was trouble and that I was being too honest. I said there were others I suspected more.

'Nick was very nervous. He hated losing at games. He came close to blowing his top a few times. When the clay pottery-making wasn't working for him, he was well close to spitting his dummy out. For someone so cool and calculating, he's close to the edge.

'I'd definitely like to meet him again, just to talk to him about it all. Was he really as dastardly as everyone made out? After all, he wasn't doing anything criminal, just playing a game. But on the other hand, if I meet him again I'll never be able to trust anything he says. It's a shame because we could have been good mates; we share the same sense of humour.'

Although he did not get on with Nichola, Andy feels he could have connected with her if she had not been so close to Caroline.

'In a different time and space we could have got on. But with Caroline she would just get drunk, talk their own language and be very catty.'

With Anna, he noticed 'a definite unpleasant edge to her personality when she is drunk. I'm one of the few who picked up on it, mainly because it was directed my way. I hugged her at the end, because we have shared an experience, but I could never feel close to her.'

He admires Darren's street-smart ability to handle people. 'Darren acts naive and juvenile, but he's streetwise. The day Nichola was so upset about the plot of the play being changed without consulting her, he turned the situation round so smoothly I was left gasping in admiration. He made her believe it was her idea to change it. In one sentence, he both slagged off her original idea and yet made her the reason we changed. I don't have that kind of diplomacy. But I think Darren was deeply disturbed by not having his kids around, and that made it hard for him to join in everything.'

On the whole, Andrew feels most people in the house did not want to pull their weight when it came to fulfilling the tasks they were set.

'They were all so lackadaisical about the pottery-making challenge. They were sunbathing, doing nothing, and it was actually quite difficult. It was a good task because we had to read the rules and measure the pots we made. But I was the only one who cared that we did it properly. Although it was an individual task, we had to work as a team – and we just didn't.

'Caroline made the most noise about the bike riding, but she covered the smallest number of kilometres. We had individual totals. Craig pedalled slowly, but he kept going – she'd get off after half an hour. In one of her sessions she only did eleven and a half kilometres.'

Andy is not intending to go back to his old job, although he loved the people he was working with.

'I'm hoping that *Big Brother* will lead to new things happening in my life, exciting things. I'd like to write, or work in television, probably behind the scenes. I gave up the best job in the world when I stopped being mechanic for my brother Anthony. We travelled the world to go-kart meetings, and it was a great high, watching him win. If I had to choose between my fame and his, it would be his every time. I'm not envious of him.'

He says his parents were not upset about his honest talk about using prostitutes. 'My dad knew, and I bet my mum suspected. There was no shock for them, and I knew they would be supportive. I went in there determined to be honest, and one of the main things I think people are dishonest about is sex. I love it. It's not dirty or smutty. I'm normal. In the end I would like a marriage and a long-term relationship, but I don't believe that closes off all sex, not for either partner.'

He believes that after *Big Brother* he will keep in touch with Tom and Craig, both of whom he likes. Most of all, he wants to stay in touch with Mel. 'I'm not in love with her, because love comes from knowing someone, and I don't know her yet. But I'm in love with the idea of her, and I want to see what happens next.'

> *'I'll have a hard time beating Caroline,*
> *she's the queen of this now.'*
>
> THOMAS

4 TO 11 AUGUST

The house is developing a rhythm of moods. The tension of eviction night is followed by real highs and lows the next day. Sunday, when the shopping arrives, is calmer and less fraught. Then Monday brings more nominations and more stress. Thursday is the weekly house meeting, which can be difficult if grievances are aired. And Friday is eviction night.

Caroline is, for a second time, thrilled to have survived to fight again. She and Nicky are equally thrilled to have got rid of their arch-enemy Andrew and celebrate his disappearance by singing 'Ding, Dong the Witch is Dead'. The adrenalin rush on Friday night, when they catch a brief glimpse of the outside world and dance frenetically to the music that is piped into the house during the live shows, means they all stay up late, struggling to come down from the excitement. In the quiet of the early morning, Tom tells Mel and Nick that life in the *Big Brother* house is profoundly affecting him and helping him to face up to the decisions he has to make.

'Am I going to stay home and do farming or move out into the world somewhere? I'll probably find my real personality in this show. I wasn't really self-aware before.'

To Mel's surprise, he talks about how his father did not allow him or his sisters to cry, and how the last time he cried was at his grandfather's funeral twenty years ago.

Mel questions him about his sex life, asking him how many women he has slept with. Tom says he has never counted, but it's quite a few. Mel persists and eventually Tom says that from the age of eighteen it works out about one every two weeks. As he is now thirty-one, if he's got it right the total is well over 300! Mel is impressed.

The three of them talk quietly for hours and, inevitably, the question of the next round of nominations comes up. Despite Mel's distrust of Nick, she's happy to join him in plotting the future for the house. Anna is their target.

'If Anna wasn't there, I could easily manipulate the way Caroline and Nicky think. I could make them vote for you. I know that I could. I could just go in and say a few bad things,' Mel says, but also acknowledges that if she can manipulate them, so can Anna. Nick pushes forward his plan to get Anna on to the hit list. They agree that Darren is unpredictable, so if they want more support for the scheme they will have to enlist Craig.

They are not the only ones talking late into the night. Craig tells Darren his worries about his building business because of battles with the local council. He's worried about how it's going while he's away from it.

On Saturday morning, Big Brother gives them the week's challenge: 'You must learn the semaphore flag signalling system based on waving a pair of hand-held flags.' Nicky remembers learning it at Brownies and Guides, but can't recall any of the signals. Before they can start, they have to make their own flags. They

◀ A bird's eye view of the house in Bow.

▲ The housemates explore their new surroundings.

▲ With a restricted shopping budget the housemates would often prioritise alcohol over food.

▲ Everyone went Nichola's favourite colour – orange – to celebrate her birthday.

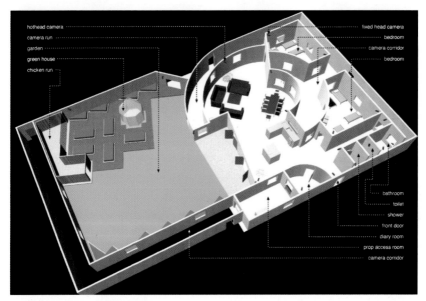

hothead camera
camera run
garden
green house
chicken run

fixed head camera
bedroom
camera corridor
bedroom

bathroom
toilet
shower
front door
diary room
prop access room
camera corridor

▲ The plan of the house.

▲ Nichola makes her imprint on the house.

▲ And so do Andy and Mel...

▲ Craig and Nichola – still trying to get rid of that sticky clay.

▲ Nichola knitting the wire dress she left the house in while Sada snuggles up.

▲ Nicky in her warpaint.

▲ Marjorie, the only chicken with its own website.

▲ Darren spends more time in front of the mirror than all the girls put together.

▲ At first the girls have fun with the nominations in week seven.

▲ But fun turns to tears when Mel hears Darren say her name in the Diary Room.

▲ Darren tries to make up with Mel and later demands for the nominations to be re-run.

▲ Leaving the real world behind, Claire joins the Big Brother house in week six.

▲ Craig and Claire sharing one of their many jokes.

▲ Braving the cameras, Claire takes her first shower in the house.

▲ Craig particularly enjoyed the kissing game.

▲ 'Those two can just amuse each other for hours.' *Anna*

▲ Craig's honesty won the public's heart.

▲ Anna in scouse mode: complete with liverpudlian accent and bulging sleeves, she gets Craig off to a tee.

▲ Craig holding Nichola under the shower after the clay-painting session.

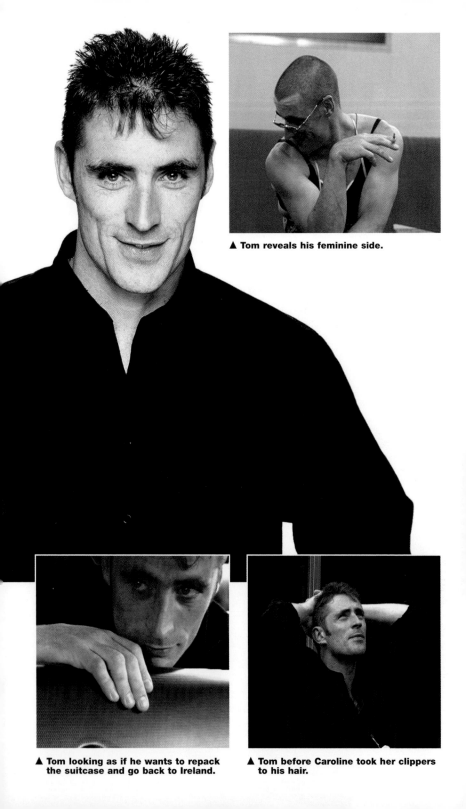

▲ Tom reveals his feminine side.

▲ Tom looking as if he wants to repack the suitcase and go back to Ireland.

▲ Tom before Caroline took her clippers to his hair.

▲ Mel and Nick size each other up in the early days.

▲ Mel's sensational looks sent the male temperatures soaring in the house and across the nation.

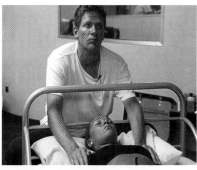

▲ Nick working his magic on Mel.

▲ Enjoying getting close to Mel, Tom gives her a massage.

▲ The extent of his enjoyment is clear for all to see.

▲ Mel kisses another man goodbye.

◄ An intimate moment between Mel and Andy in the garden.

▲ Andy's birthday party is a real drag.

◄ 'You shouldn't have done that.' *Mel*

▲ His new-found celebrity as a *Big Brother* contestant means that Andy appears on *The Big Breakfast*.

are not as sure of this task as they were of the bike ride, so decide to wager only 35 per cent of their shopping money on it, which means they stand to lose or gain £25.73. Craig is worried that his poor spelling will drag the others down.

Before he left the house, Andrew gave his remaining cigarettes to Nick. Despite the chronic shortage of tobacco, which is leaving tempers frayed, he does not share them with the others. He sneaks away every hour or so and hides to have a smoke. At first, Mel is the only one who knows, but eventually Tom is also in on the secret. Nick continues to home in on individuals and question them. He corners Darren in the garden and asks if he has upset him in any way, as he feels Darren may be a bit off with him. Darren says, 'Not at all.' Nick wants to pursue it, but Darren is growing adept at fielding Nick's probes, and walks away. Nick then moves on to Tom and offers him a place to stay when he is in London.

Darren confesses to Nicky that he had a wild, erotic dream about Mel on Friday night, only hours after Andy was evicted. Mel chased after him, and they ended up having sex in the shower and the bedroom, and the whole of Britain was talking about their porn show. Although it was only a dream, Darren is worried that viewers would not like him for it. Just a couple of hours after he tells Nicky his night-time fantasy, Mel teases him about his designer underpants and insists on putting on a pair to show how small they are. They parade together, in matching pants.

Anna has also had a dream about an affair with one of her housemates, only in her case it is Nichola. She dreamt that when she left, Nicky picked her up and drove her home but then told her she didn't love her.

Caroline is coming down from the high of surviving the eviction process and is very tearful. She cries for fifteen minutes before dinner, and then again a couple of hours later, alone in the girls' bedroom. Craig, who is walking past, hears her and goes to offer help. The two of them have not been close friends – they have had the worst row yet in the *Big Brother* house – but Craig genuinely offers comfort. Stroking her back, he listens to her explain: 'I've got post-eviction blues. I was the same last week. I wish I wasn't on such a roller coaster.'

It is a lovely evening, and the whole group sit outside watching the sunset. Mel thinks she sees a UFO falling from the skies. Caroline sings a song about the sun coming out tomorrow, which proves to be prophetic. Later, Mel is called to the Diary Room and she talks about missing Andy.

'I don't know what it's like to be in Caroline's position, to be nominated and stay in two weeks in a row. Yesterday, she was elated and I was down, today she's just on an emotional roller coaster and it's not doing her any good at all. I get a bit annoyed about it. Andy was a better person for the good of the house. He contributed in every way he could. He had a lot of good qualities to offer the group, and that was his downfall in the end. I can't see Caroline making the same contribution.

'Her presence, if anything, drags you down. It's difficult enough for any of us in here, without having that added factor, like a time bomb. I can't honestly see her making it through another week.'

She says that Caroline's elation over Andy's eviction was in her face, rubbing salt in the wound, and that she strutted around when she was feeling fragile. She says she'll use the next few days to try to bridge the gap between her and the other girls. Her skin is becoming thicker. When she was very emotional she remembered it was just a TV programme and that they are nearly halfway through. She says that Anna is a big driving force behind the girls. 'She's very clever and can manipulate the situation.'

Nick, too, has a long session in the Diary Room late in the evening. He describes it as his worst day there because Andy has left. With another nomination day coming up, he thinks the atmosphere is bringing out the worst in people.

'People are becoming more tactical. It's tending to bring out the worst side of everyone's character – as well as the good side because it's a competition.' He says he believes the others are ignoring group dynamics when choosing who they want to nominate.

'Even if you are a good team player, which I think I am, it doesn't matter because at the end of the day people are judging you for you. So you can be the best team player and not be liked so much as someone else and so you're in danger of being evicted. I think people have in mind the next three or four people who they're going to vote. If it's tactical it's a shame. It should be based on how good that person is in a team. A lot of people have lost that premise. I haven't, but a lot have. It is the greed factor, wanting to be number one and wanting that end prize.'

He says Darren is all 'me, myself and I', and that he asked Darren if he had a problem with him. He doesn't believe it when Darren said no. Yet he can't blow up at Darren or Darren will nominate him.

He talks to Big Brother about his fears as to how the viewing public see him. He has had no clue about the campaigns being waged against him outside the house by national newspapers, but he is uneasy about his public image.

'There's obviously a fear, for me personally, that parts of my character that I thought were not there have come out. You're with people all the time and so perhaps certain things in your character that you knew you had but had always put a lid on, are coming out. And it's the realization that eventually, when one leaves the house, are people going to think you're a nice or a nasty person?'

When questioned by Big Brother as to which parts of his character he worries about, Nick replies: 'Everyone has a certain amount of selfishness, a slight devious streak in them. In this environment, it can just bring those to the surface because we're all here to enjoy ourselves primarily. But, secondly, we're all here to take part in a game show that has an ultimate prize at the end of it.'

When Big Brother asks him for examples of how his nastier side has come out, he says he doesn't think it has come out, except perhaps in the way he has hogged Andy's cigarettes when the rest of the group have been without tobacco. 'I may come across as extremely selfish to be seen puffing away in the garden knowing the whole group is out of cigarettes. But it's crazy to share everything, otherwise it just goes.'

Then Big Brother asks Nick the question: if the *Big Brother* game was a sport, what sport would it be? Nick answers with a smile that it would be fox hunting, and that he would be in the chasing pack. 'Let the others run out of steam and then overtake them,' he says.

As they succeeded with their last task, they have a reasonable budget when they tackle the shopping list on Sunday morning and opt for luxuries like Earl Grey tea and Stella lager. They also order some more playing cards and some birthday candles, in preparation for Nicky's birthday in a week's time. However, the serious business of choosing their order is interrupted by a security alert and they are all ordered to go into the girls' bedroom. A remote-controlled helicopter has been buzzing around the garden, dropping leaflets printed by the *Sun* telling the housemates to boot out Nick – just as Caroline's song forecast. Luckily, the wind has carried the leaflets off target, and security men are able to collect any that have strayed on to the roof and on to the security fence.

Feelings about Nick outside the house are running very high, with unofficial 'Nail Nasty Nick' T-shirts being printed and newspapers running stories on a daily basis. There are rumours flying around the country that he is a plant and not a real contestant. However, as well as being bombarded with e-mails demanding Nick goes, the *Big Brother* internet site is receiving plenty from his supporters. He now has a cult following and his own fan club.

While the 'heartfelt plea' from the *Sun* is being removed, the contestants carry on with their list. They are not sharing the luxury money anymore, but are each having £7 of their own to spend. They notice that Nick is not ordering cigarettes or beer, but is spending his pocket money on doughnuts and chocolate biscuits.

By mid-afternoon, another helicopter, this one full size, zooms over the house, and Darren and Tom begin to semaphore messages. Darren goes for HELP and Tom tries HELLO MUM. They are all called inside and Big Brother summons Tom to the Diary Room to tell him that they must not use their newly acquired semaphore skills to contact the outside world. It's a light-hearted reprimand. But there is a much more serious one to come from Big Brother. Tom is given a written notice, warning them all once again about discussing nominations. Anyone guilty of breaking the rules by discussing or trying to influence the votes of others can, the note says, in extreme cases be ejected from the house. 'Your vote is your own private decision. Do not be swayed by others. Big Brother is, as always, watching.'

Caroline also gets a ticking off from Big Brother for not wearing her microphone. She erupts into a session of pillow thumping and swearing. 'I want to get out of here. I'm sick of being watched by a bunch of fucking twats!' she screams. Nicky comforts her, and Anna reassures her that the message about the microphone was aimed at all of them. Having calmed down, Caroline goes into the Diary Room and talks over her feelings with Big Brother. She doesn't need a counselling session, she says, and she isn't seriously thinking of leaving the house.

However, one person is. Anna, probably the most level-headed of the whole group, tells Big Brother that she has had enough. 'I want to leave. I knew before I came here that it would be difficult. But I thought I would have got more energy, more food for thought, from the group. Progressively over the past few days, I've gone more into myself. I don't think I will be missed when I go, it won't make that much difference.'

She compares life in the house with life in the convent. 'But there was a valid reason for being there. The reason for being here is... there isn't one!'

There are some good things about the experience, she concedes. 'Caroline making me laugh, teaching Darren the guitar and the cycling task. It's my fault I feel down about the whole thing. Maybe if there were different people – but that's a bit harsh because they're all lovely. A few different people would have made it more interesting.'

Big Brother suggests she discuss her feelings with the group. Anna says she is not looking for an ego boost, she doesn't want everyone telling her she's lovely. But she agrees to talk about it. Before facing the whole group, she tells Caggie and Darren as they all potter about the kitchen together, and they both hug and reassure her. Later they sing her a song.

Outside, Mel has joined Tom and Nick and they are discussing whether the men use condoms. Both Tom and Nick say they don't, and Mel rounds on them for risking disease and pregnancy. Nick says they dull sensation and he does not like the mechanical business of putting them on. Mel accuses him of being selfish. As evening falls, Mel and Tom indulge in more horseplay with the hose, with Nick joining in.

Dinner is dominated, perhaps for the first time ever, by Anna, who does what she promised Big Brother, and discusses with the group her desire to leave. 'I'm not really happy here and I kinda want to go home. I'm not content here. It is not to do with anyone or any situation. I said I'd stay as long as I'm enjoying it, but I'm not enjoying it.'

She cries a bit. Darren talks maturely about how the group cannot really help because it is her own decision; it is obviously something that he, missing his kids, has wrestled with before. Craig lightens the mood by getting Anna a Snickers bar from the stash he has in his suitcase.

Caroline goes to the Diary Room to talk about Anna's bombshell. 'With me and Nicky it's easy to read emotions, but it's different with Anna... We need to get her to be honest about her feelings. She's been doing too much mothering of other people.'

Caroline says she's not dealing with being in the house too well herself. 'I had a bit of a chat with a counsellor again. It's quite traumatic being here and being tired all the time. We go through lots of emotions, more than you would normally have in a month. Yesterday I felt like running, I just wanted out. It was just a reaction. I've been under pressure because of the evictions. I feel better today, and if I can get Anna to open up she'll feel better too... She's so wonderfully balanced, she's the only balanced one in our room. She can comfort me when I need it so I hope I can do the same for her.'

Darren also shares his feelings about Anna with Big Brother. 'I'm sad, but it was not much of a shock. I saw it coming, but I've not had much chance to talk to her. I want to help her make the right decision for her peace of mind, but it's hard. I'm going through it. Mel's going through it. Anna won't let you in, she doesn't share her feelings.'

In bed, Caggie comforts Anna, who says she does not really want to be the first person to walk. Caroline says, 'You're rock solid. I love you to pieces. Don't go, little Irish lassie.' They both laugh and Anna changes 'lassie' to 'lezzie'.

The next morning Craig is up early and does T'ai Chi exercises in the garden with Nick. His confrontation with Caroline, in which she accused him of being lazy, seems to have had an ongoing effect on him. He's sleeping less, joining in more, and making a definite effort to contribute more to the housework, having voluntarily cleaned all the windows. Nick takes the opportunity to tell Craig that he thinks Anna will walk out 'within the next two or three days'. He says he told her there was no point staying if she is unhappy.

Anna herself does not agree with his suggestion that she will walk out. In the Diary Room, she tells Big Brother that, despite the doubts of yesterday, she has decided she will stay.

'I'm a lot better than I was yesterday. I've had a good chat with the group, which was lovely. I had a wee cry, which was embarrassing. I decided I'm not going to walk. I'll go when nominated. If I go now I won't really have shaken up my life. I don't want to chicken out.'

When asked what changed her mind, she jokes, 'Craig's bar of chocolate!' But she adds that Nicky and Mel have both told her to regard it as just another few weeks. 'They were so sweet, they were all giving me different pieces of advice. I kind of knew they'd do that though. They were so lovely. Darren talked to me, Mel gave me practical advice, Craig gave me chocolate... I'm going to try to appreciate more the things I am enjoying.'

She says that in future she will confide in the group more, and feels it would be possible to talk to Mel, Caroline, Nick and maybe Darren. 'I want to try to use my time more positively – but I'll probably get nominated and evicted on Friday. That would be ironic, wouldn't it?'

She says the group as a whole is calmer and more stable. People are being more honest, and 'we seem to be sitting round chatting as a group a bit more. A couple of weeks ago there were smaller groups, but as there are less of us we become as one.'

After talking to Big Brother, Anna has a session with a therapist. Afterwards, she tells the others how good it was to talk to him, and over the course of the rest of the day and evening, every one of the housemates spends time talking to him. Nick has a very long session.

It is three days since Andy left and Mel seems to have recovered from her initial depression. She tells Nick that her final chat with Andy consisted of 'hollow words' and that relationships in the house are 'very different to the outside'. She says she'll speak to Andy as they have friends in common but 'I couldn't guarantee we would have been as close if we were not in here'.

Craig's rapprochement with Caroline continues. She jokes about him being up so early and he tells her how at home he walks his dogs before work every day. The two have a quiet chat about the death of his father. Caroline asks to see a picture of his sister, and he shows her his sister and his mum. With his family obviously very much on his mind, Craig later reads a poem written by his sister Bev to the other lads:

'Big Brother, Big Brother,
What a lot of bother
Wants my little brother
Cameras, games, whatever else?
First things first, be yourself.
You play against the other nine
You're sure to have a whale of a time
Radio One with Mark and Lard
Wants people to phone, trying hard
To break the ten
To tell again
Live your life through the lens,
Everyone wants to be your friends
My little brother
Wants to win Big Brother
He'll be last in the house and king of the Kop
£70,000 he doesn't want to drop
All jokes aside I wish him luck
And hope he wins, doesn't get stuck
We've both had things taken away
Painful memories live with us each day
Win this Craig, make Dad proud
Show the world, shout very loud
All good things that will pour
Go knock 'em dead on Channel 4

To while away the time until the dreaded nominations, Darren initiates an impromptu music session, with an assortment of bins and bowls doubling as drums. Nicky is distracting herself by creating a huge papier-mâché hand on the wall of the living area. She uses discarded food packaging and flour and water paste. The others are concerned about the amount of flour she uses and talk about asking Big Brother for extra supplies to compensate. Darren suggests that when she has finished the hand she should do other body parts on other walls, including a *Big Brother* eye.

At four o'clock, they are summoned one by one to the Diary Room to make the dreaded nominations. They won't know the results until the next day. It's an unsettling process, and afterwards they are offered counselling. Most of them decide to accept. Nick has a particularly long session, well over an hour, and comes out telling Darren it was thought-provoking. His image outside the *Big Brother* house is worrying him and he tells Darren about his fears that the viewing public may not like what they have seen of him. Darren has no sympathy. He tells Nick that if he says two-faced things, he cannot expect them not to be broadcast.

WHO NOMINATES WHO

ANNA	Craig and Thomas
CAROLINE	Melanie and Thomas
CRAIG	Caroline and Nichola
DARREN	Craig and Thomas
MELANIE	Caroline and Nichola
NICHOLA	Melanie and Thomas
NICHOLAS	Caroline and Nichola
THOMAS	Caroline and Darren
REASONS:	
CAROLINE *on* **MELANIE**	'It will be increasingly difficult for her now that her lynchpin has gone.'
DARREN *on* **CRAIG**	'He's got a business to run and it would be nice for him to see how it is going.'
MELANIE *on* **NICHOLA**	'I've seen an unpleasant side to her, she was nasty to Craig, swearing.'

Tom's voyage of self-discovery is continuing, and Mel is fascinated by it. 'I've never been in an environment where people show their emotions,' he tells her in an early evening chat. When she says that is not normal, he says, 'It is where I come from. It's pretty stifling. As a person I'd like to better myself. I've allowed myself to give in to a routine where I don't really count and basically do things to please other people. I've been pleasing people all my life. I've never had the opportunity to go up to someone and say, "Just hold me."'

He tells her that he's never given himself fully in love, and that he realizes there are things he has let slip away, like travelling. As he and Mel get more and more intense, Nick strolls over. Just as he was always on hand to interrupt Andy's passionate moments with Mel, now he appears whenever she and Tom are getting close. He gives them his thought for the day: 'Life's a shit sandwich. The more bread you have the better it is.'

Over dinner, Darren tells his housemates how he delivered his son, when his girlfriend gave birth before they had time to get to the hospital, which is only fifteen minutes away. The baby was two weeks early, so his girlfriend ignored the first warning signs. Then she dropped to the floor and shouted, 'It's starting, it's starting!' Darren wanted to get her to hospital, but she couldn't get up. He called for an ambulance. She was screaming and the ambulance controller told Darren they wouldn't get there in time and he would have to deliver the baby himself. In his panic, Darren wanted to get the emergency services off the line so that he could ring his mum. But he managed to calm down and help with the birth, and by the time the midwife arrived, he was able to cut the umbilical cord. He tells the housemates that this was the proudest moment of his life.

Darren's story has everyone paying rapt attention, and for a time it diverts them from their worries. But Caroline is on edge. 'I wonder who's going to be on the list with me this week?' she asks. Then she says that if she is on the list, she wants to stage another play – only this time she'll kill them all for real.

As it is early in the week, they have plenty of alcohol and cigarettes, and they drink steadily all evening.

Nick is still worrying about life beyond the *Big Brother* walls. He corners Mel and Tom in the garden and tells them, in confidence, that his story about his wife dying in Australia is not true. He justifies it by saying a friend told him to tell an outrageous story. He is clearly very worried that it was broadcast. 'If it was, I'm doomed,' he says. Tom does not seem surprised that the story was untrue, but Mel's face registers complete shock. Then she puts an arm around him.

'I've been feeling bad about this for three weeks,' he says. 'It's not the people in here I am worried about, it's the people outside.'

At ten minutes past eleven at night, Nick goes into the Diary Room, and stays there for more than half an hour, unloading his worries about the lie he told about his dead wife.

'I was given a very bad bit of advice before the show started to tell a really wacky and untrue story. There was so much stress with the first week nominations, that when we told our stories of first love I told an untrue story. I've discussed it with two of the closest people to me here, and now I'm discussing it with you.

'I don't know if the story has gone out or not. I made a fundamental mistake and I regret it. It's like having a car balancing on the edge of a cliff, and you don't know whether it will edge back or be toppled over. You don't know if it has been picked up by the tabloids. If it has they will crucify me at the press conference. It will hurt my family and friends. If it was broadcast and the footage of me talking to the two others just now is also shown, then that nullifies the first, no problem. Otherwise, I will be going out into the world and people will get hurt. I just feel like walking out rather than facing a studio audience shown that scene. I would hate to have that shown with me sitting there. It would put my mind at ease if there was an undertaking not to show it in the studio when I leave.'

Big Brother tells him that it is not possible to give such undertakings.

'But I've come forward with a problem. If I'm going to have to worry now until I'm evicted that's an unfair burden to have to carry,' Nick says.

Big Brother encourages him to relax and not to think about it, and not to bottle up his feelings.

'One always hopes that when one leaves this place eventually... one would hate to be branded a scoundrel or a liar because of a statement made under a great deal of pressure. There are a lot of pressures here and it gets to you sometimes and we all have different safety valves and mechanisms.'

Nick goes on to say that he finds the whole *Big Brother* experience 'challenging mentally, physically and emotionally'.

'There are pitfalls with helping and counselling people on one hand, doing reiki and giving them a shoulder to cry on, whereas on the other hand you have to show them the red card... Everyone says I'm like a father figure, which is very complimentary. I probably come across as very good to the public. Then I thought this [the story] could be a thorn in my side, so it was better to confront it.'

He is very concerned about how the public see him, and tries several times to elicit feedback from Big Brother about the world outside. When Big Brother suggests he tells the rest of the group about his lie, he declines.

'Telling Mel and Tom and Big Brother is fine. But there are too many ulterior motives with the others, and it could be something for them to use to undermine me. I wouldn't trust anyone else. They've forgotten the story, so it's best to let sleeping dogs lie. It's the viewers and family who count – I'm in competition with these people in here, not allegiance.'

He says he was on the verge of walking out this afternoon. 'I made a mistake and sometimes it's very easy when under pressure to run away from a problem. I've been trying to decide since four o'clock whether to run, who to tell, then I decided to come in and say I made a mistake and hold my hand up... I'm a practical joker and I like telling people stories. But the hushed silence meant that I'd said something important. There's so much chaos in the house I forgot about it, then realized that something was niggling me.'

Just after midnight, a huge pillow fight erupts between the boys and the girls. The boys booby trap the house, with Marmite on the door handles and a trolley pushed against the girls' bedroom door. The girls plot their revenge – Caroline's suggestion is that they use their bras as catapults and fire tampons at the boys. In the end, they paint their faces with war paint, and rush out into the garden, pursued by the boys. The two sides bombard each other with eggs, straw and rice, and the boys eventually concede defeat after Craig has had his armpits liberally daubed with egg. It's a tension-releasing end to another of the house's difficult and emotional days.

The alcohol and the late-night exercise take their toll, and the whole household oversleeps, missing not just the one hour of hot water but also the hour that the Store Room is opened. Their supplies are kept in the Store Room and they have between 10 a.m. and 11 a.m. every morning to take out what they need for the day. Now they won't be able to take anything out, because by the time Nicky realizes, it's too late. She checks with Big Brother, because she has no way of telling the time. There are only two clocks allowed in the house, one on the cooker and the other an alarm clock, and, somehow, they have managed to reset both, so have no way of working out the real time.

It's a miserable day, with rain pouring down outside, and everyone is suffering from the exertions of the night before. With very little milk and not a lot of food, they're not feeling cheerful. By three o'clock, two of them have even less reason to feel cheerful, when the nominations are announced. It's Caroline and Tom. Predictably, Tom takes the news quietly and with little obvious emotion. Equally predictably, Caroline races around making a lot of noise and putting two fingers up energetically to the other contestants.

In the Diary Room, Tom talks about the effect of the nomination on him: 'It brings back a state of reality. The outside world is again going to have an influence on my life. It's always unreal when you are not making decisions about your own life, it's a bit like an extended holiday. I'd like to see it through to the end... but it's out of my control now. That's the exciting thing, that it's the viewers, the public, who choose.

'Being nominated is the first real excitement since I got here. I know I'm up against it with Caroline, because she's the queen of this now.'

Big Brother asks him how life in the house has changed him. 'The house is full of people who have sampled and tasted life outside Britain and their stories have made me realize I want to do these things also, and I believe I am more confident, and I have a will to experience these things, like the Far East, Australia.'

He says he is not bothered about being nominated. 'I'm very easy-going, it's not a problem. I don't dwell on setbacks, I get on with it.' He says that even if he gets evicted, the whole experience has enriched his life.

Outside, Caroline tells the others that she had been sure she would not be nominated this week. She'd had a really strong hunch that she'd be let off for a week, so the nomination has hit her hard. Tom tells her that his hands are shaking and she says it is because of the adrenalin rush.

During her turn in the Diary Room, she tells Big Brother that none of her housemates can give her an answer as to why she is being nominated week after week.

'I'm shocked rotten. This week I thought I would get a reprieve. I just thought I was getting on with everybody... I know you must be getting bored of me at home, but please, please let me stay... The second week I was upset and it made me quiet. I've given everybody space to be what they want, but after my upset with Craig I came back, I'm not going to let anybody get me down. I have changed myself. I am perceived in a certain way [but] I hope I'm a nice person anyway, and I'm hoping everyone out there will think the same and leave me in the house.'

In a later, brief visit to the Diary Room she requests a session with a therapist on Thursday. And she has a question for Big Brother. She intends wearing her stilettos when she leaves – will she have to crawl over the grating? Big Brother tells her that she has to cross some earth to get from the house to the path.

The housemates are not the only ones who are going short of food. The hens are now on a restricted diet, having been given far too much food at first. However, Darren's favourite, Marjorie, the plumpest of the six hens, has decided that short rations are not for her and she's eating more than her share of the feed. She viciously pecks any chicken who tries to stop her, and even takes on the cockerel.

To help while away a rainy afternoon, the boys enjoy a fantasy session about going out for the night. Darren says, 'The public who watch this show don't know that we are allowed out, so we don't talk about it much, but we are going to a wine bar tonight.' Craig chips in by saying they have a few 'Julies' lined up. Anna says she hopes they have a nice time, and Nick tells her to come along. They even discuss the location of the wine bar and how to get there. When Mel asks the name of the bar Craig says, 'I bet there will be 5,000 people there tonight waiting for us to show up.'

Craig, who rarely goes to the Diary Room unless summoned and then has to be probed by Big Brother rather than making the long, confessional speeches as some of the others do, now goes to see Big Brother. He gives his reactions to the nominations, saying that Tom is showing no unhappiness and seems to be excited. Caroline is not happy, but has taken it better this week. He says he's not pleased to see her or anyone go, but he would prefer it to be her than Tom.

Big Brother takes pity on the starving housemates and says that if they all perform good deeds for one another before 7 p.m., the Store Room will be opened for half an hour. Craig suggests the girls should clean the boys' bedroom, but Mel says she'd rather clean the chicken run. In the end, he settles for an all-over massage from all the girls, who take to it with a will. Caroline asks for a manicure and asks everyone in the house to paint one of her nails. Darren gives

Anna a shoulder massage. Big Brother asks Nick to go to the Diary Room because he seems very subdued. He says he is surprised and saddened by Tom's nomination, but Tom has been very relaxed about it.

Bored and confined indoors by the rain, they've been making music again with any bit of kitchen equipment that comes to hand. When Mel gets a bit carried away on the drums, Craig grabs her, upends her and spanks her bottom. Tom joins in.

Mel is suffering because of Tom's nomination. Having lost Andy, she now faces losing her new best friend and confidant, the quiet Irishman who has slowly begun to open up to her. As they dig up potatoes together, she tells him that it is strange that he has been nominated. They briefly discuss the possibility that the votes are rigged, to shock the housemates but also to keep the viewers interested. In the end, they decide this is not possible. Tom thinks he has rubbed some people up the wrong way – Caroline by something he said and some of the others possibly because he is Irish. Mel is not despondent. She's sure that this week Caroline is going to be evicted.

They complete their good deeds and rescue enough food from the Store Room for dinner – a curry. Afterwards, Big Brother sets them a discussion topic: which of their parents has had the most influence on their lives. Nichola is prompted to tell them a story of how her father helped her cope with an unpleasant trip she had after taking Ecstasy. She believed her body was being invaded by electricity from a pylon and she was melting. Her dad got out of bed, went downstairs and came back with the meter that reads the amount of electricity in a car battery. Fixing the bulldog clips to his daughter's fingers, he demonstrated to her that there was no electricity in her and told her to get back to bed.

Mel and Tom have plenty of excuses to spend time together, as they have been drawn as partners in the semaphore exercise. Anna watches them and mischievously suggests to the others that Mel's signal reads 'Fancy a fuck?'

The day ends quietly, with Nicky and Caroline talking about how lovely Nick is. They wonder why he is so nervous.

On Wednesday, Thomas and Nicholas are up early by the house standards – they are in the kitchen by 8.30 a.m. Tom sings about having done his time and going home, but says that he does not really want to go. The song is to cheer Caroline up.

Craig joins them, and the three of them sit outside in the sunshine debating who in the house they would have sex with. Craig ponders the question of having sex with Nicky for a moment, but then says no. 'She's got a nice body, but when she opens her gob... She's well-oiled, pissed a lot. I'd do Mel though. I'd do Mel right there in the grass.'

Nick says, 'She's the sweetest of the bunch.'

Craig asks Tom about her, 'You've got a little hot spot for her, haven't you?'

Tom rubs his head slowly and then says, 'I enjoy her company. She's vivacious. Lush. She's got a fiery personality which I find attractive.'

Craig then ungallantly describes Caroline as 'an old slapper'.

A few hours later, the girls and Darren are having a very similar conversation. Darren says he would choose Sada. 'The yoga was enough for me. She was my kind of woman.'

Caroline says she would have a threesome with Nicky and Anna, but if she had to choose a boy, it would be Darren. Anna agrees that if heterosexuality was the only option, she'd go for Darren. 'Because I know it would be a very special moment,' she says with a smile.

Anna's sense of humour is well to the fore today. Big Brother wants to know what has happened to several batteries from the radio microphones, which they are all supposed to hand in when they are issued with new ones twice a day. Nick is called to the Diary Room and genuinely replies that he does not know where the batteries are. When he returns to his card game, he tells the other players, Tom and Craig, and Tom volunteers the information that Mel has some batteries stashed away. Anna and Nicky find the batteries in Mel's locker. They are puzzled as to why she took them. They wonder if she likes to be seen as a naughty girl, or whether she's a kleptomaniac and a hoarder. After finding five batteries, Anna whispers into her microphone for Big Brother to send in the SAS. 'We're frightened,' she says and gestures to the camera with five fingers held up. Nicky suggests that perhaps she didn't get enough attention as a child, but Caggie dismisses this and says, 'I think it's because she's been the focus of attention. She's an only child.'

A need to stash things away has taken over the whole house this week, although Mel's batteries are the most bizarre treasure. As the group ordered their own personal luxuries, there has been much hiding and hoarding. Darren has accused Mel of hiding his socks and everyone else is jealously guarding their possessions. Nick has Andy's cigarettes hidden, Nicky has a bottle of Chianti that the others don't know about, Craig keeps his biscuits and chocolate locked in his suitcase. Anna is not hoarding, but as the weeks go on she shows signs of nicotine desperation – she collects everyone's cigarette butts from the ashtrays, to try to find enough tobacco for a smoke. Unfortunately for her, everyone is smoking every cigarette right down to the filter.

Nick has now turned his attention to Craig. In the washroom with Tom, he simply says, 'He's a treacherous one, Craig,' and then walks out.

The girls are discussing how they will 'capture a human' if they can and keep him hostage. They think they have a chance of capturing the man who repairs the leaking roof.

It is the day for the semaphore task and they fail it miserably. One from each pair is asked to transmit a message, which is their horoscope from that day's *Sun* newspaper. Nichola has to send Nick her Leo horoscope: Love and money are mixing together today which can mean sharing a cash prize with a partner or, if you are single, meeting someone wealthy. Melanie has to send Tom her Capricorn horoscope: As Venus settles into your home zone you can talk about moving in together, or work at home on that product that others will want to buy. Darren has to send Anna his Cancer horoscope: It's important to measure your words with the greatest care when a friend asks your opinion, so coat the truth with lots of fact. And Caroline has to send Craig her Aries horoscope: A healing moon makes it easy to let grievances go in the family. The dream-spinner planet promises some unusual love meetings tonight.

They have fifteen minutes to send the signals with their red and yellow flags, and the receiver has to write the message on a blackboard. Craig, who is dyslexic, has special permission to print out the alphabet at the top of his board. Unfortunately, Craig and Caroline don't finish in time, and two words are wrong. Nicky and Nick also stop short. They've lost their wager, and their shopping money is down to £47 for next week, less than £7 each.

Craig knew before they started that he might let them down, because of his problems with spelling. However, he's using his time in the house profitably. Both he and Nick brought Richard Branson's autobiography in with them, but it's Craig who is ploughing through it. Also dyslexic, Branson dropped out of school to start his own business. Craig is impressed.

'This Branson fella doesn't give a shit about nothing. He's got balls. He's just got a £30 million overdraft. Mine's just twenty-five grand. Thirty million. Can't imagine it, can you?'

They make a big effort in the afternoon to clean up the house, which needs it. Thomas tells Nick he is getting worried about the nomination, and Nick advises him to go to the Diary Room and give a speech designed to sway the voting public. He even offers to coach Tom. 'Say "I was really disappointed to be voted out, I have a lot of things I want to achieve." The public will say "this guy wants to stay",' says Nick.

Tom thanks him for his advice, which is to work out what he wants to say before he goes in to see Big Brother. Soon afterwards, Tom goes to the Diary Room.

'My attitude yesterday was my normal response of so what, I don't care. But, thinking about it, I need to stand up for myself, to make changes in my life. My emotions today are that I would be gutted to walk out of here on Friday night. It would be a setback at the stage I've reached in my life at the age of thirty-one, and not having made a proper decision about my life.'

He says he thinks he is already a better person for the *Big Brother* experience, talking about his emotions more, and he doesn't want to leave until he has completed the transformation.

Craig also has a session in the Diary Room, one of his usual short sessions. But he is a little more forthcoming about himself. 'The hardest thing for me in the house, maybe a lack of freedom to watch a bit of telly and walk my dogs. TV stops you thinking about your own life, it's a distraction and it stops me going down.' He says he feels guilty because he doesn't spend much time with his family, so he doesn't miss them that much. But he loves them to bits and he knows they will be there for him when he comes out. He misses his friends, a couple of glasses of wine and his dogs, who help him relax.

Yesterday, Mel flirted with Craig and Tom, and today it is Darren and Tom. They are playing ball games in the garden and she ends up rolling around on the floor with them both.

Darren then makes the whole household some biscuits, using oats and eggs and golden syrup. While he takes them out of the oven, Nick cheats with the pack of cards.

In the evening, they are talking about making love in unusual places. Craig says he was caught having sex on a speedboat.

'The engine cut out and we drifted back to shore. I couldn't get my pants on because I had a hard on.' He also admits having done it on hotel stairways. Mel pretends to be shocked, but then admits she has had sex in a park and in a toilet in a club.

The subject of George Michael comes up. Nick is scathing about him being arrested in a public lavatory, saying that if he was going to have sex in a public place it would be on a beach. He then causes uproar by suggesting that George Michael might proposition a kid who came into the toilet. Anna, Mel and Caroline go nuts, pointing out to him vociferously and indignantly that being gay is not the same thing as being a paedophile.

Darren enjoys chatting with the girls, but they give him a hard time because he has objected to one of them leaving a box of tampons in the toilet. 'Why do women have to show me what they are doing in there?' he says, in mock disgust. Everyone, even the other boys, thinks he is being unduly sensitive. Later in the evening, he wraps the offending box in toilet paper, which makes Caroline, who finds it, laugh. Darren suggests Nicky could make a papier-mâché cover for it.

Having talked for ages about glossy mags and other girlie subjects, Darren suddenly starts to cry. The others are astonished – until he laughs and tells them that he discovered when he was thirteen that he can turn tears on to order, just by yawning.

The day ends with Anna entertaining the others with her recollections of a television programme about a man who stretched his willy every day to make it bigger.

In the early hours of the morning, with the house quiet and everyone asleep, Caroline sneaks out of the bedroom and into the living room for a good cry. She goes into the Diary Room to tell her troubles to Big Brother.

'I can't sleep. I need a pen and paper. I have too many thoughts in my head. Someone made a comment yesterday which I just can't get out of my head, they said, "Who will knock the queen bee off?" I didn't ask to be in this position... I was so convinced last week that I wouldn't be on the list this week... I am enjoying myself, but it is all so temporary. I have two days and then I hear my name again, then the whole cycle begins. I want to be here to the end but there is no peace. Just to be happy all week would be great... You don't know why the public voted me in. It could be because they hated the other person.'

'I had a conversation with Tom for the first time. He was open – that was nice. That comment, about being the queen bee, really bothered me. I don't want people thinking that it will be an extra bonus if they stay. I hate it that they think there will be some glory winning over me, like it would be an honour. It's sick.'

She asks for painkillers and goes back to the Diary Room a few minutes later to collect them.

During the course of the next day, Nick tells both the nominees individually that he has had a positive dream about them and he believes they will survive on Friday night. His first encounter is with Tom over their regular porridge breakfast. He tells him, 'I think you are going to survive after my ingenious coaching.'

Mel makes a mid-morning call on Big Brother. Her main reason is her disappointment that Tom is on the list and the fear that she will lose another of her friends on Friday. But she also wants to sound off about the semaphore task, which she believes they failed because Nicky and Caroline were up until 6 a.m. the night before and that's why they've got no money for food. She thinks Anna will leave and she's feeling guilty about judging her harshly a week ago. She can see similarities between herself and Anna, in that neither of them will really confide in anyone. She says everyone really likes Anna and would miss her a lot if she left.

She describes Darren as 'sweet, loving, compassionate but he is concerned about himself. It bothers me a bit.'

She talks about Nicholas and his confession to telling an untrue story. 'He's very paranoid, very strange. His wife story was a lie. I was startled; shocked that someone would do that. I told him to talk to Big Brother. His story is an example of how manipulative someone could be. It makes me not trust him. If that is something he can do, what else can he do? I'm worried that you won't be able to see how he wins people over. It's not my place to say "Nick you're very manipulative, you're trying to win people over." I question if he is genuine. I would never sell myself out to stay in the house. Someone who cannot be themselves in order to stay here, I don't like.'

She says she won't talk to Nick because there is no value in it. Caroline stays in bed until after lunchtime, having had no sleep last night. The boys discuss the fact that the girls have PMT. Nick describes talking to them being 'like setting a match in a petrol factory'.

When she does get up, Caroline goes with Darren to collect the eggs and they decide they would like to try to hatch one. They don't know how to go about it, but Mel says that four days in a warm oven should do it. Darren asks Big Brother if they can do it, because he wants to make sure they are not upsetting any animal rights' campaigners. In the end, they don't go through with the plan.

At their weekly house meeting, they decide that as Big Brother has not set them another mini-task, they'll set one for themselves. The first suggestion is that they kidnap a cameraman, but in the end they opt for playing rounders with a frying pan and a cushion. With Caroline breaking her fingernails and the rest being pretty inept at cushion batting, they soon give up and have a sing-song about Caroline:

> *'I get nominated every week, Can't see how they've got the cheek*
> *(Darren sings, 'It wasn't me'), When they come round again, try these names,*
> *I'll prepare a list for you, This is what you've got to do, Anna Craig Nichola*
> *or Darren Melanie Thomas or Nick, But don't call her name.'*

Mel continues her probing of Tom, as they tend the vegetables together. She asks him if he just accepts everything in life. He tells her that he tries his best in his work and in his friendships, but he doesn't pay too much attention to personal things. Mel suggests he starts now.

When Nick gives Caroline a reiki session he tells her a straightforward lie. He claims he nominated two boys this week, when in fact he nominated her. He tells her he can see her surviving on Friday night.

'I'm a traitor to the male camp, but I'd rather be with fun people when we are down to five,' he says.

The big drama of the day interrupts their session when a security alert has Big Brother ordering them all into the girls' bedroom. There have been allegations in the *Sun* that Nick has smuggled a mobile phone in and is in contact with a mate outside. According to the newspaper, he has a tiny Motorola mobile which he leaves switched off, but switches it on for a 4 a.m. chat with a friend who keeps him up-to-date with public reaction to the show. A security expert and two members of the production staff carry out a search but find nothing.

Ironically, Nick, who knows nothing about the reason for the security alert, pretends to housemates Tom and Mel that he has a phone. Using his radio microphone as a fake handset, he pretends to dial up a pizza delivery service and places a huge order. Tom and Mel join in, adding their favourite toppings to the list. Nick even gives the imaginary pizza company directions for getting to the house, although Mel points out that they'll have a few problems getting in. Continuing the fantasy, Nick then pretends to order three videos, telling the non-existent person on the line to debit his account. 'My password is "Kill the pigs",' he says.

Over the course of the day, both Anna and Craig, two of the quieter members of the group, have opened up a bit. Anna discusses with Craig his attitude to work, which is very different from hers – she admits she just likes to plod along and get by. She tells him how she would like to be more involved with the music industry.

She's the most musical member of the house and she has been teaching Darren to play the guitar, showing him a new chord each day. Craig decides to join her master class and also tackle one chord each day.

Like Tom, Craig finds that his much-travelled companions have given him itchy feet. Although he has travelled around Europe, usually he only takes short breaks because of his business. But the *Big Brother* experience is making him feel that he could afford to take six months off and travel around other parts of the globe. He talks to Nick about his experiences in Australia.

It's Nichola's birthday in two days time and the housemates are told they can have a party, but they have to decide on a theme. They decide on a masquerade and Nicky wants it to have an orange theme because that is her favourite colour. She goes with Caroline, Anna and Craig into the Diary Room to request materials. They want orange netting and fabric; cardboard to make masks; sticks for masks; elastic; orange wigs; orange dye for T-shirts; sarongs and tutus; Terry's chocolate oranges; carrots; oranges; salmon; melon; cheese biscuits; sun-dried tomato bread; and (because they are vaguely orange in colour) tobacco and lager.

They say that bored men will bet on anything, and Craig and Nick start bickering about how many nights the *Big Brother* winner will actually have slept in the house. Craig says it is sixty-three nights, Nick is adamant that it is sixty-two. They decide on a wager, with £100 at stake. Darren checks the house rules and it's Craig who is right. He says he will let Nick off, but the others all demand that Nick spends the £100 taking them all out for a good time.

But where will they go? The lads invent another fantasy night out, discussing lots of different clubs and bars that they would like to visit. Nick announces that he is going to take Tom around the London night scene. 'I'm going to take Tom to a "dog shit bar". It's a bar where older women drink. It's called dog shit because the older it is, the easier it is to pick up.'

He tells the others how he scores women out of ten. A 'shenanger' is a stunner, worth seven or more. A 'shahala' is OK and gets between five and seven. A 'woohara' is five and under. But there is an even lower category, which he calls 'wolf trap'. The name comes from a morning-after feeling which Nick describes as waking up next to a female so undesirable that a man would chew his own arm off rather than wake her up. Tom says he has never been to bed with an ugly woman. 'But I've woken up with a few.' They decide there is only one shenanger in the house and the rest are wooharas.

While the boys are sharing lads' talk over another of their unending games of cards, the girls are bitching in the bedroom about their obsession with cards. They plan to hide the pack, or, even more exciting, use them for one of Nicky's papier-mâché creations. They decide to use them to spell the word Cheat – the boys' favourite game – on one of the living-room walls. Despite their threats, they don't do anything.

Most of the housemates stay up talking until 7 a.m. and it's on nights like these that Craig's storytelling skills come into their own. He tells the tale of a dark and stormy night when he and a mate were driving home in his van. The rain was coming down sideways and the wind was howling. They passed a forlorn figure at the side of the road with his thumb stuck out, hitching a lift. Although he would not normally pick up hitchhikers, Craig stopped for him. The man had a large, heavy bag with him, and it took Craig and his mate to haul it into the back of the van. Intrigued, they asked the man what was in it. He refused to tell them, which only made them more curious. Eventually, the stranger got angry at their questions and said, 'Mind your own fucking business.' At which point Craig and his mate decided they'd had enough, and turned him out of the van.

'We left him at the side of the road and drove off with his bag,' he says.

'What was in the bag?' the others ask.

'Mind your own fucking business,' says Craig.

In the long hours of the night, Tom opens up, chatting first to Caroline and then to Darren. He tells Caroline that after a lot of thought he has finally made a decision about the farm. He does not want to be a farmer.

'Being here has helped me think. I shouldn't be doing what other people want me to do.' Caroline says she doesn't know him well, but she gets the impression that he does not want the farm, but that he's under pressure because he is the only son.

'I'd like to keep it in the family. I never really faced up to it but being here has given me time to see different views. I will take the farm on, but I will pay for others to look after it.'

Caroline asks how his parents will feel, and he says they will not be happy. He thinks it will break his dad's heart.

'He's always wanted me to do what he's wanted me to do. But I want to make something of myself.'

As the sun rises across the *Big Brother* garden, Tom is out on the patio with Darren. He admits he is not confident about the results of the voting. He is not as nonchalant as he has appeared over the past few days.

'People said I didn't seem bothered. I've been thinking about it now. I think I was wrong, saying I didn't care. Obviously, I care.'

He says he hopes the voting public is more sophisticated than to go for Caroline. 'I think they'll go for my charm,' he says, with a smile.

Just before they finally turn in to sleep, Darren grabs hold of Mel and pulls her under the duvet on his double bed. They wrestle together for a few minutes, before Mel threatens to scream. Darren lets her go and grins, 'I needed that.' Nick got a kiss, too, from Caroline, who firmly believes he did not nominate her.

Lack of sleep means tempers are frayed the next morning and the house witnesses its second major row. This time it is Darren and Nichola. Nicky is one of the first up and at quarter to twelve she is shaving Tom's head again. He says that if he gets evicted he's going to leave the house the way he has lived in it, without hair.

An hour later, with some of the others, including Darren, still asleep, Nicky launches into a loud rendition of 'Nothing Compares to You', a serenade for her best chum Caggie. Darren, who is never at his best when he first wakes, tells her unequivocally to keep the noise down. Nicky, who is under the stress of facing Caroline's possible eviction, and has the most volatile temper in the house at the best of times, gives him a mouthful in reply. She sounds off at him, and finishes with, 'Come and sit on my face.' This is an insult too far for Darren, and he unloads on her, accusing her of letting the whole side down in the semaphore task because she was too tired to keep up. Caroline weighs in to defend her friend, but Darren stalks away in disgust and anger. He tells Nicholas and Craig, 'She told me to sit on her face. I'm not one of her Bolton friends.' Upset, Nichola goes to see Big Brother.

'I'm pissed off, fuming, really bloody annoyed. That pillock Darren came out there, I was singing and he told me to be quiet. He's got a booming voice, it carries throughout the house. I told him he had no right to say that to me, it's not my problem if he went to bed at 7 a.m. ... His me, me, me attitude pisses me off. I love the guy, he's a great laugh, but his attitude pisses me off. I got up, made scones, cleaned the house and now I'm getting abuse from the pillock... He needs to apologize to me, but I doubt I'll get one because he's so full of himself. I'm sick of being in this house with people who don't understand who I am. I'm prepared to apologize to him if he does to me. Some of the people don't get my sense of humour. I've said "sit on my face" before and he's laughed along with me. To take it seriously he is being a pillock.' She cries quietly as she talks.

'I'm not showing that I'm upset. I don't want to give him the satisfaction... I always get upset when people have a go. I don't like having cross words. It's fucking pathetic, but if it's not resolved it does upset me. I try to be hard but I'm not really.'

When she leaves the Diary Room, she goes to wash her face and tries to disguise her red eyes. Nick, with his instinct for being where the trouble is, walks in and compliments her on the 'yummy' scones.

Two minutes later, Nichola goes to the boys' room and apologizes to Darren for what she says was a trivial remark. He isn't taking her apology. 'That's cool. I saw the respect you gave me outside and I'm not going to forget it. Let's end it there.'

Back with her friend Caroline, Nicky says she has now taken Darren off the pedestal she had him on. 'He's getting fuck all from me now.'

But the row eats into her soul and, as the day wears on, she becomes more miserable. When one of the lads asks Anna to go out into the garden, Nichola misreads the situation and thinks that Anna has been invited to share a cigarette and that she is excluded. Never one to bottle her feelings, she erupts, shouting out, 'I hate it in here. I'm not staying here with those c...s. You selfish c...s!' Then she turns to Caroline and says, 'If you go, I'm going tomorrow. I don't give a fuck any more. There is no point in staying here. I hardly get on with any of them. I don't want to try any more. Everyone has their little cliques and I can't be arsed.'

Anna is desperate to put the situation right by telling Nicky why she was invited outside. It was to sign Nicky's birthday card. But the card is a secret, so she says nothing. Caroline sums up the situation: 'I know it is because you like him [Darren] that you are feeling so upset. You've got to remember why you are here.'

Caroline seeks out Darren and pleads with him to make it up with Nicky, but he says he won't. 'I'm doing her a birthday card and I can hear her screaming that I'm a wanker,' he says. Caroline tells him he's wrong – Nicky is calling them all wankers.

Because they all got up late, the evening comes quickly and it's time for them to hear who is going to be evicted.

It's Caggy. After three weeks of being nominated, she finally hears Davina announce her name. One and a half million people have voted, another record rise, and 62 per cent of them have opted for Caroline to go. In the two hours before she leaves the house, she makes another plea to Darren to make friends with Nicky and he agrees.

Wearing a blue spangly suit, the stilettos and the trademark pink lips, she walks to the studio, to cheers from the crowd, for an ecstatic reunion with her family. Back in the house, her old enemy Craig says that her eviction has restored his faith in human nature. "She was just a tit,' he says.

WEEK FOUR FACT FILE

MAIN TASK PASS ■ FAIL ☒	Semaphore signalling.
MINI-TASK	Performing good deeds for each other. They are rewarded by the Store Room being re-opened.
BOOKIES' FAVOURITE TO WIN	Anna, with odds of 7/4. In second place is Tom, at 2/1.
TO WALK	Nichola is favourite at 1/3 odds on.

WHAT THE EXPERTS SAY

WHY DID MEL HOARD THE BATTERIES?

'Hoarding is often resorted to at times of anxiety and a feeling that one's territory is being violated. This is a way of re-asserting her own power and trying to cope with the fact that nothing is her own. As an only child, she may not be used to sharing. Mel's past behaviour supports this. She has been very possessive over food, labelling her cheese with notes such as "Mel's. Hands off".

Linda Papadopoulos, Counselling Psychologist

'Some of the housemates have started to hoard things like chocolate and cigarettes which they can exchange for other things. Another kind of hoarding is going on, as shown by Mel, who has been found to be hoarding batteries. It is reminiscent of what prisoners do. They are often found to hoard useless items. It's a way of exercising free will and breaking free of the rules provided for them by the prison.'

Geoffrey Beattie, Professor of Psychology, Manchester University

CAROLINE LOOKS BACK

Like Andrew before her, Caroline is gobsmacked when presented with the video evidence of Nick's treachery. 'That guy followed me everywhere, this is a real shocker,' she says. 'And he wants me to live in his house? He was obviously just working us. These lot [she gestures to the studio full of her friends and family] are always saying how naive I am. How naive can a girl be?'

The highlight of the live show is a letter from George Michael, who saw himself valiantly defended by the rest of the household against Nick: 'Hi guys. I just wanted to tell you I saw the Thursday show. It was great to see a diverse bunch of people making it clear they know the difference between a gay person and a paedophile. So to say thank you for your kind words, please let me buy you all a drink when they let you out on parole – but preferably on a night when Nick's not available.'

With champagne and chocolate – her favourites – delivered to her by Andrew and Sada, Caroline ends the night on a triumphal high.

For Caroline, like the other evictees, leaving behind the cocoon of the *Big Brother* house means finding out what the world has been saying about them. And the world – or, at least, the whole of Britain – can't stop talking about them. The massive press coverage is, like the numbers voting, growing all the time. Anything to do with any of the housemates is hot news.

The *Sun* has printed raunchy pictures of Caroline dancing on stage. Both Craig and Andy have been the subject of kiss-'n'-tell stories by ex-girlfriends in the past week, Craig for the second time. The Nasty Nick campaigns continue, but there's a backlash with stories from neighbours and friends about how nice he really is, underneath it all, and there's a growing swell of e-mails arriving at the *Big Brother* website in support of him.

Even the serious broadsheet newspapers have come round from their original sneering condemnation of voyeuristic television. They analyse and speculate about the fascination of the show, but they all concede that it is compulsive viewing.

'We can't help ourselves. Night after night, in our millions, we tune in to watch a group of peculiarly egotistical people behaving in an unlovely way...' says the *Daily Telegraph*.

'Just this once, believe the hype. *Big Brother* was billed as the summer's monster hit, and it is,' says the *Guardian*. It describes the programme as what American television executives call 'water cooler television' – in other words, in offices across the land, staff gossip about it at the water coolers (or in Britain, round the tea trolley).

The Times describes Nick as the undisputed star of the show 'stirring up in less than a month the depth of public loathing that took Jeremy Beadle and Chris Evans years to achieve'.

The *Observer* covers two pages paralleling what happens in the show with what happens in every office in the land.

On trains, buses and in shops across the land, people are talking about it. The disco crowds in Ibiza are getting a nightly update on what's happening from DJ Pete Tong, who turns the music down to give them a summary of the goings on in the house, to cheers and stamping. Academics at Birmingham University announce that they will be running a course on *Big Brother* as part of a BSc degree, because the show is ideal for psychology students studying human behaviour.

Over in Tom's hometown in Ireland, his friends even organized a concert to show their solidarity with the nominee. Top-rated Irish folk bands gave their services free to express support for the boy from Greencastle.

Even the Labour Party gets in on the *Big Brother* act, by setting up a website aimed at finding the country's least favourite Tory politicians. Ten people, 'forced to share a political house', were put up for public voting. 'Secret rivalries, cynicism and intolerance are breeding an air of mistrust among the group. The language used is becoming more extreme and they are increasingly out of touch with reality,' says the website.

Caroline knows nothing about *Big Brother* mania when she first comes out, but when she faces the press the next morning she hears that more than four and half million viewers watched her walk out of the house. That was a 38 per cent share of all viewers and the highest rating programme in that slot.

Having had less than an hour's sleep, she is remarkably lively and composed, and after facing a barrage of questions from journalists which centre around Nick, she settles down to talk about life in the house.

'I wondered how long my luck would last and it was third time unlucky,' she says. 'I didn't dare to think I was surviving because the public loved me – that would have been too vain. So I always thought it might be because they hated other people more than me.

'The first time I was nominated, I thought everyone in the house hated me. You don't realize that it only takes three or four nominations to get you on the list. You assume it's all of them. So I hated them all and felt physically sick.

'It got easier in the next two weeks, but it never got easy. If I'd gone out in the first round I would not have been able to say anything positive about the experience. I thought it was all horrible and cruel. But the longer I stayed in the house, the more I enjoyed it.

'The first week was so hard because I am so used to living on my own. You don't sleep well, even when you get to sleep. You feel constantly wired, probably because there is so much electrical equipment around.'

She says the thing she will remember most is the laughter. 'We had some really, really, good laughs, and considering we had hardly any alcohol, I learnt that even sober you can have great fun. In six months' time, when I look back, it's the laughter I will think about. We called it the Betty Ford Clinic because we were all off alcohol and everything else.'

She is particularly close to Nicky and is convinced they will remain friends for the rest of their lives.

'We're so different – me with all my hair and her with her shaved head; me wearing my knickers in the shower and her wandering around the kitchen area wearing a T-shirt and no knickers. But she's not an exhibitionist, she's just totally natural.'

The downside to her relationship with Nicky is that they are both volatile 'and could work each other up into a nightmarish state. I'd be all right, then she'd get in a state, then I'd be in a state, and left to ourselves we'd have thumped some people. And that's when Anna was our saviour. She'd say, "Let's just think about it this way." And we'd calm down and have a laugh. She started calling us "The Loopy Twins". She was the real calming influence in the house, and she's clever, too.'

Although she only spent two weeks with Sada and they come from such different backgrounds, Caroline feels she's made a true friend there, too.

'She's a lovely person, and she's had such an interesting life. I felt inspired by her. She has such a searching spirituality. I envied the things she's done. I've only been out of Birmingham on holidays and I've never travelled on my own, I'd be too scared.'

Caroline also hopes she'll stay in touch with Darren.

'I nominated Darren in the first week, but that was before I knew him well. He is bone idle. I called him the armchair director because he sat in a chair ordering the rest of us about. I thought he must have had a load of handmaidens at home, attending to every wish. And he was a real hypochondriac. When I nominated him, I said, "he needs too much attention", which he did.

'But before long I found that he's got a wicked sense of humour, and he tuned into my humour, and we had some great laughs. He's a wonderful cook, and when he's up, he's brilliant.

'But as for the rest, I couldn't care less if I never see them again in my life. Before I came out, I would have included Nick as a friend. He was so sweet, so caring – so cunning. I think he's out-and-out evil. To think I shared my last packet of cigarettes with him, and then when Andy left he let us go without cigarettes for days, sneaking off to have them himself.

'In the first week I thought he was peevish, but then I thought it was just his nerves. Then when I heard how his wife died, I felt really sorry for him and thought he had been so hurt by his experiences I could forgive him anything. To find out that was all a lie was a great, great shock. He staged telling it so well. He refused to go first and, in the end, he went last. There was a huge silence after he spoke and everyone felt so upset. What a dreadful lie to have told.

'They were an unappealing bunch of men. The women were much more interesting, even Mel. The guys had nothing going for them, they'd have been happy playing their stupid card games twenty-four hours a day.'

Caroline and Mel did not get on.

'She followed me around at first telling me I was glamorous and saying how wonderful my colour co-ordinated underwear is. I thought straightaway it was a bit over the top. Sada thought I might be jealous of her, but the boot was on the other foot, she was jealous of me.

'She didn't want anything to do with the women. We didn't expel her from the women's group, she just kept away from us. If we asked her to exercise, she didn't want to. If the boys got up to exercise five minutes later, she was there.

'I actually felt sorry for her with Andy at the beginning. I thought he was using her, and I took her on one side and warned her that he was a gamester. I didn't want her to get hurt. But later I realized it was only a game to her, too. It was so funny when she went after Tom before Andy was even out of the house. And when Tom came up for eviction, she started flirting with Craig. But she finds Craig repulsive – you should have seen her face on the day we all did good deeds and he asked for a massage. She could barely bring herself to touch him.

'She said everything was "divine" or "hilarious". If she'd said those words much more I'd have had to punch her. And she talked about how her pierced clitoris made her permanently aroused – well, if that's her idea of arousal and her idea of hilarity, she's sad.

'And why did she stash those batteries? We never sorted that one out. Anna said she could cope with my madness and Nick's madness, because it was obvious. But this was something else, bizarre.

'It may just have been another reason for her to go to the Diary Room. I hated going into that box, but Mel loved it, she was always in there. I think she wanted attention from Big Brother like she wanted attention from the men.'

Caroline's biggest row in the house was with Craig, but she says that in the end 'I found a place in my heart for him, although I can't say I like him.

'I hope when he comes out of the house something clicks when he watches the programmes and he realizes he owes me an apology. I did something for him when I sounded off at him. The rest were cowards, they didn't back me, although they'd all be complaining about Craig. But after I'd laid into him he was awake more and he read a book. He thinks he's going to be the next Richard Branson.'

She took a dislike to Andrew before they had even crossed the bridge and walked into the house.

'From the moment I clapped eyes on him, I knew we wouldn't get on. We'd been smiling for cameras all morning, and there were lots of press photographers there to see us walk in, and we were all trying to look cheerful. Later on, we all confessed how at that stage we felt like crying, leaving all our friends and family behind. But Andy was saying "It's great, isn't it?" And we weren't even inside.

'Andy wanted the money, he wanted romance, he wanted to become a gay icon, he wanted everything.'

Tom she describes as 'dull and cold'.

'I shaved his head, plucked his eyebrows, made him attractive – and he turned into a monster. He fell in love with himself. It was thanks to him that we had to split the luxury money – we'd have carried on sharing if he hadn't made a fuss about giving up smoking and not wanting to pay for other people's tobacco. Not that he did give up.

'When he came up for nomination this week he tried to turn himself into the new Tom, Mr Gregarious. It would last ten minutes, then he'd slip back into the old Tom, until he remembered to try again.'

She describes life in the house as 'a real encounter with myself'. She says, 'I've had to act and behave in ways that I never expected other people to see. When I'm at home, if I'm upset, I hibernate. I take the phone off the hook and I don't see people until I feel better. I do my crying alone. If I hear myself bitching, I take myself away until I am a better person, and don't affect others with my bad mood.

'But there I had to let the whole world in on my mood swings. I'm not a pretty sight when I cry, but you all know that by now. And I had to cry in front of people I believed had betrayed me. I felt I was letting myself down. But now I believe that being true to my feelings was right – some of the others were play-acting, but I was just being me.

'The girls thought I was strong, and Nicky told me that because I was the first to cry I made it all right for everyone else to show when they were down and shed a few tears.'

She will never regret her *Big Brother* experience.

'My life was stagnating and that's what I fear more than anything else. I wanted to shake things up, make things happen. There was nothing about my life that I missed while I was in there, apart from my family. I love my flat, but it's only a place to live and I'm going to sell it now and move to London.'

With a demo tape for one of her songs already released, she's hoping that a singing and recording career will now take off.

'I need to re-work my song, "Prince Charming", and hopefully get it mixed properly and released. The words say, "Like Cinderella, my life is going to change for the better". And I really think it is after *Big Brother*. I want to be famous. I'm up for it.

'The great buzz coming out of the house is that people recognize me in the street and it's wonderful. I love it.'

PLACE YOUR BETS ON CAROLINE'S FUTURE

5/1	She'll star in a lipliner ad.
6/1	She'll have a number one hit record.
66/1	She'll marry Craig.

*'I didn't murder anyone. I didn't commit a crime.
I just broke the rules of a game show.'*

NICHOLAS

11 TO 18 AUGUST

Immediately, the house seems quieter after Caroline's departure. As Friday night slips past midnight into Saturday, Tom
goes to the Diary Room and talks to Big Brother about the relief of surviving
the nominations.

'I spent all day preparing myself to leave for the real world, and I'm disappointed not to be going. Now I have to tune myself back into being here.
Friends and family are very much on my mind tonight. It was nice to see my
mum, sister and friends. It's an emotional thing, being so close to them and yet
so far, and I know it will play on my mind. It was good to know that they will
be there for me. It is disappointment mixed with jubilation that I can carry on.
I'm on an emotional high.

'The hardest thing is gearing up for leaving, not knowing what people think of
us. You have to gear yourself up to leave, and then you have to re-adjust to staying...
It got easier tonight for the rest of us to see someone leave, we're getting into the
groove. Nichola will find it hard, so we'll try to take her mind off it. She has been
somewhat distant, but will now have to get back into the main group, and that will
be good for everyone in the house. She has enough common sense to get back in.'

The rest of them start taking Nichola's mind off her mate's departure even
while Tom is in the Diary Room. As they realize it is technically Saturday, they
burst into a rousing chorus of 'Happy Birthday' for her. Shortly afterwards,
Nichola herself goes to the Diary Room and repeats what Tom has just said,
about how she will now find herself joining the main group again.

'Caz and I had a strong bond so we were segregated, so now I will mix
more.' But it is Darren who is most on her mind.

'My apology was crap... I messed up badly, and I've seen a side to me that
is embarrassing... It was a bad day. I was panicking about losing Caz. There's a
destructive side to me, I can't control my temper.'

Mel follows the boys into their room at quarter to one, and joins Tom, Craig
and Nicholas on Darren's double bed. As she leaves, they decide to play a practical joke on Darren, and remove the wooden slats under his mattress. He notices
straightaway, before he gets into bed, so the joke falls a bit flat. But when Craig
leaves the room, they do the same to his bed.

Nick takes his late-night turn in the Diary Room.

'Thought for the day: I was quite pleased that Thomas stayed in the house
this week... It was good that I sat down with him and gave him some advice, told
him to talk to Big Brother to drum up support. It is quite nice to give someone
some good advice, see it acted on and that advice working.'

After talking about Caroline and Nichola, he tells Big Brother how he sees
the future of the house unfolding.

'I think the next person to go will be a girl, then a boy then a girl and then
there will be four: three boys and one girl. It could go awry. People are not overtly

plotting against each other. There's still a long time left – the days will go on longer as more people are evicted.'

Then he retires to sit outside in the garden and watch the dawn come up with Tom.

Anna gets up first on Saturday morning and spots a radical change that has happened to the garden overnight. An assault course has been delivered. She wakes the rest of the household, and they read their weekly task, which is to erect and arrange the assault course according to instructions, and then practise on it. Twenty-four hours before they are due to be tested, Big Brother will give them the time limit in which they have to get round it as a relay team.

They have to work out how much to wager on it and decide to go for the full 50 per cent, despite some misgivings from the girls about being able to swing across the monkey bars.

It's a very hot day, over 80 degrees in the *Big Brother* garden and as they clean out the chicken coop together, Mel complains to Tom that it is unfair that men can take their tops off and women can't. Tom tells her that she doesn't normally stick with tradition and she replies that some prudes among the viewers might find it offensive if she removed her bikini top. When Tom suggests that having her tongue pierced is offensive, she says she doesn't walk around with her tongue out. Because of the way he asked the question, she senses disapproval, and asks him if he has done something to upset him. 'You've got a strange tone with me,' she says.

They carry on talking in the kitchen, while everyone else is in the garden making masks for the orange party. Nichola is delighted with all the goodies that have been delivered and has already tie-dyed lots of white T-shirts. Mel and Tom are now discussing Nick, and Mel tells Tom: 'He was saying yesterday you've got to be one step ahead. He's got this overwhelming paranoia. I think it's weird... He says you've got to plan who to nominate.'

Tom says, 'He's going to do whatever is necessary to keep himself here.'

Mel agrees, but says it will backfire in the end. Tom tells her that for two weeks in a row someone has tried to influence his decision of who to nominate. 'But I won't vote tactically to save myself.'

Perhaps Nick senses that they are talking about him, because he strolls across to join them. When he asks Mel what is wrong she says, 'I don't feel like being here today.'

She cheers up when Nichola gets her to model a floating net orange skirt... Then a birthday cake made by Nichola's mum is delivered, and with it a card from Big Brother which offers Nicky a choice from a list of presents, including a space hopper, an instamatic camera and some celebrity wigs. But it has to be the unicycle for Nicky, whose ambition is to join a circus. She tells the gang that when they are all dressed in their orange gear they will go to the Diary Room to thank her mum, and, in the meantime, she is going to make a card for Big Brother.

(Nichola does not know, but another birthday cake, in the shape of a leopard-print bra and knickers, is delivered by the *People* newspaper for her – but is turned away by security at the *Big Brother* site. The feature writers at the newspaper enjoy eating it when it is delivered back to them!)

They have assembled the assault course, under the direction of Craig who goes to the gym several times a week when he is at home. There are tyres, monkey bars, a camouflage net and a seesaw. The monkey bars are being used to dry sheets. After four weeks, one or two of the housemates have finally decided to wash their bed linen (Craig was the first to tackle it). Nick, wearing the crash helmet, knee pads and elbow pads supplied with the assault course, is struggling to cross the monkey bars and falls heavily. Tom, watching from inside the house, says it is hard to believe he spent three or four years in the Territorial Army.

'Do you think it's all lies?' says Mel – she and Tom are the only two in the house who know that the story of his wife's death is a lie. 'Have you heard about this escort agency? He thinks he's a male prostitute.'

Tom says, 'When he first came in here he said his first girlfriend left him on New Year's Eve, and now he's saying a friend's girlfriend left on New Year's Eve.'

'He's going to end up hurting himself,' says Mel.

'There's no way he could have been trained in the army and be that clumsy,' Tom says.

When Nick strolls in, Tom says it looked as though he was struggling on the monkey bars.

'I never struggle,' says Nick.

Mel takes advantage of the pens that have arrived in the house as part of the materials to make the orange party gear, and gets all the housemates to sign their names on a white T-shirt. One of the lads draws a large penis, so she probably won't be wearing it much when she gets home.

The food for the party arrives and also the unicycle. Nichola is excited. It will be her first birthday party for eight years, since her twenty-first. Despite wearing the skimpiest of thongs, she climbs on to the saddle and, with help from Darren and Tom who hold her upright, tries to ride the unicycle. The birthday provisions also include frizzy orange wigs. In addition, they are delighted to find salmon among their orange food. With four bottles of champagne, it's a good party. Everyone dresses up, with the boys covering their legs and arms in orange paint. After they've tucked into the meal, cooked as usual by Darren, and the birthday cake, they all pile into the Diary Room. With Darren on the guitar, they tunelessly serenade Nicky's mum and dad.

Afterwards, Nichola sparks a lively after-dinner discussion by asking 'What's the most shocking thing you have ever done in bed?' Darren talks about having oral sex with a girl with a pierced tongue but is completely eclipsed by Craig, who tells tales of taking part in orgies. Even Nichola, no prude, says, 'I wish I'd never asked the bloody question.'

Darren wants to know how an orgy starts and even suggests they should have an orange orgy. Craig says he doesn't know how they get organized. Nick confesses to bedding a mother and daughter in a single weekend and Mel admits having sex in the loo on a plane with a man she had known 'for a few hours'.

One of Craig's stories is about picking up a married woman and driving her home, with her husband. He ended up making love to her in a muddy field, while the husband waited in a service station down the road.

As the party winds down, Nicky takes time out in the Diary Room, and this time confesses her true feelings about Darren.

'I think I freaked him out yesterday by imposing on him. Darren is into people respecting him, which I didn't. I have a lot of feeling for Darren and I stick him on a pedestal... I'm not going to hold a grudge because I've nothing to hold a grudge about. I hope Darren sees that what I said should not be taken personally, it was just Nichola having a bad day. Today he's been fine, but I feel he's not there 100 per cent. I'm probably expecting more than I'll ever get. He's not into me like I'm into him. It's not that I'm falling in love with him, just that I'm into him as a person. I think he's lovely, but he's also a pain in the arse. I love his energy, laughter, creativity, and I love the way he is.

'I know he has a thing for Melanie, but I feel I should tell him that I think the world of him. It needs the right time and the right place, but it will happen.

'If I'm nominated and thrown out on Friday I will tell him how I feel... but only if I know I'm able to leave. I would never tell him otherwise.'

The boys are having trouble removing the orange paint, so Big Brother does them a favour and puts the hot water on for fifteen minutes. While they are showering, Anna goes to the Diary Room to give Big Brother a slice of birthday cake.

'I was a bit weepy last night with Caroline, because she was the one I was closest to. In here you learn to get over things really quickly, you never know what you'll get thrown at you. It's quieter. Because Caroline was repeatedly nominated, people weren't at ease with her. Now it's calmer... It was easy today. I was surprised how easy it was.

'There's no one I'm getting on particularly well with... I like them all, there's no one I'm mad about but they're all lovely... I'm in good form, but I miss home. It was a dead good party, nice to see Nichola happy... She freaked yesterday because she needed someone to love her, she needs to have a best friend, it was scary without a best friend. She's prone to flipping anyway. She works herself up into such a frenzy... She made the others not like her because she was worried they didn't like her. But she's definitely all right now. She's making a good effort, which is what she needs to do.'

Outside, Darren is practising on the monkey bars, doing some impressive gymnastics. Anna is cornered by Nick for a late-night chat. He accuses Caroline of being sneaky and underhand. 'If people do that, the public see it and it affects our chances,' he says. 'This show brings out our good points, but it also shows our bad points. These things are magnified on TV.'

Anna agrees with him that Caroline and Nicky were the high maintenance members of the household. She tells him she referred to them as 'the two loopers', and to everybody else simply as 'the group'. 'It was the group and the loopers,' she says.

Nick laughs and tells her she is astute. Then he reverts to a theme that is increasingly bothering him – the public perception of the housemates in general, and himself in particular. 'What would it be like if we leave and they boo us? I think we should be given a hint by Big Brother as to how we are doing.'

Getting up late on Sunday morning means they have only fifteen minutes to compile their shopping list. As they have less than £50 to spend, it's a very basic list, but they still manage to overspend, and Big Brother sends Anna back to make some economies. Chocolate and biscuits and cheap cider are all reduced.

The assault course dominates the day, with Nick getting in lots of practice, to the amusement of the others due to his lack of co-ordination. Out in the garden at 5 o'clock, he and Darren hear shouts from beyond the walls of the house. It's not the first time that fans of the show have got close enough to make their voices heard. In the early weeks, before he learned to love the hens, Darren was shaken up when he heard someone yelling, 'Chicken-hater!' This time, he cannot make out what is being shouted. But Nick, who stays outside longer, does hear, and seems to be very upset by it. He tells the other lads he has heard abuse being called, that he heard someone being described as 'a fucking nutter'. He says he does not know who the insult was aimed at, but it was 'horrible'. Darren tells him he coped with it last time by thinking, 'I'm in this project – you're not.'

In the Diary Room, Darren tells Big Brother that he is having a hard time at the moment, missing his kids badly. He doesn't want to tell the rest of the group because he feels he is letting them down, and letting the production team down.

'When I first got chosen I was happy... I'm generally a happy person. But I keep thinking this is crap... I know we are lucky to be doing this. I'd do it again if I had the chance, it's just that the whole environment is strange. But I don't want to load all this negative stuff on the group or it will bring them down.'

To keep their minds occupied, Big Brother gives them a task on Sunday evening. They draw a name of one of the others in the group from a hat and have to write a poem about that person without naming them. The poems must then go into the hat, to be read by whoever draws them out, and the group must guess not just who the subject of the poem is, but who wrote it.

Here are the poems they wrote – it's not hard to guess who they are describing...

Tom's poem:
Incredible as it may seem to be
He is a man with the strength of three
He doesn't really smoke or drink
But a party animal, I would think
On one hand, he wears his mother's ring
This shows he appreciates a wonderful thing
If the rest of the world cared as much as him
It would surely be a nicer place to live in
At the end of this poem I really must say
I would hope to party with him some day
Because I know on him I could depend
And I believe I have found a good friend.

Mel's poem:
I would like to introduce you to a very special person
They are an important part of the BB production
If you knew half the things I do
I am sure you would like me to introduce you
Just to give you a flavour I will encapsulate her
In a few lines on this piece of paper
The randiest nun in the world
Teaching drums is a speciality of hers
With the wickedest grin, a love for cider drinking
She is a music loving bird
Of a night you may find her in Soho Square
But please beware, you may get a shock at her state of undress
Pendulous breasts and the stuff she likes to wear
She will strum like a tart till her fingers are raw
Or play continuously with a basketball
She will never give up, and has the strength of a wench
With her you are sure to have a ball
I am wondering if you know who this
Remember this is a bit of a quiz
One last clue she loves Davina McCall
And will love to watch you on the loo.

Nick's poem:
There was a girl from Bolton
Who refused to wear an apron

Her knitting was good and fast
Because she had no time to bare her ass
She has a heart as big as Big Brother
But that did not give her any bother
It was the men you see who could not pee straight
That would give her reason to exasperate.

Craig's poem:
She thinks she's right, she won't accept she's wrong
She always thinks she can smell a huge pong
Even though she is wrong and thinks she is right
She then always starts a fight
And when the fighting is over and we know she is wrong
She won't accept she's done the huge pong
So the fight goes on and on and on
Until one day we are all gone
Then when there is no one left to fight
She still thinks she was always right.

Anna's poem:
He is quiet at times, you won't hear a word
You will see him just watching, taking in the absurd
He will sit back and observe your laughter and cries
It's hard to work out what's behind those blue eyes
And then he will jump up and giggle with glee
After beating all six at a cool game of Cheat
When we all feel low and are filled with dread
He will brighten our day with his weird, wacky bread.

Nichola's poem:
He loves to rhyme, he does it all the time
In his Prada shoes and Dolce vest
He really does think he is the best
Even though he is the armchair critic
And always loves to take the mick
One thing I would really love to know
Why I really love him so.

Darren's poem:
When you need somebody to talk to
This person will be there
When you need somebody to help you
This person will take you somewhere
With a warm heart, kind and gentle
Rhyming is hard, so I will just say pencil
Very mature, intelligent, funny
Sometimes childish and a dummy
I'm sorry to whoever has to read this poem
I can't think of any more, so sod him
Yes, I give it away, it's a male not a female
I might as well tell you who it is, what the hell

But before I do, knowing me, knowing you
I have to put something in about me, you know who
You may know me, myself and I
The man who is gorgeous, tall but shy
OK, enough about me, me, me
The person I'm writing about does reiki.

After the fun of the poems, Big Brother sets them a serious discussion topic: homelessness. The argument is heated, with the girls saying they would give money to beggars regardless of what they spend it on, and the boys feeling that if it was wasted on drink or drugs it would be wrong. Nicky says that she buys takeaways for down-and-outs when she can afford it, preferring to give food rather than money. Both Craig and Anna admit to having been on the receiving end of charity – Craig when he was travelling in Europe and had to beg for money for food and accommodation and Anna when she was drunk and broke with a friend and they propped themselves up against a wall and put their hands out for money for more booze. She is disgusted at her own behaviour.

The insults he heard in the garden are preying on Nick's mind, and he shares his worries with Nichola and Mel. They reassure him. He says he is thinking of walking out, but Mel tells him he is worrying too much and should have a good night's sleep.

At 11 o'clock in the evening, Anna is in the Diary Room chatting with Big Brother. She talks about Nick's strategy for winning, how he works out who he wants to be with him in the final week.

'It was really interesting and I started thinking about who I would want with me in the final week.' She admits that she now sees herself as a contender to win, and wants to win.

'It's about time a girl won. [In the other *Big Brother*s, the winner has always been a man.] They say all the voting goes towards the hunky young boys, and I'm gonna do the girlie thing and be like Girl Power.' She holds up two fingers to Big Brother in a victory sign. 'I'll be the girl who wins it.'

She tells Big Brother she had a dream that she was out on the lash with a group of friends, but they were all famous women who she admires: Jane Middlemiss, Zoe Ball, Cat Deeley, Jo Whiley, and Davina McCall.

'We were sitting round this table having pints and a laff. I'm gonna give it my all and try and win and perhaps if I do, I'll be able to have a pint with all those girls.'

When she comes out of the Diary Room everyone is in the sitting area, apart from Mel and Tom. She has dragged him into the bedroom to give her a massage – she asked him to do it in the morning, and now she's not letting him avoid it any longer. She tells him to undo her bra straps, and says he is 'surprisingly gentle'.

Despite Mel telling him to sleep on his worries, Nick can't put them out of his mind. Just after midnight, he goes to talk to Big Brother. He is still very unsettled after hearing the abuse shouted over the wall. He says he doesn't care if it was only four or five people, or that they sounded like young children, they are still viewers.

'In this environment, paranoia sets in. Not knowing how people feel about us is very important to us. It is like living on a knife-edge, not knowing what reception we will get when we leave the house. People on the inside see 360 degrees of me, but the public only see limited bits. It's distressing because they could read it in certain ways which would determine the reception I get when I leave here.

'Everyone can't like you. The only thing that concerns me is do I walk out of here with a blanket over my head or with head held high.

'We're protected in here, guards patrolling the perimeter, you [Big Brother] monitoring us verbally, watching us twenty-four hours a day, nothing can happen to us. It's like being a child in a womb. Then suddenly we're out in the big world. It's a terrifying thought, especially if you are worried that you may have come across in the wrong way. It just could be one of those things that haunts you for the rest of your life. It's a fairly mind-provoking thing.'

He tells Big Brother that he is terrified that he has been received in the wrong way by the viewing public and that on eviction night, when they hear the crowds and get a glimpse of the families of the two who have been nominated, they wonder what their families are thinking.

'We have had so much exposure, it has been life changing. It will be hard to resume a life outside if people dislike us or think we are bad.'

Nomination day starts late for most of the housemates – Nichola is the only one up before lunchtime. Despite her outrageous appearance, she's secretly a homebody. She does more than her share of clearing and cleaning, likes baking, and makes the effort to bring flowers in from the garden to cheer the place up. When the other two girls, Anna and Mel, eventually join her and the lads are still asleep, they sit around chatting about how much fun it will be if the three of them are left together in the house. They will, they decide, all grow fat from the cakes and biscuits they will cook and eat.

Much later in the day all the boys have a similar chat about what they will do when they are left in the house at the end. Darren suggests they trash the place, as they won't have to clear up the mess.

Nichola has a good chat with Big Brother, saying that she feels better because she has done some yoga. She's still missing Caroline, her energy, laughter and jokes. She wants to stay in the house till the end, but has a feeling that people might not want her, and she's preparing herself to leave on Friday.

'I feel relaxed within the group but at times I feel on my own. But so does everyone... I enjoyed playing cards with them yesterday. I haven't played before. I was surprised to enjoy it. It's nice that Craig got on the unicycle. He does have his good and bad points. I don't communicate with Tom, he's so quiet. I get on with Mel a bit, Anna is lovely. Nick, the reiki man, he's more a one-to-one man. I don't know why that is. I do like him one-to-one, but in a group he is a bit quiet.

'To be in a house with ten strangers can be hard. They don't understand your moods or sense of humour... I spend most of my life on a massive high, but sometimes I feel on my own.'

She says the others have also been through mood swings, and some of them have cried. She knows Darren misses his family. Big Brother advises her to talk about her feelings to the others.

'I find it really hard. I get that thing in my throat. I don't want to start crying again after the other day. I am a really weepy person.'

She says she doesn't want to bring the others down before the nominations, but may talk to them afterwards. She says her cleaning is an effort to keep herself busy because she feels a bit out of sync with the place and the others. However, there are plenty of things she is enjoying, like her papier-mâché art (which Darren is joining in with), cooking, lounging in the sunshine, playing cards, writing the poems and doing the task because it brings everyone together.

Expecting to be nominated and to leave on Friday, Nichola announces that she is going to decorate the door through which the evictees go with a shooting star design.

When Craig surfaces, he chats with Mel about the nominations they are all going to have to make within the hour. He likens it to waiting at the doctor's. Their anthem, 'It's Only a Game Show', has been heard a lot less since Caroline's departure, but they sing it again as each of them is summoned to the Diary Room to go through the routine they all dread.

WHO NOMINATES WHO

ANNA	Craig and Thomas
CRAIG	Darren and Nichola
DARREN	Craig and Thomas
MELANIE	Darren and Nichola
NICHOLA	Craig and Thomas
NICHOLAS	Craig and Nichola
THOMAS	Anna and Nichola

REASONS:	
NICHOLA on **THOMAS**	'Tom is really quiet, I don't connect with him.'
NICHOLAS on **CRAIG** and **NICHOLA**	'I feel the group would operate better without them.'
THOMAS on **ANNA** and **NICHOLA**	'They are the two people who are most unhappy here.'

To relieve the tension they all have another go at the assault course. Mel insists that she won't be able to do the monkey bars, even though Big Brother has now provided gloves. Afterwards she has a reiki session with Nick, and he talks to her in code about the nominations, referring to 'Delta' and 'Charlie', and then to 'Dogfight' and 'Nicosia'.

Darren is preoccupied with the chickens, which don't seem to be at all well. Some of them have diarrhoea, and he asks Big Brother if anything can be put in their water to get them well again.

Tom tells Mel and Craig another of his future plans. He's going to build himself a house on a hill with views all around, including one down a valley to Donegal. Craig asks him if he will do all the work himself, and he says he will do most of it. Craig is impressed that he can lay bricks.

The evening passes cheerfully with a special treat. Big Brother gives each of them a riddle and fifteen minutes in which to solve it. They then have to take the first letter of their answers and rearrange them into another word.

The clues given to them are:

Anna: *Beyond* Big Brother *the world is waiting, but what divides you from the debating?*

Craig: *Best foot forward, sure and deft. Work it out, it's not what's left.*

Nick: *Numbers are pitted against each other, but how many souls can win* Big Brother?

Mel: *In the room where teeth get clean, look in the mirror and describe what's seen.*

Tom: *He's out of the door but always game, to win this quiz you must guess his name.*

Nichola: *Music, which you can't disparage, you'll sweat a lot when you listen to...*
Darren: *A gift from Marjorie amidst the clucking, a perfect shape but not for chucking.*
The answers are: Fence, Right, One, Melanie, Andrew, Garage, and Egg.

The group manage to solve the anagram, yelling out FROMAGE well within their deadline. Big Brother rewards them with pizza and fizzy drinks.

Afterwards, Mel talks to Anna and Nichola about taking the Pill. She tells them she's been on it for about ten years, but came off it when she went travelling for a year. 'It was great. I felt fantastic. But when I came in here I didn't want my libido to be going through the roof. So to control my libido and control my periods I went back on the Pill. Honestly, that's what I was thinking. I just wanted to control my libido and then when I get out of the house I'll come off it again.'

None of them are sleeping well, but Nick seems to have an even more disturbed pattern than most. At twenty past three on Tuesday morning, he goes into the Diary Room to talk once again about how the public outside the *Big Brother* house are thinking about him.

'Yesterday I was concerned about what was happening outside, but I'm over it now... There is nothing we can do about what might have been broadcast... Everyone so wanted to be in the show that they may have overlooked that people may hate them.'

He says it would be good to have an exercise bike or a rowing machine, because they are not getting enough exercise. He also asks if he can be given the Fulham football results, as it is the first time in ten years that he has missed the opening game of the season. He says he is prepared to do an individual task in return. To demonstrate his willingness to help, he cleans the camera lens before leaving the Diary Room.

He goes to bed, but finding it impossible to sleep he gets up again, and sits with Craig who is also awake. He tells Craig, 'Anna's a dangerous one... She has started to befriend people to lull them into a false sense of security.' He tells Craig his plan is to get rid of Darren, Anna and Nichola – he does not mention, of course, that he has just nominated Craig. On the subject of Nichola, he gestures to all her art work on the walls and says, 'If Nicky goes we can get that shit down and paint over it.'

The next day the hens are still poorly and a vet is called. Darren takes two of the chickens, one at a time, to see the vet. He's most worried, of course, about his beloved Marjorie. The vet says they are not as sick as he feared – their temperatures are normal. He thinks the problem is down to feeding. Darren tells him they love banana skins and the vet replies that they may love them, but they shouldn't be eating them. The vet arranges to send in a treatment for worms, which the housemates will have to administer, and it's strictly chicken food from now on, none of Darren's tasty treats.

At three o'clock the news of the nominations comes, and it's Craig and Nichola. They both take it very calmly, giving each other a big hug. Craig says he's not bothered and that he'll worry about being evicted when the time comes. Nichola is a little bit more wobbly but goes into the Diary Room to say that in many ways she's relieved. She's ready to go. She's bored with the others:

'Most of my friends are artists or singers, and these guys work in offices. They are just not my type of people,' she says.

She has been busy getting her dress, which she's knitting with wire, ready for the day she leaves. The others have all been admiring it and Darren has even had a go at knitting – which prompted Nick to label him as 'slightly gay'.

The phlegmatic Craig does not volunteer to talk to Big Brother, but is called to the Diary Room. He says he doesn't feel anything, probably because the news has not yet sunk in.

'I don't feel disappointed. I'm a little bit excited – life could change on Friday, or I could be back in here. I'm not upset about it.'

He says he feels he could have brought a bit more fun into the house given a chance but he hasn't had the chance.

Shortly afterwards, they are given the time in which they must complete the assault course. Working as a relay team, they have to get round in a total of eight minutes, with penalties for missing out one of the tyres or one of the monkey bars and bigger penalties for falling off or not completing.

Craig has been quietly coaching the others, particularly the girls, but Nick is keen to assume the role of leader, telling everyone they should take it easy and not rush it or they will make errors. 'Errors are for the weak,' he says.

In a chat in the kitchen, he teases Mel about burping, farting and smells in the loo that the girls make. He even accuses her of 'having a wee-wee in the shower', which she hotly denies. Tom says that he hopes Nick hasn't peed in the shower either, as he has sometimes followed him in there. 'I never do,' says Nick. His housemates may believe him, but the production team know better – he's been caught on camera having a pee in there some mornings.

Nick, again preoccupied with life outside the *Big Brother* walls, talks about the betting that will be going on, on matters like who in the house will have the first kiss, who will throw the first punch. He teases Mel about the first kiss, hinting that Andrew told him (as he did) that he had kissed Mel. She denies it, calling Andy a 'lying little toerag' and insisting she said, 'You shouldn't be doing that,' when he tried to kiss her. She did say those words, but after the kiss.

Mel asks Tom for another massage on the sofa, and it turns into a very erotic, if public, encounter. He climbs on her back, and obviously enjoys the encounter hugely, his baggy shorts failing to conceal his erection.

While Darren starts to prepare the evening meal, the others go outside for another rehearsal of the assault course. Deciding that they would like to do a full run-through, timing themselves by counting, they call Darren out to take part. Unfortunately, he leaves a pan of oil on the stove, and while they are busy cheering each other across the monkey bars, and practising their pit stop changeovers of the crash helmet and pads, the pan catches fire. The first the housemates know is when Big Brother orders them all to stay in the garden. Craig, ever practical, dashes inside to turn off the heat under the pan. Their home is then invaded by two security men who put a damp cloth across the flames and carry the pan outside. A frisson of excitement runs through the whole group at the sight of 'human beings'.

In an early evening chat, Nick tells Craig that Darren voted against him. He urges Craig to go to the Diary Room and tell the nation why he has been a benefit to the house. He tells him his familiar story of having accurately prophesied each time which one will survive the nomination process. 'I think you're going to stay,' he tells Craig. They talk about Darren, and agree that he spends his time charming the girls.

The housemates sit up late talking and, again, their favourite topic – sex – dominates the conversation. Mel asks Tom and Nick how many times they have masturbated since being in the house. Tom is uncomfortable about the questioning which she persists with, but eventually says he has, in the shower. Nick says he has three times, including once in the greenhouse (although this is not true). Mel says she has not masturbated since being in there.

When they are joined by some of the others, the talk widens to sexual positions. Craig uses Nichola, fully clothed, to demonstrate a sexual position, and then dumbfounds the girls by telling how he has twice made girlfriends faint during sex. He and Tom discuss how they have matured sexually over the years, from being teenagers when, in Craig's words, 'you want to do it all the time, you want to do everything that moves' to becoming fully fledged sex experts. They agree that they now know a lot more about giving a woman pleasure. Craig says he prefers mature women.

'Women are most sexually active at thirty-two,' he says.

Anna goes to bed before the late-night talk, so she's first up the next day. To her astonishment, she finds that a garden candle has been left burning in the living room all night and has burned right through. Just a few more minutes and another fire could have started. Anna blows out the flame. Later in the day, when the others are up, they are given a collective reprimand from Big Brother for being so careless. Nicky admits under her breath that she brought the candle in from the garden. Big Brother tells them to search out the fire-extinguishing equipment so that in the event of anything else catching light they will know what to do. Anna suggests that Nicky should knit them a fire blanket.

Nicky is responsible for another problem in the house. The papier-mâché decoration she made for the door of the boys' room is beginning to smell unpleasantly. They decide it is because she used an egg in the flour-and-water paste mixture. In the end this remains on the door.

Darren is told to bring his beloved Marjorie to the Diary Room, as the vet wants to take her away for observation. He threatens to keep her, to refuse to give her up, but the girls persuade him that it is in Marjorie's best interests to be seen. The chicken dutifully follows him when he makes a clucking noise at her and he takes her through to the Diary Room. Anna asks if she has to sit in the big chair and talk about her problems.

Nicky, still convinced that she will be leaving on Friday evening, tries on the multi-coloured wire dress she has been knitting. The others are impressed. Anna tells her she looks 'sassy, sexy, wild and wicked, too'. Darren asks the others what they think she would look like with hair, because he can see that she's really pretty, with very big eyes.

In the garden, Nick tells Craig that he will survive the eviction process – he's seen it in a vision. He brags that he was able to prophesy Tom's survival the previous week.

While Darren cleans the boys' bedroom, Melanie goes to the Diary Room, summoned there by Big Brother. She says she is in a bad mood because seeing the same old faces all the time makes her irritable, and she know it is going to get worse. She's getting irritated with some individuals. Big Brother asks her who, and she says Nicholas.

'I'm annoyed about being irritated, because I like him. But he thinks he knows exactly how all the nominations and evictions will go and how everything will unfold. He doesn't know, he's not psychic, he's just making educated guesses.

'I'll be sad to see Craig go on Friday. I've very much changed my mind about him. He is a real sweetheart, such a nice bloke with a heart of gold. I know for a fact that Nick doesn't feel that way because he's told me. I find it sickening when he says to Craig that it's terrible he's been nominated. I find that two-faced attitude sickening, and I think he's probably saying the same sort of things to me.'

She says she thinks certain people are trying to sway the voting of others 'quite obviously and blatantly'. She asks Big Brother for helpful suggestions. She says she still misses Andy and wishes he was there, but that there is a much more united feeling in the house since Caroline's departure.

In the afternoon, they have to tackle the assault course. Just before they start, Craig goes to the Diary Room. He reckons they will do it – they've worked out that even if the girls cost them some penalty points, they should be all right. The girls don't cost them any penalty points. Nick is the cause of the heart-stopping tension with the housemates watching as 50 per cent of their shopping budget is put in jeopardy when he slips from the monkey bars, touching the floor and incurring a 20-second penalty, then emerges from the cargo net with his knee and elbow pads falling off, which uses up precious time in re-fixing them, and then falls from the seesaw and has to go back to redo it. Despite this, with very fast performances from all the other boys and no mistakes from the girls, they sail through in three quarters of the allocated time. Mel, who thought she would not be able to do the monkey bars, puts in the fastest time of all the girls. Darren turns up for the course wearing smart jeans as if he is about to go out for the night, but they don't impede his progress, and everyone is jubilant at the prospect of having £94.50 to spend.

Nick's confidence is undiminished. Within minutes of finishing the assault course, he is teasing Darren about his sister, Julie. He says that 'Julie Bateman' sounds good. Darren laughs at the prospect of Nick marrying his sister but says it would never happen because his sister would not have Nick.

'I could put a spell on her. She would say, "Darren I want that man's phone number. He was very cute and helpful and supportive of people in the house and that's the sort of strong man I want."'

Darren is unconvinced. 'My sister wouldn't have you mate – I'd tell her about your sneaky and conniving ways. Mind you, she has her own mind, she might find you attractive.'

But then, as a clincher, he adds, looking disparagingly at Nick's footwear, 'My sister does not do white socks with shoes.'

The conversation moves on to Darren's children and Nick gives him a pep talk: 'Your children are very lucky to have such a wonderful and magic father as you. Eight or nine weeks in here is but a short time. The longer you are here the more they'll grow to love you and miss you. The time you are away gives you time to reflect that they are the most important things in the world. They will be so happy when they see you it will be a beautiful scene to behold. It will make you a stronger and better person being away and missing them.'

Darren, unimpressed by the speech, says, 'You're still not fucking my sister.'

Mel and Craig are getting on much better than they did in the first few weeks and she joins him on the settee for a flirting session.

In the evening, Big Brother sets them another mini task. They must write an original song, to be performed in twenty-four hours' time. It must not be not a parody of an existing song and each housemate must perform a separate function in the band: singing, dancing or playing instruments. Mel suggests it should be a rap song and Tom suggests they called themselves 'The Wannabes'.

Craig retires to the bedroom with a blackboard and chalk, to work on some lyrics. Finding him there, Nick strolls over and starts another discussion about nominations and evictions, trying to write something down on Craig's board. Craig rubs it off and simply says, 'I know what you mean, mate.'

Another of the endless card sessions starts, and Darren and Nick have a spat over it. Nick tries to cheat by looking in one of the mirrors to see his opponent's hand.

Thomas goes to the Diary Room at 11.30 p.m. and at first talks over his own feelings and the way life in the house has changed him. 'I am learning when to put my views forward. Within the house I've gained more confidence, which is quite a step for me... To become a member of the team is quite a confidence booster for me. I have some pretty major decisions to make, and I now have more idea what I want for myself. I think at thirty-one I should be more confident and looking out for myself more.'

When he moves on to discussing the others in the group, he shares a similar disquiet about Nick to that which Mel has been expressing for a few days.

'I do find that some members of the group try to have an overbearing influence that you should see things their way and their way only. I don't agree with them – they can give me advice and I don't have to follow it.'

When asked by Big Brother to name names he says: 'Nicholas would be one of these characters... he's like an overgrown schoolboy who likes to whisper in your ear, likes to lead the directions of your thoughts, likes you to be in his way of thinking, likes to guide the conversation like the headboy in class.'

With thoughts of Nick's machinations on his mind, half an hour later, Tom finds a quiet moment to have the seminal talk with Craig which precipitates the events of the next twenty-four hours. They are both in their beds, side by side.

'I'm saying this as a friend to you,' says Tom, 'I was influenced to vote a certain way this week, which I didn't.'

'Were you instigated to vote against me?' Craig asks. 'Who by?'

'Nick has a habit of writing things down... On Friday there was something like that. On Tuesday last week, he said "Craig's the traitor." I said I didn't see it that way. I'm getting more wary of him. He's coming up with wee stories...'

Craig says, 'The whole thing is diverting from him. I appreciate you telling me this.'

'It has made me so uncomfortable with him. It's not very often we get room in here to talk,' Tom says.

'He's tried to divert me,' says Craig. 'I was writing lyrics for the song, bits of a poem, and he started to write on the blackboard... I feel like finding these papers because he has shown me one.'

'I think he has two sets,' says Tom. 'One in his locker, one in his bag.'

'I feel like going out and knocking him out.'

Tom tells Craig to keep cool and goes to find Mel. She's in bed but comes to join them and confirms to Craig that Nick has shown her written slips of paper with names on. Craig then brings Anna into the boys' room. She tells him she has never been shown anything and is shocked by what Craig tells her.

'Tom said we should look in his bags. I said no, but I'll ask him at the table tomorrow if I can look in his bags. Hopefully, if anyone else has experienced it they'll put their hands up. If they're honest enough. Even if they're not honest to me and the others round the table, they'll make themselves look a fool in front of their family and millions of viewers.'

Back in the girls' room, Anna and Mel talk.

'He's giving different names to different people,' says Mel. 'It's really weird. I thought "What are you doing?" It indicates to me that he doesn't remember what he is doing. I started to freak out. This doesn't make any sense, I feel like I'm going mad.'

It's now Darren's turn to be brought in on what is happening. While Tom stays outside with Nick and Mel, who are playing backgammon, Craig fills Darren in.

'How can he write your name? He's got nothing to write with... I can't believe he's got papers in there. We should have a look now, then we know we have seen it, because tomorrow when we say it he's going to say he's not got them. We should look now, to make sure we know we've seen them.'

He strides across and pulls open Nick's suitcase, with Craig, uncomfortable, muttering, 'Don't do it.'

After a hasty rummage, Darren produces two slips of paper, one saying 'Caroline and Nicky' and the other 'Craig and Mel'. 'Fucking hell. Don't go out there. It's there, we've seen it, I've seen it. I can't say I went through his stuff.'

Unaware of the problems that are about to hit him, Nick continues his machinations. He tells Tom and Mel that 'on Friday, it will be goodbye Nicky.'

He adds, 'Then next week Darren and Craig, Darren goes. The weeks after that, Craig and Anna, Anna goes. The week after that, Craig and Tom, Craig goes. We're left with the three of us, and Tom wins by three per cent. I've seen it all in my dream.'

Craig and Darren have agreed to leave the confrontation with Nick until the next day, at the group meeting. At ten past four, when Nick finally comes to the bedroom, Craig tells him there will be a meeting 'because everyone's upset about different things'.

'What's it going to achieve?' Nick asks.

'Everyone's got to say what's on their minds,' Craig says.

'I think it's a good idea. But at the end of the day there's always a hassle on nominations day, and generally it's the girls who are unhappy.'

'On this occasion, Nick, I'm not very happy,' says Craig.

Nick says he did not realize this and asks if Craig has taken his concerns to Big Brother. Craig says he has, and the advice was to bring it up at the meeting.

'I look forward to that,' says Nick.

'So do I,' says Craig, forcefully.

The household settles down and goes quiet, but it's unlikely that they all sleep easily tonight.

It is after midday before they are all up on what will turn out to be possibly the most momentous day in the *Big Brother* house. They assemble round the table, Nick in the centre of one side, with Craig facing him diagonally and Anna next to him. Craig addresses the meeting.

'I've got a very important thing I want to bring up. It's everyone's concern. I'm sorry to have to say this Nick, but I'm very disappointed in you. I not only feel, I'm positive and have evidence, you are plotting a very dirty plan on everybody here to vote against each other and divert from you.'

'That's absurd, Craig,' Nick says.

'You may think it's absurd Nick, but facts are here,' Craig continues. 'A number of people sitting round this table have come to me over the weekend and said you showed them paper with various names on, i.e. my name on a number of occasions.

'I have witnessed you giving me a piece of paper with various people's names on, and so have other people around this table, whose names I won't mention, if they want to add in. What disappoints me most: how can you be so two-faced? You have sat and had a one-on-one conversation with me, made arrangements for the future when we get out of here, to go and visit Tom, things like that. How can you do that knowing full well you've passed paper around in a conspiracy to get me out?

'You may think I'm paranoid or upset and feeling personal because I've been nominated, but you're wrong, I don't feel that. I feel everyone in this room is strong enough to make up their own minds. I feel I'm fairly nominated this week. I don't know the reasons. Everyone's entitled to vote and in my thinking it's been done fairly. What I cannot understand, please explain – what's your game, what are you playing at, what's your motive?'

Nick hesitates for a split second, and then speaks: 'Craig you have made a number of wild accusations over the last couple of weeks. When you accused Caroline of drinking too much – you tend to, when you are cornered, jump up...'

Several of the others interject and try to stop him speaking, but Anna calmly tells them to let him have his say.

'We've all been told we can't discuss nominations, but you told me who you were voting for this week...'

'No, I didn't,' says Craig.

Darren asks Nick if the allegation that he has been showing names is true.

'No, it isn't,' says Nick.

Both Mel and Tom chip in that they have been shown names. Darren says he hasn't. Anna asks Nick again if he has showed names, and this time he admits to showing Mel and Tom, but says he cannot remember which names he showed them.

Anna, who has calmly taken on the role of mediator, asks if he can explain his actions.

'I've had this discussion with people in this room. People will back it up. I've seen each time, and I've said, I've seen Tom jumping up in the air the Friday before... Regardless of the bit of paper, people don't have to act on it...' Nick says.

Anna questions him about when he has shown the paper, before or after the nominations. When he says it was before, she asks for his reasons.

'In retrospect it was a mistake to make. But well before... even just after the person has gone... It shouldn't have been done. Just a vision... It's been misinterpreted now...'

He stumbles, stutters and looks uncomfortable. Anna asks him why he only showed his piece of paper to some people.

'Some people you share things with, some people you don't. Some might take it the wrong way, some might take it the right way,' he says.

Mel interrupts: 'It seems to me it is not a vision, showing different names to different people.'

Nick says that's not true. When asked by Darren to confirm that he shows the same two names, he says yes.

Mel speaks again: 'I get the feeling that it's not the same two names, so I went to Big Brother about it because I was not comfortable.'

Nick tries to defend himself by saying he doesn't show the names just before nominations, but Anna stops him:

'Nick, it's against the rules. It's wanting other people to know, and you're not allowed to do it. You've just admitted you've broken the rules.'

Tom says that he hasn't followed Nick's recommendations. 'You've given me names and indicated you wanted me to vote for those names. I've not been happy with it. I never realized it was on such a scale until I talked to Craig last night and blew the whole thing open. I find it very disappointing.'

Craig says: 'You've told me that you have seen me, yourself and someone else in here...'

Nick speaks: 'I told Darren that I can see the final five, one person I can't see, I can see four out of five.'

Anna then says that he has told her she will be in the final three, and also Mel.

'In your version, whoever you are with, you see them jumping up and celebrating,' says Tom.

'I said, Tom, I could see you winning it and jumping up...' says Nick.

Darren gets the subject back on to the pieces of paper, and Craig says: 'It's quite insulting, thinking that you can divert us. I said to Big Brother, I feel a fool. I voted for one of the people you had on the paper. I voted for my own personal view. I don't want them to think I'm weak enough to be led by you or anybody in here because I'm not. The only weak person in here is you, Nick. You've lowered yourself and it's backfired on you.'

Darren asks where the pieces of paper are, and Nick says most of them are destroyed. 'Most of them' alerts Darren and Nicky who both want to know how many there were and where they are.

Craig speaks again: 'No one wants to make a fool of themselves. I went into the box a couple of weeks ago and said in front of five million people and my family and friends that you are a genuine guy and I would like to spend the duration with you. I feel a c... in all honesty. I feel you're responsible for making me feel a c... in front of millions of people. I would like to see the paper with my name on it.'

Darren's indignation takes over: 'You're a grown man. I can't believe you would do this in a situation where we're being watched by so many millions. There's kind of no excuse. You're a grown gentleman. That's childish. Pathetic.'

Tom adds: 'Last week you came past me and you said to me "Craig's the traitor" as if to say Craig was the one who voted for me.'

'What game are you playing?' Nicky asks.

Darren says: 'There's no traitor in here. As much as I may talk to Anna, when it comes to nominations I can nominate her. Why is Craig a traitor? Is it a boy/girl game? Is that what you think? What's the game to you? I'm not here to get the girls out. I'm seriously shocked at the fact that you're showing people's names. That's fucking sick.'

'You're making more of a fool of yourself by saying you only put two names on there,' says Craig. 'You've been caught out and you're blatantly lying about it. Will you go and get the paper?'

Nick: 'I will not do that.'

Craig: 'Will you give me permission to go through your things?'

Nick shakes his head. "I'll pack my suitcase and go.'

Craig: 'That's your decision, but you've dug your own grave.'

Nick: 'I accept that.'

Darren: 'Do you really want that £70,000?'

Nick: 'I've done something wrong.'

Darren: 'Not just in front of us, in front of millions. I feel sick.'

Craig: 'I've lost all respect for you. I thought you were a clever guy.'

Nicky: 'A lot of people had respect for you. Caroline used to sing your praises at night-time. I'm gutted. Caroline's name could have been on one of those pieces of paper as well, and you were telling her "Caroline you're fine, you're not going this week, you'll be fine" and you were flashing her name in front of other people. She'll be so disappointed in you. It makes me feel sick.'

Darren then says that he now understands why Nick constantly referred to nominations being rigged, because names were nominated that 'weren't supposed to be'. He says he kept wondering how Nick knew who would be nominated. Nick accuses him of taking the matter to extremes. Craig tells him that his behaviour has made people paranoid, made them feel insecure within the group.

'We're all having a hard time in here, it's a difficult environment, we're missing our family and friends, breaking our minds on what's happening outside. Nick, you've made the whole thing harder. I was doubting other people in here, and I'm sorry for doubting them. You've really disappointed me.

'We can drag this out all day but it's humiliating. I don't think it's fair, and we should put it to an end now. But I've got one question, and then I'll walk away: What was your motive? Why were you plotting against each other?'

Nick says there was no plot. He says, 'I just showed two names.'

It's a major tactical error, because he has brought them back to the question of the number of names he has showed. Anna checks with him that it was only two and he repeats that it was.

Craig says, 'We don't want to humiliate you any more. We just want you to be honest and tell us. If you consistently say you have not written it on a piece of paper I will embarrass you. I will go into the bedroom and take the pieces of paper. Just answer me an honest question.'

Nick: 'It was one bit of paper. There were six names covering three weeks' nominations.'

Craig: 'How many papers? If I'd known you were this organized, Nick, I'd have given you a job in my office. I feel bad humiliating you. Just answer the question.'

Nick: 'I showed two people round this table names for this week.'

Mel challenges him, and he says it was her and Thomas he showed names to. She says she got the impression they were shown different names, but Nick insists they were shown the same ones. Mel says that she and Craig were shown different names, and that it happened the week before. 'And I think you showed my name to people,' she says.

Nick says, 'I've never showed your name.'

Nicky asks if he showed hers, and he confirms he did.

Darren jumps up and announces he's going to get the names. As he leaves the room, Craig says: 'I gave you the opportunity a moment ago not to drag this out.'

Nicky says, 'You could have done it with Sada, Caroline, Andy.'

Mel reassures her that he hasn't influenced anyone's vote, and Craig says he has confidence that they are all strong enough people to make their own decisions about voting.

Darren returns with Nick's suitcase and puts it on the kitchen worktop. He goes through it and pulls out three pieces of paper with different combinations of names on: Craig and Mel; Caroline and Nicky; Craig and Nicky.

They all start firing questions at him, in particular Darren who wants to know where the pencil came from.

Mel tells them all to leave it to Big Brother now and the meeting breaks up. Craig puts water on to boil and asks who wants a cup of tea. Nick picks up his suitcase and takes it back into the bedroom. He swears softly under his breath and then puts his shoes on. He kneels on the floor by his case and Mel comes in. As she talks to him, he slumps forward with his head on the bed and tears run down his face.

'You can't just walk out. You can't. The reason is that it's going to be hell for you out there. You can't. OK, it's something that has gone wrong, but you can't walk out. Big Brother is there to help you, you need to talk to them. It's something that got out of control. It's OK.' She rubs his shoulder as he hangs his head in despair. 'Sit down. You can't go. You need to work it out. You are going to have to speak to Big Brother first. If you walk out now your life will be hell, absolute hell. Don't worry about us in here, it will be hell out there. This is on national TV... Big Brother will give you advice on the best way to deal with it. You need to talk to them and then come and tell us what they said. Just walking away is the worst thing you could do.'

Nick says that if he stays he will be voted out next week, anyway. He is starting to give her his verdict on Craig, who he describes as a hypocrite, when Craig walks in with a cup of tea for him. Mel tells him to worry about now, not next week, and she takes him to the Diary Room and rings the bell for him.

In the Diary Room, he is subdued. He looks down. Big Brother asks how he is feeling and he says he is upset. Big Brother asks if he thought the others wouldn't notice the games he was playing.

'Eventually, yes,' he says. 'Like all things, in retrospect it was an error. If you live by the sword, you die by the sword. It's a game show, a game. One has to try and do the best one can with it.'

He says he is not sure about his future in the house.

'It's probably easier to walk. I'm worried about the obvious perception people will have when this episode round the table goes out. I don't want to leave the house at all, but if the perception of me outside is bad I'd rather leave. There's nothing more terrifying than walking out of here and people booing and hissing.'

Big Brother promises to let Nick know what is happening, and Nick goes back to his bedroom and crawls under his duvet to cry. The others want to talk to him again and Darren asks him if he is coming out. He says, in a voice cracking with sobs, that he will be thirty seconds. He gets no sympathy from Darren.

Darren says: 'I don't know why you're doing that. You shouldn't have done it in the first place. I'm disgusted to think that I thought Nick's a cool man... If the whole reason was money, you can sell loads of stories and get that. I'm fucked off that these guys are thinking about Nick and how's Nick feeling. I'm not. You should have thought of this before.'

Nick rouses himself and says, 'You're selfish anyway.'

Darren: 'I'm glad you said that and everyone knows you said it.'

Nick: 'I don't care what you think. Everyone can see that you're selfish.'

Big Brother then interrupts and calls Darren to the Diary Room where he is assured that the production team had no knowledge of Nick writing notes or they would have stopped him.

'He never came to me as he knew I wouldn't accept... the names. He's treated others badly, and the ones he's shown the names to are feeling sorry for him... The reason I stay here is first that I feel lucky to have been chosen to do it and second to benefit my family. Someone like him, he's sick, crazy. I feel isolated now that it feels [it's] just me who wants him to be punished for what he's done wrong.'

Big Brother sympathizes with Darren's feelings, and says that they are still working out what the procedure should be. In the meantime, Nick is going through a hard time right now and Big Brother would like Darren to be calm and supportive, and the positive influence he usually is on the group.

Tom goes into the bedroom to talk to Nick as Darren leaves the Diary Room. 'You know yourself that Darren is your biggest critic, the most strong-minded. Darren's not going to be happy if you stay, but other people will give you a second chance.'

Nick says, 'It's such a minor thing, in a way. It's bound to happen. It's in the rules that we shouldn't discuss or write down nominations...'

Tom tells him not to try to justify what he has done, as it comes across as arrogant. 'Don't say rules are meant to be broken, which is what you are telling me now... There are a lot of people out there feeling hurt that they were party to this. They feel guilty, ready to make you the scapegoat for their guilt. That's what you have to consider. Get yourself tidied up.'

Nick goes into the living area to talk to the group, who gather round the table again. 'First, I want to apologize to you all for my actions. I'm not going to justify them, but I will tell you why I did them. I feel ashamed and I will give you the reasons. I come from a big family, and when you come from a big family you tend to compete, for attention, for everything. I spent ten years at boarding school where you fight and compete for everything, and people constantly try to do one over on you, constantly try to make you come second or third. It's a very competitive environment. I've also worked in a very aggressive environment where people will gladly stitch you up to further their own careers.' Nick adapted this same aggesive policy to the *Big Brother* house – of getting rid of rivals before they could threaten his position.

'We're all here to partake in this show and do as well as we'd like to do. I chose a way I thought was the best way. Of course, I was wrong. I fully admit that. I thought I would walk out the door but that's the coward's way out. I made a mistake. People do make mistakes. I've been there for people when they've been down... I'm asking you as a group – yes, I made a mistake, a bad mistake...'

Nicky reminds him that he broke the rules.

'Yes, I understand, I've spoken to Big Brother about it. Everyone has done things in our lives that have been a mistake and you regret it but you have to go "Fine, that's done, this is the reason." I apologize. As adults, mature people, we go "Fine," and give that person a second chance.'

Nicky says, 'So you think tomorrow me and Craig should be up for nomination and you stay? Why should me or Craig walk out the fucking door? I'm very angry. I don't think we should go, I think you should go.'

Nick tells her she would have been nominated anyway, and she agrees, but says she's done nothing wrong, apart from losing her rag a few times, but nothing in the same realm as trying to influence nominations. She calls him sly, and says, 'You think you should stay? You're a joke.'

Tom suggests that they should all talk privately to Big Brother, so that they have some input into the eventual outcome of the situation. Nick announces that he has an idea for a compromise that will enable both Nicky and Craig to stay.

He goes to the Diary Room and says: 'I would like to stay but the group are still raw with this problem. I was wondering about a compromise where I walk out on Friday and those two stay, but under the terms of me feeling that I should leave rather than face the accusations... Obviously, under the circumstances, one contestant decided he had to go rather than face the humiliation of being accused directly and being upset in my room.'

He is trying to extract a promise that the scene of his humiliation at the table will not be shown on television. Big Brother tells him that nothing is private, apart from chats with a psychotherapist. He has already requested a counselling session.

Half an hour later, the situation still unresolved, Craig goes into the Diary Room and makes the same suggestion that Nick has made. He says that because Nick has broken the rules and could have influenced the nominations, it would be fairer if Nick left and that both Nichola and he stay. He says he won't walk away too happily if he knows the rules have been broken and that person is not punished. He would lose complete faith and trust if the matter is not dealt with fairly. He tells Big Brother that if Nicholas stays, and Nichola is voted out, he will leave with her.

Outside, Nick is telling Anna that the viewers want a bit of 'skulduggery'. She asks him if he lied about the story of his wife dying, and he admits he did, but says 'one hears dozens of lies'. Anna says it is the most shocking thing of all and what she will think about when people ask her about Nick.

'This kind of environment has brought out the worst,' says Nick. 'I think it has been blown out of all proportion. Perhaps people should have told me I shouldn't do it...'

Anna stops him and lectures him briefly on the importance of taking responsibility for his own actions and not blaming other people. 'That's kiddish. You did what you did. What people are thinking deep down is "I thought he really liked me." And you didn't. I don't like some people, you don't like some people. But you took it a step further. You gave them the impression you really liked them. The flatterer.'

Nick starts to tell her: 'I think you out of all the people are the most understanding...' But before he can get any further, Anna cuts him off. 'Don't start that,' she says.

Craig is sitting on his own on the patio and Mel joins him and sits on his lap. They both reassure the other that they did not vote according to Nick's recommendations. Craig says he feels sick and wants to go home. 'Whatever happens with anyone in here, I'd love to take you out for a drink when the show is over. You can see my dogs,' says Craig.

'I'm coming,' says Mel. 'You're not stopping me.'

At twenty past four, Nicholas is called to the Diary Room to hear Big Brother's verdict. Big Brother reads out the rule about tactical voting, which finishes with the clause that 'in extreme cases we can eject you from the house'. He tells Nick this is an extreme case and that the decision has been made that he should leave. Nick bows his head and weeps.

At quarter to five, he gathers the others together to tell them what is happening. 'I shall be leaving in about fifteen minutes, at 5 o'clock. I've broken the rules so I should have to face the consequences. I do like all of you. I've been here six weeks [in fact, it's five]. I would see any of you any time. I know I've betrayed your trust with this. For me this was a competition. I wanted to go as far as possible. I did it in ways that were unnecessary on reflection. I'm sorry I've let you all down. It's been a very enjoyable six weeks. I wish you all every success for the remaining four or five weeks and for the rest of your lives.'

Tom tells him that he should be concerned for his family, not for them. Facing his family will be the hardest part. 'You have to face the music, you can't run away from things,' says Nick with a shrug.

Mel says, 'None of us are happy that you are going through this.' Nicky agrees, saying that the prospect of going out and facing people is bad enough under normal circumstances.

Craig says: 'You obviously haven't considered the aftershock this sort of behaviour can have, not just for your personal self, your selfish self, but for everyone else. To go about it that way you mustn't have had any pride, to be that two-faced. I do advise you to look into your background and work out what made you think of being that two-faced and do something about it before you go around upsetting your friends and family. Or eventually you will be on your own, you'll be lonely.'

Tom consolidates this by saying that if Nick can come out of this with a positive attitude, it could make his life a lot better. Then Craig, ever the practical one, points out that it is five to five and perhaps Nick ought to pack his things. When Nick has gone into the bedroom, he tells the others that Nick is obviously very insecure and paranoid and that they should all see him to the door and pat him on the back.

Tom goes into the boys' room to help him pack, and Nick says: 'I know the trust between us has been broken, but I hope that you at least can forgive me.'

Tom replies, 'There are two emotions I'm going through, anger and pity. I'm angry with myself that I didn't speak up sooner, that I somehow put you in that position. And pity that you have to go out there and face it.'

Nick says, 'See you on the outside if I'm not being crucified or ostracized.'

He and Craig carry Nick's bags to the gate in the garden – he is going out through the back entrance. Everyone hugs him, even Darren. The sky has been grey and heavy all afternoon, and as he leaves the heavens open and rain pours down. Outside, a car waits to whisk him away from the Three Mills site to a hotel in Hertfordshire, away from the long lenses of the press pack.

Back in the house, the others take it in turns to go to the Diary Room. Nichola comes back with chocolate fudge cake and wine, and Anna comes out to tell the others that their song performance is postponed, and they can choose a video to watch. They decide on *Stigmata*, a religious thriller.

Tom tells Big Brother that he feels he has betrayed everybody in the house, and he knows some of the others feel the same. He wants Big Brother to tell them what is happening to the nominees. Mel, who goes in ten minutes after Tom, explains to Big Brother that she also feels guilty for not nipping it in the bud earlier. She also says she is very worried about Nick and the reception he will get outside.

When they eat their evening meal, they drink a toast to him and his family with the wine that Big Brother has donated. At half past ten in the evening, they are called into the Diary Room one by one to have the decision to eject Nicholas explained. Nichola and Craig are told that they still face eviction the next day. Craig asks if there will be a replacement for Nick and is told a new housemate will arrive on Saturday. Outside, when he tells the others, they have a big group hug, and Craig jokes that the new recruit may be a transvestite from Transylvania.

When Tom sees Big Brother he praises Craig: 'I think a special word should go to Craig. He can be volatile but he showed an amazing level of control. He showed another side to him which some of us hadn't recognized before.'

Finally, the most exciting, upsetting and ultimately tiring day in the history of the *Big Brother* house draws to a close – and there is another, unexpected, empty bed in the boys' room.

The next morning, the world outside the house is going mad for Nick. His picture is on the front page of every national newspaper, and, when he faces a press conference, 130 journalists are there and twelve television cameras.

Inside what they all now describe as their 'cocoon', the housemates have no idea about his phenomenal reception and they have to get on with their own routines. It is an eviction day, when tempers are often frayed and tension runs high. However, after the events of yesterday, everyone is remarkably calm. Nichola jokes that when the new person comes they can clean out the chicken run. Craig and Mel collect eggs, which they are not allowed to eat because the hens have been ill. So instead they throw them at one another and Mel has to be hosed down to get the eggs off her clothes.

Craig tells Tom that, after a night's sleep, he feels no animosity towards Nick, and he hopes everything works out well for him. He says he will contact him when he leaves. Yesterday, he felt that, although he would not be rude if Nick contacted him, he would not initiate any meetings. Now he wonders if the whole thing was blown out of all proportion.

They are curious about the new arrival, and spend time speculating whether it will be a boy or a girl. Big Brother tells them the rules: the new person will not be up for nomination in their first week, nor will they be able to nominate. Anna and Mel agree it will be difficult when the numbers are down to five and they still have to nominate two. They also realize that whoever comes in will have difficulties.

'It's going to be hard for them to make an impact without overdoing it,' says Anna.

Mel says the new person will know a lot about them all from watching the show.

Nicky, convinced she's on her way out, starts her beauty preparations early, plucking her eyebrows and re-shaving her head, and then having a face mask and a shower. She tells Craig she's not feeling nervous, but when Darren offers her some crisps she turns them down because her stomach is churning.

Craig goes into the Diary Room during the afternoon, to announce that he's finished reading Richard Branson's autobiography, and he's feeling good, despite the eviction threat. 'I think my time's up and I'm looking forward to going, but if I manage to stay in I can go the distance. I just feel really positive. My life outside is so busy I don't get time to think and read a book.'

He says his time in the house has taught him how to handle different people in different ways. 'I tend to learn from other people's mistakes, like Nick, and I think we've all learnt a lesson here about honesty, respect and breaking the rules. I've always had a high level of honesty. I expect it and want it back.' He says it has made him realize that doing even the slightest thing to mislead people is wrong. He also says that although he specifically wanted to win the money, he's philosophical about it. He's also unsure about the prospect of being famous when he leaves the house.

'If we are famous, we haven't done anything in here. But not anyone could have done it. Five weeks is a mere fraction of a lifetime, but it's been the longest five weeks of my life. I used to think the school holidays were a lifetime, and in here I knew it would be long, but not this sort of long, because I've never been able to experience time like this. In here, having this time is amazing. I think people should set aside so many weeks, not to go on holiday, but to look back and plan ahead. It would open people's minds more.'

He hopes that things are going OK for Nick, and thinks that the pressure-cooker existence of the house made them all react more extravagantly than they would have done outside.

It is the longest talk Craig has had in the Diary Room and he has opened up more than he usually does.

Darren causes the biggest stir of the afternoon by appearing with a black bandana round his head and lapsing into Jamaican slang.

Before they get down to the serious business of the voting results, the housemates have to put on a show: their song. They've called it 'It's True' – and the lyrics for the first verse were written by Nick, so his spirit lives on with them. Dancing, singing and making music out of anything they can bang, they perform it for the cameras. The chorus, D, C and G, are the first three chords that Darren learnt in his guitar lessons from Anna and 'Veuva' is a nickname given to Nichola based on a funny little noise she makes. (All the boys have nick-names: Darren is 'the Count' or 'Me myself and I', Nick's name is Ross Hunter, the name that was thought up for the murder-mystery play, Craig is the Incredible Sleeping Man and Thomas is Mouse, a name given him by Nick who started pronouncing his name Tom-mouse, which contracted to Mouse.)

Wanna tell you about a house in Bow
Where ten people had to go
It's true, it's true

Who will stay and who will go?
Just remember it's only a show
So what, so what

D, C and G

Loving friendships all around
Feel the wonder of our sound
It's minging, it's minging

In this house we're so frustrated
It's been so long since we have dated
For weeks, for weeks

We sleep all day and talk all night
Most of the time we just talk shite
It's Veuva, it's Veuva

D, C and G

The announcement from Davina about the eviction comes soon after the song. The *Big Brother* programme has been specially extended, as it was on Thursday, to cover the extraordinary events in the house and to show an interviewDavina conducted with Nick. By the time the news comes, Nichola is sitting on Craig's lap. As soon as it is announced that Nichola is to depart, Craig hugs and kisses her, and allows only the smallest expression of relief to cross his face. Nicky's greatest fear is that there will be no friends and family there to greet her, and she asks while the live link to Davina is open, 'Who's there for me?' In the noise and confusion she gets no reply and is momentarily despondent, until the housemates rally to cheer her up. Craig picks her up and runs away with her to the bedroom for a snog. 'We should have done this weeks ago,' he tells her. She says she'll miss him and will fantasize about him.

More than a million people have voted, and 72 per cent of them chose Nichola to leave.

Mel and Anna go to the Diary Room to plead with Big Brother for extra supplies of alcohol and cigarettes to see them through the evening, as they are now down to two girls in their room. The boys follow them in, congratulate Big Brother on making it to the halfway point of the show, and add their pleas to the girls'. They are told that they must buy anything they want from next week's shopping money, so they decide to spend £12. It gives Nichola a great send off – she's quite pissed when she walks across the bridge with Davina.

Mel helps Nichola dress for her arrival in the outside world. She wears high leopard skin-boots, a tight black dress and, over the top of it, her multi-coloured wire creation. All dressed up, she fulfils her pledge to talk to Darren to tell him how much she likes him.

'I think you're absolutely fantastic. I think the world of you. What I want to say is just crack on and go for it 'cos you're brilliant. You put lots of smiles on my face, you and Caroline. I think you're wicked.' With that she stepped out to the cheers of the scores of fans awaiting her.

Back in the house, Craig goes to the Diary Room to expiate his guilt over nominating Nichola. The group discusses their best moments in the house, and he and Tom agree that surviving the eviction process, and catching a glimpse of their families, are the highest points in their stays. Mel says she constantly appreciates the special bond that has developed between them all and Anna values the warmth and support she received when she wanted to walk out.

Soon after the discussion is over, Anna goes to the bedroom. When she pulls down the duvet on her bed she finds that Nicky has left her a present: her teddy bear. It is a touching moment and tears run down Anna's face.

The late-night card-playing sessions continue, but with Nick gone it is down to Mel and Tom to take each other on. At quarter past five in the morning, they hear a noise outside in the garden – the fox is back. Tom dashes out and sees it, but it scrabbles up the wall and away. Mel follows him outside but is not in time to see the four-legged visitor.

Ten minutes later, Tom and Mel are lying on different sofas in the living room, covered with sleeping bags. Tom is questioning Mel about why she kissed Andy and she's uncomfortable. As usual, she does not enjoy answering questions about herself.

She says she did not want Andy to go and seriously thought about walking out. But she insists she did not kiss Andy – he kissed her. Tom then tells her that he feels attracted to someone in the house, and he does not know how to approach the subject because he does not want to lose a friendship. As there are only two women in the house – and one is a lesbian – it's obvious that he means Mel. Eventually, he drops the pretext of talking hypothetically, and admits he finds her attractive. He asks if that upsets her.

'You're making me blush,' she tells him.

'How do you think I feel?' he says.

WEEK FIVE FACT FILE

MAIN TASK **PASS ☑ FAIL ■**	Assault course.
MINI-TASKS	Write poems about each other. Solve riddles. (They received pizza and pop for completing this successfully.) Write a pop song.
PARTIES	Nichola's orange masquerade party.
BOOKIES' FAVOURITE **TO WIN**	Anna remains the clear favourite at 2/1, with Darren second at 5/2. Craig has risen spectacularly from a 20/1 outsider to become third favourite at 4/1.
TO WALK	Tom and Mel are joint favourites at 9/2.

WHAT THE EXPERT SAYS

Nick managed to avoid being rumbled for five weeks. 'He tried to find out where people were coming from and then build on that. People love talking about themselves. It's a control thing. The more you let someone talk about themselves the more you know about them. He realized who everybody wanted to be and he allowed them to be just that person when he was with them. He played them. He also conducted his conversations intimately; it's much easier to show yourself up in a group.'

Linda Papadopoulos, Counselling Psychologist

NICHOLA LOOKS BACK

Nicky's departure is frenetic. Arriving in the studio after a rapturous welcome from the crowds outside, she hugs and kisses her own family and then makes a beeline for Craig's to tell them all that he loves them. She tells Davina that she was ready to leave. And she's delighted to discover that she's going to have six weeks training with a circus – there are belly dancers, jugglers and acrobats there to greet her when she leaves the studio at the end of the programme.

On Saturday, Nichola faces the press and insists that her departure from the house has not been overshadowed by Nick's ejection. But most of the questions directed at her are about Nick.

'I was quite upset to find my name and Craig's name had gone around the house on a piece of paper. But me and Craig were both prepared for eviction, we expected it. What went on with Nick has been going on for weeks, and at the end of the day the people in the house did what they wanted to, not what Nick told them to do.'

Asked to sum up Nick in three words, she says: 'Liar, confused, dreamer.'

She says she bears him no ill will. 'What he did was quite bizarre, but it's no crime, no big deal. He played a game, broke the rules and got caught... He really wanted to win. Perhaps he had to prove something to someone, maybe his family. But he hasn't hurt me.

'I would never be able to trust him again, so I don't think I'll be taking up his offer of somewhere to stay in London. We spent a lot of time yesterday trying to work out who he is. Is he really a reiki master? Is he this? Is he that? We don't know the truth of anything anymore.'

After the press conference, Nicky talks about life inside the *Big Brother* experience.

'It was the weirdest few weeks of my life. But it's time to leave. I have things to do, and I didn't feel I could create much more in there. The saddest thing for me, more upsetting than what he did with the nominations, is hearing that Nick intended taking my artwork down when I left. He was always so complimentary about it, always encouraging me and telling me it looked lovely. It is so disappointing to hear that he wanted to destroy it. Anybody who destroys something that has been created destroys its energy and its magic – to me, that's much worse than breaking the rules of *Big Brother*.'

Nichola was really moved to find that her mother, her sister, her cousin and the landlord of the pub where she works behind the bar were all there to meet her when she came out of the house. She is very close to her mother and her sister but it has not always been an easy relationship. Nicky admits that her years of heavy drug use drove a wedge between her and her family, which she regrets. 'They were worried about me doing *Big Brother*, so I was surprised that they turned up. It made me so happy to see them. I know I've hurt them in the past but I can't regret the way I've lived my life because it has made me who I am. I knew my dad wouldn't come, because he's a very private person.

'I've taken lots of drugs, everything except crack. I've injected heroin two or three times, but I found it the most boring, pointless drug in the world, it stopped me being creative. I've taken lots of Es – at one time I was taking ten or twenty a week. I've been on lots of LSD trips. I've done the lot. I've had kidney failure through drugs. I was in intensive care for four days that time. I'd taken a cocktail of drugs and collapsed in a club. I was in a coma and saw my whole life, from the womb through to dying, pass before my eyes, and I really did think I was dying. I saw heaven, hell, the devil. I was surprised to wake up. I've been told that if I use drugs heavily again I'll kill myself.

'My sister told me that the day I started using drugs was the day she lost me as a sister and that's the thing that has hurt me most. But now we're close again and I wish I could undo all the things we said to each other in those bad years.

'I don't do drugs anymore – maybe once a month, if I'm with mates and I want to stay up all night and someone's got some speed, yes. But now I enjoy drinking champagne and having a nice meal – that's much better than the come-down from drugs.'

Nicky's shaven head was the subject of a lot of speculation across the nation, with many viewers echoing Darren's comment that she could be very pretty if she had hair. But being bald is proof to Nicky that she is finally happy with herself, after ten years of suffering from the eating disorder bulimia.

'I've had hair, and I know I can be a lot more attractive with hair. But when I was bulimic, I was very self-critical. If one hair was out of place I couldn't go out. Now, if I haven't got hair, it's one less thing to be self-critical about. I enjoy being bald. It's freed me from worrying about hair and buying mousse and gel and paying for hairdressers to do it. I know I can look good with a shaved head, and if I can look good bald I can look good with any hairstyle. Also, if someone loves me when I'm bald, they love me for me. If I sleep with someone, they don't get a shock about the way I look the next morning, because I look exactly the same as the night before.'

One of her past relationships came back to haunt her in the days immediately following her eviction from the house. The Sunday papers carried details of her being involved in a three-in-a-bed situation with a girl and a man.

'I have had relationships with women in the past. I describe myself as bisexual, and if an attractive woman comes on to me and I fancy her, why not? But I definitely prefer men. This girl made a play for me in a club and my boyfriend of the time took us both back to his place. But after a week or so, he got off with her and I was excluded, and that's all there is to it. I'm just sorry that dragging it all up upsets my parents.'

If this was the downside of coming out, there are compensations. She is really looking forward to her circus training and hopes to be able to improve her trapeze skills. In the long-term, she wants a career designing costumes for television or theatrical productions.

She believes that in ten years' time, Caroline and Sada will still be part of her life.

'I hope I will see them all, and if I move to live in London, I hope we can meet up on a regular basis. *Big Brother* may only have lasted a few weeks, but it made up a big part of all our lives.

'Caroline is very special to me, and I think we're going to remain very close. I'd love to see Darren again, he's wicked. He loves himself, but I love people who love themselves. He can be self-centred and selfish, but I love him for all his bad points because he makes up for it with his wit and energy.

'Craig and I have got plans to go clubbing together. He's a great guy, like a brother. I love him to bits. I think he must be a wicked son to his mum and a fantastic uncle. He's a very special guy, very focused, knows what he wants, but still very playful.

'Sada and I really connected on a spiritual and creative level. She is also a very creative person and she understood my need to be creative in there. Anna is a great mate and I'd love to see her for a few drinks.

'Mel is very beautiful but I never got deep enough with her. I'd love to know the real Mel but she doesn't let you get close. She's very logical, very in tune with her masculine side, which is hard for me to understand because I'm much more in tune with my feminine side.

'Andy is the one I connected least with. He talked about sex all the time, but he was really very straight. He was trying to be all things to everybody – he wanted the romance, he wanted the gay vote, he wanted to be in charge of everything. He was too busy controlling the game to play the game.

'Tom I were OK on a one-to-one basis but he was very private. You could fish for information from him but you often didn't get any feedback. But as time goes on, he opens up more and when there are fewer people in the house he will be even better.

Speaking about Nick she says: 'I hope Nick is all right. I think he has problems and he should get help but I hope in the end that everything works out for him.'

Nicky describes the whole *Big Brother* experience as 'wicked' and says she would do it all again – she has no regrets. She believes the production team looked after all the contestants 'fantastically'.

'They really care about us, they did everything possible for us, and we felt completely safe.'

Her main problem going into the house was 'doing a poo with the camera watching me'.

The first couple of times she wore a big sweater and pulled it up over her head. 'But that wore off very quickly. You get bored worrying about it. Everyone else just got on with it, so in the end you just forget the cameras.'

NICK'S EVICTION

A week before Nick was ejected from the house, the senior members of the production team held a daylong meeting to draw up plans for how they would handle the day when he left. It was clear from the near-hysteria of the popular press that however he went, whether he was nominated and voted out, or walked out, or, as happened, he was asked to leave, it was going to be very different from the normal Friday night evictions. Media interest was going to be overwhelming and contingency plans for dealing with it were needed. More importantly, there was the effect on Nick of coming out to discover that he had been turned into the nation's favourite hate-figure. He could find it very hard to deal with. All the contestants have counselling and support when they leave and the television company offers them a personal manager to handle the business offers and requests for interviews that come flooding in. It was obvious that this interest would be multiplied by a factor of ten at least in the case of Nick.

So, the meeting came up with contingency plans which involved double-booking hotels, having dummy cars ready to lead the press pack astray, booking cars with blacked-out windows, having extra security men on standby and making sure that a psychotherapist was available to spend as long as needed with Nick.

Throughout the week before he left, Nick's future within *Big Brother* was under constant discussion. Even though he managed to avoid the eagle eyes of the cameras when he showed written notes to other contestants, it was clear that he was breaking the rules by persistently discussing nominations. He had been given both a verbal and written warning, and neither had worked. How much longer his behaviour could be tolerated was a matter for debate.

However, in the early hours of Thursday, 17 August, the residents of the house took over the decision-making process from the production team once again. When Darren pulled the notes out from Nick's suitcase and showed them to Craig, it was clear that exciting events were in train. The immediate fear was that violence might break out and because of this, the website was closed down for two hours. In retrospect, the production team regret this and regard it as a mistake. The whole idea of *Big Brother* was that it should be played out in public, be transparent, even in its worst aspects. Nonetheless, the decision to close the website was made in the middle of the night in a crisis.

Closing the web, especially after the events which preceded its shutdown, alerted the press to the fact that something big was happening. When Craig went into the Diary Room to talk to Big Brother, he was advised to sleep on the problem and bring it up at the house meeting the next day. As well as allowing tempers to cool, this bought time for everyone at the Three Mills site to begin to put their contingency plans into operation.

By eight o'clock the next morning, Ruth Wrigley, the executive producer, Conrad Green, the series editor and Liz Warner, commissioning editor for Channel 4, were at the *Big Brother* site, watching the tape of the night-time activity. All the key players in the Nick Action Plan were alerted: the psychotherapist, Keith Woodhams, whose services as agent are offered to each housemate when they leave, and Matt Baker, head of the press office at Channel 4 who would have to deal with the enormous press interest. Hotels were booked, cars organized, extra security men drafted in, and production staff contacted on their days off and asked to come in. Even before the house meeting, it was clear that something major was going to happen and that the chances of Nick still being in the house by nightfall were slim.

By the time the meeting in the house started, there was a growing band of reporters and photographers gathered by the gate to the house (there is a public right of way along the footpath on the riverbank). The senior production team watched the meeting and decided soon afterwards that they were going to have to ask Nick to leave. He was not told immediately as it was important to get the cars on to the site.

'We did not want to tell him too early and leave him to stew, but, on the other hand, we knew we had to tell him with time to talk to the others and say goodbye,' says Liz Warner. 'Five o'clock was the time we decided to bring him out and we gave him about forty minutes to organize himself in there.'

When he did walk out, through the garden door so that he did not have to cross the bridge of shame, he was shepherded into a car, where Ruth Wrigley was waiting for him. He travelled with her, the counsellor and Matt Baker to a hotel in Hertfordshire. The decoy-car ruse worked and the press did not track them down until the next day (the *Sun* arrived by helicopter). They were joined at the hotel by Keith Woodhams, Jonathan Francis, who had been the liaison with Nick's friends and family throughout the programme, and one of Nick's closest friends.

(When the press pack did arrive and lined up outside the hotel with their telephoto lenses trained on the door, it caused consternation for the father of a bride who was having her wedding reception there. As he stepped out of the car and saw the battery of cameras, he turned to his wife and said, 'Dorothy, I told you one photographer was enough. What's this lot costing?')

In the meantime, there were programmes to be produced. Liz Warner quickly decided that the day's events merited an extra long programme that night, so the half-hour slot was doubled to an hour.

Although she is in charge of ten other projects as well as *Big Brother*, throughout the weeks of its run she was based at the Three Mills site and on the day when Nick's activities were exposed she worked for twenty-four hours on the production of the show. Although extra staff came in, everybody was working frenetically to keep pace with events and to prepare the enlarged programme. The internet site, already Britain's favourite site, trebled its normal traffic to 7.4 million hits and 8 million tuned in to the live video stream (more than treble the normal 2.5 million).

A decision had to be made about the nominations. With Craig and Nichola both up for eviction, would the vote be held over for another week? Or should the show stick by its own rules and carry on? Public voting dried up on Thursday night and most of Friday as the public were unsure what was happening. The television trails, giving the telephone numbers for voting, had been pulled off air in case it was decided not to go ahead with the eviction. Liz Warner argued strenuously in favour of carrying on with the vote and she was backed by Ruth Wrigley (who stayed with Nick for most of Friday). It was then a matter for Liz to persuade the senior staff at Channel 4, who were in favour of letting both Craig and Nichola stay on for a week, that the eviction vote should go ahead. Ultimately, she prevailed and by the time the early Friday evening programme (also doubled in size) came on air and the voting telephone numbers were given again, the telephone lines went mad. It was the biggest surge in voting for any programme. At the beginning of the show there was only 10 per cent difference between Nichola (who had 55 per cent) and Craig, however, by the time the lines closed, it was 72 per cent wanting Nicky to go and only 28 per cent wanting Craig out. His exponential rise in popularity was the obvious result of his commanding performance at the confrontation with Nick.

It was decided on Thursday evening that the extra-long programme on Friday would include an interview with Nick and Davina McCall was diverted from normal rehearsals for the evening show to go to the hotel to question him on Friday morning. An extra film crew had to be booked and it was an early call for Davina, organized so much at the last minute that make-up for her had to be bought at the local Tesco.

After the interview with Davina, Nick faced the press – 130 journalists turned up to cover the press conference on Friday afternoon and there were 12 television cameras there. The *Big Brother* information line, normally receiving 2000 calls a day, was up to 15,000. Keith Woodhams, who was reacting to all commercial interest for Nick, took 360 calls in four hours. Eventually, because the demand was so great, it was decided that his interests needed to be looked after by another manager too.

'The atmosphere was incredible for the whole two days,' says Liz Warner. 'Because it goes out live on the net, people knew what was happening in the house as soon as we did. I was taking lots of phone calls from friends and colleagues, all lobbying me not to let Nick come out, or not to go ahead with the eviction, or whatever. I've never known a programme which involved people like this one did. I really thought the days of 'water-cooler television', where everyone discussed the same programmes in the office the next day, were gone, simply because with so many channels viewing it is much more fragmented than it used to be. But *Big Brother* proved me wrong.

'The programme has had a profound effect on the people who work for it. Normally, when you go home at night from a television programme, you leave a lot of rushes in the edit suite, ready to pick up again the next morning where you left off. With this show, you leave a group of human beings in a house and it's impossible to cut off from them in the same way. And by the time you get into work the next day, they may have done and said things which completely change what you thought you were leaving the night before.'

When the early programme went on air on that Friday evening, it had 6.3 million viewers, a 29 per cent share of the whole tele-watching total and the highest figure ever for *Big Brother*. The 11 o'clock show, when Nicky walked out of the house, had 4.8 million viewers, a 36 per cent share. Across the whole day, Channel Four had an 18.5 per cent share of all viewing, compared to their normal average of 10 per cent (and against normal BBC and ITV figures of 27 to 30 per cent).

Every national newspaper covered the end of Nick's time in the house, with the tabloids devoting acres of space (in the case of the more downmarket tabloids, the whole of their front pages) to it, and the broadsheets carrying intellectual pieces comparing him to Machiavelli and analysing what it is about the public imagination that is so captured by a villain.

Nick's first major business deal was to secure an exclusive series in the *Sun* (which for several weeks had been labelling itself 'the official *Big Brother* paper', without any justification), but that did little to quench the interest of the rest of the media. He was forced to move hotel twice because of other reporters tracking him down (in the case of the *Daily Mirror*, even infiltrating his protective entourage).

In his interview with Davina McCall, he stressed that he was taking part in a game show and that he went into it with a strategy to win and that he selected the names for his nominations on the basis of who was valuable to the team. He admitted playing 'mind games' with people.

'In that kind of arena there is psychological warfare,' he said. 'My over-competitiveness came through in a bad light.'

The whole confrontation was magnified, he said, because the group was bored and 'a small thing became a huge mountain'. He said he had no hard feelings towards any of the others and would be happy to see them again. He described *Big Brother* as 'an extraordinary and fascinating show that has turned me into Nasty Nick'.

A week later, when he had had some time to reflect on everything, he talked about the fundamental change to his life wrought by *Big Brother*.

'I'm still not sure what it all means. I'm not enjoying living out of a suitcase but I think it will be a while before I can go back to my own house. There's no sign of it calming down.'

The previous evening he had attended the premier of the movie *Snatch*, and found himself upstaging Brad Pitt and Vinnie Jones. The crowd went wild for him and it was all cheering, no booing.

'It was incredible, an amazingly positive reception. I find most people are really supportive. Since my mobile phone number was given out by a radio station and broadcast on the internet, it has never stopped ringing and there have been very few nasty calls. I feel sad for the other contestants who have already left the house because this interest in me eclipses them all. When they do get interviewed by the press they get asked questions about me.

'I've been out for a drink with Andrew and I assumed people would recognize both of us but they only realized it was him later, after they spotted me. I've discovered that a baseball cap and dark glasses are not enough to stop people recognizing me. It was good to see Andy, we share a sense of humour, and only someone else who has been in there can really understand what it was like.

'The version of *Big Brother* you see on television is edited and it misses out a lot of the pressure of being in there. Sleep deprivation is the main thing and the food is like being a student, you have to eat lots of cheap stuff. The lights are the worst thing. You are literally living in a studio within a studio and even the chickens became disorientated. I worked out that I had 160 hours sleep in the forty days I was in there, an average of four hours a night. Some people could sleep during the day, but I couldn't.

'We had discussion topics set by Big Brother but these were often almost moronic. We had much better discussions when we came up with our own subjects. I came up with these and Darren also had ideas.'

Nick never completely forgot the presence of the cameras. In fact, he was so aware of them that he gave them all names. Charlie, one of the cameras in the garden, was his favourite, because one day he and Tom got a reaction from it.

'It shook its head at us – only once, never again. Arthur, the camera in the washroom, was the coolest, really dinky and smooth, and made this little whining noise when he turned. Cuthbert and Cecil were the ones in the garden, really boring because they were just viewing the landscape all day. Cassandra was the one in the living area, near the television screen.'

He also saw the cameramen behind the glass occasionally. 'They looked very sinister, draped in black. Occasionally, you'd be woken in the night by the sound of noises in the camera run.'

He claims to have identified three blind spots in the house, where the cameras could not penetrate.

'There is a place in the garden, near where we put the cargo net, where, if you lie down, you are out of camera range. There is a place in the boys' bedroom, near the door, and against the lockers. Also, to the left of the shower unit.

'It was just fun finding them, not anything sinister. There were times when you felt the need not to be seen. Times when you felt the lack of privacy more acutely.'

He was the first of the household to use the loo on the day they arrived and admits he peed in the shower, 'I think all men do that.'

He admits going to considerable lengths to talk to the others without it being picked up on the microphones.

'If you tapped on the microphone just as you were speaking, they wouldn't hear. And if you let it drop down, by the time they realized and told you to fix it back on properly you could say what you wanted to. It was if you wanted to talk about other people in the house or if perhaps you wanted to tell someone something that you didn't want to share with five million viewers.'

The housemates were always aware of the noise of planes and trains. 'It was very comforting, knowing there were people on those trains going to work or going on holiday in the planes. It reminded us that life was still going on outside. It would have been much worse if we had been in the middle of the countryside with no noises.'

He would have liked to have stayed longer, but is, in the event, glad he left when he did. 'Ironically, I've given up one form of imprisonment for another – I'm holed up because of my fame. Now that I'm outside, I don't miss the inside at all.

'The whole confrontation in the house came as a shock to me. It was a lynch mob, a kangaroo court. I felt like a trapped animal with nowhere to run to, and my stomach was dropping away. It is not like me to cry in public, but it was the sheer shock of it all.

'Coming outside and finding out what the press had been saying about me was another shock. I only got two hours sleep on Thursday night and when I saw all the press coverage on Friday I felt very low. I was tired, and susceptible to criticism. But when I got to the press conference I loved it, really enjoyed it. I told the journalists that how they portray me is not how I portray myself.'

'Of course, I was worried about my family and friends, but I knew that the people who really know me would realize that it wasn't the real me that was being talked about and written about. I didn't contact my family at first, partly because a newspaper had managed to hack into my voicemail on my mobile phone and partly because I needed time to stand back from it all, take a few deep breaths, try to make some sense of it. When I did speak to my mother and sisters, they were all very concerned about me and wanted to see me as soon as possible.'

He tried to rationalize his actions: 'Everybody in the house was not telling the truth 100 per cent of the time. It's like men in pubs, boasting about the size of the fish that got away. That's all. Nothing worse than that. I did apologize to Mel and Tom for telling an untrue story, but by then the damage had been done.'

Nick is proud of the fact that he never received a nomination. 'They all liked me and I'd be happy to meet any of them again and have a drink with them. I think Andy, Tom and Mel are the only ones I will maintain as friends, particularly Andy. My game plan was working, that's why I was never nominated, and at some stage I'd have stopped showing notes. If I'd known how much they all liked me I might have played it differently, but I have no regrets.

'We had no control of what was going out and people became increasingly paranoid about it. The lack of food, lack of sleep and the Trojans bellowing at the gate [fans who shouted things that the contestants occasionally heard] fed the paranoia. We knew it was a TV show and they didn't want pictures of us all having tea at four o'clock in the afternoon and a jolly singsong. We knew they would pick negative things.

'Everyone was concerned about it, although some of them didn't express it. If you went into the Diary Room they would never give you an answer as to how it was being seen outside.

'When Andy gave me his cigarettes, I shared one with Tom and I later gave some to the girls. That wasn't shown. Nor were the girls shown guzzling down wine and chocolates in their room and not sharing them with the rest of us.'

Most of the housemates believe the pencil he used for the famous notes was one that went missing after a task. Nick denies this.

'I took it in with me. I picked it up in the hotel where I spent my last night and without thinking I put it in the pocket of my jacket. It fell through a hole into the lining. I knew it was there and I thought it would come in useful because I wanted to write a diary while I was in there.'

Learning to share with nine strangers was not too difficult 'because I've been to boarding school'. He says alcohol was a constant problem because 'it was just hoovered down'.

'In the first week I think we completely underestimated how much food ten people would need. Also, we knew they would never let us starve. But it was very annoying that the vegetarians were given extra food – we weren't given extra Mars bars or baked beans.'

He's now hoping to capitalize on his high media profile. 'There are lots of avenues opening up for me. I hoped the show would give me a new career but I didn't rely on it. Now I think it has. I want to write my own version of events. Remember: we are here tomorrow but our dreams may not be.'

He is not planning to take his seat at Fulham football ground for some time. 'Football crowds are fickle and can be vitriolic. They turn on their own people very easily. I think I'll stick to following their progress on the internet for the moment.'

Another downside is that he thinks relationships with girls will become trickier. 'I'm going to be reticent about entering into a relationship. When you are a public figure you have to ask whether people like you because of that or because of who you really are.'

However, on the plus side he is loving signing autographs, having been an autograph-hunter himself as a child.

'I always daydreamed about signing autographs. I love doing it. And I love talking to all the people who ring my mobile number to give me support. I know some famous people turn on their fans but I think that is wrong.'

Despite having experienced 'the full kaleidoscope of human emotions, from happiness to sadness to joy to despair' he says he would do it all again.

He goes on to talk about his housemates: 'I was very worried about Tom at first and within the first few days I told Andy that he was so unhappy I thought he would walk out. He was monosyllabic. But I spotted early on that the way to bring him out was to get him to join in playing cards and it worked. At first, none of us could understand his accent and he was very aware of us constantly asking him to repeat what he said. In the end, he let his guard down and became more boisterous. The turning point for him was when he was nominated and I told him not to take it lying down, but to go into the Diary Room and plead his case – which he did, to great effect. That's why it was hard to believe he turned on me. He was never good mates with Craig, yet he had that bedroom chat with Craig. I thought he could have said it to me because we were good companions.

'I got on well with Caroline. Much has been made of the fact that I was two-faced, talking to her after nominating her and saying the same things to her as to Sada. But when two people have suffered the same problem, naturally you comfort them in the same way. Having lots of sisters, I am used to the company of women and it is easy for me to comfort them. She had her bad points – she was very loud and in a small environment that's hard on other people. But she had a really good heart.

'She and Sada both took it far too personally when they were nominated, instead of realizing it was just a numbers thing. Sada was the nearest to me in background and I think, as far as the production team was concerned, she was the choice for me, romantically. But there was no interest on either side. She was very unhappy. She didn't enjoy the experience at all. She couldn't adapt to the life in there and she was greatly relieved to leave. She was used to having her own way and her creature comforts.

'Nicky was the most temperamental. One minute she was really high, the next really low. There was no equilibrium. She spent a lot of time away from the group, doing her own thing. She was a maverick personality. She behaved extraordinarily on the day Caroline left and although she improved slightly afterwards, it was probably just the lull before the storm. She didn't fit in and she knew people were anxious about her behaviour, so she was glad to go.

'I talked a lot to Craig, he was full of stories about his life, his holiday antics and romantics. He's not the quickest man on earth, but his heart is in the right place.

'Anna is intelligent, calculating, perhaps slightly devious. She's intellectually bored and didn't get on particularly well with the other girls. After Sada and Caroline left, she became the Queen Bee but she was always waiting in the wings, like an understudy, for that role. Out of all the women in there, she was the only one you could have a proper conversation with about all subjects.

'Mel uses her sexuality for her own agenda. She gets men hooked. She likes to ask questions but she doesn't like to give answers to questions. She never went with the girls so she was a Judas within her own ranks, a Judas personality.

'Darren was on the one hand very mature for his age, with his head screwed on, and obviously a very loving father to his children. But on the other hand, he could be very childish and churlish. He was very sycophantic to the women, making them banana fritters. He talked about himself a lot, so I nicknamed him 'me, myself and I'. He refused to give me much personal information about himself and he could be very touchy, like on the occasion when I joked that people might mistake him for a drug dealer. Sometimes I got on really well with him and sometimes I just wanted to knock him over the head with a pillow.'

WEEK SIX

*'It's not as though you're sending
someone to the electric chair.'*

CLAIRE ON NOMINATIONS

18 TO 25 AUGUST

The sadness at losing another of the housemates is lessened this time by the excitement – and worry – about the arrival of someone new in their midst. In the early hours of Saturday morning, both Anna and Craig tell Big Brother how much they are looking forward to it.

'I think the next person will have a big impact. It will be very strange... I feel that someone new from outside will create a spark. God help the new person... I don't think I would like to be in their shoes. They know all about us but they will be a stranger to us. We are all looking forward to seeing who it is. A fresh start should make the time go quicker,' says Craig.

Anna also says they will all be glad to meet someone fresh. 'Someone we can all bully,' she jokes. She, too, says that it is going to be very hard for the newcomer.

The next morning they are given their new task, described by Big Brother as 'a test of memory and reaction speed'. They have to record and memorize in sequence a series of large photographs which will be held up over the garden wall, all pictures of the ten original contestants plus the new arrival. Every time a head appears a klaxon will sound, and the only time they can guarantee there will be no heads is between 3 a.m. and 9 a.m. They decide quite quickly to wager the full 50 per cent of their shopping money on the task.

They notice that Nick's picture is still hanging on the wall with the other portraits they painted. Anna jokes that she feels drawn to him, and Darren asks why the ears are not attached to the head. 'Because he never listened,' Mel says.

The task starts almost immediately, and the first face to appear over the wall is Caroline's. What is most exciting for the housemates, though, is the realization that a real person is holding the sticks which support the head. They call out 'human being, human being', and the disembodied head responds by doing a little jig. Each head that appears is recorded on a master board with a tiny copy of the photograph.

At 1.25 p.m., Mel comes out of the Diary Room with some important information. She has been told that the new arrival is a woman. One by one, they are all called in to be given the same news and some coaching on the ground rules of how to behave towards her. Craig and Tom have to be brought from their beds.

Big Brother tells them: 'It's not based on gender, but the best person for the house. She will enter the house either today or tomorrow. For the first week, she can't nominate or be nominated because she needs the same period of grace that you had, and you need to give her a chance...You can't talk to her about anything after July 15, the day you came in to the *Big Brother* house. You can't ask leading or abstract questions like "How do you think I'm perceived?" You can ask her what she did in spring but you can't ask what she did two weeks ago. You can't ask her viewing figures. We've all seen the mess that can happen when people push the rules. We don't want to have to deal with that again, so follow the spirit of the rules and not just the wording. We know that the rules may be broken by accident, but we will clamp down hard if it is deliberate.'

Outside, Darren is initially delighted by the news, and dashes around singing, 'We're getting a girl.' Mel looks slightly shocked by the news and Anna says her heart goes out to whoever it is.

'It will be awful. We'll have to make it nice for their little stay. It's probably going to be someone quite mature, a mature lady.'

Melanie describes the prospect of opening the door and encountering a stranger as 'weird', and she and Anna discuss which bed she is going to sleep in. Thomas says, 'God help her,' and when the others agree he modifies it to 'God help her, some other person has to meet Darren.' They laugh, which breaks the tension of the sombre moment, and Craig makes everyone a cup of tea.

The lads discuss initiation rites, debating whether they should insist she walks in naked. Craig has a plan: 'We could really wind her up. Tell her that the rules are for her to give us a massage every morning and every night. And do the cleaning!'

Darren goes to the Diary Room and tells Big Brother, 'We are hoping she can bring out excitement in us. We feel that we won't be able to lounge around. She will lift us back up, shake us up. We are not bored but it is going to be exciting finding out about someone new.'

WHO IS THE NEW HOUSEMATE?

FULL NAME	Claire Strutton
AGE	25
DATE OF BIRTH	15.9.74
STAR SIGN	Virgo
HEIGHT	5 feet 10 inches
WEIGHT	10 stone 7 lb
DRESS SIZE	12
PIERCINGS AND TATTOOS	Belly button piercing
CLAIRE'S FAVOURITE SONG	No favourite but likes 'Optimistic' (Sound of Blackness) and 'Little Bit of Luck' (MC Neat and DJ Luck)
BOOK	*Mr Nice* by Howard Marks
FILM	*Sixth Sense*
AMBITION	Doesn't really have one.
WHAT'S IN HER SUITCASE?	Two bottles of wine, cooking sauces, 200 cigarettes (although she doesn't smoke)

Claire is 25, and comes from Gerrards Cross, Buckinghamshire. Before *Big Brother* she was running a florist's shop for her mum: she belongs to a family empire of flower shops. Although she loved the job, she had already decided to leave before being whisked into the house: she is planning to do an I.T. course and work in the computer industry.

'Being a florist brings you into contact with people at both the happiest and saddest times of their lives.' she says. 'But I feel it wasn't stretching me enough. I went into it to help Mum out, and six years later I was still doing it. I also started to get very attached to some of my older customers, and was getting very sad when they died.

'I grew up with flowers. I'd spend my weekends and evenings after school doing hundreds of buttonholes for weddings. I love flowers, but I feel I should do something different.'

She's been going out with her boyfriend, a mechanic and semi-professional ice hockey player, for ten years, since they met at an ice rink. He is six months older than her. She first saw him when she was thirteen, but didn't start going out with him seriously until two weeks before her sixteenth birthday. 'He was my first proper boyfriend,' she says. 'When I first saw him, it was like being hit with a thunderbolt.'

It's been a stormy relationship: they've broken up three times, once because she caught him in bed with another girl. She took a hammer to his VW Golf and did 'a substantial amount of damage – he's never told me what it cost'. The next day, she was driving to her mother's home for a comforting hug when she ploughed her car into a skip full of concrete, fracturing her skull in three places, and landing herself in hospital for a week. Six weeks later, she was back with her boyfriend, and they lived together for a year.

'But I could never completely trust him, he's such a ladies' man.'

Then Claire discovered that she has coeliac disease, which means she is allergic to wheat, and which was making her tired and irritable. She moved out of her boyfriend's home, and she found another boyfriend. The relationship lasted eight months, ending six months before she went into the *Big Brother* house. Predictably, as soon as it was over, she was back with her previous boyfriend.

Claire's family life is complicated. When she was eight, her parents' marriage broke up, after her mum Mandy discovered that her husband and Claire's dad, Bob, was having an affair with Mandy's younger sister, Zoe. It caused ructions at the time, and for seven years Mandy and Bob did not speak, but the dust has settled and Zoe and Bob are happily married, with two young sons, including baby Josh who was born on the day when Claire went into the house. Her mum Mandy now gets on well with them, and the whole family goes on joint holidays.

'It was difficult for a while, but Mum and Dad always said that their love for me and my brother Mark was more important than any animosity they had for each other.'

At first after the break-up Claire and Mark, who is now twenty-three and fast becoming a successful DJ, lived with Mandy, but they now live with Bob and Zoe, after their mum moved away from the area where they grew up.

'My family is really cool. My half-brother has exactly the same family and upbringing as me. My brother is also my cousin, and my step-mum is my aunt.' Her step-mum's six-year-old and the new baby are both her half-brothers and her nephews. Claire describes babysitting the six-year-old as the most difficult job she has ever done 'because he's the sneakiest, most cunning six-year-old I know. He's so smart I can't wait to see what he makes of his life when he's grown up.'

She's big mates with her forty-five-year-old mum: they often go out together, and Mandy has nicknamed her daughter 'Saffy' after the character played by Julia Sawalha in *Absolutely Fabulous*. 'She's always trying to make her mum behave better – and so am I,' says Claire, who describes her mum as 'a nutter' and her dad as 'a softie'.

'Mum's a real adventurer. She's got her pilot's licence and her yacht master certificate. She takes after my nan, who's just as mad. One of my favourite memories of when Mum was on her own after Dad left is of all her friends coming round and getting ready to go out at our house, with Shalamar blaring, and everyone dancing. I loved it. Our house was always full of music.'

The marital upheavals of her parents is not the only skeleton to emerge from Claire's cupboard. Her uncle is serving a seven-year sentence for smuggling cannabis, and one of her cousins has also had problems with the law.

'I can't be responsible for what others in my family do. My close family are all law-abiding.'

She also stunned the others in the house, and gave them something to talk about for hours, by announcing that she had a boob job last year, boosting her measurements from 34C to 34D.

'I waited ten years to have it done, so it wasn't a rush decision. One of my breasts was bigger than the other which meant my bra strap was always sliding down, and they were both, I felt, too small for my body. So I had them evened up and enlarged. It cost £4,000 and I'm still paying for it. But I reckon it was worth it.'

She's also got a pierced belly button.

Claire was educated at boarding school for two years, and then at a private girls' day school, where she passed nine GCSEs, and is remembered for landing the whole class in trouble by daubing paint over a teacher's marking book. After school she did a year at a crammer and passed two A-levels, in Maths and Physics. She's had lessons in the piano and the double bass. She describes herself as 'scatty, with a hedge-hopper mind, moody at times, abrupt when unnecessary but also level-headed. Not too much fazes me.'

Although she's far from stupid, she's used to people thinking she's dim. 'I remember when my mum pinned my GCSE results on the wall, a boy from my group of friends came round and said "Where did you get that printed? It can't be yours." I asked him why not and he said "Because you're stupid." I realized then that people don't see me as bright.'

It could be because she laughs and fools around so much. According to friends and family, she's thoughtful and happy to accept criticism, is cheerful, never moans and sees the funny side of most situations.

'I can be selfish, smug and rude.' she says.

Although she's pathologically late herself, she hates others to be late. She loves juicy gossip, and she can be a bit lazy. But she has not been lazy as far as her career goes: she was thrown into the deep end of running the shop five years ago, and is proud of the success she has made of it.

She doesn't have any deep ambitions: she simply wants 'to be the best I can... and to never have any regrets, or be the cause of someone's misery or disappointment.'

She plays every week for a league netball team, watches her boyfriend playing ice hockey regularly and enjoys singing and doing puzzles.

Her favourite film is *Sixth Sense*, but she also likes *First Knight*: 'the bit where he catches them kissing, and the bit where he dies – I guess I'm a romantic fool.' Her favourite book is *Mr Nice*, by Howard Marks.

She says that if her life story was to be portrayed in a film, she'd choose Meg Ryan or Julia Roberts to play her 'because both are "nice but dim" experts.'

Before going into the house she was worried about the twenty-four-hour filming 'because I could find out I'm not normal. What a prospect to look forward to, finding you're a loony in front of the whole country.' Using the loo and the shower under the all-seeing eye of the cameras doesn't bother her because she's used to chatting to friends while in the loo. And she sees being cut off from the outside world 'as a chance to take a break from the madness and see life in a new environment.'

Claire did not know she was going into the Big Brother house until Saturday morning. Ever since Nick was ejected, the production team had been going through the ten names they had in reserve. They decided the replacement should be a girl, to help balance the numbers in the house, and Claire's ebullient personality made her a good choice to take over in difficult circumstances. Nick's dismissal was much more dramatic than a contestant choosing to leave, and coming, as it did, halfway through the series, meant that the others inside the house already knew each other very well.

When Claire was called she was given one hour to pack and get ready – she's complained since that she packed so hurriedly she took the wrong clothes. Then she was whisked away to be briefed, photographed, and taken to the Big Brother set. Massed ranks of photographers watched her go in – a bigger turn out than five weeks earlier, when all ten went in.

At ten to eight, the housemates are all told by Big Brother to go to the door to welcome their new guest. Outside, the eleventh person to enter the *Big Brother* household walks up the path carrying her suitcases. On command, the housemates open the door and she walks in, to be greeted by kisses and introductions. She tells them her name is Claire and Craig takes over, telling her their names, and then taking her on a conducted tour of the house. She brings with her a present from Big Brother: a Chinese takeaway, wine and cigarettes.

She tells them she is feeling stunned. They toast her with the wine she has given them and then they all rush outside to see another beautiful sunset over London. They tell her about Nick's departure, as though she does not know the reasons for it. 'At the end of the day, he cheated,' says Anna. 'It's sad because he was a nice bloke.'

They give a performance of their song for her and tell her about the tasks they've had to do in previous weeks, and the one they have already started on for this week.

When Big Brother asks for someone to go to the Diary Room, Anna suggests Claire. While she's away, the others talk about her. Craig says she's a good sport. Anna says she's lovely and Darren says he thinks he recognizes her and thinks she recognizes him from somewhere. Tom says he'll find out when he starts talking to her. When he does mention it, Claire agrees that he looks familiar to her. (It isn't until several hours later, at two o'clock in the morning, while Mel helps Claire make up her bed, that he remembers that she may have been at the same interview session for *Big Brother* that he attended. 'I remember getting on really, really well with someone,' he says. Anna and Tom agree that she may not be sure who he is because he's now got a shaved head – he had hair then.)

Claire shows she's got a good sense of humour and it's obvious that Craig has warmed to her. He tells her about the trains they can hear and about the hens and the cockerel. She asks if the cockerel has a girlfriend among the hens.

Craig says, 'It does them all, one after another.'

Anna adds, 'It's got a harem.'

'So the only person who's getting it in the *Big Brother* house – the hens,' says Claire.

'On the subject of that, are you up for any sex, Claire?' Craig asks.

She laughs and says, 'I'm glad you waited until I felt at home before you asked.'

Craig replies, 'I didn't want to embarrass you when you first came in the door. Have a think about it – you can give me the answer tomorrow.'

Mel seems a bit put out by the arrival of another young pretty girl and drags her mate, Tom, off to the boys' room to give him a massage. She uses it as an excuse to sound out his views on the new arrival. She stops when the klaxon sounds and in her rush to get off the bed she bangs Tom's teeth against the metal frame of the bed.

At midnight, Claire goes to the Diary Room again to talk to Big Brother about her impressions of the house.

'It's surreal coming in here. Whatever you see on TV, it's nothing like it looks. It's real here. It's weird – when you are a kid you want to put your hand in the TV and take out the chocolate bar. I feel I'm in the TV and it's really strange.

'They're telling me some stuff that I know and that I can't know, can't tell them I know. I feel a bit of a traitor. But they haven't asked me anything.'

Outside, Craig also thinks the situation is weird. He reminds the others that Claire could have read a great deal of gossip about any of them in the newspapers.

She stays up late, chatting to the three boys. In the girls' room, Anna and Mel get closer to each other, united by the stranger who is entering their domain.

'Our cocoon has a crack in it,' says Mel. 'She probably knows more about us than we know about each other.'

Anna apologizes to Mel for back-stabbing her in the first couple of weeks.

'I said some things about you spending too much time with the boys. I'm really sorry.'

This leads Mel to open up to her about why she was with the boys: Andy. She admits she shared an instant bond with him and says she was gutted about him leaving.

'But he abused the situation a bit,' she says, and then goes on to tell Anna that she prefers kissing someone better looking and with a bigger chest. Then they talk about the first evictee, Sada.

'Even though Caroline and Nichola loved her, I've never met anyone so conceited,' says Anna.

In bed, in the early hours, Craig and Tom talk about new girl, Claire. Tom says he thinks Anna fancies her. Craig asks Tom, 'What's the score with you and Mel – have you got a grip of her yet?'

Tom tells him they talked about it and agreed that if there was a spontaneous moment for both of them, they might go further. Craig reminisces about his snog with Nicky and Tom points out that he was getting on very well with Claire. Craig says he was only joking.

'She's a big girl. Must be five feet ten inches,' says five-feet-six-and-a-half-inches-tall Craig.

Claire is initiated into the Sunday morning ritual of ordering the shopping but leaves the list to Anna and Mel. The smokers insist on lighter fluid, flints and tobacco going on the order. It's another warm day and Claire joins Craig and Tom sprinting around the garden – but not for long. They jeer at her lack of fitness. But if she can't run as much as they can, she soon proves herself a very good shot when she and Craig have an egg fight. Because of the illness of the hens, the eggs cannot be eaten and Craig has already pelted Mel with them a few days ago. Claire doesn't play the girlie 'I can't throw' card but zaps him energetically, later attributing her skill to her netball training.

Afterwards she has her first shower, leaving her shower gel behind to Darren's delight. He's impressed that she's got over the hurdles of her first trip to the loo and her first shower.

The housemates are finding out more about Claire. She's shared with them the details of her tangled family and she tells them about her problems with cars – she tends to write them off. She's wrecked four cars in all, including pranging one against a skip and swerving another into a telegraph pole.

'When I hit the telegraph pole I rolled the car,' she says, 'and I was still in shock from that when I had another accident, going into the back of someone on a dual carriageway.'

The skip accident happened after she found her boyfriend in the arms of another woman. She was driving to her mother's the next day.

'I didn't see the skip. But it was dark and the skip was on a bend.' She tells the others that she's a whizz at computer car-racing games but just can't drive the real thing.

With fewer people in the house, sound seems to carry more. Mel says that she heard Tom and Craig talking and giggling in their room in the early hours of the morning about their sexual frustrations, and Craig confirms, 'We're like volcanoes about to erupt.'

Darren has other problems. He goes into the Diary Room and tells Big Brother: 'Over the last three days, I keep lying in bed and thinking that I'm not really happy inside. But I decided that I'm going to change my thoughts and be really enthusiastic, and it has worked and I'm feeling better. Before Claire came, I was feeling really down, but now she's here I'm kinda settled. I'm much more up.

'I'm really scared of seeing my kids if I get nominated and not evicted. I'm envious of Thomas and Craig when they see their families because it's like a fresh start, but being nominated and not evicted would be the worst thing for me. Craig said it was a good experience, it made him happy, but I'm scared of it.'

He says the best thing that has happened was the film of his daughter's birthday party.

'I didn't bring any pictures into the house. I completely forgot. That's mad. I worry about the kids, what they are going through.'

He says he has realized what he is missing in terms of family life and how important it is for both parents to be involved in a child's life.

In the afternoon, Anna goes back to bed. She's had a restless night and needs more sleep. Mel sits with her, telling her how she does not like having an extra person in the house. After chatting to Anna, she tells Tom that she is dying to go out for a Sunday drink with her mates. He replies that he is dying to go to bed with a woman. Mel tells him that she wants to share a bed 'with someone I know cares about me and I care about them'. Darren demonstrates by cuddling up to her that it is cuddles that he misses most and they all agree that they crave physical contact. Anna, who has joined them, says she cannot have contact with anyone she does not know.

Darren cooks them another amazing West Indian meal with fish. Claire joins him while he is doing the preparation. Before the meal is ready, Anna goes into the Diary Room to share her thoughts about the newcomer with Big Brother. She says it's a moan because she is finding life in the house hard.

'We've just reached a stage where everyone is really relaxed and comfortable, we could talk at our ease. Now I'm watching everything I say again. Mel is, too. It's not Claire, she's the most perfect person you could have chosen to come into a situation like this, a balance of being quiet and a lot to say as well.

'She's smacked a bit of reality back into us because we have built a whole cocoon around ourselves and I'm sure you've noticed the way we've changed and developed. In a way, we're happy not knowing about reality... She knows so much

▲ Big Brother Is Watching You.

▼ Anna watches as Mel gets every detail right for her wire model.

▲ The arrival of the hot tub provided hours of fun for the housemates.

◄ Anna spent a lot of mornings perfecting her basketball technique in the garden.

◄ Anna finds solace in her music.

▲ Work goes on to get the house ready in time.

▼ Sada and Caroline get cosy together.

▼ Sada's yoga classes were very popular.

◀ Caroline pours out her heart to Big Brother.

▲ Caroline's unforgettable laugh.

▲ Caroline in a rare quiet moment.

▲ Nick really offends Darren when he suggests that the public might think he's a drug dealer.

▲ Nick and the other housemates were all warned about discussing the nominations.

▲ Nick managed to pull the wool over everyone's eyes with his charm.

▲ The moment of truth: Darren discovers the notes in Nick's suitcase.

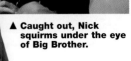

▲ Craig takes the lead in calling Nick to account.

▲ Caught out, Nick squirms under the eye of Big Brother.

▲ Tension mounts as Nick and the housemates await Big Brother's verdict.

▲ He came in through the front door, but he must leave in disgrace through the back gate.

▲ Nick faces the music – and the media.

▲ Davina tries to calm down an ecstatic Nichola.

▶ The treat all evictees look forward to – a chat with Davina.

◀ Davina breaks the news that Sada will be the first to leave the Big Brother house.

▲ Despite her short stay, Claire's stint brought lots of fun for the housemates.

▼ Goodbye for now – Tom leaves the housemates behind.

▲ Tom's fans make their feelings known.

▼ The first of the final three to leave the *Big Brother* house, Darren runs to his family.

▲ Another 2 per cent and Anna would have been £70,000 richer.

◄ Only ten minutes to go for Craig, whose winnings will go towards a heart and lung transplant for Joanne Harris.

more than we know, we can appreciate only a little part of her but she knows us...There's another area of non-trusting that has come into it, I don't want to open up again.'

Anna says she's missing her close friends. It's not that she's not getting on with the group – 'they're all lovely' – but she thinks at this moment she's finding it harder than anyone else in the house. She says she's chatting more to Mel recently and the boys are more tactile, but she hasn't really chatted to them on an emotional level. When Big Brother suggests she shares her feelings with the group, she says she can't do that again. She says she knows the feeling will go away and she'll soon feel all right again.

Craig has both Mel and Claire hanging on his every word when he tells them he tamed a wild falcon but that the RSPCA took it from him because he did not have a licence and because the bird had not been bred in captivity. When Claire loses interest in the subject and wanders indoors, Mel stays close to Craig and probes his knowledge of birds, letting him see how impressed she is.

Darren's Caribbean meal is, as always, very well received. Afterwards, he unwittingly starts a discussion on a subject close to Claire's heart: cosmetic surgery. She quickly admits that she's had surgery and Craig guesses straightaway that it's 'a boobie job'. He then tells her 'Get 'em out – you can't have spent all that money and not show everyone.'

Mel comes through from the bedroom, probably drawn by the excited shouts of the others. They tell her that Claire has had surgery and ask her to guess where. She suggests 'ears'. When she finds out it was a breast enlargement, she is fascinated and asks how much bigger they are now. She also asks why Claire had it done. Claire says she gives different answers to that according to her mood: either to have them made into the same size or to make them bigger. They all want to know what the inserts are made of, and Darren wants to know if they feel like normal breasts. Claire says yes and makes a comparison with boys' balls. Craig suggests a wet T-shirt competition and everyone laughs and agrees Anna would win. Craig gives Claire a lollipop for her bravery.

The evening ends with another interminable game of backgammon between Mel and Tom. Darren takes Claire outside to show her the Canary Wharf building on the skyline.

Craig, who is staying up later since the arrival of Claire, has volunteered to do the early morning shift watching for the heads to appear over the wall. He sleeps on the sofa, being roused from his slumbers whenever the klaxon sounds. None of the others is up before 11 o'clock.

Claire's revelations about her silicon boobs fuel a great deal of speculation among the housemates. Melanie is surprisingly happy to share with Anna a dream she has had about Tom, in which he gave a T-shirt she wanted to Claire and, as a result, she failed a job interview where she was intending to wear it. She says she understands what the dream means.

Craig's fascination with Claire's superstructure is more explicit. He simply loves talking to her about it. And she's happy to chat, too, revealing to him that she worries about her £4,000 investment.

'I was in a car accident and when I got out the first thing I did was check my breasts.'

She's worried about what happens to them after death: 'I've imagined what will happen if someone ever dug up my coffin. Would they find a skeleton and two plastic lumps?' Cremation also bothers her – what will happen to her implants? Craig suggests they could be 'taken out and reused, sold at a car-boot sale'.

Craig manages to keep the boob conversation going for hours. He tells Claire about a girl he knows who puts inserts in her bra, which he says look like chicken fillets. Claire tells him that the skin on her boobs tans differently since she's had the enlargements although there's no medical reason for this.

Darren's chat-up lines with the newcomer are a little bit smoother. He tells her she reminds him of Kelly Brook. When Claire says she doesn't like her and prefers Catherine Zeta Jones, Darren tells her that she looks like Catherine Zeta Jones – only better. He promises her that she will end up on the cover of *FHM* magazine. Reciprocating, she tells him that he looks like a model.

Mel and Anna are getting closer, sharing intimate chats. Mel opens up more to Anna than she has to either of the men who have pursued her, Andy and Tom. She tells Anna that there was a time when she wondered if she was gay.

'The whole idea of women became really appealing,' she says, referring to when she was in her late teens and visited gay bars. 'It all seemed simple and sexy.'

She tells Anna that she enjoyed women making passes at her but that her first real love was an older man. 'I had this feeling of "I want to be with you so much". I would be on the other side of the room and I still wasn't close enough to him. I would have to walk over and touch him, then it would be OK.'

After he dumped her, she pined for him for years, but when she finally bumped into him she thought he was pathetic. 'He looked so weak and I felt so strong.'

This vulnerable side to Mel has never been exposed before to anyone in the house. She's boasted of breaking a boyfriend's nose and she's been at pains to let both Andy and Tom know that she's feisty and wild.

Anna reciprocates the confidences, telling Mel how she came to enter the convent. It was a spur of the moment decision.

'I had a funny holy experience. I was trying to decide what I wanted to do in life. And then I decided one day I would go to the convent and become a nun. But, I ended up getting very tormented about it. I didn't even read the Bible. I just opened the page and it was St Stephen and it said, "You will follow me," and I did.

'It was awful telling my mother. I said it wasn't definite but I'm going to give it a try and she just said I wouldn't be suited to a nun's life.'

She was so unhappy in the convent that she began to lose her hair and was eventually called to see the Mother Superior.

'She asked me if I wanted to leave and I just had to say yes even though I wanted to prove something to myself by staying. She told me, "You'll spend three days thinking you'll stay and three days thinking you'll leave and then you can choose the route you are most at peace with."'

Anna explains to Mel that this is a Jesuit technique for making decisions and she has used it again when she has faced major decisions. She says she has no regrets about leaving holy orders. She tells Mel how she discovered she was gay, after Mel asks her if she has ever been attracted to men.

'I've never been in love with a man. Sex is all right – sex is sex – but I've never been attracted to a man. In a group, I'd be looking round and thinking I find the women so much sexier than the men. And when I was younger and watching a love scene in a film, I always wanted to be the bloke kissing the woman. Then I thought 'Fuck, I bet I'm gay.' And I so obviously, blatantly am.'

She says she told her sister first and her sister was great about it. Then she plucked up the courage to tell her mother who said she already knew, to Anna's great surprise.

It's nominations day and tension inevitably mounts. When Claire tells them all to cheer up ('It's not as though you're sending someone to the electric chair,'), they treat her comment with disdain. She has no idea how it feels. They will not know it until tomorrow but they have managed to distribute their nominations so equally that four of the five who were up for nomination will have to stand for eviction. The rules say that if two or more get the same number of nominations, the public must decide. Darren receives three no minations and Anna, Craig and Thomas each receive two. Only Mel and Claire (who was not eligible for nomination) can rest easy this week.

WHO NOMINATES WHO

ANNA	Craig and Thomas
CRAIG	Anna and Darren
DARREN	Melanie and Thomas
MELANIE	Craig and Darren
THOMAS	Anna and Darren
REASONS:	
CRAIG on DARREN	'He's still a bit selfish, allergic to everything. I'm going to see if he's allergic to nomination.'
MELANIE on CRAIG and DARREN	'It's just I get on better with the other two.'
THOMAS on ANNA	'I think she's still the unhappiest.'

Claire and Craig, the two non-smokers in the group, have amused themselves by hiding the only lighter on top of the boiler. The others are running out of matches but, so far, they are taking the loss light-heartedly. They suspect Craig and Claire and Anna warns the newcomer: 'We've turned before and we can turn again.'

Anna goes to the Diary Room to tell Big Brother that she's feeling better than she was yesterday.

'I was sad yesterday, agitated, annoyed. But today is a nice day, everyone's relaxed. Nominations are a pain but they always are. The new resident is settling in well, she's brilliant. The first day there is so much to take in, but today it's a lot quieter. Things will get more difficult for her but for us she's great, dead chatty, nice, so I hope she is finding it OK. Every time we ask her, she says it's fine but it takes a while in here before you say it's horrible.'

Mel cooks the meal and they discuss cleaning duties. To the delight of all the boys, Mel dresses for the evening in a stunning little white outfit.

The evening is livened up by Claire teaching them a US army marching song. She soon has them all tramping in step around the living room, repeating the lines she sings out:

Whoa, oa, Captain Jack
Meet me by the railroad track
With a bottle in your hand
I will be your fighting man
To the left, go left
Go right, step right
Go left, go right, go pick up your step
Go left, go right, go le-e-eft

You've gotta stand up on your left, your right
You've gotta stand up on your right, your left
Sound off: one, two
Sound off: three, four
Bring it on down
One, two, three, four
One, two, three, four

Once again, they stay up late into the night talking and, as usual, the subject is sex. Anna asks the others what is the 'minxiest thing you have ever done', which paves the way for the boys to outdo each other with tales of their sexual exploits. Craig recounts being involved in a foursome with another guy and two girls but says he was not involved with the guy. Tom also admits being in a threesome, with another man and a girl. But Craig can top that, and to the horror and amusement of the others, talks about one girl being shared between him and three mates – and coming back the next night with two friends! However, the discussion does not stay on this level – for once the *Big Brother* residents get on to something more serious and the conversation topics change to fate, the meaning of life, religion and the confines of space.

On Tuesday, the main item on the agenda is the nomination results, which come at 1 p.m. – when most of the housemates are only just up. Mel explains to Claire that it is more difficult for the person who is up for eviction but stays because they look out of the door and see their friends and family.

'Me and Anna get jealous every week when someone goes. And we had to hold Craig back last week when he saw his family. Thomas saw his mum, whom he didn't think would come and heard his sister over the tannoy.'

Despite being so new into the house, Claire says she will miss it if she has to leave.

Just before the announcement comes, they are joking about the possibility of three, or four, or even all five of them being nominated. To their astonishment, four of them are. The immediate reaction is to point and jeer at Melanie, the only one who has escaped the vote.

Somehow, all being up for the chop together makes it easier to take and they are already beginning to get excited about the prospect of seeing their families, even if only a glimpse. Darren improvises a song which sums up the feelings he will run with all week – he hopes his children are not brought to the studio because he knows that if she sees them he will just run.

He tells Anna how he feels about *Big Brother* and about being nominated for the first time.

'I always said someone's got to be nominated...When your time is up, it's up. I've had some real tough times in here. I've had some fun times. What I expected of this place, in respect of the ten people here, is totally different from what it is. This is much better. I pictured everyone singing, playing, being in your face, showing how much they can do. It's been really good.'

Of all of them, Mel is perhaps the most dismayed by the nomination news. Once again, her mate Thomas faces eviction. She sidles up to him on the sofa as he sits quietly thinking about the news. Her chat-up line does not work.

'Look,' she says, 'I've got a hairy belly.' She pulls her T-shirt up to show him. 'Don't worry, so have I,' he says and refuses to rise to her flirtatious approach.

Called to the Diary Room, Anna is asked by Big Brother what qualities she brings to the household. Pausing for a few seconds, she replies that she makes great roast potatoes, which is a valuable contribution to the community. She pleads with Big Brother to tell her where the cigarette lighter is hidden but he refuses to get involved in this ongoing problem for the smokers.

'I can't comment,' he says.

'I hate it when you get all stern,' Anna says. 'Actually, I do like it when you get all stern. Thank you, Big Brother.'

Craig also goes in and tells Big Brother that he is buzzing. Seeing his family last Friday was his best day so far in the house and he's looking forward to seeing them again although he doesn't want to leave.

'I'm just settling in, just getting warmed up, starting to get the chance to do things and say things. I think I should be in here longer.'

They decide that they will re-create 'It's a Knockout' on Friday night to celebrate the great eviction event, with pillow fights and egg fights.

The drama of the day is when they are all ordered into the girls' bedroom, so that the vet can come into the garden to administer medication to the chickens. He also brings back the two chickens – including Marjorie – that have been away for observation.

In the bedroom, Craig climbs on to Claire's bed. She helps him get comfortable with a pillow and then he dives under the duvet with her. There's lots of giggling and they stick their feet out at the end and cross their legs to confuse the cameras. They also throw out various items of clothing. But it's all fun, no real action. The closest they get to sex is to talk about it. Claire asks Craig:

'Did you look at anyone when you came in here and think "I'll shag her"?'

'After five weeks I'd say that about anyone,' Craig replies.

'It would be easier not to think about sex because if you are used to having it all the time you'd miss it more,' she says.

'But you have all the time in the world in here and it's difficult not to think about it. By next Friday, you'll be pulling your hair out!' Craig warns her.

In the Diary Room, Claire tells Big Brother she is getting on really well with everyone in the house. Big Brother asks if there is anyone in particular and after a moment's thought she realizes this is a reference to her closeness with Craig.

'Oh, you're talking about Craig! You can't ask me that. I like them all equally,' she says. She's having a few inevitable problems sticking to the rule about not discussing events in the outside world before the start of *Big Brother*. She says she was about to mention an advert she'd seen but couldn't remember whether it was out before the others were locked into their strange *Big Brother* world. She also wants to know from Big Brother whether she is going to have her own guinea pig – the Friday evening television programmes include a slot of a replica house peopled by guinea pigs, each given the name of one of the contestants. Big Brother replies that he does not know and advises her to be careful what she talks about. 'If in doubt, leave it out.'

Marjorie's return causes Darren some concern because he finds it hard to recognize her and she seems to have forgotten the bond she had with him, failing to respond to the clicking noise he makes which she used to follow. Obviously, chickens' memories are not as good as the housemates', who are doing well practising their memory test!

For once, Darren joins the others sunbathing – most of the time, he avoids the sun. But he is happy to lie down alongside Claire, who has loaned him one of her T-shirts because his are all dirty (Big Brother orders him to wear it inside out, because it has a huge logo on it.) When he goes to the Diary Room to talk about the chickens, Claire excitedly tells the others that he should go in naked.

'That would keep him in the house,' she giggles.

It's another late-night session for Craig and Claire, who while away the night looking for grey hairs on each other's heads. Then they plot more mischief. They've already caused consternation in the household with the missing lighter and now they discuss sneaking into the boys' room and shaving off Tom's eyebrows. Then it's on to their favourite topic – anecdotes about their wild behaviour. Craig has finally met his match – Claire can rival all his tales. He tells her how he burned his sister's entire wardrobe when he was young. She tells him how she staged a huge waterfight at school and all the girls had to sleep in soggy sheets. He tells her about throwing bottles into the pool from the balcony in the middle of the night at a hotel in Tenerife, while the security men hammered on the door. She tells him about locking her friend in a room in Majorca and leaving her there for a day and a night. Craig tells the story of propositioning a scantily clad housewife while working on a building site. Despite her husband being around, he arranged to go back at a better time – and did. Claire tells how she won a prize at a Kiss FM radio roadshow – but only after the original winner said she would spend her winnings on an eighteenth birthday party, revealing she was under age.

Wednesday morning brings a very welcome addition to the household. A £9,000 hot tub has been donated and installed overnight. Craig is the first up and does a double take when he sees the massive tub in the garden. He shows Claire and tells her he was tempted to carry her from her bed and dump her into it, but realized it was not hot enough. The water will take several hours to warm up.

The others are delighted when they see it, especially when the jacuzzi switch is thrown and the water swirls around. Anna has never been in a jacuzzi and has one major concern – she didn't bring a swimsuit with her. Claire says she'll lend her a bikini.

They lie in the sunshine and Anna starts to plan her Friday night leaving party. She wants everyone to dress and act like someone famous, without telling the others who they are meant to be. The others ask if it's a bring-a-bottle party and Claire says she'll organize a minibus. But the others tell her they always stay at home on Friday nights. 'Davina comes round on Fridays,' Anna says.

Darren goes to the Diary Room. He's had a session with a psychotherapist and now he wants to talk to Big Brother. His one huge worry is that his children will be brought to the studio for Friday night's show.

'I wouldn't want the kids to see me and not be able to hug me and not know why I can't go down there and hug them. I'm scared to see the kids, for my own sake because of the emotion it will bring back, but more so for their sakes.'

He says he's very happy for other members of his family to be there, but he wants Big Brother to give a message to the children's mother so that she does not bring them.

'The kids might really want to come and they could be hurt, they might cry, if they can't.'

He suggests to Big Brother that as his family only live twenty minutes away, one solution would be to only bring the children for the 11 o'clock show, if he is being evicted. Big Brother reassures him that it will be discussed with the children's mother and something will be sorted out.

At three o'clock they all pile into the Diary Room to take the memory test, after first psyching themselves up and chanting 'energy, energy, energy'. They each have to recite seventeen names from the sequence and they manage it, despite almost collapsing in giggles. They are relieved to have done it – their shopping total is now £78.70.

They've got the perfect way to celebrate by plunging into the jacuzzi. The water may not have reached the correct temperature but they can't wait. Craig chases a bikini-clad Mel around the house and carries her in.

In the garden, Claire flirts ostentatiously with Tom, to Mel's irritation. She tells him first that he has lovely toes and then that he has lovely eyes that 'kind of disappear into your head'. Tom deflects the flattery by saying that sunken eyes are a sign of 'interbreeding in a small area'.

Mel goes into the Diary Room to talk through her reactions to the nominations list.

'Weirdly enough I felt guilty that I was not on the list. Then I felt kind of a bit left out. If Anna goes on Friday, I'll find it very hard in here. We can talk about how we feel within the household on quite an emotional level. I'd miss her most out of everyone. She is calm, level-headed, sensible but fun too.

'Claire is fitting in well, she's very relaxed and calm, much more than we have been. Everyone likes her as well. It's nothing to do with her but having a new person in here has made me feel slightly worried. What makes me unhappy is that she has probably seen us nominate people. That is the most secret, private part of being in here, like your sanctuary, the part no-one can get into, and she has seen us justify picking two names and those people possibly being evicted. That is the most horrible part of being in the house. It feels like there is a little gap that the outside was getting in. It's suddenly made me feel a bit vulnerable, like this is our bubble and it has kind of popped or deflated.'

She says she has felt as vulnerable as this once before and Big Brother asks her about it.

'My ex-boyfriend, who I split up with three months before I came in here and who I was going out with for four years. Things didn't go well when we split up. I still love him, he is an important part of my life. Just before coming in here we saw each other again and became close again and I'm sure everyone out there has seen what happened between me and Andy, which I'm not regretting because it was just a kiss, not that meaningful, but I'm regretting it because it happened when I was really miserable, I didn't want to be here. I'm kind of worried that my ex-boyfriend has seen this and it's going to really hurt and upset him.

'I've been worried about it, I mentioned it to Anna. Then Claire came in and she said, "Has anyone got partners?" and Anna and me both said "ish", and Claire looked me straight in the eye and said "Aren't you worried that your partner will take it badly if you say stuff?" and I knew that she meant Andy. I felt strange again, like the cocoon had fractured.'

When she leaves the Diary Room, Big Brother asks her to take out some chicken wire. The chickens are still sick and it could be because they are getting on the vegetable patch, which has been treated with pesticide. Big Brother wants the housemates to rebuild the chicken coop, making it harder for them to escape. Craig, the builder, takes charge, with Claire acting as his assistant. When she goes to make tea, Tom and he chat about her. They both agree that she's good fun. Craig comments that she's got a fella but Tom points out that he is not here.

'Believe me, that thought has crossed my mind,' says Craig.

As she prepares the evening meal, Mel casually drops into conversation with Anna that she once lived with Norman Cook, aka Fatboy Slim, for about a month while she was at college in Brighton. Anna is impressed and wants to know about him.

'He's lovely. Very strange, eccentric, nervous, but so interesting, such a nice bloke. I used to spend hours chatting to him,' says Mel. 'His basement was just bright orange and yellow, absolutely mad. The bathroom had green turf on the floor and an enormous jacuzzi-like bath in green. The wall was a life-sized photograph of a palm beach.'

The downstairs' bathroom, she says, was 'tacky', black with lots of mirrors and little strip lights. Overall, she says, the house in Hove was 'mad'.

She found herself living there after meeting the promoter of the Big Beat Boutique, who was sharing the house. As she had nowhere to live, he invited her to move in.

She tells Anna that she used to come up to London with Norman when he was playing clubs here.

'I saw some incredible things. To me, he was Norman but he'd have all these girls knocking on the DJ booth. A girl knocked on the booth one night and, assuming she knew him, I let her in. I got totally told off about it, but she asked for his autograph and when he said yes lifted her top for him to sign in permanent pen across her chest. It was good fun, I really miss those clubbing days.'

She had one major row with him, she tells Anna, over her habit of writing lists.

'I am really passionate about lists, they are just so satisfying,' she says. 'But we had a massive argument because he thought Post-it notes were better. When I got up the next day to walk his dog, Pickle, before going to work, there was a Post-it note stuck to her collar saying "Walk me", and another on her bowl saying "Feed me". He had spent four or five hours sitting up and writing them everywhere. It was so funny. He just loved talking to me.'

Just after 9 p.m., Big Brother gives the group a mini-task. They have to use their fashion sense and creativity to customize jeans and T-shirts for each other and put on a fashion show. They are given a huge bag of clothes and told they can use any other materials they find in the house. They draw names from a hat to see who designs for who: Mel designs for Darren; Claire for Craig; Tom for Anna; Darren for Claire; Anna for Mel; and Craig for Tom.

Claire is delighted to have 'Mr Prada man' designing for her and he promises her: 'You're going to be rude, sexy, crazy, cool.'

The evening ends with a long chat in their wonderful new possession – the hot tub. If they are nervous about the nominations, they are hiding it well. There is a great sense of comradeship among the four who are on the hit list.

On Thursday morning, Tom and Craig are so fed up with the chickens (described by Melanie as 'problems after problems'), that they seriously discuss killing one a week to supplement their food rations and to reduce the amount of fowls they have to care for. They have reconstructed the fence around the coop but it still does not keep the birds in, and they are going to have to redo it with a lid over the top. As they're still not allowed to eat the eggs, the chickens are beginning to seem like more trouble than they are worth. Even Darren's relationship with Marjorie has not picked up where it was before she went away with the vet.

Craig decides to go to the Diary Room, where he asks permission to 'neck a chicken'.

Big Brother asks how he intends to kill the bird.

'Well, like you would normally kill a chicken. Pull its neck and wring it.'

'Certainly not, Craig!' snaps an alarmed Big Brother.

When he tells the rest of the group, they feel mutinous. They believe that the chickens are there for them to do what they want with and they don't need Big Brother's permission. Darren even concedes that they can kill Marjorie if they choose.

Big Brother calls Craig back to the Diary Room and says a vet has been consulted and they must not eat the chicken meat for twenty-eight days, because of the medication the birds have been given.

Marjorie's stock doesn't rise any higher when she is caught eating a frog in the garden, which upsets Claire. Craig tries to rescue the frog but Darren watches fascinated while Marjorie demolishes it.

The day is dominated by work on the fashion designs and rehearsals for the evening show. Melanie is commandeered by Darren to model the T-shirt he has designed for Claire, as Claire is too busy working on her own creation for Craig. Mel happily obliges but loves the T-shirt so much she is reluctant to return it.

'It's wicked! I want it!' she says, strutting round the garden in it. But Darren insists on having it back. Mel tries to enlist Craig's help, asking him to tell Claire it doesn't suit her. Craig looks bemused by her scheming.

Claire and Mel are beginning to talk to each other more, although Mel is still not relaxed around the newcomer. But when Claire tells them of the time she caught her boyfriend with another woman and attacked his car with a hammer, Mel joins in with the story of how she broke her boyfriend's nose when he cheated on her. Darren says the *Big Brother* house has given Claire the perfect chance to get her own back on her boyfriend, by being unfaithful with all of them.

'Tom can go first because he is last in the alphabet, then myself, and then we will unleash Craig,' he offers.

When they take an afternoon plunge in the hot tub with him, Darren questions all three girls about whether they would appear in *Playboy* for £10,000. When Claire says it's horrible, he modifies it to front page in a bikini and centre-spread discreetly nude. Anna still says no but Mel says she'd do it for £20,000. Claire is still against the idea but says that if she had the body for it she'd do it with minimal clothing.

Later, when Claire's in the hot tub with Craig, he tells her, 'You are in my heart.' She asks him about his girlfriend, Shelley, but Craig says, 'It wasn't that serious, it was better that we split up.'

He then tells Claire of his recipe for a perfect evening: 'I love it when you've had a lovely day and then go for a lovely meal just as the sun is going down, with music in your ears. You can feel your skin glowing.'

Claire cooks her first meal for the household but needs some help from Darren, who is the acclaimed master of the *Big Brother* kitchen.

The catwalk show takes place at 10 p.m., and they've all worked hard. Tom's design for Anna is called 'Oppression' and is an allegory of life within the *Big Brother* house. Craig has designed an outfit for Tom which he calls 'Lightning'. Claire has come up with 'OTP' for Craig, the initials standing for On The Pull. However, the really creative designs are Darren's, who has created an outfit called 'Release' for Claire and Mel, who has named her design company Aesthetic Armour and has persuaded Darren to wear make-up to enhance his blue and white T-shirt. Anna's design for Mel may not be the most striking fashion contribution but with the help of Darren she makes the presentation of it a worthy grand finale to the show.

Afterwards, Claire is keen to carry on with the fun and pleads with Thomas to let her paint his nails. He resists for ages, but eventually capitulates and lets her paint one finger.

Tom and Mel spend the night together until dawn comes up. Neither of them know that this is Tom's last night in the *Big Brother* house but perhaps they suspect it. Under questioning from Tom, she tells him that she was three when her parents separated and that it is her father's departure that has made her so cynical.

'I trust very few people in my life. I trust my mother and my grandmother, very few others.'

Tom asks how someone can gain her trust, get past the barrier she puts up.

'I don't know. Very few do,' she says.

Their closeness continues throughout Friday, with them sharing the same bed for an afternoon nap and Mel giving Tom another massage. Tom tries to take the encounter further by stroking her leg, but Mel says, 'Now, Tom, what do you think you're doing?'

Anna feels ill, having spent a restless night tossing and turning, worrying about the possibility of eviction and what she will make of the world outside. 'What a day to feel ill,' she says. 'What if there's nobody there tonight? Maybe all the cheering we hear on a Friday is just a recording.'

Craig shows no sign of any worries and whiles away the afternoon with an exhausting pillow fight with Claire. With empty beds in the house, they have been using the spare mattresses for sunbathing – now they are pressed into service as crash mats. They place upturned buckets in the middle of the mattresses and try to stand on them Gladiators-style while whacking each other with pillows. Craig quickly won against Claire and then against the rest of the housemates who lined up to fight him. Darren, acting as referee, makes them all bow to each other in martial-arts style. Mel, abandoning all attempt to play within the rules, eventually just pushes Craig off his bucket.

When the news of the voting comes, they are all looking edgy. Craig gets the least of the million-plus votes, with 19 per cent, Anna is next with 22 per cent and Darren and Tom are very close, with 29 per cent and 30 per cent respectively. Not that the housemates are told this – all they hear is Davina announcing that Thomas is the one who has to leave. He looks surprised and then a wide grin breaks out on his face. Mel looks bemused and cross.

Ten minutes after getting the news, Thomas goes to talk to Big Brother. He has a request: can he please have two bottles of red wine to share with the others in his final two hours in the house. He thanks the *Big Brother* team for giving him the chance to be part of the project.

'The margin in the voting will have been narrow this week and it's good that it wasn't a competition between two people. Even if I'd made it through to the final week, I wouldn't have won.' He says he is very much looking forward to meeting all his friends and family and he knows there will be lots of people there because of so many being nominated.

'I will miss the friendships I have made. The days are long and hard in here and being in an enclosed environment you begin to depend on each other. If I can carry that on outside, it will be good.'

Big Brother turns down his request for wine. Within half an hour of the news Mel enters the Diary Room and says why she will miss Tom:

'I'm feeling sad and pissed off. I'm going to miss him. He didn't want to go, he wasn't ready to go. He didn't think it would be him and neither did I... He probably feels it is the end of something that could have gone on longer.

'I will miss the glint in his eye when he's up to mischief; I will miss him teasing me; I will miss having him to talk to; I will miss him to play backgammon with; I will miss not having someone to do the vegetables with. It's a shame. I was just starting to get quite close to him. We are not similar people really, although I can talk to him and he is intelligent and on the ball. We have come from very different backgrounds and areas. It's such a strange situation in here, you latch on to people. Tom and Anna have been my support. Your feelings in here get warped, you don't see things straight in such an intense environment.

'I really hope to see him afterwards. It will be exciting to see him. I have really good hopes for him and I hope he fulfils his dreams, takes new opportunities. I will be really excited to see him in London. I hope he comes to see me. Out of everyone here, I really want to see him and have an in-depth chat with him outside *Big Brother*. Even though you can talk quite freely, you can't talk as freely as you would like to, and can't say everything you would like to say, and I'd like to say things to him outside the *Big Brother* house.

'I just want to see how we are together outside, being normal, away from the cameras and lights... At certain times, you really notice the cameras. I wanted to be by myself when the announcement was made today. As time goes by, it will get quieter and we will be more aware of the cameras. I feel it is becoming a strain on me.'

She tells Big Brother that Craig is 'over the moon' to have survived but both Darren and Anna are a bit disappointed not to be going.

She joins Tom in the boys' room where he is packing his suitcase and tells him that he will have to come to London to meet her mum. Tom tells her that there is a place in the house where the cameras cannot see them but she does not rise to the bait. Instead, she lets him kiss her gently on the lips, but it is not a passionate kiss and lasts only a few seconds.

'I can't do this to every boy who leaves here,' she says.

'You'll get a name for yourself,' Tom replies.

He teases the other housemates by telling them how he intends to eat steak and ice cream tomorrow and then he demands a massage from all the girls to while away his last twenty minutes in the house. Craig gives him a present of a packet of condoms. Then Davina's at the door to take him away and the rest of the housemates are fighting for a glimpse of their family and friends.

Just before midnight, a violent storm erupts over the *Big Brother* house, the weather in tune with the disturbed emotions of the residents. Craig goes to share his thoughts with Big Brother.

He says he is sad to see Tom go and will miss him. The atmosphere is not as good this week as it was last week, as there has been no alcohol in the house. Last week was the first time he had seen his mum and his sister and it was great to see them again, as well as his sister's children.

'With this place, things tend to get back to normal quite quickly after someone leaves. Saturday comes, we have the task, then the shopping... But we're getting closer and more attached, and it's harder to nominate and say goodbye... I hope I'm here to witness all the new tasks and experiences. I was lying in bed thinking about all I've done and achieved in here compared to what I do at home. It's been amazing and makes me want to be here for the duration.'

Anna is next in line for a Big Brother chat.

'I feel a bit emotional. It was awful seeing people I know waving madly. It's quite subdued now but I'm a little bit chuffed that my name wasn't called. It wasn't like winning or beating other people at all, I just feel a bit happy that I'm staying. It was easier last week because Nichola wanted to go, and Tom didn't, which is sadder.

'It's on our minds that there are only three more weeks to go and only two more people to be evicted and the nominations become harder and harder. You never know how things in this madhouse will turn out. We could all be laughing – or smothering each other in our sleep.'

Claire and Craig talk long into the night in the living area, her telling him about the second time she broke off with her boyfriend when she went to Ibiza with another guy. Even Craig is shocked and says, 'Bloody hell, Claire.' Craig tells her a story from his life, but it was altogether gentler than his usual wild anecdotes. He explains how he cooks pasta and other special meals for his three dogs. When she relays this on to Anna and Mel at bedtime they raise quizzical eyebrows – Craig has spent much of his time in the *Big Brother* house avoiding cooking duties on the grounds that he is hopeless at it.

Darren, who now has only Craig as a roommate, stays in the girls' room talking to Anna and Mel. He is pleased his children were not at the studio, especially when he saw the size of the crowd.

'I'm pissed off with myself. I've said all along to Big Brother that I will work on staying. I felt an idiot because I really wanted to go and I felt it was shit for Tom. That was so hard. I was so looking forward to hearing my name and then I didn't. I was devastated big time. Then I hugged [you] Mel and you said "three more weeks". It was like you said another year. That was so bad. But tomorrow will be fun again.'

After he has gone, Anna tells Mel that they should start trying to win.

'Not to win so much, as not to think we'll lose. The boys don't think of losing.'

They decide that Craig is only in it for the money and that he's rather vain. Mel says she frequently sees him glancing at himself in the mirrors that surround them.

Anna asks Mel about Tom and, although he's not been out of the door for more than three or four hours, Mel describes their relationship as weird and says it made her uncomfortable. Later on when Claire has joined them, she tells them both that she still loves her ex-boyfriend.

'He might hate me after this. He might see me picking my nose and think "that's disgusting".'

Claire, who is having her first bout of homesickness, borrows Nichola's teddy bear from Anna for a cuddle. The final act of the night is Mel killing a very large spider that has come into the room on her shirt. She drops the shirt and prances around naked while all three of them become very girlie about the spider. They have the sense not to call the boys, who they think will just torment them with it.

WEEK FIVE FACT FILE

MAIN TASK **PASS** ☑ **FAIL** ■	Memorize 100 heads in sequence.
MINI TASK	Design and present a fashion show.
TREATS	Chinese meal, wine and cigarettes when Claire arrives and so does the hot tub!
BOOKIES' FAVOURITE TO WIN	Craig is favourite at odds of 5/4. Anna is just behind at 6/4, Mel is third at 5/1 and Darren is next at 10/1.
TO WALK	Claire is hot favourite at odds of 1/7.

WHAT THE EXPERT SAYS

'It's interesting that Claire has allied herself straightaway with the most dominant male in the house, Craig. This may be because of Craig's irresistible charms but it may be a way of Claire ensuring that she survives within the house. Her interaction with the dominant female, Melanie, is also of great interest. Although we see Claire comforting Mel when she is upset, she has also been provocative in her interactions with Mel. She's even dared to flirt with Tom right in front of Mel's eyes. By doing this, Claire is saying: I'm not afraid of you Melanie, and I'm not afraid to play your game either.'

Linda Papadopoulos, Counselling Psychologist

THOMAS LOOKS BACK

For Thomas, there is only two hours' sleep that night. He sits on the window-sill of the London hotel where he stays on his first night out of the *Big Brother* house and watches traffic and people in the street below, phones his friends in Ireland who are partying through the night in his honour, and tries to get his head around the amazing experience he has lived through.

When he came out of the house, there was the biggest crowd to date waiting for him – about 500 people. Many of them were young girls all desperate to see the man Davina McCall described as *Big Brother*'s Mr D'arcy and 'Ireland's latest superstar'. After his initial wild excitement at seeing his mother, six of his sisters and a crowd of friends, Tom predictably took it calmly. He was genuinely delighted to be reunited with Andy at the end of the show and the following evening the two of them were out on the town together.

However, before that he faced the press and talked about his time in the *Big Brother* house. 'Coming out is such a shock. Seeing my own face, filling a television screen, was very strange. I'll have to deal with the fact that people have seen a great deal of me. I'm very glad I did it and I would definitely do it again if I had my time over: I recommend it. It gave me a chance to share experiences with other people I would never normally meet. Although it's a strange goldfish bowl atmosphere, it is still very refreshing to encounter other people's views.'

In the first couple of weeks, when the viewers were worrying that he wasn't settling in, Tom says he was behaving exactly as he predicted he would to the production team.

'I told them that I would be very quiet for at least the first week, then I would establish myself more. I'm not competitive for attention like some of the others are, so I was quite happy to sit back and let them all talk.'

Splinter groups were established very quickly, with Tom joining Andy, Nick and Mel in late-night card sessions and Sada, Nichola, Caroline and Anna congregating in the girls' room.

'Darren was the only boy they would talk to. Mel tried to be with the girls at first but found it very hard. There was no real reason for the two camps to develop. Before it happened, I had the chance to have good chats with Nicky and Sada and a short chat with Anna. Caroline was always difficult to approach and the more the other girls were drawn to her the less friendly they were with me.

'Nicky told me all about her travels and her art. Sada appears to be shallow but she's not at all and she has a beautiful view of the world, although I don't know if it's genuine. She does things to contradict herself, like saying she's a Buddhist who never kills anything and then becoming the best mosquito-catcher in the house.

'In the beginning I thought Darren was really selfish. It was all me, me, me and I don't normally get on with that sort of person. But when I was nominated the first time he showed a different side to his character: he was very decent, friendly, considerate. I think Darren has matured in there. He's less self-involved, more rounded. Towards the end, we were getting on well although it would never have been a close friendship.

'I enjoyed Andy's company, he's very witty. I admired his motivation. If something had to be done he got on with it. He was determined to succeed. If he had a fault, it was trying to make the group do it the way he wanted, trying to control the group. He also upset the girls by talking so much about sex before we had all had time to get to know each other. I was surprised he went out so soon because I saw him as a real contender to win it. On the other hand, his eviction showed that it was fair, that boys would go out as well as girls.

'There are lots of similarities between me and Craig. He was quite quiet at first, taking it all in. Then as the weeks went by he came out of himself more, became more playful. Craig is the most honest person in there. He's very genuine. I look forward to meeting up and partying with him.'

Despite being the one who initiated the unmasking of Nick, Tom still feels that he would like to meet him and stay friends with him.

'If he's played it all deliberately to get all this attention, then I must congratulate him. He's done an excellent job, manipulated everything quite cleverly. I knew he had Andy's cigarettes and he did give me one behind the greenhouse – we laughed and waved it at the cameras. I didn't think that was unfair – the girls kept chocolate and alcohol in their room. We'd stay up late and we'd be aware that they were drinking in there, when we had none. They'd stash some of the cider from the supplies that were meant to be for the whole house. And in the morning, there would be chocolate wrappers in the bin and they didn't share it.

'There was a lot of naivety from the girls. They seemed shocked by the nomination procedure and Caroline and Sada took it very personally. Caroline was wearing clothes in the shower and they claimed they didn't know there were cameras in the bedroom. They hadn't thought through the whole picture.'

When he spoke to Craig about Nick's duplicity, Tom says he knew that something would happen.

'I had no idea of the scale of what Nick had been doing but I knew something was going on from a brief chat with Mel. We never finished that conversation because as usual Nick came and joined us. He was always turning up when we were talking. But I'd even mentioned twice in the Diary Room that something was going on and I guessed that Craig would do something about it.

'Darren was the most angry, but Darren had never been approached by Nick and shown any names. That was one of the worst feelings for me. Did he not approach Darren because he saw Darren as very strong? In that case, did he think I was weak enough or stupid enough to listen to him?

'Craig dealt with it well, he showed great temperament. The meeting at the table made me feel very uncomfortable because in life we never normally confront things like that. I was angry with myself that I hadn't done something sooner.'

Although he was instrumental in sorting out the Nick problem, Tom guessed that he would be on the nomination list the following week.

'In the back of their minds people were glad that I started the ball rolling but at the same time I think they blamed me for going along with it. I wasn't the only one who knew he was showing notes but because I was the one who spoke up about it I think there was a reaction against me.

'At first, I thought he might be able to survive in the house but as soon as he displayed arrogance, talking down to Nicky and trying make Craig look stupid, his days were numbered.'

Tom hopes that Nick is enjoying his new stardom and that he can see the funny side of it.

'He's got a sense of humour, so I hope he's able to laugh about it all.'

Tom believes that in ten years' time he will still be in touch with Andy, Craig, Mel and possibly Nick.

'They are the ones I got on with. I didn't really know Mel at first. She was half with the girls and half with the boys and she spent a lot of time with Andy. I think I'll see her again, but the relationship would never have developed any further in there. We were always aware that we were on cameras and my final kiss was a farewell kiss to a friend. She was a good friend, someone to argue with. She needs that and Andrew was her first choice. Nick was not so good, so I was the next.

'I'd like to see her and sit down over a meal and talk to her. Would it be the same attraction? I don't suppose so, but I'd have to try it to know.'

The only embarrassment he has about his time in the *Big Brother* house was the occasion when, as one of the reporters at the press conference delicately put it, his 'manhood was on display to the nation'. He told the press that he felt no shame about something so natural and normal but he admits that it does worry him.

'I'll have to learn to live with the embarrassment,' he says.

He only had one week to get to know Claire but he feels she was very well chosen for her role as an interloper.

'I suspect the production team consciously chose her to spice things up a bit. She's got a bubbly personality and she mixed in very quickly – probably because she already knew us well from the television programmes.

'I think the biggest shock for her was how lazy and laid-back we all were. She came in bursting with energy, wanting to do things and we were all five weeks into it and quite happy to lie around all day. She read three books in her first week, she was so keen to always be doing something.'

Tom's dilemma about his future – does he take over the farm or does he go out into the world – preoccupied him, and the viewers, while he was in the house. He admits he is no nearer to making a decision.

'But I have had time to think about my options and I've now got the confidence to express my opinions. The house hasn't given me any answers but it has given me more questions. And that's probably a good thing.'

'I was born beautiful.'

DARREN

25 AUGUST TO 1 SEPTEMBER

The task that the housemates are given to take their minds off Tom's departure initially thrills them and they feel confident that they will be able to do it. They have been challenged to make photo-sculptures of their own bodies. Each of them must make a life-size model of themselves with chicken wire and cover it with photocopies of photographs of the appropriate parts of their body. They are provided with a photocopier, an instant camera, five black-and-white films (so they can take ten photos each) and lots of chicken wire, paper, staples and sticky tape. They must completely cover the wire frame.

Although Anna concedes that 'we could have done with Nichola for this one', she says they can do the task, although she admits they don't really have a clue what it entails. They decide to wager the full 50 per cent of their shopping money. Darren gets stuck in straightaway and discovers that the pliers supplied to cut the wire are not as good as the ones Nichola had.

He goes to the Diary Room to ask if they can have different ones and when he discovers that it is his 'favourite Big Brother' – a female voice – he goes back to have a chat. He tells Big Brother that having four of them nominated made the week easy.

'We totally forgot about it. Nobody was asking how we were feeling all the time. But I really was missing my kids, wanting to go home. It's hard because when you hear Davina over the speaker you think, who do I think the audience would choose, who do I want them to choose? I think it's stupid and pathetic but I wanted them to choose me. I even started packing, getting ready. I felt it was over. I'd done it, loved it, didn't regret it, hoped it was over. It was stupid 'cos it made it worse for me. How can I wish to do that? I'll be much prouder if I'm here for the full time, winning or not. It makes you realize how hard it was for Caggie and the others.'

He says he wasn't surprised to see Tom go. They were all upset, but Mel most of all because she used to sit up late talking to him. He says they are going to set up a rota system for staying up with Mel.

Claire tells the other girls that she packed in such a hurry she has not brought enough clothes and is running out of things to wear. She tells them she has no clean underwear and they tell her that they are both washing their knickers in the shower every day, a trick Darren taught them. Anna is rotating three pairs; Mel is managing with two. They both laugh in genuine disgust when Claire says she will start wearing hers inside out. She goes on to explain that a thong can be rotated and used six times!

She provides further amusement about the coarser side of things when she goes into the boys' bedroom and climbs into Tom's bed, but only after inspecting it for stains and asking Darren and Craig if Tom made any 'dodgy noises' in the night. They assure her that he washed the sheets regularly.

Anna and Mel talk about whether or not they are ambitious. Mel says she is, but possibly only because of the environment she works in. Anna says philosophically that some people are not ambitious because they are happy with their lot and others are not ambitious because they are afraid of failing. Mel says that she has a good idea of what all the other housemates want out of life, but she is nervous of asking Claire because Claire knows what kind of reception the evictees have had outside and whether or not ambitions can be fulfilled.

The problems with the pliers persist and both Anna and Darren have cut themselves.

At half past five Claire goes to the Diary Room to chat to Big Brother. Something is bothering her which, she says, she 'has to get out'.

'Some people in here can MOAN! It's like why do we have to do this, why do we have to do that? If they didn't want to do it, they shouldn't have come in here. I feel better now I've said it to someone... Every time you ask us to do something it's a big, I dunno, it's like a requirement that we have to disagree with you... I think they have been in here too long. You have my permission to shoot me if I whinge at requests. They're pissing me off every time with the moaning, the moaning.'

She says that although she's not as close to the others as they are to each other, she has no problem talking to them. She is generally very happy, enjoying the sunbathing, the jacuzzi, the gourmet meals and the lack of responsibility. She especially likes just being able to be silly and stupid. The most difficult bit is holding her tongue and not just to avoid giving the others clues about the outside world.

'Once or twice I've started to express an opinion and then realized that it wouldn't make any difference so I've given up. How do I put this nicely? Sometimes I think it doesn't matter what I think and I don't mean that in a jokey way. There are stronger opinions in the house... they're more opinionated... If I was outside I'd probably walk away and let them get on with it... It's fine to have an opinion but to go on and on and on about it and not push it on other people, but express it quite strongly when you're blatantly not listening to anything anyone else says... Shoot me if I do it.'

She says she thinks the rest of the group have been worn down by this, but refuses to 'name names'. She thinks she can see it more clearly than the others, coming in from outside, and although she finds it annoying the others probably find it endearing. She wants to say, 'Just stop moaning and do it.'

Before she leaves she tells Big Brother that she is dying to see her baby brother, born on the day she came into the house. Twice in the course of the chat, she says she is worried that her voice can be heard outside and Big Brother reassures her this is not possible.

Early in the evening Big Brother gives them a mini-task that delights them. They are given three bottles of wine, one a supermarket red costing less than £3, one a Spanish Rioja costing £8 and one a £14 claret, and they have to identify the most expensive. Their prize for getting it right will be five bottles of the wine. With such a serious prize at stake, they agonize over it for an hour. Eventually, Darren tells Big Brother their conclusion and is thrilled to hear they got it right. He tries to pretend to the others that they failed, but can't keep it up for long.

Another session in the hot tub brings the housemates back to one of their favourite subjects: Claire's breast enlargements. Always happy to introduce her boobs into the conversation, she tells Craig and Anna, who are in the tub with her, that they float. Craig asks her if they weigh more than normal tissue. She says she doesn't know. Darren and Mel are sitting in the garden listening to the conversation and Darren asks if Claire weighed more after her operation. She says she did – a couple of pounds.

The others are fascinated by the subject and listen intently while she tells them that she saw the implants before they went in; the surgeon encouraging her to feel two different types. Darren, who seems even more intrigued than the others, asks how they felt at first.

'I had this tight elastic thing fastened with Velcro around them at first. When I took it off, my boobs were like rockets. I was really, really upset; gutted for about two months. Apart from the pain, I hated them. Then, I'll never forget it, I was walking somewhere quite quickly and they cracked, just like a nut and then they were normal.'

She says she was in agony immediately after the operation and had ' big cuts where they put them in'. Darren says he cannot see any sign of scars, so she lifts the bottom of her bikini top to show them. Mel comments that they look no more noticeable than the marks a bra leaves. Darren, unable to leave the subject, asks if the surgeon told her to be careful when having sex. When she says no, he says, 'So it's all good then?'.

He says he reckons that he can normally tell when a girl has had a boob job and he gestures to indicate that the breasts are unnaturally high. But, he says, Claire's are not like that. Prompted by Anna, who mischievously whispers the words to him, he describes Claire's breasts as 'pendulous' and 'voluptuous'. Claire says, 'So they were worth the money, then.'

Later in the evening Craig tells Claire: 'Before either you or me gets chucked out, I have to feel your tits. I've never felt plastic ones before. I'll get you before you go. I only want to feel one. Perhaps I'll do it when you're asleep.'

Claire does not make any promises but tells him she's certain she'll be walking out of the *Big Brother* house on Friday.

More stories from Claire's past come out during the wine-fuelled evening chat. She tells the others how she blew her cousin's tooth out of her mouth by booby-trapping her popcorn. When Claire, who was eleven at the time, discovered her cousin was helping herself to Claire's popcorn, she put some small bangers in – and her cousin bit into one.

'To this day she still says she can't believe I put the bomb in and I can't believe she was stealing my popcorn,' says Claire.

Anna says, 'I get more and more scared as the days go by.'

But for Craig there's a moral to be drawn: 'Don't steal people's property.'

By eleven o'clock three of the five bottles of wine, plus the three they had for the tasting, have been consumed (they've carefully stashed two bottles for eviction night). Craig and Claire are still in the hot tub, splashing and fooling around with Darren and Anna who turn the hosepipe on them. Craig tries to throw Darren in, then goes into the house, leaving Claire alone in the tub.

Later on, back inside the house, Claire and Craig go over to one of the mirrors to see if each other's eyes are bloodshot and then work out more pranks to play on the smokers in the house. Inside, Darren simulates sex with Mel's model, which makes Craig laugh.

Craig asks Claire what she was talking about in the Diary Room. She tells him that she is fed up that certain people's opinions are forced on others and that everyone moans about the things Big Brother gets them to do. She says she didn't tell Big Brother who irritates her. Craig has more success persuading her to name names – she admits to him that it is Mel. She says it stems from Mel moaning about having to redo the chicken coop, even though she wasn't the one having to do the work. Claire says she doesn't want to make a big deal of it.

By one o'clock in the morning Darren, Mel and Anna have all gone to bed and Claire is in her nightie. Craig remembers that they have to give the chickens their medicine and the two of them spend a chaotic ten minutes catching the hens.

Shopping is the main preoccupation on Sunday morning. The group has just under £80 to spend. Claire donates £1 of her allowance to the smokers so that they can get some Rizla papers, putting her stock up with them and compensating for the prank of hiding the lighter.

The sculptures are taking up lots of time. For all her complaining in the Diary Room about the others moaning about the tasks, it is Claire who has not yet started. The rest of the group is concerned that she won't have made hers in time and they press-gang her into getting going.

Anna, Mel and Darren improvise a new song: Anna plays the guitar and the other two come up with words using the names of all the housemates. Afterwards, they discuss the bits of film that will not be going out to viewers, the X-rated bits, which leads on to a debate about whether Andrew was the only one to masturbate in the loo and how many of the men did it in the shower.

After the story of Claire's disappearing popcorn and how she booby-trapped the bag, you would think the others would be careful about stealing from her. However, the lure of Maltesers is too great and when she leaves a packet on the kitchen counter she comes back to find it empty, but with an egg inside it.

'I'm not even going to guess who did it, I'm going to get you all back,' she says. Anna, who is the only one who owns up to taking one, offers Claire a beer because she feels so guilty. While Mel is out of the room the others hatch a plan. They send Claire to the bedroom to make it seem as if she is really upset about the missing sweets. Then Anna suggests Mel goes and talks to her. With the other three listening at the door and suppressing giggles, Mel tries to reassure Claire that she is not being picked on.

The highlight of the evening is the arrival of a new guest: Barry. Barry is Darren's sculpture of himself, and he's finished – although the group soon demonstrate that he's not going to be able to stand up unaided for a full minute, which is one of the rules of the task. He's also got to survive until judgement day – Wednesday – and for a time that looks unlikely. After Darren and Claire hide some of Craig's Yorkie bars, he gets his revenge by kidnapping Barry and holding a knife to his throat. 'The Yorkies – or Barry gets it,' he says. When he takes Barry back to the bedroom, with nobody around to see, he delivers a quick punch to the head and then kicks him when he's on the ground.

Three hours later, when Craig is in the loo, Darren and Claire are laughing over the missing chocolate bars. Mel sees them and immediately calls Craig to say she's got them. While the rest of the household settle to sleep, Craig photocopies Claire's empty Malteser packet and lays a trail of copies across the floor. Hearing a noise, Claire comes out of the girl's bedroom and jumps in alarm as Craig surprises her from behind.

The next day is nominations day and Tom is on Mel's mind. She tells Darren and Claire that he had a way of stepping into arguments and calming things down. She reminds Darren of the famous Caggie and Craig row, when Tom simply spoke over them and said, quietly but forcefully, 'We will talk about this later.'

'He was so quiet, so when he spoke up he was really assertive,' says Mel. Claire, who only knew Tom for six days, agrees. 'Tom was cool,' she says.

The house is looking a mess. In the early hours of Friday morning Darren gave it a thorough clean, but it has deteriorated rapidly and Mel and Craig tackle the mess. Anna has a breakfast of cheese on toast and coffee, which she describes as 'heaven', and this sparks a discussion about what the others really think would be heaven right now. For Mel it is fresh croissants, good coffee and the Sunday papers in bed with someone she loves. Anna jokes that the food and drink would be enough. For Darren, heaven is 'being here with you'. But for Craig it is a really wistful vision: he is walking through the woods with his dogs, with a girl he loves and it's wintertime so they are snuggled inside thick coats.

Mel has consulted Big Brother and been told that it is OK for the life-size models to be on all fours. After the problems with Barry they feel this is going to be the only way they'll pass the test of making them free-standing. Mel demonstrates by going on all fours on the dining-room table. Darren says it's a very sexual pose and leaps up behind her to demonstrate how Barry will climb on to her model. Laughing, he picks Mel up, spins her round and puts her down. Claire asks him if he is a bum man and he says he is. They all talk about which bit of the human anatomy most turns them on. For Darren, breasts come second to bums – to Claire's surprise as she thought he would choose legs. Claire says she looks at eyes and comments, for a second time, on how nice Tom's eyes and eyelashes were. Anna says she never falls for anyone on their looks. Mel jokes that she looks for a big penis, but then says she is actually turned on by nice hands. Claire admits that she is very shallow: 'I see a bloke and I think "fitness on legs".'

Darren and Mel talk about their first few days in the house. Mel says she didn't speak to Tom or Anna at first. Anna agrees: 'For weeks and weeks she ignored me. And she tripped me up, twice.' Darren says he didn't talk to Craig at first. Fooling around with the chicken wire he pretends to have an enormous willy, to the amusement of the girls. He tells Mel that she can talk him into having his genitals pierced, by telling him how it will improve his love-making.

Claire and Mel have not really established a rapport, but when Claire asks her how she acquired her skills with make-up Mel is happy for a girlie chat. She tells Claire how she modelled for a make-up artist and now gets a discount on the range of products that were used. Darren joins in the chat. Mel says she used to hate her skin colour and her hair and, when she was eleven, she had all her hair shaved off. 'I looked like a boy and I had a large unconventional bum.'

Claire confesses that she was a heavyweight teenager and that when she ran the ground shook and people scattered before her. Both girls agree that they used to hate their feet. Darren listens with interest and then says: 'I have no complexes. I was born beautiful.'

It's time for the nominations and the three girls decide to express their feelings for the process by wearing knickers on their heads and lashings of make-up. Anna lends a pair of clean pants to Claire.

When Darren is in the Diary Room making his nominations a huge shock runs through the rest of the group, who are in the living area – they clearly hear him name names. To reinforce his nominations he repeats the names, quite loudly, but oblivious to the fact that he can be heard; the Diary Room has always been the private sanctum where secrets are shared only with Big Brother and the viewing public, not the other contestants. Perhaps Claire, who was worried that she could be heard outside, was right – now the house is much more empty and quiet, voices carry more.

When Darren comes out, cheerfully singing 'It's only a game show', he soon senses that the mood of the group is dangerously changed and, when they tell him that they heard him, he is visibly shaken, thinking at first that they are winding him up. When Craig whispers the names to him, his jaw drops. Mel has followed him into the Diary Room to make her nominations – she's the last on the list – and when she comes out busies herself with her photo-sculpture. Darren asks if he can have a private word with her. In the bedroom she tells him she is fine, but there are tears on her face and she admits she is gutted. Darren describes it as 'fucking sick' and tells her that he nominated her because he hadn't nominated her for ages and that was how he chose. He tells her later that he wants her to go home to see her mum.

After thinking about the mess for a while Darren goes to the Diary Room.

'This is terrible. Mel is crying in there. I want to change my nominations. She said she is gutted and that hurt me more than it hurts her. I feel really sick. I just don't like it. I want to change my nominations.'

He goes to the Diary Room three times in half an hour.

He tells the group that he has asked to change his nominations. Mel is still in the girls' bedroom and Claire goes to comfort her, giving her some chocolate. Craig and Darren discuss the fact that Darren also nominated Craig, but Craig's reaction is very different to Mel's. He shakes hands with Darren and, when asked, tells Darren that he nominated him. Darren says that's cool with him and Craig says, 'We're all in here to win and I think you'll win over me.'

Darren then gives his reason for nominating Craig: 'I wanted you to see your business is all right, see if your garage is OK.'

Craig, honest as ever, replies: 'I told them you were a pussy.'

At quarter past four there is an announcement to the whole group from Big Brother – the nominations for this week have been cancelled and they must all go to the Diary Room to do them again. 'Big Brother understands the nominations should be confidential. Big Brother is sorry,' says the voice.

This time the girls take it seriously – no knickers on their heads, no OTT make-up. Everyone makes exactly the same nominations as before, with the exception of Darren. He substitutes Claire for Melanie. The rest of the group is ordered to stay in the garden while the nominations procedure takes place to avoid any more sound leaks from the Diary Room. They play football, arriving in the Diary Room out of breath.

WHO NOMINATES WHO

ANNA	Claire and Craig
CLAIRE	Darren and Melanie
CRAIG	Anna and Darren
DARREN	Craig and Melanie on the first round of nominations, then Claire and Craig on the second round
MELANIE	Claire and Craig
REASONS:	
ANNA on CLAIRE	'She's lovely, really nice but she's new, and I've known the others longer.'
CRAIG on DARREN	'He's so vain, such a wimp.'
DARREN on CLAIRE	'So that she can see her little baby brother.'

The incident with Darren and the nominations doesn't stop the others from seeking sanctuary in the Diary Room, though. Both Mel and Anna have a lot to get off their chests. Anna starts the ball rolling by telling Big Brother: 'It's doing my head in. It's changed my opinions of some people.' She says Darren explained his reasons for nominating and she's genuinely shocked that he tackles the choice that way, especially now they are so near to the end.

'Then he wanted to change his nominations. That to me spoke volumes. Utter guilt. He didn't say, "I want to do them again," he said, "I want to change them. I didn't mean it." So why did he nominate them in the first place? It's very interesting and has completely changed my outlook on certain people here. Craig also told us how he voted. I'm gobsmacked by both of their ways of thinking. It's so wanting to win, which I suppose is fair enough. It's a game show, there's money up for grabs, but voting people that you get on with... I want to go to Darren and say, "You little shit, you. Voting for Craig and Melanie over Claire, who fair enough is a lovely girl, but she's only been here a week and a half. What is your reason for doing that?" I think it's crap, a stupid game show and I just want to go home again. I want to switch off and get pissed tonight and not talk to anyone for a week. Sod them and their stupid, selfish ways.'

As soon as Anna comes out Mel goes in. 'I was really shocked at how I responded when I heard Darren say my name. It kind of makes everything a bit sour. I don't want to know why people are nominated, who they're nominating. If I'm nominated that's fine and I don't care who did it. But if I do know I can't help but think why, why is it me?

'We've got a new person come in, Claire. If I was in her position I'd find it very hard to get involved in a group that's already very solid and very well formed.'

She says that Claire sometimes misreads the mood of the group.

'There's only the odd occasion. For instance, today after we had this mess up and I was in my room and Darren came in to speak to me, I was quite tearful and Darren was emotional about it and she came in and kinda tried to make a joke of it. I feel in those situations a tiny bit of sensitivity wouldn't go amiss and I think that's something Claire might be lacking.'

Darren copes with the crisis by retiring to the boys' bedroom and going to bed. Later in the evening Mel joins Craig in the hot tub and they discuss the fiasco. Craig asks if she is feeling disappointed with Darren over the reasons he gave for the nominations. He describes Darren's reason for nominating Mel – so that she can see her mum – as 'pitiful'.

'Over the last few weeks, I'm seeing a wimpish, two-faced person in Darren. I feel let down by him. It's just shit.'

He says the reason Darren gave for nominating him – so that he could see his business and his garage – is as phoney as the one he gave for nominating Mel. She asks what Craig thinks Darren's real reasons are.

'He's thinking about people who could win over him,' Craig says. 'Don't you think he's false? All love and nice things he says. I've just got some doubt. He's really trying to use it that he's got children, he thinks it will benefit him, which I think it will.'

Darren is being comforted by Anna and tells her that he is coping with the fallout of the debacle.

'I'm cool. I keep remembering it, but I just say fuck it, there's nothing I can do, they heard it, it's too late...'

By bedtime Craig and Claire are back on practical-joke form. He plans to put her bed in the hot tub, but when this proves too much for him he settles for removing the slats under the mattress, so that she will fall through. He's thwarted when she spots that someone has been messing with her pillows.

She solves the problem of reassembling her bed by sleeping in the boys' room, in Tom's bed. Into the early hours she talks to Darren and Craig about what turns a woman on and what turns her off. In the latter category she lists grubby, saggy underwear, kissing hard and dodgy shoes and socks. Although the boys don't know how Nick went about kissing, they reckon he fails the other two tests.

The conversation degenerates and the boys try to impress Claire with their farting noises. In the meantime Mel and Anna, kept awake by the giggles, get up and go to the kitchen for a crisp sandwich.

Anna is in a cynical mood triggered by the events of the day. She tells Mel that Craig 'tells stories about himself all the time to make us think he's worthy of something. He so wants to win.'

She's feeling generally fed up with all the others, with the exception of Mel, to whom she is drawing much closer. Talking about life after *Big Brother* she says:

'I don't think I would enjoy the company of many people from this house… less than a handful I would actually go for a drink with.' She says she wouldn't mind if she never saw Nick again. She doesn't even want to watch the TV programmes when she gets out. 'I never want to see it – I don't like looking at myself on TV.'

The comfortable collusion between Mel and Anna continues the next morning, with Claire still asleep in the boys' room. They make tea and go back to bed to drink it and smoke cigarettes, and Anna jokes that they are turning into 'two fat, loud-mouthed sloths who spend the day eating and smoking in bed'.

They are all out of bed by 1 p.m., in time for the results of the nominations. Anna thinks there may be four names on the list; Mel thinks three. They are both nervous and Anna says she's 'sick of feeling sick'. To while away the final few minutes before Big Brother's voice breaks the news to them, Darren and Anna have a quick tidy-up. The constant photocopying and cutting up of paper for the models is making the place messy.

When the announcement comes, it is Claire and Craig. Unbeknown to the housemates Darren's change in nominating made a big difference – if he had stuck with Mel, then Craig would have had three votes, and Claire, Darren and Mel would all have had two, so all four would have been up for the vote. Darren's change saved his own skin and Mel's and meant that Claire had an equal number of nominations with Craig. They both take the news very calmly. Claire, who has never had unrealistic hopes of surviving beyond her first week in the nominations, says 'It's been nice knowing you.' Craig suddenly realizes he now equals Caroline's record of being nominated three times and he points out that on her third time she was evicted.

Called to the Diary Room, he tells Big Brother: 'When you are nominated three times you start to think if people inside may not like you – do the viewers like you? You tend to think because Mel has not been nominated at all the viewers will think she's a perfect girl. There's nothing wrong with Mel, but the audience may think she deserves to win it because she's not been nominated.'

Darren teases Mel in the same vein, saying that she will go down in history as the girl who was never nominated for eviction. Mel reminds him that there is still one more week of nominations. For Darren, there is a sense of relief at not hearing his name, although he admits that there are times when he just wants to go home. Claire said she was pissed off yesterday, although the evening was great.

'In the day I just had the feeling that this is crap,' she says.

'You get that feeling a lot in here,' Darren says.

Mel brightens the day up by announcing that her sculpture of herself will be nude, with just three carefully placed photocopied leaves. She gets Anna to take photos of her naked. They spend half an hour in the bedroom together; Mel striking various artistic poses and Anna clicking away with the camera.

Afterwards Mel announces she is not happy with the bum pictures, but instead of doing one large photocopy she will do lots of little ones. Later, when the boys are out of the room, she and Anna giggle as she copies her boobs and her belly button by lying on top of the photocopier. Anna, who after Nick is probably the housemate most conscious of the ever-present cameras, comments, 'This will make great television.'

Mel is hyperactive in the afternoon, possibly suffering from a delayed reaction to yesterday's trauma or simply out of relief at not finding herself on the nomination list. She bakes bread, cooks herself lots of snacks, dances, sings to herself, and, eventually, goes to bed, undressing and turning out the lights – only to get up five minutes later. She even peers closely at one of the cameras, trying to decide if it is a boy camera or a girl camera. Her verdict is that is a girl.

In the Diary Room Darren talks about the aftermath of the nominations furore.

'Mel broke down and I still feel sad for the fact that she broke down because when I asked how she felt she said "gutted" and started crying. Next day I said, "Forget about it, throw it over your head, squash it." I'll be fine, I know I will. It's not worth thinking about. It's too late. Last night I wanted to come out and say, "Forget about it. It doesn't matter. I've said your name and you've heard me saying it. It's too late, there's nothing you can do about it, so squash it."'

The late afternoon and early evening are whiled away in idle chat, Craig and Claire together and Anna and Mel together. Darren, who is making a lot of progress with his guitar lessons, tells the others that his true ambition is to become a rhythm and blues star, like his idol Craig David.

He remains slightly isolated from the group all day. Anna and Mel cook a Spanish omelette for the evening meal and Darren, who does not eat eggs, makes himself a sandwich which he takes into the bedroom to eat.

Claire has been very unsettled by the events of the past twenty-four hours. She genuinely expected to be nominated, but she finds the process distasteful. She tells Anna her feelings when they share the hot tub.

'I feel cool about being nominated. I knew my name would come up, from day one. I've got the hump a little bit but it's nothing to do with my name being called. Normally, when I've got the hump, I open my mouth but it's not the same in here. But if my friends are watching they'll think I'm not being myself. In here, there's nothing to do, nothing else to think about, so naturally your brain goes over something a bit more interesting, over and over. I'm actually beginning to bore myself in my head.'

Anna tells Claire she can offload on her.

'Either way round my name would have come up, so that's not the issue,' Claire says, 'but there were two names heard. One person didn't react at all and one did. I feel it stinks a bit, there's a bit of manipulation going on.'

'Are you angry with someone's reaction or the decision?' Anna asks.

'Both, equal. I think it was really pathetic. It's easy for me to say. Obviously, it's a lot harder if you've been in here a long time and it happens. But because there's someone else and he's been here the same length of time, that's why I say it about both of them and not just the one. If it was just the hurt about the decision, regardless of whether Big Brother said we could change our nominations the mood would stay the same. But the minute Big Brother said we could change, they were all laughing, happy, all buddies again. The mood has changed too quickly. That's a bit sick. Whether there are lingering things or not, the initial reaction was really, really happy.'

She is implying that Mel was more concerned with the outcome of the nominations than with the hurt of hearing Darren name her. Anna defends Mel, saying that she was very shocked by Darren.

Claire says that Darren announcing he was going to change his nominations was 'like getting caught nicking sweets from a shop – you can't go back and change the consequences'.

Anna agrees that it is Darren's reaction, rather than the technical fault, that has upset her.

'Why was he acting like that?' Claire asks. 'It's like pure guilt. It's fair enough to do the whole thing again, but not to change the names.'

'He basically wants Craig and Mel out of the house and that speaks volumes,' says Anna, who seems to be agreeing with Craig's reading of the situation – that Darren was nominating those he saw as his strongest competitors.

The talk with Anna does not assuage Claire's unhappiness, but it does open up the line of communication between her and Anna. Anna takes her time about getting to know anybody and she has snubbed Claire once or twice, possibly without realizing it. Earlier in the day she blanked her twice, once by stopping talking in midsentence when Claire joined her and Mel in the garden, and once while talking to Mel about the sculpture challenge.

Claire is still not happy and four and a half hours later, just after 1 a.m., she goes to talk to Big Brother.

'When I came into the house I knew a few things were certain almost. I knew it was very unlikely that I would win and that it was likely there would be bad stories in the press and stuff. So, when I ask myself why I came in, I have to think it was for the experience and that was why it was, and I was happy that even if I got nominated out in the second week (which I was pretty positive I would) I would have had a really good fun time here. But it gets you down a bit. People disappoint you and it's really sad. I didn't expect that.

'When you are watching at home, looking in, you see people sitting around a room and you can't feel the tension that's in the room. But you can when you are in here. And it's intense sometimes. Definitely for some people, not everyone, there's another agenda going on. People ask if you are OK and you know they are not asking 'cos they really want to know if you're OK.

'I promised to myself I would be true to myself... Things do get magnified in here, there's nowhere to hide or run... That's why it feels so bad because there's nothing else to think about. I understand their behaviour is not natural. Some people want to win. They behave the way they do for that purpose. I feel negative about the motives, not about the person. They've been saying that when we leave here we won't want a reunion because we won't be friends, but I would like to meet up with them. I don't feel bad towards any of them, I just don't like some of the behaviour.

'I've watched nominations on television and it made me laugh, the way they are nice to people and then nominate them. I prefer being on the other side watching it: it's not nice nominating and then being nice to people.'

She is not the only one who is still unsettled. Later on, sharing another session in the hot tub with Craig, Claire jokes about giving him a present of a blow-up doll because she feels he's about to explode with sexual frustration. She asks him what presents he would give the others in the house and he replies without a moment's consideration: 'I'd give Darren a right hook.'

Before they go to bed Craig and Claire rearrange the life-size sculptures into a tangled mass of limbs, as if they were all taking part in an orgy. They place Mel and Anna in a '69' position. When Mel sees the mess the next morning she is not amused and calmly removes her model before she has her breakfast.

Two days ago Craig cracked a tooth, and a dentist has been summoned to see him in the Diary Room on Wednesday morning. He sets the alarm clock the night before because none of the housemates can rely on being awake by 9.15 a.m. Unfortunately, he leaves the clock in the girls' room but Mel goes through to wake him. He needn't have been up so early as the dentist is stuck in traffic and turns up nearly an hour and a half late.

Eventually he is summoned to the Diary Room and instructed to take his toothbrush. The dentist, who has a nurse with her, tells him off for over-zealous brushing of his teeth and says his toothbrush is not fit to clean anything but the loo. Craig protests that it is a new brush, bought specially for his sojourn in the house.

Claire is still sleeping off her late-night session in the tub, but at 11 a.m. Mel and Anna start to worry that she will not finish her sculpture in time for Big Brother's judging. She eventually gets up at 11.30 a.m., with a bit of cajoling from Anna. The two boys have finished their models but the girls have still got work to do.

They complete the task with half an hour to spare and as the sun is out they all lie in the garden to make the most of it. Darren once again turns the conversation round to Claire's boobs. He tries to persuade her to remove her top and he sings 'Get your tits out for the lads...'.

Claire tells him she doesn't want to subject her scars to direct sun. Then she tells him that she could never appear on Page Three in the *Sun*, as all the boobs in the pictures are natural. This prompts a discussion on why girls have the operation and whether it's available on the NHS. Darren wants to know if breast size is hereditary. Claire says no, because her mother's are huge. Anna says they're all well-endowed in her family.

Claire's breasts have provided them with one endless source of speculation, but there's also another regular theme developing in the stories she tells them about her life. She is a driving disaster, having written off all the four cars she has ever owned. She was even stopped once for driving a stolen car which she had bought unwittingly. On one occasion she was arrested after colliding with a telegraph pole, and the police stopped their car at her nan's to tell her grandmother she'd been arrested. Her nan told the policemen to look after her. However, it's not only when she's behind the wheel that she gets into trouble – she also picks up parking tickets at the rate of three or four a week.

At 1 p.m. they face the moment of truth – the judging of the models. They each have to adopt the same pose as their model so that Big Brother can assess the size. Then the sculptures are taken to the Diary Room to be examined more closely.

Mel and Darren discuss who they miss most among the evictees. At first Darren plumps for Caroline, and then Sada for whom he has always had a soft spot. 'She's just a memory now, the one we never got to know.' Mel says she misses Tom the most, but they both agree that if they had the chance to bring one person back into the house it would be Nick.

'He was so funny because he was so competitive. If he came back it would be weird and interesting,' says Mel. 'He would cause uproar, chaos. It might be horrible but he would be the most interesting to have back.'

They are all despondent when Big Brother announces the results of the sculpture challenge. They have failed. Two of the sculptures – Darren's and Anna's – failed on height, being a combined total of 17 centimetres too small. Craig's and Claire's failed because plain paper was used instead of photocopies.

Only Mel's is deemed good enough to pass. The food budget for next week, with four people left, will be a paltry £21. Darren tells them they will have to eat from the garden. Anna decides to ignore Big Brother and tells them all that they did very well, put a lot of effort in, and they don't need approval from Big Brother. Craig's comment is even more succinct: 'Kiss my arse.'

There's still some film left with the camera, so they whizz around taking photographs. Claire tells them to say 'shit' instead of cheese as it makes them pout and 'gives you a better smile'. They practise shouting it enthusiastically. They have a group photo on the sofa and then lie in a circle with their heads together. Craig climbs into bed with each of the girls in turn, so that Darren can record the moment.

Later, they photocopy all the group shots so that everyone can have a copy. Darren even makes himself an improvised album to display his prints.

In the evening Darren gives Mel a lesson in how to gut fish. When she says she is going to bake the fish without gutting them he tells her, 'Right now, my mum is throwing a wobbly and so is yours.' He lets her handle cooking the second course – a rice pudding.

Craig asks Claire if he can have her toothbrush if she leaves on Friday. She agrees and also offers to leave him her deodorant.

Big Brother sets them another mini-challenge – in twenty-four hours they must prepare and present a news bulletin about life in the house. They must all take part, but they must not play themselves. They start discussing possible news stories, like the fiasco over the nominations, the pornography on the photocopier and the scandal of a girl sleeping in the boys' bedroom. Claire is not well and goes to bed without eating. Craig takes some rice pudding through to her and is feeding her tenderly. 'Oh, you've got some on your nose, that little nose of yours,' he says, wiping it off. 'Is that better?'

'Well, better than up my nose,' Claire says.

Darren joins them and before long they are fooling around, dropping the pudding on to her. The other two girls come in to watch.

While Claire sleeps the others reminisce about life in the house. In a reprise of their earlier conversation, they talk about missing Nick and how quiet the house now is. Anna seems to need to fill the void – she's invented an imaginary housemate called Ronald. She talks to him from time to time, telling him to stop whistling. When Darren talks about being the youngest housemate, Anna says there is no upper age limit: Ronald is 108. Ronald is not the only strategy the group has developed to help them through. They no longer refer to the end of the show as two weeks and a couple of days away, they always say one week and nine days, one week and eight days. Somehow, it makes it sound closer.

They are all up late on Thursday and the girls make for the garden to enjoy the sunshine. Mel uses a pair of tweezers to pluck her bikini line and discusses with the other girls whether or not you get hairier as you get older. She apologizes to Craig for her personal preening, little realizing that one of Craig's greatest turn-offs in a woman is excessive pubic hair. The other girls in the house have been known to give themselves a quick trim in the shower, but Mel works away in public, without even a grimace of pain. Then she turns her attention – and her tweezers – on to her eyebrows.

They present an early evening news bulletin for *Big Brother Television Channel 4 News*, with Claire and Mel taking the part of the newsreaders, both sporting sensible black shirts, hair tied back and glasses. They introduce themselves as Crystal McFeisty and Fiona Cartwright Mason. Craig plays roving reporter Stigpea Bootleg, Darren plays Mel with a froth of coiled sticky tape on his head as a wig and Anna plays Dr Know-it-all, whose learned opinion is given on the important news items. These include the group failing their task, their wine tasting, Anna's excessive sleeping, Darren's obsessive tidiness, Claire's stolen chocolate, Mel's murder of a huge spider and Craig's wrecked toothbrush. The bulletin ends with the two presenters announcing that they're going off down the pub for a cider.

As a reward they have been promised a continental breakfast for the next day. Anna fantasizes about 'heaps of bacon, burgers and barbecue' until Craig brings her back to earth with a reminder that a continental breakfast means coffee, croissants and orange juice.

Claire surprises them all by revealing that she had a properly supervised test for Mensa, the society for people with high IQs – and she passed. She was told she was in the top 2 per cent of the population. But she likes to play dumb and immediately followed up by telling them it didn't mean she was smart, just that she is 'weird. Your brain's strange. If you've got a high IQ you're a bit of a divvy.' Darren comments that Sada had a high IQ – without Darren, Sada's presence in the house would be completely forgotten. Claire jokes that if she'd been there at the same time as Sada she would have told her she was 'a div', and those who knew Sada find this hysterically funny.

To while away the evening they set up a mini obstacle course in the garden and the girls beat the boys. The obstacles are a chair, which has to be leapt over; a bin, which has to be run around five times; a washing basket to hurdle over; and, a garden table, which they have to pass under. Racing side by side, Craig and Claire arrive at the table together and spend a happy few minutes struggling with each other as they try to squeeze through at the same time. Then Craig improvises a water slide with bin liners and he and Darren have great fun hurling themselves along it. The only girl who joins in is good sport Claire, but she doesn't quite have the boys' knack. However, because she's wet and dirty from the ground, Craig has a great excuse to hose her down afterwards and they play-fight enthusiastically, writhing on the ground together.

Next the pair of them devise another prank, only this time one with a barbed edge to it. They know that Darren's switch of voting caused a change in the nominations and neither of them is happy about his behaviour. He's also used Claire's toothbrush, the one she promised to give to Craig when she left. It was a genuine mistake because it is the same colour as his, but after taking it he wound Claire up by telling her that he also used it to brush his pubic hair. So the two Cs decide to wipe their sweaty bottoms on his pillow. They also wind a few of Craig's grey hairs around the bristles of Darren's own toothbrush.

'People will think we're disgusting, wiping our arses on pillows. And afterwards, when I'm at home, watching them go to bed each night will give me intense pleasure,' Claire says, giggling.

Then it's everyone into the hot tub and Anna comes up with a game for them all to play. One of them has to dive under the water and one of the others will then kiss them. The trick is to guess who has been doing the kissing. Anna's only rule is no tongues. It comes as no surprise when Craig volunteers to go first, and he gets his guess right by identifying Anna as the one who gave him an underwater smooch. When it is Darren's turn under the water Craig takes the plunge, causing Darren to leap out screaming, 'That was Craig!' Craig is shocked to be rumbled so quickly. 'I had a shave this morning,' he says.

They move on to above-the-water eyes-closed kissing, concentrating on ears and then backs. Craig enthusiastically licks Claire's back after gently unhooking her bikini top. But he fails to identify his favourite lady when she kisses his ear, guessing that it was Mel. The antics are getting wilder and both Mel and Claire begin to feel uncomfortable. Anna jokingly asks for her nipples to be sucked and Claire gives Mel a kiss, but in the end Mel calls a halt by climbing out.

When the others retire from the fray, Craig and Claire carry on playing together. They blow bubbles through a plastic tube and Craig describes it as the best blow job he's had in ages – then remembers it's the only one he's had in ages!

'Look at those two – they can just entertain each other for hours and hours,' says Anna.

On cue, Craig says to Claire, 'It's our last night together, Claire,' and they plunge across the water for a hug.

They play in the water for a time and Craig tenderly inspects a bruise on Claire's leg. She's worried about it because she wants to wear a dress that will show her knees when she leaves the house tomorrow, which she assumes will happen. Craig has a horrible thought – supposing the film of the kissing session in the hot tub is edited and only the clip of him kissing Darren is shown? He goes to worry Darren with the thought and, together with Claire, the two boys go to the Diary Room to plead with Big Brother. Craig begs Big Brother not to show the film of him and Darren kissing. Darren butts in to make it clear that they did not kiss: it was Craig who kissed him. Claire winds things up by saying they looked happy together and Craig points out that Darren did nothing to stop the kiss. Everyone collapses in giggles.

Later they talk about the other possibilities for film editing, and Claire wonders about the effect on her boyfriend. She tells Craig that her boyfriend is a ladies' man, and that she does not trust him completely. She hopes he will be there to meet her tomorrow. They talk about the possibility of ex-boyfriends and ex-girlfriends selling stories about them to newspapers and they wonder how much the going rate for one of these stories is.

Before they go to bed they prepare the table for the morning feast, with Claire picking fresh flowers for the centrepiece and Craig attempting to fold loo paper into posh napkins.

Craig looks at one of the cameras and says: 'Why are we doing this? They all voted us out. Shall we poison them?'

Friday starts late, at 12.30 p.m. The girls wake first and both Mel and Anna are anxious because it is an eviction day. Claire, who is confident that she is leaving, feels 'chilled out'.

Anna says: 'I just want Tuesday to be here because you know who's nominated, you know who's staying, you know who might be feeling nervous. That's the day I want to be here, that's the final nomination list. After that nobody has any control over anything.'

When Mel says the prospect is making her feel sick Anna tells her and Claire to close their eyes and breathe deeply and visualize. But instead of the usual stress-busting picture of a palm-fringed tropical beach, she tells them to imagine they are on the edge of a cliff, about to fall over. 'And then you die,' she says. Her dry, black humour breaks the tense mood and they all laugh.

Then they remember the continental breakfast. Anna finds the goodies in the Store Room and they don't wake the boys until they have steaming hot coffee ready to serve with the *pains aux chocolats*, the croissants and the Danish pastries. It's a first for Claire – she has never had a croissant before.

As they sit around enjoying the treats, a few regrets begin to creep in about the activities in the hot tub. Craig can't believe he actually kissed Darren. Claire says that after she leaves her father is going to give her a bad time about her language.

Mel is feeling low and goes for an afternoon nap. But instead of going to her own bed she curls up in Tom's. Later, she joins Anna and Claire in the girls' room and Claire regales them with stories of her boarding-school days, where the austere regime was similar in some ways to that in the *Big Brother* house.

The kitchen table has been put to lots of different uses by the housemates and, on Friday afternoon it becomes a massage table for Anna, who is given a massage by Craig. He checks first with Mel that the massage he gave her wasn't too hard and, when she gives the thumbs up, lays his hands on Anna, who is impressed. 'Heaven' is her verdict.

There are a few minutes of excitement when they find a mobile phone left behind in the Diary Room. They discuss using it to make a few calls or ransoming it to Big Brother. In the end, they behave themselves and leave it in the Diary Room to be removed by the production team. What none of them realize is the mobile actually belongs to Davina McCall, who has been rehearsing the evening show which will include film of her in the Diary Room. It sets them all off thinking about phone calls and who they would like to ring.

Claire cooks her last food in the *Big Brother* house – she makes some soup. Mel really appreciates it. She also appreciates Claire's singing voice, commenting to Anna that Claire should get a recording contract when she leaves.

Despite being so relaxed at the start of the day the tension is building up for Claire by the evening. She and Craig lie together on one of the beds and he puts his arm around her and strokes her hair.

'It will be a good night anyway, whoever goes,' Craig tells her. 'Out there it will be rocking, they'll be rocking their socks off.'

'I think it's safe to say it's going to be me,' says Claire, telling Craig that he must not feel nervous.

'I do, I still worry. There's been loads of things here that have surprised me. Andy evicted in the second week and getting won over by Caroline – I could not believe it. It made me want to go home. I felt it was a fucking fiddle, leaving Caroline in here because she was annoying people and that makes good television, while Andrew was a sound and funny guy.'

Craig reassures Claire that her family and her boyfriend will all be waiting for her.

The group decides to greet the eviction news from their favourite place – the hot tub. They have saved two bottles of red wine from their wine tasting and they drink these as they wait for Davina to give them the news. When it comes, it is what they all secretly expected – Claire is going home after only thirteen days in the house. She takes the news well, with lots of hugs and kisses for everyone.

She teases them about their pathetically small shopping money for next week and tells them she'll think of them when she's eating in a restaurant and her starter costs as much as their whole £21 budget.

Perhaps sensing that Craig and she should have a few moments on their own together, the others go back into the house. The inseparable pair hug and kiss and she whispers to him that she will miss him the most and that she hopes he wins. As he hugs her he manages to fumble one of her breasts, and she laughingly accuses him 'Oi! You just copped a feel!' He feebly defends himself by saying she pushed them against him.

Mel and Anna have already moved on in their thoughts to the next round of nominations: the last round. Mel thinks it will be great if all four of them get nominated while Anna predicts it will be Darren, Craig and herself.

Claire and Craig are so relaxed together that they stay in the tub until 10.15 p.m., when Big Brother has to order them into the house. 'Spoilsport,' Claire whispers under her breath as she goes inside to start packing and getting ready for her grand exit. Mel and Anna take her off to the bedroom 'for girlie things'. She models a slinky black dress but then changes into a stunning blue one for her exit. Mel does her make-up and they all discuss whether she should wear her hair up or down. The other two reassure her that she looks good:

'You are so beautiful, you are gorgeous, you're going to knock 'em dead, you're a million dollars,' says Anna.

They are called to the door. After a group hug and individual goodbyes, Claire tells them, 'I love you guys, seriously.' Then she's out, walking along the grille to meet Davina and her family at the gate.

'And then there were four,' Anna says, wistfully, after the frantic minute of waving from the door to the outside world. There's the usual Friday night music booming through the house, to mask the chants of the crowd, but for once there is no frenetic dancing by the remaining housemates. They seem more subdued than normal on an eviction night – the depression has kicked in early. Craig admits that losing Claire is more than 'my little mind can handle'.

Just before midnight, Craig discovers that Claire has left a bag behind. He takes it to the Diary Room and then talks to Big Brother about his feelings after surviving the nominations procedure for a record three times.

'Claire leaving was sad as I'd have liked to spend the rest of the duration in here with her. We snapped together straightaway, had a good giggle, she was up for a laugh, up for winding up the rest of the group. I'm sorry to have to say to her that I'm glad I'm still in.

'What I wish now is to be able to complete the show. That'll be a dream come true. It's hard to describe the mixed emotions of being happy that I'm still in here, of seeing my family for a brief time, but then knowing that you are losing a friend.

'A couple of weeks in here is like a couple of years outside. I can't put into words how the short time can drag out. But I fit so well in here. We've done so many things. I've seen a different side to my thoughts, emotions.'

He is worried that the rest of the group keep nominating him and feels he may even ask them why.

'All the people in here voted for me. What I'm worried about is the viewers thinking, he must be a right idiot because everybody is voting him out. Personally, I don't feel that way but the people in the house must feel something. Everyone says it's only a game show and you've gotta pick somebody. I've been in this seat and I know you've gotta pick. But I just hope their reasons for picking me aren't too bad... I'd respect them more if they said something to me and I could hopefully amend it... No one has approached me. I'm at a point where I may ask them but I don't want them to feel I'm being intimidating.'

He says he is certain he is going to be nominated again. 'If I'm not, I'll demand a recount!' he says. He predicts that Darren and Anna may also be nominated.

While Craig is pouring out his heart to Big Brother, Darren is pouring out a different feeling to the girls – disgust at the state of their room. Darren, the household's Mr Clean, tells them he thought that with one girl less in the house the room would be tidier.

'It looks as though twenty people are living in here. Every nook has got something in it.'

Mel and Anna chorus that the room is their 'walk-in wardrobe'.

'It's a walk-in mess, girls,' says Darren.

Within ten minutes of coming out of the Diary Room, Craig decides to ask the others why they keep nominating him. They listen in silence, as he makes a very similar speech to the one he made to Big Brother:

'I'm very aware that you all voted for me last week. I have no objections, no quarrels. I'm positive it will happen again this week... When it comes to this level, so close to the end, it does partly become a personal thing. If there is anything in particular that I'm doing that is aggravating or annoying anyone... I know that in here the tiniest little thing, like you tie your shoelaces wrong, can annoy people. If there's anything, I would respect you if you told me. I don't want anyone to feel intimidated or feel it would embarrass me. If there's a problem and I'm doing something wrong hopefully I can amend it, make it more comfortable for you.'

The others listen in silence, Anna nodding now and again, and finally saying, jokingly, 'We'll let you know tomorrow, Craig.'

An hour later, as Mel prepares for bed, Craig tells Anna how much he will miss Claire.

'We clicked on. It's not a fancying thing, because obviously she's got a long-term fella and I wouldn't put her in a position, or humiliate myself. But it was nice, messing around, flirting. It's good, nice, when you know for sure that nothing's going to happen and she probably knew the same.'

Later, the two remaining girls discuss Craig's unhappiness and Anna comments that he must find it very hard losing his soulmate, Claire.

'I'd go mad if I didn't have you to chat to of an evening. And being nominated three times in a row...'

Mel says she doesn't think Craig really talks, anyway. She says he's 'really sweet and nice, and I think he's hurt because he realizes I've nominated him. I feel guilty. He feels hurt and crushed.'

The girls go on to discuss whether they could have prepared themselves better or handled things differently in the house. Mel says if she had her time again she would make more effort to get on with everybody and be interested in everybody, from the beginning. She says she did not click with Sada or Nicky, who she says

WEEK SEVEN FACT FILE

MAIN TASK PASS ■ FAIL ☒	Make photo-sculptures of their own bodies that must stand up unassisted.
MINI-TASKS	Wine tasting. Prepare a news bulletin about life in the *Big Brother* house.
TREATS	Five bottles of wine for correctly identifying the most expensive bottle of wine in the wine tasting. Continental breakfast is their reward for the news report.
BOOKIES' FAVOURITE TO WIN	Craig's still the punters' favourite to win with odds of 1/4. Anna comes in as second favourite at 9/4, Mel third at 16/1.
TO WALK	Darren is the hot tip to walk next week.

was difficult, or, to a lesser extent, Caroline. Anna says she didn't click with Sada, although she felt she knew as much as she wanted to about her. She also had some problems with Nicky and she didn't establish any rapport with Tom.

'The last two weeks are going to be the most difficult,' says Mel.

Darren is coping with another problem, not related to nominations or depression about the eviction. He has eaten some Brie cheese and he feels sick. He is sick.

WHAT THE EXPERT SAYS

'It's obvious that both the guys and the girls are missing sexual contact. What's interesting, however, is how the two go about expressing this need. The guys are much more prone to throwing in off-the-cuff remarks about missing sex, joking about it, actually bringing it in to nearly every situation. The girls are more likely to discuss this in the context of longing and in the context of missing emotional bonding.

'Although in the early days all eyes were on who would be the dominant male, it's now apparent that the dominant people in the house are female. Mel was the dominant female from the start of the show. Now we are seeing a whole new side of Anna. She's emerging as the leader... She effectively emasculates the boys. What Mel and Anna have is a very powerful alliance, more powerful because the boys are split.'

Linda Papadopoulos, Counselling Psychologist

CLAIRE LOOKS BACK

For Claire, real life starts again within a few yards of the blue door she walked through thirteen days earlier, with her *Big Brother* suitcases and a box of Chinese takeaway. She is preoccupied with not catching her heels in the metal grating that leads from the door, but when she catches sight of her mum she breaks into a run. There are 800 people in the crowd to cheer the new girl out of the house and they give her a great reception. The usual bank of flashlights pops as she passes the press photographers and, to her astonishment, by the following morning she has knocked President Clinton and Britt Ekland off the front page of *The Times*, which runs a huge picture of her.

Once again, the viewing figures for the Friday night programmes are enormous with 5.3 million people watching the early slot and 4.4 million tuning in to see Claire in the studio with Davina. With the Tuesday to Thursday programmes moved forward by an hour to a 10 p.m. slot, viewing figures for the whole week are up, averaging 5.6 million (the Wednesday show got 6.4 million, second only to the 6.9 million who watched Nick's departure). The website is being hit an average of three million times a day, a million clear of its nearest UK website rival.

For Claire, there are family and friends to greet her and, to her surprise, her stepmother arrives carrying her baby brother, Josh, born in the early hours of the day she went into the house. It's not the name she would have chosen for him. She wanted her dad and stepmum to call him Brandon. But that's a very minor disappointment. Among the friends in the studio is her boyfriend, who watches with a pained expression while clips are shown of the moments in the house when Claire got close to Craig.

The following morning, at the press conference, it's the question that the journalists come back to over and over again. Does she miss Craig? Does she plan to see him again? How does Claire's boyfriend feel about her friendship with Craig? She fielded all the questions expertly, stressing that Craig is just a great mate, an ally, and refusing to comment on whether the relationship would have gone any further if she had survived longer in the house.

Afterwards she talks about her time inside and the effect being chosen had on her life.

' I wasn't upset or relieved to leave so soon – I totally expected it. I knew that if I came up for nomination the viewers would vote me out because I'm the newcomer. I didn't take it personally and I certainly didn't want to beat Craig. I hope he wins.

'I went in there for the fun of it and I had a brilliant time. I loved it. It was fantastic. There was nothing about it that was disappointing. Of course, I would have loved to stay longer but I knew I wouldn't, so I was cool when I heard my name.'

Claire knew that she was a standby a couple of weeks before the programme started, having gone through the same selection procedures as the others and making it to the final twenty-strong shortlist.

'At the beginning of the second week it looked as though Sada might walk out and I had a couple of phone calls to see if I was still OK about being a stand-by. A camera crew came to make a film of me to use as an introduction if I went into the show. So I felt quite excited, but when she stayed until she was voted out I thought it was unlikely to happen again. I put it out of my mind.

'When the Nick thing blew up I had phone calls from everyone who knew I was on standby, but I told them because a boy had gone he would be replaced with a boy. I had a call on Thursday telling me in strict confidence that they might be putting a girl in, but I still did not think it would be me.

'Then my stepmum was starting in labour and the phone was ringing all the time because of that, and I put *Big Brother* to the back of my mind. Dad went to hospital with her on the Friday, so I stayed at home manning the baby hotline. Toni Cox [from *Big Brother*] rang me and said she could not tell me what was happening but would let me know by ten o'clock on Saturday morning.

'I was up all hours waiting for news of the baby, drinking wine while I was answering the phones and watching *Big Brother* on the internet at the same time. I was so sure it would not be me going in that when I got the news about the baby I rang Toni and said, 'Hello, *Big Brother*, I just thought I'd let you know I've got a little brother.' It was the early hours of the morning, so she probably wasn't pleased, but she was very nice about it.

'In the morning, I went out to buy orange juice, two bottles of wine to replace the ones I'd drunk and some food. I was expecting to have a nice lazy weekend chilling with the new baby.

'My boyfriend was with me, and as it got closer to ten o'clock I was sure I wasn't going in – I felt they had probably arranged it all with someone else and that I was just one of the others who would receive a phone call saying not this time.

'Then Toni rang and asked me where I was. I said I was at my dad's house. Then she said she was outside in a car. She said they were putting me in the house. I had to pack as fast as I could. I knew I couldn't take in any clothes that had logos on them and when I looked in my wardrobe I thought I must be such a sad person because almost everything had names on. And lots of my stuff that I took was damp because I had to grab it out of the tumble-dryer.'

After a day at a hotel being photographed, and then briefed by Ruth Wrigley and Conrad Green, Claire was taken to the *Big Brother* site and walked through a battery of photographers to the blue door.

'I wasn't nervous. People kept asking me if I was OK and I really was. I knew I would not be in for long – I told my mum I would see her in a week, then Toni told me I would not be up for nomination the first week so I changed it to "See you in a fortnight."

'Conrad told me that after the Nick problem they wanted me to go in "in the spirit of *Big Brother*". I told him there was nothing to worry about – I was just looking forward to having a laugh and a good time.

'I was pleased that I had not been watching every episode of the show. I'd deliberately not got too involved watching it, which helped when it came to talking to the others. If I said I knew certain things I'm sure their minds would have been focused on the fact that I had seen them on television and they'd be wondering which bits had been shown. They'd be wondering what I knew and didn't know.

'I didn't want them to feel uncomfortable around me. The last thing they wanted was a smug, gobby git. There were lots of times when I nearly said things. Then I'd remember and cover up by looking vague and saying that I'd forgotten what I was saying. They were so pleased to have someone new to talk to that within the first few days they'd told me so much about life in the house that it was no longer a problem. I was glad to listen to them telling me things, like all about Nick, and give no sign that I already knew it all.

'For the first couple of days they would jokingly try to ask me things, but it was never serious and someone else would always say "Leave her alone".'

Claire took in with her two bottles of wine, some cooking sauces and 200 cigarettes – even though she doesn't smoke.

'I thought it might look a bit creepy, but then I guessed that if you are a smoker and you are running short you'd just be glad of them. And they were.'

Claire had already briefly met Darren, at her audition. They'd clicked then and for her first couple of days in the house he was her best mate.

'We've got the same taste in music and he's feeling really starved of music so I was able to remind him of songs that were in the charts just before he went in. I didn't recognize him instantly. For some reason, I thought that the guy I got on so well with at the audition was called Philip. And when I saw Darren on television he looked familiar, but he had hair when I met him before.

'I don't think he's vain or selfish – he's just sending himself up when he seems vain. He's into his designer labels but I can understand that. And he joked about it. He'd say things like "Craig dared to look at my Prada shoes". I think he was worried that Craig would go too far and throw them in the hot tub or something. He and Craig do rub each other up the wrong way a bit. I got the hump with him when he changed his nomination but you have to remember that, although he seems mature, he's actually very young. After he'd done it, he was very nice to me, putting in a lot of effort.

'Tom was very funny and I'd love to see him again. I don't think Anna or Mel would think it was any great loss if they never saw me again but I'd hope to keep in touch with them all. Because I was hyped up when I got in there I couldn't sleep for the first few nights and as it was the boys who stayed up late playing cards I tended to be with them more than with the girls.

'I said to one of the producers before I went in that I expected to get on with Mel best because in the programmes I had watched she seemed to be really fun, up for a laugh, similar to me. But I did know about her kissing Andy and then getting close to Tom, and within minutes of Tom going she moved on Craig, rubbing his head and asking him for a massage. I knew she'd do it and Craig knew what the game was, too.

'I was aware that I was getting on her nerves. At one point Craig said to her, "You're not the feisty one – she is." He pointed at me. She wasn't pleased. But I never felt I was in competition with her. She's got a stunning figure, a beautiful face and she's very bright, she need never feel threatened.

'I thought she made too much of a song and dance over the nominations. Craig behaved admirably and it was just the same thing that happened to him. Then I shared my Maltesers with her because I was trying to lift her spirits and she went into the Diary Room and slated me. She got what she wanted. Darren changed his nomination. That made her happy.

'Anna is really easy to get on with, very funny and nice. But you don't get close, you don't get past too many walls. I think she thought I was a silly, giggly girl, but she listens to you and sees into you quite quickly. In the last couple of days, I was joking about being "nice but dim" and she said "I don't think you're dim".'

But it was obvious to all the viewers that Craig is Claire's favourite.

'I am very, very, very, very fond of Craig. We were good mates. I felt like I'd known him for years. He is just a great guy. If people don't like him, that's their problem. He doesn't care. He hasn't got an agenda and with the others you did have to wonder. If they asked if you were OK, you were never sure whether they really cared or whether they were performing for the cameras.

'Craig asked me to tell his mum how much he loved her and that he was sorry he didn't say it enough, and to give a message to his two nieces.'

What she really loved about Craig was his willingness to have fun.

'Being in there is like being a kid again. You've got no responsibilities and you can have a laugh. Craig doesn't mind making a fool of himself, looking silly. I don't mind either. When we had egg fights the others didn't want to get egg in their hair, but we didn't mind. How can you not have fun when you can go to bed and get up whenever you want, and there are vegetables and chickens in the garden?'

Claire never saw taking part in *Big Brother* as the passport to a different life. She was leaving her job running her mother's flower shop anyway and hopes to train in IT because she believes 'I'll never be out of work'. If she ends up working in television or singing she will be happy, but it's not an important goal for her. As for her relationship with her boyfriend, it has survived plenty of ups and downs and she feels they can weather the storm of the publicity over her fondness for Craig.

'I can't imagine life without my boyfriend in it. We have a laugh together, he's laid-back and easy-going, he doesn't take himself seriously. We have lots of shared history.'

At the same time, she hopes she never loses touch with Craig and that she's there for him when he comes out of the house.

Summing up her experience in three words, she says: 'Brilliant, awesome, fantastic.'

'I'm dead chuffed to still be here.'
ANNA

1 TO 8 SEPTEMBER

At quarter past ten on Saturday morning, Mel wonders whether Claire is 'at home, in a hotel, or at a press conference'. She's scored two out of three: at that precise moment, last night's evictee is en route from the hotel where she spent the night to a press conference. The fact that Mel is wondering about the outside world shows that the end is getting close and the contestants are beginning to dwell on the reception they will get when they leave the *Big Brother* house.

Anna reminds Mel that there is less than two weeks to go. They agree that this is nothing and that the time will fly. They may be whistling in the dark because experience has shown that the fewer of them there are in the house, the harder it is to entertain themselves. Anna shocks Mel by saying that she was kept awake in the night by a strange noise coming from Mel's bed.

'You were making clanking noises with your teeth. I couldn't work it out. I have a friend who grinds her teeth and I thought it was that, but then I worked out it was your tongue piercing.'

'That's horrible,' says Mel.

They brighten when they talk about the next task and Anna says prophetically that it will be a skill, like juggling. She is right, but juggling is only one part of it: the challenge is to put on the *Big Brother* circus. They must walk 3 metres of a tightrope unaided and without touching the ground, unicycle for ten seconds unaided and juggle three balls for thirty seconds. Between the four of them, they are allowed only three mistakes. They all know how difficult the unicycle is – when Nichola had hers in the house, Craig spent a whole week struggling to do it before he was competent enough to cross the living area. They decide that, after the fiasco with the photo-sculptures, they will wager only 20 per cent of their budget on this one.

Big Brother provides them with everything they need, including a supply of multicoloured clown wigs and red noses. As Anna reads out the rules, they all laugh at the one that says they must not attempt the tightrope under the influence of alcohol.

'That would be a fine chance,' she says.

Craig's low mood has not lifted and he admits to Mel that he already misses Claire. He says he thinks they are all getting lazy and, as a group, they should do more, like writing poems and playing games. But obviously not yet – he goes out into the garden and falls asleep!

Anna is also in a very wistful mood, but for her the sadness provides inspiration and she writes a melodic little song:

Today I know that I will see your face again
You will be waiting there for me
And when I put my arms around you, you will see...

She struggles with the last line and comes up with 'That I hate being on TV', and 'How much I am needing a pee'.

Darren, who is musically very in tune with Anna, picks up the gentle melody and whistles it.

Craig and Anna reassure each other that they can make it through the next two weeks and, whatever happens, they are glad to have been part of the *Big Brother* project. Craig says he thinks about Nick's tricks every day and Anna wonders if Nick would really have wanted to win that way.

'I want to watch the shows when I leave,' says Craig. 'There will be twenty-seven hours of footage... I wonder how long it will take to watch.' He's obviously missing Claire with her A level maths!

After his experience with the Brie yesterday Darren gives everyone, including the audience at home whom he addresses through one of the cameras, a lecture about the dangers of eating too much cheese because, he says, it blocks arteries and causes cholesterol.

Shortly afterwards, Big Brother calls Anna to the Diary Room. She says she is sleepy but otherwise feeling brilliant.

'It feels great. I'm in much better form with two weeks to go. It's great. Craig wants to chat to everyone because he's so fed up being nominated. It's hard for him. He wants to know why. There is no why. It's just different personalities. He's always been the one who says it's nothing personal.

'He's a little bit down and also he gets bored. He is cleaning a lot, which is great. The days are longer now because there are fewer people.'

She says that when it is down to three people each day will seem like a year.

'I would be so nervous if I was here. It would be so mad. But I might not be, I might be out this Friday. I told my friends I would just last a few weeks, so I'm dead chuffed to still be here.'

When she leaves the Diary Room, she tells Mel, 'I just talk absolute pants in there.'

In the kitchen, they start on their vegetable feast – they know that for the next week they are going to have to rely on the garden for many of their meals. Mel is making vegetable soup, and they have plans for vegetable curry and vegetable stir-fry.

Darren goes to the Diary Room at half past six. He says he's pleased with the task but thought it might be bigger, like the assault course.

'I didn't think I would have been here this long. It's so cool to have made it this far. You sit down sometimes and think of what you are missing but then it's nice to know it's only two or one weeks to go.'

He says he thinks the whole of next week will be as quiet as today or perhaps quiet periods with outbursts.

'We're thinking of things to do. We know it will be quiet and there will be dull times, so we're thinking of things to lift us.'

After preparing and serving the meal, Mel is called to the Diary Room. She is worried about the next two weeks as she knows they will get bored and tension will mount, irritations will increase.

'It's going to be the most difficult two weeks. I'm already sleeping too much. I was sorry to see Claire go, despite nominating her, as she injected a lot of life and energy and she will be missed.

'Talking about nominations, I regret making those I made last week because of what happened on Monday hearing Darren. I was shocked at the reasons he gave for making the nominations and I know those reasons are not true. Craig was quite angry. You should have a more solid reason.'

She says it was cowardly of Darren to change his nomination from her to Claire, which is what she suspects happened.

'I'm really surprised at Craig asking why he had been nominated three times. I feel guilty for nominating him a lot. I can understand why he is asking, wondering what the hell is going on. It is difficult. I'm now nominating on the basis of people I'd rather be with and nominating the other two. It's not that you want them out of the house, but that's the way the show is designed. I felt sorry for Craig in that respect and tried to talk to him today. I said I made a mistake last week and told him my reason for nominations. Part of me feels really guilty as Craig has said he has never nominated me and he will look back and see how many times I've nominated him.'

She says she cannot have the same close relationship with Craig that she had with Andy and Tom. 'Craig and I are very different people. I get increasingly frustrated with his anecdotes. He is funny but he'll talk and exclude others from the conversation... It is more for the cameras than for us. It may be paranoia but...

'Craig is a sweetheart, a diamond, heart of gold, but he has a very different life from everyone in here. I can't have the same level of conversation I have with the other boys... He wanted to ask me out. In that respect, I can't see any kind of relationship developing of any length. I think I'll see him a couple of times afterwards. I'd love to visit him at his home. He's talked about having a marquee party. I'd like to see how he is outside the show. I feel he will be different as all the people in here will. People are trying to win. I hear Craig often saying "Can the cameras see this?" – little comments which disappoint me. I hoped that people would be themselves in here. The same goes for Darren. The reason he nominated me and Craig – Anna and Craig think – is that either one of us might win.

'I've thought about the end of the show. There's a one in four chance of winning. Few would say they want the money but now there is a possibility of winning and I'm thinking "Could I win?". I think the boys have a better chance of winning. From the beginning, I thought a man would win. For Craig, winning is a real possibility... I think about the next two weeks, the possibilities of who will be here. It makes it exciting, it's something to hold on to and look forward to... I get filled with this kind of panic... One of the last three will win and the others will have a shit time. They will have lasted nine weeks and be left behind. The next weeks will be tough.

'Everyone has wanted to go home at some point, except Craig, and the next two weeks will be trying and difficult for Craig if he feels unwanted... I'm at a slight disadvantage as I've never been up for eviction. Craig knows the public like him. I haven't a clue what they think of me so I think the worst.

'Leaving is now real, it's here. In the next two weeks all of us will leave... I'll miss it once I leave as we are all looked after by Big Brother. We are in this bubble and in two weeks, the bubble will pop. It's going to be really weird and frightening and exciting.'

Two hours later Mel is still talking about the last two weeks, but this time she is discussing it with Anna, in their beds. Craig and Darren are in the living area and Craig tells Darren that it was exciting to hear the roar of the huge crowd that was there for Claire's eviction.

'What was making me feel good was that noise we heard on Friday. That was a massive crowd. I felt the majority must be there for me more than Claire because I'm more known. That made me feel... well... overwhelmed.'

He and Darren discuss how the people in the crowd have given up their Friday night in the pub to be there to see him. It cheers Craig up.

Mel and Anna's late-night talks have become a regular bedtime feature. Mel allows Anna to get closer than anyone in the house has to her real inner feelings. She talks about the trauma of not seeing her father.

'It would be so weird to see him. I think about it, but what would be the point? This strange man. I think, "Why the fuck should I?" This is my life and I would be cold to him... I'd want to punish him.'

She tells Anna of her childhood with her mother and grandmother and of the family friends who have a daughter the same age as her. She regards the father of this family as her father figure.

'I could never have a relationship with my real dad like the one I have with my surrogate family. And my real dad's young. It's not like he's going to die tomorrow.'

Anna probes Mel's feelings gently, aware that this is a subject she finds it hard to open up about. She asks how Mel's mother feels about her seeing her father.

'She'll say "If you don't do it you'll regret it." She'll keep pushing and pushing me and one day she'll get her own way because she always does. And she's right, but I get resentful of being pushed into something and I'm still very, very angry with him for not being there.

'I have friends whose parents split up but their fathers were still supportive through their schooling and my dad wasn't. He was just there when he wanted to be. I don't understand how you can have a child and be prepared not to see it growing up. I obviously don't mean anything to him, otherwise he would have made the effort.'

Anna suggests Mel release her anger by meeting her father and shouting at him for four hours. Mel laughs.

'I'm not sure I could do it. I'd ask him how he could have no contact with me for ten years, though. I just can't imagine how he would justify that.'

Anna asks her what she would like to happen.

'I don't know. A huge part of me wanted him to disappear, go away. When I was younger, I know it's awful, but I used to wish he was dead because it was actually easier to deal with than the fact that he just couldn't be bothered to see me. I've only been forced to think about it in the last couple of years and, even then, I haven't really. It's easy to run away and hide from it.'

The next morning they have to agonize over their meagre shopping supplies. Despite their best efforts, they spend 62p too much and Darren is called to the Diary Room to sort it out. He begs to borrow the small amount from the following week's total, but Big Brother is unrelenting and he has to cross off the bananas, their only fruit.

Most of the day revolves around their attempts to get to grips with the circus equipment, particularly the unicycle. Craig can do it, having practised for hours on Nicky's. Darren does not expect to be able to do it but gets the knack very quickly. Mel and Anna both swear and curse, falling off the unicycle, bruising their shins and, occasionally, kicking the bike. To compensate, Mel quickly gets the hang of the tightrope and Anna is the first to master the juggling balls.

They decide that they will insist on being tested inside, not in the garden, because even Craig could not unicycle on the grass. Anna fantasizes about them being blindfolded and taken to the nearby Tesco car park to do it, but admits that she'd run off if she got that much freedom.

There's a moment of comedy when Darren smears Mel's face with jam from a slice of bread he is eating. The rest of them object to this waste of their precious food supply and Craig makes sure nothing is wasted by licking it off Mel's face.

Darren's major task for the day is his ablutions and he spends ages working out the order he should do everything in. Should he shower before he shaves his head? Or have a jacuzzi first? Decisions, decisions. He thinks he's got a rash on his head through lending his clippers to Tom and Nicky, so he gives his scalp a quick soapy wash at the kitchen sink. Then the shaving ritual begins, until every hair on his head (apart from his moustache) has been shorn off. He finishes by giving the dome of his head a vigorous polish and then applies cologne to it. The girls are baffled by the amount of smelly stuff the boys use on their bodies, complaining that the clash of their different aftershaves, deodorants and colognes is making them feel sick.

They discuss the walkway they have to go along when they leave the house and how Claire nearly fell off when she turned excitedly to wave to them all. Craig, who has always said he intends to cycle out on a unicycle, wonders whether they could get plywood boards to cover the grating.

At five to seven in the evening Anna is on her own in the garden when she spots something land in the grass. She asks Craig if he threw it. When he sees it, he thinks it is a firework. Big Brother quickly orders them indoors and sends them to the girls' bedroom while two security men remove a plastic rocket toy. While they are holed up in the bedroom they hatch a plot to trick Big Brother into letting them have a video for the evening. Anna pretends that the rocket hit her and damaged her leg.

Darren carries her into the Diary Room, where she shows Big Brother the bruises she acquired by falling off the unicycle. They both explain that a video would take her mind off the trauma and they even know which film they want to watch: *East is East*. Big Brother says he will get back to them. After half an hour Anna strides back into the Diary Room – her 'injury' no longer troubling her – for the decision. It is no.

They discuss the celebrations for the end of the whole show and speculate as to whether the final three in the house can spend their last evening drinking champagne, agreeing that they will need truckloads of Moët to get them through. Darren says that in a year's time he can imagine reading a newspaper and seeing the headline 'Big Brother Ruined My Life: Contestant Tells Story' and thinking 'Shit, which one is it?'

Monday is the last day for nominations in the *Big Brother* house. There will be none next week, the final week, when viewers will vote for a winner rather than an evictee. Although this last round of nominations has preoccupied the four finalists all weekend, they sleep late. Mel is the first up, at twenty to twelve and, after making herself a cup of tea, goes straight to the Diary Room to share her thoughts with Big Brother. She has spent longer, and talked more, in the Diary Room than any of the other contestants.

'I am getting increasingly irritated with people, getting wound up by them, and that's probably because I have no way of getting away from them now there are only three others here. I've got a short fuse and have kept my temper very well in here, but now it's starting to get difficult. It's exciting but nerve-racking being so close to the end.

'Anna I get on with really, really well. I'll be really sad to see her go. She comforts me the most. She said she would have gone mad if I wasn't here and I would definitely have gone mad without her. My relationship with her is a big turnround from someone I didn't really speak to.'

She says the difference between the boys and the girls in the house is that the boys entered to win and the girls for the experience.

'Darren, I find he was cowardly, a real coward when he probably – and I can only guess – changed his nominations in the second slot. He should have had the guts to stick by his nomination, not change it because the person knows about it, because the person cries a little bit.

'I find it difficult. He doesn't want to talk about his life. I don't know him very well. I don't really know anything about what he does when he's not here. I don't know why he's here – probably to get a better contract, a better job to support his kids, which is great, but I don't know whether he is here to be part of the project. I don't think he is because he won't open up to people. He's always checking whether the cameras are on him, got the right angle or whatever.

'Craig's fairly constant throughout this. He is here to win for whatever reason, we don't know. He's always been the same to me, solid as a rock, but I'm just getting really wound up by him, but that's more me than him. Perhaps it's because I have the least in common with him. He tells a story and it excludes everyone from the conversation. He's made it clear you've got to look out for yourself in this kind of environment, got to look after number one. I feel it's very strange when people play up to the cameras and both boys do that – like when we were doing the water slides the other day they were saying, make sure the cameras can see this. I think you should just be yourself all the time.

'With Craig I have no idea what he's like out of here. I expect he would be an excellent friend to have, with a heart of gold, but he's in here to win.'

She says the days are getting longer and harder to fill with just four of them. Also, she and Anna are not enjoying the task and she has the bruises to prove it. The weather is getting colder and that makes them all think that winter is coming.

All of the housemates have been grumbling about how unfit they have become in the *Big Brother* house. Craig has tried all the way through to maintain some exercise regime but since the end of Caroline's aerobics classes, there has been no organized session for the others. Because of the low food rations, there has been no risk of any of them running to fat (most of them have lost weight – Anna has lost a noticeable amount and even Claire, who was in for only two weeks, came out half a stone lighter). However, they are finding themselves out of breath just doing their circus practice. Mel joins Craig for a training session, running the length of the garden and then doing handstands against the wall. Then Craig fills pillowcases with tins of food and uses them as weights, nagging Darren to join in.

The exercise effectively takes Mel's mind off the main activity of the day and, when Anna eventually gets up and says, 'I think we have to do something today,' Mel genuinely has to be reminded that the nominations are only a couple of hours away.

Big Brother calls Anna to the Diary Room – she has not been sleeping well and looks tired.

'I'm just not sleeping at the moment and I'm quite grumpy. I'm finding it quite difficult, I suppose because there are less people here.'

She says she is looking forward to talking to people she knows, as she finds it difficult to talk to the people in the house. At night her mind races and then she sleeps during the day and she doesn't know why. She says she has started to think about what is happening in the outside world and she feels a combination of nerves and excitement about being so near to the end.

'It's nice, as everyone is being non-competitive, and people are just getting through the day... It feels amazing to have been here so long. It feels like forever compared with Sada. I was looking around and thinking I wouldn't miss it but it has been funny. I've had thinking time, which was good.

'The people in here have not changed but maybe my feelings about them have. It took me ages to get to know Mel. We didn't talk for the first few weeks. Now I get on with her really, really well. She's very easy to talk to, a lovely girl.

'Initially, I got on well with Craig and in the first few weeks I really liked him. Recently, I've withdrawn myself from him a little bit. I don't find him easy to talk to. But that's more me than him. He's like a little kid sometimes – he is always looking for praise. If you are tired, you can't be bothered giving him praise. Darren, I just liked all the way through. He's brilliant, entertaining, a good laugh and I find it easy to talk to him.'

The nominations happen at three o'clock. It's a subdued time as everyone knows they must nominate two of their three mates. Darren says he's not going to do it 'because I love you guys'.

Anna goes in first and, while she's in there, the others sit in the garden. As she mentions Craig as one of her nominations the camera picks him up, sitting next to Mel, looking fed up. He rubs his ear with one hand. None of the housemates nor the viewers know that this is a secret signal to his missing mate Claire – he has promised her that whenever he is pining for her very badly, he will rub his ear.

WHO NOMINATES WHO

ANNA	Craig and Darren
CRAIG	Darren and Melanie
DARREN	Anna and Melanie
MELANIE	Craig and Darren
REASONS:	
CRAIG on MELANIE	'She's still not been nominated and you've got to have at least one experience of it.'
DARREN on THE GIRLS	'Craig has been nominated three times in a row which makes him feel he's not wanted and he is.'
MELANIE on THE BOYS	'Because I feel they are both not as genuine as Anna. Anna is the most genuine person – along with myself – in here.'

As soon as the nominations are over, they bring mattresses out into the garden and use them for gymnastics and as a trampoline. They all join in energetically and there's a lot of physical shoving and pushing going on – the group are re-establishing themselves after the divisive nominations procedure.

Then it's back to practising their circus skills. Craig is getting on Mel's nerves by nagging her to practise on the unicycle, which she still finds impossible. She complains, 'My piercing doesn't help.'

They seem to have the tightrope licked, but the juggling is also causing problems because the thirty-second minimum time is quite long.

Big Brother gives them a mini-task for the evening – they each have to impersonate another member of the household for two hours, dressing and talking like them and visiting the Diary Room in character. They draw lots for who gets whom: Craig is Anna, Darren is Mel, Anna is Craig and Mel is Darren. There are huge screams of delight from all of them when they hear that their reward will be a video.

They throw themselves into the task. Anna is best at it. She stuffs socks inside the sleeves of her T-shirt to pretend she has Craig's muscles and she lapses into a strong Liverpudlian accent, telling Craig-style stories of wild, womanising holidays. Craig does his best as Anna but it's more a pastiche of femininity, with lots of eye fluttering and a squeaky voice. Mel and Darren don't bother with voices but go for personality traits: Mel talks about sex, imaginary illnesses and the cost of the exclusive designer clothes she is wearing. Both she and Anna make loud farting noises at regular intervals. Darren talks about missing Tom and how he tried it on in the greenhouse and makes a reference to genital piercing.

To the astonishment and genuine dismay of all four, their reward is a Bobby Davro video. Craig says, 'I've never been so insulted.' Anna, who has been looking forward to *East is East*, says, 'Bobby bloody Davro... Even my mum and dad hate Bobby Davro.' Craig says even his nan and granddad hate Bobby Davro.

Mel, believing that Big Brother is winding them up, goes into the Diary Room to ask if they can have something else to watch. Big Brother is being very stern and turns them down. The only thing that cheers them up is the arrival of snacks to go with the film. After they sit through the recording of the Bobby Davro television programme in stony silence Big Brother asks for one of them to go to the Diary Room. Mel volunteers. She laughs out loud when Big Brother tells her that there are another two episodes of the programme on the video if they want to watch them. However, she's really quite annoyed, feeling that they wasted time on the impersonations when they could have been practising their circus skills. The girls go to bed, leaving Craig and Darren glumly watching the 1980s' Davro programmes. Darren says, 'Is Bobby still around?'

Despite their disappointment with the choice of video, the next morning they drink a toast (in tea) to Bobby Davro or Debbie Bovro, as they have christened him. After all he has, they say, bored them all into the best night's sleep they have had in ages and they're grateful.

They get a temporary reprieve from the unicycle practice because the bike has to be taken away for repairs.

It's another day of tension, in many ways worse than yesterday. They are going to hear who has been nominated for public vote. With so few of them in the house they know that at least half their number will be involved. When the news comes Anna is the only one to escape – Craig, Darren and Mel are all facing eviction. They hurl juggling balls and cushions at Anna in mock attack and then they all hug each other. Mel smiles but she's shocked. She tells Anna that she was expecting it but that now she will be sick with nerves on Friday, so nervous that she will pee her pants. Anna admits that she's 'dead chuffed' knowing she will be there to the end.

They are each called individually to the Diary Room. Craig says, 'I wouldn't try to steer the viewers into voting me over anyone else. All I can say to the viewers is thank you very much for all the times they voted me and, hopefully, they'll do it again this week. I'm looking forward to it. We're coming to the end now, I'm up against the biggest competition.'

He says every Friday when he survives eviction is a confidence boost, but he really thinks this week could be his last. 'The viewers might be sick of me by now.'

Darren says he is excited whatever happens, whether he stays or goes, because he hasn't seen or heard his children in ages. He says he's really chuffed for Anna.

'I'm feeling really good. Last time I made the mistake that I wanted to go, probably missing my children. Now I'm excited either way. It's been a brilliant experience and I'm lucky to have been chosen for the project.'

But he slips into his unhappy face and tells Big Brother off for rewarding them with a Bobby Davro video when they really wanted *East is East*. Then he cheekily predicts that he will survive into the final three because 'the audience want me to cook banana fritters for them when I get out'.

Anna says, 'I'm dead happy, really happy. It means I'll be in the final week, which is brilliant. I never thought I would make it this far. I'm just really happy.'

But she says she feels for the other three in the house. 'It is going to be a tough week. It's the biggest eviction because it's the last one. I know they all want to stay whatever they say. They'd all like to be here for the final week. My heart goes out to them.'

She says it helps her to know definitely when she is leaving. She went into the jacuzzi on her own, she says, because she did not want to be too happy in front of the other three.

Big Brother asks if she would like to talk about anything else and she says she just wants to say two words: 'Bobby Davro.'

Mel talks to Big Brother and, as usual, has the most to say: 'I feel I am one of the most genuine people. I feel I've bared my soul to everyone out there. I've offered myself up entirely as it were, warts and all. I feel I've done that much more than most people. I'm not just here to have a laugh. I also think I'm quite diplomatic. I think people like me and I like them. I'm good at getting on with people.'

She says she wants to send a message to her mum. 'I just want to say: Mum, I'm doing this for you. I love you and I hope you still love me – you are the most important person in the world to me. I hope you're proud of me being here and I hope I'll be in the final three. I hope that I stay next week to make you proud of me. I just want to see the whole thing out. I suppose it's now got to the stage where I really want to win.'

It's Mel who is most aware of the cameramen working just a few feet away from them. On a previous occasion she told Darren there was a female camera operator, much to his delight. She'd heard a cough that was 'definitely a woman'. Today, she hears one of them stumble and decides to initiate a relationship. 'Are you all right, chuck?' she asks, peering into the mirror. 'We'll make you a cup of tea and then we'll go into the girls' bedroom for three minutes and you can come and get it.'

They all get carried away with the idea and make two mugs of tea, which they leave on a tray, with sugar and biscuits, by the Store Room door. They go into the bedroom and time how long they are there. 'Can you imagine if it goes? It will be like Father Christmas,' says Mel. To their disappointment, the tea and biscuits are still there when they emerge. Craig and Anna drink the tea and Craig holds it up to the camera and remarks, 'You don't know what you're missing.'

They are still practising their circus skills and Mel is being given lessons in juggling by Darren. However, it is to no avail – she still seems unable to get the hang of it. Darren, on the other hand, is perfecting his unicycle skills on the repaired machine, precariously threading his way across the living area and collapsing on top of Mel on the sofa.

It's the boys' turn to cook and they take a piece of beef from the freezer. They have been saving it. They have cut a picture of a roast dinner out of a magazine and pinned it on the wall and Anna tells them they should touch it for luck. Darren does and says, 'Please let my dinner turn out as good as this.' He makes a cauliflower cheese for Mel, the vegetarian. The meal is good and the girls appreciate it.

Darren then amuses them by making them decide which Spice Girl they would like to be. Anna wants to be Sporty Spice and Mel settles for her namesake, Mel C. Both the boys agree that if they could date a Spice Girl it would be

Posh Spice. Darren says he likes her because she is slim, which draws outrage from both girls.

'She has a sense of humour. She's really dry, quite cutting, a little bit cynical. That's the reason to like her,' says Anna. But Darren insists that in the absence of knowing any of them well enough to judge their personality, he ranks them Posh, Mel, Baby and Ginger and he would refuse to date Sporty.

They get to bed at 1.30 a.m. and Craig tells Darren that he is getting up at 8.30 a.m. – a time that long ago ceased to exist for the *Big Brother* residents – because he wants to work on his juggling.

The girls talk, discussing how long it is since they had sex.

'Fancy a shag, Mel?' Anna whispers and they both giggle. They stay awake talking for another couple of hours.

Craig is the ringmaster of the *Big Brother* circus and he's up the next morning, as he said he would be, when the alarm clock rings at 8.30 a.m. He spends the next hour working out with his bags full of baked bean tins.

At half past nine, worried about the amount of work Mel has to do if they are to complete the task, he wakes her up with a cup of tea. She promises him she'll get up in half an hour.

One hour later, at half past ten, he has another go at rousing his sleeping housemates. One by one, over the next twenty minutes, they get up. Anna and Mel do battle with the unicycle, which has just been returned to them after adjustments to its seat. They can both pedal a couple of metres now, which is an improvement on their past performances. But it is not enough.

Craig goes into the Diary Room and tries to persuade Big Brother that they should only be asked to cycle one length of the room, as they are finding it hard to turn round to complete a full ten seconds. Big Brother will not give them a reprieve, but because they lost several hours of practice yesterday while the unicycle was away for repairs, they are each allowed two attempts at riding it. Anna tries to bargain further with Big Brother: if the boys do the unicycle twice each will that count for all of them? Big Brother says an emphatic no.

Painting clown faces on is the best bit of the whole task for the girls and they show more enthusiasm for it than for any of the skills. Mel opts for a black face with silver diamonds over her eyes. Anna's look is Gothic horror – a chalky-white face with purple eyes and large purple lips painted in an unnerving smile, like the Joker from the *Batman* films. Craig teams an orange face with an orange wig, with a tear painted on one cheek as a finishing touch. Darren goes for a restrained look, with two little stripes between his eyebrows. He adds a plume of foliage to his yellow wig which is worn inside out, and a necklace of leaves.

Before they perform for Big Brother they have a dress rehearsal. Allowed three mistakes, they manage to scrape in, with both girls failing the unicycle and Mel dropping her juggling balls. They are delighted and, for the first time, success seems a possibility. However, luck is against them when it comes to the real thing. Both Mel and Anna fail on the juggling and the unicycle and Mel even falls off the tightrope. As the others struggle to scrub the thick paint from their faces they all envy Darren, who has so little to remove. They decide that the only way to get really clean is in the hot tub.

Mel and Darren spend the afternoon outdoing each other with tales of their wild schooldays. Darren admits he was expelled from one school for winding his teachers up. In one incident, he said 'fuck' to a teacher, then tried to pretend he had said 'frigging' – not realizing that this was also an unacceptable word in polite society. Mel tells how she behaved so badly on two school trips, one to

France and one to Germany, that the school stopped running the trips. A strongly worded letter was sent home to her mother, who was furious with her. When Anna asks exactly what she did, Mel says: 'Basically, drinking, smoking, smooching and discussing sex'. She was also banned from going on a skiing trip because she misbehaved on a school outing to the theatre. But her greatest triumph was being thrown out of the Brownies for refusing to pledge allegiance to the Queen.

Craig has found himself some female company to replace Claire by stealing Darren's chick. Since Marjorie's trip to the vet, her close relationship with Darren has foundered. He just isn't interested in her any more and she's pining for male attention. She's switched her devotion to Craig and follows him around the garden.

Their shopping budget for the final week will be £25.20 but they are not depressed. It is more than they have had this week with four of them in the house. The freezer will be restocked with meat and fish on Friday and there are dry goods like chickpeas in the Store Room. They happily dream of spending the whole of the amount on alcohol. To demonstrate that they can manage on short rations, Craig cooks them a meal of leftovers from the last two days: rice, potatoes, roast beef and saveloys, topped with fried egg.

While he rustles it up, the other three compare notes about what they will buy when they get out. Darren and Anna share a passion for chunky KitKat; Anna drools at the idea of dunking one in her cup of tea. Mel fantasizes about a deep-filled cheese ploughman's from Prêt à Manger, followed by cherry cheesecake. As they eat Craig's meal, Anna reminds them that they have known each other for fifty-three days and Darren reminds them that next week one of them will be sleeping in a bedroom on their own.

The food fantasies continue, with Anna and Darren sharing a passion not just for KitKat but for crisps. Darren wants traditional cheese flavour and Anna wants ham and mustard. Darren reckons that if he cleans all the mirrored windows, Big Brother will reward him with crisps and two bottles of red wine. Craig says he'll clean them twice for that. But when Mel goes to the Diary Room to enquire about this reward, she is told that all food and drink has to be bought from the shopping budget.

To amuse themselves they carve farmyard animals out of potatoes, painting them with the face paints given to them for the circus task. The 'farmyard' is an empty All Bran box with some grass strewn inside it and the animals are a motley collection, in disproportionate sizes. But just as they are really enjoying themselves, giggling over their efforts and making animal noises, Darren is called to the Diary Room and told that all the circus gear must be returned.

Anna's sardonic humour takes over as she announces that Big Brother could tell them all not to speak for the evening and that would mean there was no possible way of them enjoying themselves. She orders the others to put their smiles and their good moods in the box and hand them into the Diary Room. All jokes must go, she says, mouthing, 'Have you heard the one about the mean Big Brother person...' into the box.

To while away the evening Darren makes biscuits, with help from Mel.

Then Anna is called to the Diary Room and given another task, which they must complete by Saturday evening. They have to produce a four-page tabloid newspaper about life in the outside world while they have been incarcerated in the *Big Brother* house. Big Brother reminds them that although four of them will start the task, by the time it is finished one of them will be in the outside world, reading real newspapers.

Big Brother requires them to give themselves editorial titles, including editor, news editor, sports editor and showbiz columnist. They can also include an opinion column, an agony aunt, a horoscope column and a cartoon. Craig is immediately appointed sports editor and Darren initially grabs the showbiz slot. If they successfully meet the deadline they will be rewarded with a video and a takeaway meal – they're all a bit suspicious of Big Brother's video offers, after the Bobby Davro experience!

At their first editorial meeting they decide to write about what the other contestants are doing. Sada, they decide, is either running a helpline for tofu addicts or setting up a sanctuary to save turtles. Andy is heading a Lady Boy band in the Philippines but they are involved in a sex scandal. Caroline has landed a huge lipstick advertising contract, with the lipsticks in the shape of her pink saxophone, and the TV ads are such a success that she has started a craze for pink saxes and has become a teenage icon. As for Nick, they toy with the idea that he has become either a politician or a spindoctor.

Craig and Darren are chatting, but not about the newspaper. Craig tells Darren that he wants to buy a monkey but they cost £2,000.

Craig is called to the Diary Room and is asked by Big Brother why he thinks the circus-skills task went wrong.

'People didn't try. They didn't put enough effort in. The rest of the house didn't like the task, they didn't enjoy it so they didn't put the effort in. It's disappointing because some of the other tests I didn't enjoy, like the memory tests (and you know my spelling is awful), but I tried my hardest. The others, especially Mel, didn't try at all.'

He says the final four in the house are not the ones he expected. He really thought Andy would make it to the end and possibly be the winner. He says he really wants to make it into the final three, but if he is evicted on Friday it will just be the name of the game.

He says that everyone has had good and bad times in the house, but that it has been about working as a team. Now, with so few left, he feels that some of the people are being selfish. For example, nobody helps each other in small ways, like washing towels for one another.

'They all want to get to the finish line and so they think of themselves.'

The newspaper task is already proving fun. Darren laughs at his own inability to type. At half past ten Big Brother calls Melanie to the Diary Room. She says she was disappointed with the circus task, it was the most difficult they have had. She found it frustrating and even more so when others tried to motivate her to do it.

'I'm not very good when people are telling me to do stuff... It makes me feel more deflated about the whole thing, makes me want to do even less. It doesn't help at all.'

On the whole, though, she's finding it easier with just three other housemates than she expected it would be.

'There are boring times and times when you get irritable, but it's OK, there's a nice sense of calm in the house. We've reached the point where it's really relaxing.'

Big Brother asks her if the whole experience has measured up to her expectations: 'Yes and no. I didn't expect it to be such a good bunch of people. I expected stereotypes but everyone's nice, a really nice group of people. It's been interesting seeing the arguments, watching how people interact and work together... The disputes have all been minor. I didn't expect the nomination and eviction process to be as traumatic as it is, incredibly traumatic, the first three especially... I didn't expect how mad and crazy it's been in here. We've gone from incredible lows to incredible highs. It's been the longest eight weeks of my life, I've experienced every emotion to the extreme... I didn't expect the emotional stuff. I didn't think I would want to go home so badly at times and at other times didn't realize how much I'd want to stay.'

She says she expected the cameras to be more intrusive and, at times, she has been very aware of them, especially when she's feeling down and she's aware of them focusing on her. She notices them much more now that the numbers in the house are lower.

A very rare event occurs – the day ends before midnight even though, in the end, it was only Craig who had an early start. The girls are amused by the possibility that Craig went into the Diary Room and complained about their lack of effort. But their laughter turns to shrieks of horror when a large spider crawls over Anna's duvet. In terror, they shake the bedding and even lift the mattress, searching for it. But the spider has escaped.

'That was a big spider. A BIG spider!' Mel says.

'Imagine if it gets into our brains and lays its eggs. Because they do that,' says Anna.

Anna spots a tiny spider and asks if that was it.

'Didn't you see my face? It wasn't that,' says Mel.

Anna says the spider is probably dangling from her bed. She does a funny impression of a spider dangling. After ten minutes of spider hunting, during which Anna announces that she can feel it watching them, Mel puts towels on the floor over the crack where they think the spiders are getting in and they climb back into bed.

'It's only a teeny English spider, after all,' says Anna. 'They're nice, polite. English spiders have manners.'

Darren, Mel and Craig get up by half past ten the next day which, for the housemates is another long, good night's sleep. Anna, who is struggling to get to sleep, stays in bed. Mel seems to have been inspired by the face paints they had for the circus task, because now she paints her face white with the Tipp-Ex they've been provided with for the newspaper task. While she cleans her face Darren sets about cleaning the house, complaining that it's in a disgusting state. He shames Mel, who is lying on the sofa reading, into getting stuck into the washing-up and bleaching the kitchen work surfaces, while Craig tackles the boys' bedroom. Darren even cleans the Diary Room, pressing the bell to enter and then calling out 'Room service!' as he sets to with a brush and duster. The big clear-up results in several pieces of lost property being discovered. Mel takes them to the Diary Room. There's Claire's washbag, Nick's tie and cap and Tom's red shorts. There's also a Diesel top but Mel announces that she's not giving that in to Big Brother. Tom will have to wait till he sees her to recover it. She then asks, under instruction from Darren, if they can have some pot-pourri for the lounge.

'He says it doesn't smell very nice,' she tells Big Brother. 'He wants alpine fresh, mountain meadow or the one with the little apples in.'

When Anna gets up an hour later, Darren tells her that they have cleaned the house for her. He says that even if he gets evicted on Friday, at least Anna has a tidy home to spend her final week in. The cleaning bug is obviously infectious because the chickens appear to have unanimously decided that today is the day for a dust bath. They are lying on the dry earth, using their wings to flick dust all over their plumage. Craig, who is the first to spot them doing it, drags Anna outside to watch them. They are both fascinated by the behaviour of the hens. Darren tells them how he used to wash his budgie once a week in washing-up liquid, which draws gasps of horror from the others. 'That's not natural,' says Craig.

'He was the best-looking bird you have ever seen,' says Darren. Then he turns to the camera and adds, 'I wouldn't try that at home though, kids.'

Darren's relationship with the chickens, however, is not what it was. Marjorie shuns him and he's beginning to find the others as irritating as the rest of the housemates do. When he catches one on the cauliflowers he threatens it with a dunking in the hot tub, even holding it over the water.

Throughout the afternoon there are discussions about the newspaper and the stories they must write. Darren says that the biggest headline of the summer was 'Contestant Cheats in *Big Brother* house'. Mel laughs and says that's not a big story, it's only big news to the others in the house.

Darren has been appointed agony uncle and is getting on with his problem column, under the byline 'Uncle D'. The other three have all promised to give him a problem from their lives for him to suggest an answer to. Anna reads out the introductory blurb that Darren has written: 'Hello and welcome once again to your favourite column and uncle. This week we have some of the horrific, serious, heartbreaking and sometimes weird stories that you have faced. If you need a shoulder or someone to cry on, Uncle D is always here for you. Please do not hesitate to write, fax or visit my website with problems, queries and questions you need answers to.'

It's just as well he's getting stuck into his work, because Darren has also been appointed the astrologer and illustrator for the newspaper. He's handed over showbiz gossip to Anna, who is sharing the job of news correspondent with Melanie. Mel is also going to write about pop culture and Craig is in charge of sport.

The prospect of their reward for completing the task is preoccupying them. They're cynical about the choice of video they will get but excited by the promise of a takeaway. Darren says that Kentucky Fried Chicken is his favourite takeaway, Mel says she would like an Indian. Anna would prefer Thai but they're not sure whether it will be possible to get a takeaway.

In the meantime, they have to content themselves with a meal of fresh mackerel, cooked by Mel. They have no alcohol to drink with it because they forgot to take their two remaining bottles of cider out of the Store Room in the morning. Darren goes to the Diary Room and pleads with Big Brother for a bottle of red wine as a reward for sweeping the room or, if that is not allowed, a second chance to get their cider. Big Brother promises to get back to him.

He tells Big Brother that they keep reminding themselves that this is the last dinner they will share and that after tonight one of them will be sleeping in a bedroom on their own.

'It's going to be sad for the people left in the house and sad for the person going because we're a tightly knit group.'

Soon afterwards, Mel is called to the Diary Room where she is given the new supply of batteries for their radio microphones and a bottle of cider. She tells Big Brother how she is coping.

'I feel I am going to be evicted and I'm looking forward to seeing my family and friends. I will be so nervous but I will never experience an adrenalin rush like it. I will be so nervous I will be ill or pee my pants. Friday is going to be a long day. The eviction process is quite strange. To start with, it was quite traumatic for people, then it became quite easy. People realized it's quite fun to go out there, quite exciting to see what's going on out there. I'm fine about it. Part of me is apprehensive because I'm the only person who has never been nominated. I'm the only person who hasn't a clue what the public thinks about me, which puts me at a slight disadvantage to Craig and Darren, who have already been nominated... I hope no one hates me, hope no one's disowned me.'

Outside, when she hands over the cider, the others let out a cheer. Craig pours it for them and they drink a toast to Big Brother and to their last evening as a foursome.

Craig, who is making a real effort to improve his fitness, is up early by *Big Brother* house standards on Friday. By 9.30 a.m., he is out in the garden practising lifting his weights, the bags full of baked bean cans. Anna is the only other one to wake early. As Mel predicted, this is going to be a long day and from the start their thoughts are on the eviction process. Anna and Craig do a spoof of Davina making the announcement.

'The next person to leave the Big Brother house is... Marjorie!' says Anna, to laughter all round. Mel has twisted her red feather boa around her head like a crown.

Darren is getting stuck into his task as a journalist. He's writing his astrology column and he's modelled his style on Mystic Meg, as Mel points out. But he has a good turn of phrase – 'Love is about to hit you harder than your mother,' he tells his Gemini readers. Craig is impressed and says that people may believe it and start telephoning each other with the predictions. Craig struggles on with his sports coverage, typing laboriously with one finger. 'I only have a tiny bit left to do so I'll be here about three hours,' he says. He expresses admiration for real-life journalists. 'Shows what a lot of work goes into a newspaper, don't it?' he says. 'They must have to work through the night if it's taking us this long for one page.'

The boys are a bit concerned about the effort being put in by the girls. While Mel and Anna mull over a news story, Darren and Craig between them carry Anna across to the typewriter, sit her down and command her to write a story. She types, 'Once upon a time...'

Conversation comes back to one of their favourite subjects – sex – when Darren remarks that women visiting porn shops is disgusting. 'That's what men are there for,' he says. Mel expresses surprise at this view, so he questions her on which sex aids she possesses. She says she doesn't know their technical names. To encouragement from the boys she reveals she has love eggs, a vibrator and hand-cuffs. When the question is turned on Craig, he replies, 'I've got a whole suitcase of stuff.' Darren only owns up to 'a five-inch index finger and big luscious lips'.

Craig has told the others that he didn't tell the whole truth in one aspect of his interview with Big Brother. When asked if there was anything that might be revealed to newspapers about him, he said no.

'There's loads of people that could tell stories about me,' he tells Darren. 'I have had my moments, but it has all been good fun. But people can twist things and manipulate them.'

Anna, the only housemate not facing eviction, prepares a special outfit to wear for the evening. With nail varnish, she paints a large 'T' on the back of a T-shirt, with another 'T' on the front and the date 10.9.00. Only that date is two days away – Anna is sending a secret message to her flatmate outside. Mel wears a dark red leather jacket, white trousers and a pink top.

They all sit in silence as they wait for the announcement about who is leaving. At 8.52 p.m. Davina says the familiar words about the telephone vote being independently audited, climaxing with, 'The next person to leave the *Big Brother* house will be – Melanie.'

For a split second Melanie's face freezes and then she erupts – smiling and cheering as she hears the sounds of her friends and family on the live link to the studio. 'I'm going home, I'm out, I can see my mum,' she shouts. Craig, who has his hand over his heart at the moment of the announcement, and Darren both leap up to hug her, followed by Anna whose face registers her disappointment at the news that she is losing her roommate and close companion.

The two hours that Mel has to prepare for leaving are spent trying on several different outfits. She models the rock-chick look complete with denim jacket and then a slinky, pink shirt-dress. Then she slips on a tight black top and a tight, sequinned skirt and that's the one that the others vote the winner. Anna asks her what she feels the most comfortable in and Mel replies, 'I don't give a shit about comfort, look is all.'

Every Friday night, music is played in the house to drown out the noise of the crowd and this week it is the *Big Brother* theme tune – only the four house-mates have no idea of this. They give the sound a rousing endorsement by dancing jubilantly around the house. Mel gives viewers their final glimpse of her naked bum as she moves and grooves to the music.

To soothe away some of the stress, Craig takes a chair and collects from on top of the boiler the cigarettes that he and Claire hid there. 'You watch how I put a smile on their faces,' he says, as he walks through to the living area with his bounty.

'I've got a little pressie for you all, 'cos I know you's all nervous,' he says. There are whoops of delight from the desperate smokers, followed by a mock attack on Craig for having taken them in the first place. But there are no serious recriminations – they are all delighted with the stash.

'I've had these a long time. I hid them and kept them until I knew you were desperate,' says Craig. He offers to save more for the final night.

Then it's into the hot tub together and they toast Mel's future in cider. She drinks to them having an enjoyable last week. When she gets dressed Anna stays with her and offers a few words of comfort: 'You've been through so much in here. It will all be easy for you, don't worry, there's no pressure on you.'

The one-minute warning is given and they have a group hug at the doorway. When it opens Mel lingers to give them all another hug outside, and then she's off down the walkway. There's the biggest crowd yet, over a thousand, to greet her. She turns to shout, 'I love you, Craig, Darren and Anna,' and then runs into the arms of her mother.

All three who remain in the house have a brief and intense celebration of the fact that they have survived to the final week. The boys punch the air, Anna screams and then Craig picks her up and runs around with her over his shoulder. After this short burst of excitement they lapse into silence, each wrapped up in thoughts.

'I can't take this any more. I'm not doing it another week,' says Anna. She will feel the loss of Mel most keenly.

Big Brother calls her to the Diary Room at ten to midnight to see how she's coping.

'I'll miss her. She was lovely, dead sound. I'm sleeping on my own in this bizarre environment. I'm left with the lads, who are great, and I love them. Friday nights are always a bit loopy and I'm sad at the moment.'

She says she wasn't surprised that it was Mel who went because of the competition she was up against.

'Craig is a funny young man, he's lovely. Darren is popular – well, I can imagine he is liked because he is funny and outgoing. Lots more girls vote than boys so I think they vote for people they like. The lads have set me up a bed in their room, which I might not take up. In the last few weeks, Mel and I would chat every night and that would send us off to a nice deep sleep – we'd bore each other to sleep. It will be strange, but I will be all right.'

She says she sees the coming week as very exciting but she thinks they will all still get on well together.

'There are no nominations, just the voting. That's bizarre, it really freaks me out. So, on Monday it's tap dance, on Tuesday Riverdance, I do my striptease on Wednesday and on Thursday it's the moonwalk like you've never seen it before...

'It will be really strange leaving the house, I don't know what will happen. Well, all I know is that I meet Davina and that will be enough of a treat.'

She says it was really tough being the only one with nobody to wave at when the door was open but she shouted to Craig's sister and the others' friends.

Despite putting a brave face on it to Big Brother, when she retires to the large empty girls' bedroom on her own, she cries herself to sleep.

As she settles down for the night, Darren goes to the Diary Room.

'You hear what's going on outside and you think, what the hell is it? You just don't know what's going on. We're on the project/game show and all we can see are the cameras. We don't see anybody but ourselves. It's really exciting. I feel nervous, like I want to puke. It's an experience I was glad I was chosen to participate in. As the weeks go by you see people going and you feel the sadness and see the tears. You realize you will miss things in this house. I will miss the garden, the chickens, Marjorie. I'll miss this box, coming in here and talking to you. I love this chair... I'll miss the small things.'

When he leaves the Diary Room, he goes into the girls' room to kiss Anna goodnight.

WEEK EIGHT FACT FILE

MAIN TASK **PASS ■ FAIL ☒**	To perform circus tricks, including tightrope walking, juggling and riding a unicycle.
MINI-TASKS	To impersonate one another for two hours. They are rewarded with a Bobby Davro video. To write and produce a four-page tabloid newspaper about events in the outside world.
BOOKIES' FAVOURITE TO WIN	Craig is still in front of the pack, with odds of 2/5, Anna is in second place at 7/4, with Darren trailing at 20/1.

WHAT THE EXPERT SAYS ABOUT ANNA

'Anna has one of the strongest personalities in the group. At the beginning this wasn't apparent, and she faded into the background. But she has emerged as a charismatic, extremely funny person. She has steered away from sexual games, sexual politics. She is seen by the others as someone dependable, someone to talk to.'

Linda Papadopoulos, Counselling Psychologist

WHAT THE EXPERT SAYS ABOUT CRAIG

'Craig was never a real contender for the last three until his showdown with Nick, when he came into his own and showed himself to be both tough and fair. He's become an archetype for the public – a short, plucky, working-class lad who dispatches a lanky, Machiavellian toff. But the qualities you need to win over the public can be very different from those needed to be a good housemate. Craig is entertaining, good at tasks, a task-orientated leader. Despite this, he has not been popular. Early on there were complaints about his laziness; later on he formed strong alliances, first with Nick and then with Claire. This can count against you in a group.'

Dr Peter Collett, Experimental Psychologist

WHAT THE EXPERT SAYS ABOUT DARREN

'Unlike Craig, Darren is not afraid of showing the feminine side of his personality. This has allowed him to connect with the girls very well and at the same time set up a situation where he doesn't pose a threat to the boys in the house. At times the other housemates have criticized him for being lazy, a hypochondriac, and selfish. We see very little evidence of this. He's one of the obvious givers within the group.'

Linda Papadopoulos, Counselling Psychologist

MEL LOOKS BACK

The vote to evict Mel was a record-breaker – a massive 3.3 million viewers rang the phone lines, the highest-ever total in UK television history. The previous record-holder was ITV's debate on the monarchy, which received 2.6 million calls, ahead of *Stars in Their Eyes* with 2.37 million. It was an overwhelming vote against Mel: 69 per cent voted for her to leave, 18 per cent for Darren and 13 per cent for Craig.

When she talks about it afterwards, Mel says that she expected the vote to go against her because she knew how popular both Darren and Craig were. Nor does she regret getting so near to the end but not making the final three.

'If I'd been given the choice beforehand I would have stayed, just to see it through, but I have no regrets. It has been a truly amazing, fantastic experience, and I'm just so glad that I did it.'

She's delighted to have been reunited with her mum, the person she missed most.

'She's really cool about everything. She's very liberal, forward thinking, very accepting, not at all excited by it all. My grandmother has been upset by the things people have said to her. She's in her seventies, a very proper person, very bright. I think she's shocked by some of the things she heard in the house but more upset by comments made to her. She hates the way the press portrayed me as a flirt and a tease. Now I'm out I hope she'll get her granddaughter back, although it may take a little time.'

After her exit from the house, one newspaper tracked down her father and talked to him.

'It's true I haven't seen him for years and I did talk about it in the house. But the way it was presented was exaggerated. It is something I am going to have to resolve, but it's not something I think about all the time.'

Mel's ex-boyfriend was waiting for her when she came out of the house and her relationship with him is another thing that she feels she needs to resolve.

'He's very supportive, it's great to see him. We were together for four years, then split up about four months before I went into *Big Brother*. We saw each other just before the start of the show and I realized I still have some feelings for him. Now we will take it slowly and see what happens.'

Mel was surprised by how much she liked the other people in the house.

'I was expecting ten people all placed there in certain roles, for particular reasons. For instance, I expected there would be a gay man and a homophobic person so that there would be tension between them. But there was nothing as obvious as that.

'I think we were all chosen to fulfil certain roles but they were more subtle, more interesting. Up to three weeks before the end I was still getting to know people. I had my first proper conversation with Anna in the fifth week and I was surprised how well we got on. Out of everyone in the house, I think we got on best. I think we know more about each other.

'I was a bit disappointed that there were so many people from London and that more races weren't represented. But it was still a diverse group of people from different backgrounds.'

As a psychology graduate Mel intended to enjoy people-watching when she went into the house, hoping to turn the experience into a psychological and anthropological study.

'But it didn't work out that way. I was too busy just being in there, getting on with it, trying to be happy.'

For the first four weeks, she really was not happy.

'I wanted to get out. I did not want to be there, it wasn't what I wanted to do. It was not enjoyable. But I stuck it because I didn't want to give in. Then it became fun, interesting, and I was learning about myself every day. I learned to be much more diplomatic and to deal with people better. In the first few weeks, I dealt with things too emotionally because it was a highly emotionally charged atmosphere. It made me miserable because I felt isolated from some of the people and close to some of the others.

'It was as much my own fault as anybody's. I did what I felt was comfortable, went into my comfort zone, which meant I stayed with people I felt I understood and could get on with. After four weeks I realized that I should make more effort with other people. Anna and Darren both did that from the outset, became everybody's friends. I couldn't see the point of that but I learnt to do it. The bonus is that I will take that with me for the rest of my life. And I started to get so much more from the people in there.'

The fact that Caroline and Sada had both gone by this time helped Mel a lot. 'It was a key factor. The atmosphere became much calmer. It was more boring but it was also much easier.'

The intense boredom of the house is, she reckons, the most difficult thing to deal with.

'By the fifth week we were coping with it because we were all so chilled out and relaxed. We slowed down, mentally, physically and emotionally. We found it hard to raise any energy and we all started sleeping lots. We planned our days around our naps, all wandering back to bed for a sleep or sleeping in the garden or on the sofa. I normally have only about six hours sleep a night but I was sleeping for ten at least in there.'

She worried that the survival techniques she learned for the house would affect her life outside.

'Things change so much in there and you have to become really adaptable. Someone is evicted and you really miss them, but within a day you pick yourself up and get on with it and forget them. I was afraid that I'd be the same outside. I'd meet someone and like them but the next day I would forget them. I hope it won't happen, but it was a real fear.'

She believes that she and Sada did not get on well because they were too similar.

'We're both strong-minded independent individuals, not afraid to speak our minds, so there were clashes. I actually really like Sada; admired her. She has a beautiful perception of the world and a wonderful way of laughing off the slightly dizzy image she has. She's also witty and amusing, which is a side of her the viewers didn't see. She was unique, different. She didn't feel she bonded with the boys, and she didn't feel she bonded with me, but I think we never really had chance to get to know one another. It seems a whole lifetime ago that Sada was in there with us.'

Andy was the first housemate that she got on well with.

'We had a lot in common. We'd been to the same university. He is very bright, quite witty. Although his upbringing is very different from mine, we got on really well and I became very close to him. I was gobsmacked when he was nominated because I had no idea that someone who gave so much to the group could be chosen for eviction. The boy–girl divide had developed and he was a casualty of it. I didn't like it at all. I felt like a go-between, sleeping in the girls' bedroom and talking to them, but getting on with the boys as well. I was really miserable when Andy left but that seems such a distant memory now.'

Caroline was the next to go.

'Caroline could never understand why she was nominated and she took it so personally, which was wrong. She has spent her life getting on with people; she's very popular. She just felt it was a slap in the face to be nominated. She was emotionally so up and down, especially in weeks two and three. When she left there was a great sense of calm.

'But we missed her because she was very funny, she'd have us in hysterics in the girls' room most nights. She is very different from anyone I have ever met. I liked her and I thought I got on well with her so I've been shocked to look at the TV programmes and see some of the things she's said about me. She didn't like me.

'I expected that, in a way, because all through my life I've had experience of people disliking me for reasons I can't really understand, reasons I don't think are there. So I've learnt to live with it, and before I went in I told myself it could happen. But then because they were such a nice bunch of people I genuinely thought I was getting on well and so it came as a surprise.'

Mel believes *Big Brother* made the right decision to remove Nick from the house 'because he could not have stayed, feelings were running so high'.

'In the cool light of day he cheated. Everyone does it at times but he did it on national TV. Personally, I wasn't too upset by his cheating but I was really upset about the lies he told, particularly the story about his dead wife. At the time he told us, I was very moved by it and then to be told three weeks later that it was a lie was really shocking. After that, I questioned everything he'd ever told me. I didn't trust Nick from early on. I saw changes in his behaviour as soon as the nominations started.

'Nick was a very funny guy – he made us laugh most out of everyone. He has a fantastic sense of humour, quite childlike in some ways. I don't think his humour came over on television at all. He was certainly the most fun person to play cards with. He had this incredible ability to make us laugh, whether at him or with him, and he didn't mind if we laughed at him. Our favourite card game was Cheat, in which you have to cheat, so he was really good at it. And very, very competitive, which was good to watch. He refused to learn the rules of other card games, like Black Jack, and was constantly being penalised for making mistakes, but somehow he always managed to make something very funny from it.

'He was certainly the one I missed most when he left. In the end, the card games were so boring that I'd brighten them up by role-playing that I was Nick, just to try and get some fun back.

'I'd like to see him again but I'll never be best friends with him. I don't think he's Nasty Nick but I'm not sure that he's Nice Nick.

'I predicted he would have a big success after *Big Brother* because he was the cleverest of the lot of us. He was always thinking ahead, weeks down the line, while we were just trying to get through each day.'

Nichola is someone Mel feels she never got close to and was only just beginning to know when Nicky was evicted.

'We nicknamed Caroline and her Loopy and Loopier because they were both so outrageous and outgoing. But Nicky was also a bit of a loner, very involved with her art. She also had the fieriest temper, which could be difficult at times. After Caroline left I really began to enjoy her company. She and Anna and I would sit round the table having a cigarette and a cup of tea first thing in the morning, just chatting about normal things. When Caroline was there they fed off each other emotionally and I think they made it harder for each other.

'Nicky was the most energetic of us all. She decorated the house brilliantly. She seemed to need to be doing something all the time.'

Mel's time in the house was one of serial closeness – first it was Andy, then Tom, then Anna – each getting nearer to her than the last.

'Tom and I got really close, although we rarely had time to talk together on our own because Nick was always the first up and the last to go to bed. I was a lot closer to Tom than I was to Andy, although I don't think viewers realize that.

'At first I found him very quiet, difficult to talk to, very closed. But as I got to know him I found he was actually very open and he talked to me about his family, his friends, his dreams, his aspirations. We kept each other company into the early hours and I was really upset when he left.'

She emphatically denies ever considering either Tom or Andy romantically.

'There was no point whatsoever of thinking about romance in the *Big Brother* house. Nothing was going to happen on national TV, absolutely no way, I wouldn't even entertain the thought. It was ignorant and naive of anyone if they thought it would happen. I wasn't trying to form any kind of sexual relationship. I just thought I was getting on with them. I was aware that Tom fancied me because he told me and, after that, I distanced myself from him a little, became slightly more withdrawn. It just wasn't the right environment to have those thoughts. It was a stressed and strained environment.

'I had much longer to get to know Tom than Andy. Five weeks feels like five years in there. I really want to see him again but I will have no agenda for the meeting. I don't go out to meet people wondering whether the sexual chemistry will be there. I want to talk to him, outside the house, have a good chat and a laugh. I also want to see Andy, for the same reasons.

'Andy was very tactile but Andy is a tactile person and he was hugging other people, not just me. I really liked being hugged by him because I was missing physical contact. But I still thought we were just enjoying each other's company and I was surprised when he kissed me. But I was miserable and upset at that time. I really didn't want him to go but not because I was expecting a romance to develop.'

For all the housemates the arrival of new girl Claire was traumatic, and Mel appeared particularly unsettled by her.

'Claire had a tough time, probably the toughest of all of us, and she handled it very well, took it all in her stride. We were living in this bubble, totally isolated from the world and getting more and more comfortable in our isolation. We'd reached the stage where we didn't even need to speak. Tom would pick up the cards and deal a hand for Darren without them even discussing what they were going to play. We didn't feel the need to fill the silences with talk, in fact we enjoyed the silences.

'Claire's arrival made us all feel strange – not because of anything to do with her but just because she came from the outside world. She reminded us that there was an outside. At first I didn't even know how to talk to her.

'My vivid recollection of Claire is of sitting on the back of the sofa, with Tom next to me, staring at her and not able to speak. Then Tom nudged me and said perhaps we should speak, not just sit and stare at her with our mouths open. She was just so strange to us, so full of life and energy. We had all wound down to this really slow pace and she came in, wanting to have fun, wanting to stay up all night, getting up early in the morning. She was a breath of fresh air. We were becoming boring and stagnant.

'What I found hard to handle was the fact that she had watched the television programmes. She knew more about Anna than I did, for example. I didn't like that. I knew from something she'd said that she'd seen the kiss with Andy and that was something I was already worried about. I hadn't even discussed it with Anna and Tom, so she knew more about me than they did.

'It was weird to think that she had watched us making nominations, the most secret part of the whole procedure. But she handled it all brilliantly. She's really good fun, with an innocent sense of humour. She describes herself as 'ditzy' but that's wrong because she's not dim. I don't feel I really had time to get to know her. She bonded very well with the boys – Darren at first and then Craig. Darren knew he recognized her but he didn't dare ask because we knew we were not supposed to ask her questions about the outside world, so it took a few days before they chatted about it.'

Mel's third big friendship – the biggest, she says – was with Anna and developed during the final three weeks when the number of girls in the house had dwindled.

'I can't even remember Anna being there in the first few weeks. I can't visualize her. Then in the fifth week, we had a conversation together outside, and I discovered to my glee that we had the same perception of the world. She's got a real minxy sense of humour, which you don't realize is there to start with.

'I think we will be good friends, for the future. She wrote her home telephone number on the back of one of my photographs, in lipliner. She's the only one whose number I have. I really want her to win.'

However, she knows that Anna is up against stiff competition: 'Darren came to *Big Brother* to be on a television programme, not to open himself up, not to be analysed by anyone. He's kept himself incredibly closed. I know nothing about him, except that his mother is called Joyce and she's a good cook. He refers to his ex-girl-friend as 'the mother of my children'; he never uses her name. I don't know where he lives, what his normal life is like.

'Yet at the same time as being so closed he is very outgoing, great fun, a wonderful balance of maturity and immaturity. We often forgot that he was only twenty-three. He is fantastically diplomatic and very caring. He treated me like a child in the kitchen, which I enjoyed, telling me off for grabbing hot pans and handling knives dangerously.

'Even more than Anna, he formed relationships with everybody. The biggest surprise is watching him on television now that I'm out – he comes across as quite camp, but that's something I didn't have a clue about when I was with him.'

Mel reveals that the housemates will have a few debts to settle when they all get out. While fans were betting on their futures in the house, they were running side bets with each other.

'I've lost £50 to Anna because I bet that Darren had an identical twin brother – he told us he had in the game of truth and lies we played in the first week. But I've won some of it back because I bet she would be in the last three. I think the last six of us in there – Craig, Claire, Darren, Tom, Anna and me – will definitely meet up as a group and then we'll have to sort out who owes what to whom!'

Craig is someone Mel likes but had so little in common with it was hard to establish a close friendship.

'He played different roles. At first, he was the Incredible Sleeping Man because that's all he did. Then he became Craig, The Amazing Storyteller, with lots of stories about his girlfriends and his holidays. Then he became The Human Jukebox because he knows every word of every song. Unfortunately, he can't sing a note, which we teased him about.

'I could never speak in any great depth to him. With Craig, what you see is what you get.'

WEEK NINE

'It's been a wicked experience.'

DARREN

8 TO 15 SEPTEMBER

It's the final week and in the house there's a sense of tension lifting. They are missing Melanie, with both Darren and Anna making references to her during the day. There's also the feeling that they are all on the final leg, within sight of their homes, families and friends, and the Friday night excitement which they have glimpsed others enjoying. In addition, there's a sense of achievement – these three have gone the distance, whoever wins.

Anna is first up, at quarter past ten, wearing the T-shirt with the cryptic message to her flatmate on it. The housemates still have to complete their newspaper by nine o'clock this evening and there's quite a bit to be done. In her role as showbusiness correspondent she goes to the Diary Room to ask if comedian Bernie Winters is still alive. Big Brother cannot give her any information about the outside world, so Anna has to assume he is.

'It would be awful if he passed away last night and I'm writing a story about him,' she says into her mike. In fact, he died in 1991.

Darren and Craig sleep on until midday, leaving Anna to beaver away alone. When they do surface they complain about headaches, perhaps caused by the loud music that blasted through the house – which is now so quiet – the previous evening. Darren saw his baby girl being held up by one of his brothers from the door on Friday night. After being reluctant to see his children the first time he was nominated in case he wasn't evicted, he is now very happy to have caught a glimpse of them, knowing that he's going home in a few more days.

With the deadline looming they discuss the content of their newspaper, adding a section about Nick having a job in a nursery school showing flash cards to little children. They reckon Mel is partying away but will soon be fronting a TV chat show called *Come and Have a Go at Winning an Argument If You Think You're Hard Enough*.

Craig is the only one who hasn't been in the Diary Room since Mel's eviction. Big Brother calls him in and he says, 'I'm sorry I didn't come in last night. But I felt brilliant; words can't describe it. The moment of the announcement seemed to last forever. Darren told me that all the colour drained from my face and it took about twenty minutes to come back. It's still not sunk in that I've practically completed the show. It's a dream come true. Whether I win or not, just being a full part of the show is brilliant.'

He tells Big Brother that he is nervous of the week ahead, and also nervous about coming out on Friday to face the world. He says he thinks the last week will go faster, as he's noticed the time going more quickly as things happen. Darren and Anna are thinking about Friday, too, discussing how much cleaning and washing-up they will do in the *Big Brother* house before leaving.

At quarter to three Big Brother gives them more instructions about the newspaper, and asks them to choose which video they want, and which kind of takeaway. They haven't yet come up with a title or a masthead for the paper, but they're all working hard on it now. So hard that they fail to notice one of the chickens wandering around the house, pecking at crumbs under the table where they are gathered. When they spot the hen, Anna bundles it up and takes it outside, threatening it with the cooking-pot on the way.

She and Darren discuss Mel's absence.

'Although she had her special people she always had time for me. I always had a good relationship with her,' says Darren.

The film they want to see is *The Bone Collector*, a thriller starring Denzel Washington, but they tell Big Brother that *East is East* or *Sleepy Hollow* will do. They request a Peking/Cantonese banquet, stipulating that they want chicken, crispy duck and pancakes.

Craig amuses the others by walking around with an egg yolk in his mouth. He has read in a magazine that passing an egg yolk from his mouth into a girl's mouth will spice up his love life. Neither Anna nor Darren volunteers to try the experiment with him.

'I can't wait until I get out to try it on some of the girlies.' says Craig.

The newspaper has now been given a name – the *CDMA Evening News*. Craig may not be able to spell very well – he spells Darren with an 'o' instead of an 'e' at the end – but he's a dab hand with the Letraset, which they are using for headlines and the masthead. The banner headline on the front page is 'Dreams Can Come True', stencilled on by Anna above a piece about the evicted housemates. Cartoons drawn by Darren of all the ex-housemates serve as illustrations.

Although she isn't around to share in the glory, Mel made her contribution to the paper with a feature about a new craze about to hit the world called 'Gibrethrob' which is an anagram of Big Brother. It involves talking about sex all the time and results in 'turning to minging cider' for comfort.

Thoughts of the outside world are creeping in, and Darren and Anna discuss whether they will be invited to appear on Richard and Judy. At quarter past six, Anna goes to the Diary Room. She says the final week is not so bad and she knows she only has 'six more sleeps' in the house. She discusses how sad they are that Mel is no longer with them.

'I was surprised by how sad I felt in the room on my own... I did become very attached to Mel... It was sad being in that minging room on my own with all the mirrors... I've thought about how I should be on Friday and think I should be just the same. I'm not even going to do my hair although I might change my clothes a few times... When I get out I will get absolutely pissed and buy everyone who voted for me a drink.'

She tells Big Brother that she thinks the final days in the house will be very calm but that tension will rise as Friday gets closer. Big Brother asks her about the message on her T-shirt, but Anna refuses to explain it fully.

'It's a special date in my heart. 'T' is my favourite letter, the date's my favourite date. I'm really looking forward to going home. But I'm chilled today, very relaxed.'

A couple of hours later it's time for their final editorial meeting and they sit around the kitchen table and discuss their completed four-page newspaper, free to *Big Brother* subscribers but at the normal price of 'one video, three takeaways'.

They have all given themselves fancy bylines: Anna is Anna Conda, Mel is Melanie McFeisty, Craig is Craig Pickstick and Darren is Darren Rampant. As showbusiness editor Anna has 'interviewed' Britney Spears who she says is raving about a new young band two of whose three members have the same names as Darren's two elder children and the other one is called Anna.

Darren's problem page includes a letter from Anna J Lopez from Middlesex who is 'upset because she is showing the first signs of madness'. The sports page compiled by Craig carries a motor-racing report about 'bachelor Davidson' (or Andy, as the housemates refer to him) and his 'rocking good' car.

The newspaper is duly handed in and to their delight Big Brother says they have passed the task, and will be rewarded with their food and the film they requested. Anna is first to bed. Darren and Craig stay up until the early hours, discussing whether there was ever any real prospect of sex in the house or not.

The next morning they are given their final task that is entitled Mind, Body and Soul. For the first time instead of working as a team they are actually competing against each other on three separate challenges which they will each be assessed on. The one with the highest score will be able to choose the theme, food, drink and music for a final party on Thursday evening.

They each have to do one section of the task each day. Today Anna is working on the 'Mind' task – this involves learning the Highway Code and then sitting the driving theory test at 7 p.m. As she's the only member of the household who doesn't drive that puts her at a disadvantage, but she's determined to do well and buries her nose in the book straightaway.

Craig has been allocated 'Body'. At regular intervals during the day he will be tested on three different aspects of physical fitness. For the speed aspect he has to run between two points 15 metres apart as many times as possible in one minute. Then he must jump across a central line to a point either side of that line as many times as possible in one minute to test his stamina, and lastly to test his strength he has to do as many press-ups as possible in thirty seconds. Immediately after each of these sections he will have to attempt to score ten basketball hoops within three minutes, to test his accuracy.

But it's Darren who has the most interesting – and by far the most demanding – task on this first day. 'Soul' is a twenty-four-hour challenge; Darren has to look after a digitally controlled baby girl, a life-size doll who needs constant care: feeding, nappy changing and affection. A tamper-proof ID bracelet means that only the designated carer can look after the baby. When the baby cries, the carer must touch a contact point on the doll's back with the bracelet to find out why the baby is crying. It could be for food, to have its nappy changed, it may have wind or it may be because she is being held incorrectly or is uncomfortable. The baby may even be crying because it wants to be left alone. The microchip inside the doll records how well she is being cared for, how long she cries for, and how long she has to wait for her nappy to be changed.

The virtual baby was originally developed to give youngsters a realistic idea of what looking after a baby involves but it makes a great challenge for the housemates. As a father of three Darren has the most experience of babies although Anna also comes from a large family and is used to being around babies and small children. Craig admits from the outset that looking after a baby is foreign territory for him and that he's nervous about it. Contrasting this assignment with their previous ones, the housemates are surprised by the competitive nature of this task.

'For the last eight weeks they've combined us as a team, and now they've separated us.' says Craig.

'This is war!' says Anna.

Darren takes delivery of the baby at noon and they all decide to call her Juanita. Darren seems immediately comfortable with her even though she cries on and off all afternoon.

'This would put you off having babies. It's a good form of birth control,' says Craig, who has carried his bedding through to the girls' room as he has no intention of sharing a room with Darren and the baby tonight. Anna is not consulted about this but raises no objection.

Craig is tested on his physical prowess at 1 p.m., 3 p.m. and 5 p.m. Before the tests start he goes into the Diary Room to challenge Big Brother's definition of a press-up, because he disagrees with the instruction to straighten arms completely because he says it is bad for the elbow joints. Big Brother gets back to him – and concedes that Craig is right. He manages twenty lengths in the running test, forty-four cycles of jumps and fifty-three press-ups, scoring the maximum points for all three. Unfortunately he is not so good at shooting basketball hoops and manages only eight out of a possible thirty. To celebrate the end of his test, he enjoys a plunge in the hot tub, followed by a trip to the Diary Room to report to Big Brother that he's enjoyed the task 'apart from the basketball thing'.

He's still worrying about looking after the baby, who will be in his care tomorrow and confides in Anna: 'I've thought of a real big problem. When the baby wakes up in the night and we need to, like, walk it and things like that... All night, right, I have a hard on.'

'Really?' says Anna. 'The cameras are going to love that.'

She takes her driving theory test, and manages a very creditable thirty-one – if it was the real thing, she'd have passed. Shortly afterwards she is called to the Diary Room.

'It's been a nice day. I've got Craig sleeping with me tonight because Darren has little Juanita. Craig made a beeline for my room... I can't wait for Friday, seeing friends and family. I'm so looking forward to Friday – normality again. Maybe I'm looking forward to a pint more than anything else.'

For their evening meal Craig re-heats the leftovers from yesterday's Chinese banquet. Their final shopping list has been delivered and they've given up any pretence of eating healthily. Apart from a packet of All Bran, the list mainly consists of lager, cider, crisps, tobacco and chocolate – they've bought five of the chunky KitKats that Darren and Anna fantasize about.

They all go to bed relatively early – before 11.30 p.m. Darren expects to have a disturbed night – and he's not wrong. He snatches odd moments of sleep but it is 4.30 a.m. before Juanita allows him to really nod off.

Craig is the only member of the household who sleeps soundly. At quarter past seven on Monday morning Anna is up, this is the earliest that any of the housemates has ever stirred. Perhaps it is Craig's presence in the bedroom that disturbs her. Today is Anna's day for the physical tests and she spends a lonely time in the garden practising shooting basketball hoops. As she played for Ireland in a junior international championship when she was a schoolgirl, she's got a head start on this part of the test.

It's Craig's turn to look after Juanita when Darren hands 'my little girl' over at noon. Craig spends the morning reading the instructions – and panicking. He goes to Darren for advice and looks through the baby clothes that have been supplied for Juanita. Darren tells him which clothes are for day and which are for night and instructs him not to use one particular outfit because 'it's for a boy'.

The scores for the first day of the Mind Body and Soul task are high: Darren gets 92% for his parenting skills, Anna scores 88.5% for her driving test theory, and Craig gets 81.5% for the body challenge.

Ten minutes before he is due to become a surrogate daddy Craig makes himself some food. 'I'm going to stock up now. Might not get the chance later.'

Darren teases Anna about getting up so early. 'Craig was all over you then?' he asks.

'He was an animal,' replies Anna.

'Wait until tonight,' replies Darren as he will then be sharing the girls' room with Anna while Craig tends to Juanita.

When Darren hands his baby girl back to Big Brother he comments on the experience.

'It's very realistic about the time to feed her, the time for her to sleep. What got me was every time I fed her, I wanted to tidy her up and change her clothes. Every time I changed her nappy, I wanted to use a wipe and baby powder, get into it. Once you have a baby, it's about their routine not your routine. You think she is real.

'I'm really positive for Craig, he can do it. He's a bit scared of Juanita, but he'll be fine.'

Just how scared Craig is shows when he hears Big Brother call him to the Diary Room to take on his charge. 'Oh my God,' he says, and crosses himself.

Craig tiptoes out of the Diary Room with Juanita sleeping peacefully in her carrycot. He protects her from the other two, who want to say hello in the hope that she'll start screaming and Craig will have to minister to her needs. They have to wait a whole half-hour for the fun to start: Darren and Anna roll around on the bed laughing together at the sight of Craig trying to 'breastfeed' the new member of his family. He may seem slightly ill at ease and unsure how to handle her but he's being very gentle and doing his best.

'It's like disarming a bomb,' he says. 'Here she goes. That's my girl... I'm sweating.'

Then he tempts fate by saying that it is easy, and he doesn't know what all the fuss is about. 'If there's any girlies out there who want to take me on, I'd make a perfect Dad.'

Then it's time for Anna to do her physical tests and Craig and Darren cheer her on. She manages to do thirty press-ups and she follows the newly established ritual of downing a glass of beer between each bout of strenuous exercise and the basketball hoops. Predictably, given her practised basketball skills she manages to net an impressive twenty-one out of thirty balls.

In the middle of the afternoon, Craig is called to the Diary Room for a chat with Big Brother. He takes his baby with him, and she cries as soon as he sets the carrycot down in the corner, so the interview with Big Brother takes place with him nursing and feeding Juanita. He tells Big Brother that he does not think he has changed much over his weeks in the house. He says Darren has changed: he is less selfish and is not talking about himself all the time, which is better. Anna is her usual self – he hasn't seen much change in her.

He says he's nervous about the prospect of Friday. 'It's exciting, very exciting. I'm excited to see everybody, to meet Davina, find out how the show is going and because I may even win. But I'm bracing myself for losing.'

He says he reckons he's mastered 'this baby business' and that he's looking forward to spending the night with Juanita. Just as he says this she starts to cry.

She cries again forty minutes later and this time after struggling to pacify her, Craig discovers there was nothing wrong and she simply wants to be left alone.

'She was crying for nothing. Stupid woman. Like all women, crying for nothing. Typical woman,' he mutters to Darren. Unknown to both of them, Juanita is not the only female crying in the house today. Several times during the day, Anna retires to the girls' room for a quiet sob. During the afternoon, Big Brother summons her to the Diary Room to tell her off for wearing a top with a large logo on it because the housemates are not allowed to wear anything with a prominent brand name. Anna has never infringed the rule before – perhaps she believes that by wearing it she will avoid her sobs being broadcast. Whatever is upsetting her, she does not confide in either of her housemates or Big Brother.

Darren has been very cavalier about memorizing the Highway Code, relying on the fact that he's an experienced driver. It's not enough: when he takes the test he scores an abysmal nineteen out of thirty-five.

It's Anna's turn to cook, and she makes a lamb dinner for just herself and Craig because Darren does not eat lamb. Unfortunately Craig doesn't get the chance to enjoy his, because he's too busy taking care of Juanita – Anna has to put his meal in the oven to keep it warm for him.

Discussions turn to Friday once more and they talk about whether they will miss the house after Friday. Darren says that when he has been out for a few weeks or months he may miss it and Craig agrees. The fact that there's no stress and no bills appeals to him, although some of the other housemates have found it very stressful. Anna says she'll miss going into the Diary Room to chat.

Big Brother gives them a discussion topic: they have to talk about their proudest and their most embarrassing moments. Craig's most blush-making moment comes from a story the housemates have already heard about him making love to a girl in a speedboat he'd hired on holiday. He thought it had run aground, but didn't realize it had beached on a stretch of shore popular with holiday-makers who were watching him 'bollock naked, making love to my girlfriend.'

His proudest moment was 'getting dressed up and getting out of a sixty-four-year-old Rolls Royce and walking my mum down the aisle on her wedding day'.

Anna says she has a whole raft of embarrassing memories to choose from, but settles for one where she was chatting up a girl she fancied in a gay café where she worked in Edinburgh, only to discover afterwards that she had tomato sauce all over her top. Now, she says, showing her bum to millions of viewers must be the most embarrassing thing. Her proudest moment was her mum going to university to study for a degree four years ago after Anna suggested it.

Darren's embarrassing moment came when he had to give a presentation about how he approached his job. Everyone else took it seriously but when it was his turn Darren took to the stage and did a striptease in front of his bosses. Although he says his managers were 'a bit iffy' about it everyone else enjoyed it and nicknamed him 'The Body'. As for his proudest moment – no prizes for guessing what has made him most proud: his kids.

Knowing that they may not get an unbroken night's sleep, they all go to bed by 10.30 p.m. Craig sings a Scouser's lullaby to Juanita in the hope that it will send her to sleep. But they're all wide-awake at quarter to four, including Darren and Anna who don't have Juanita in the room with them. The baby is crying non-stop and even with Darren offering advice Craig seems unable to pacify her. Anna does not get up but groans resignedly. Darren, concerned about Juanita, goes to the Diary Room and suggests to Big Brother that there may be something wrong with the doll.

'Can you ask someone if the doll's knackered? I think she's broken because she keeps going back to abuse crying. She's keeping us all awake. We're all very tired. There's only three days left in this house and Juanita is driving us crazy.'

Big Brother tells him to give it another twenty minutes, and if it is still crying to come back. Eventually, Juanita settles down and Darren goes back to bed. Craig sighs with relief and mutters 'only eight hours left'. Then he tells anyone who is whiling away the night watching the activities in the house on the internet: 'If there's anyone watching at home, don't have children!'

When he wakes the next morning at ten past ten he's pleased to tell Anna that there are only two more hours of parenthood ahead of him. 'I love her really,' he says. 'She's got some lungs on her. It seemed so loud last night. She can scream for ages.'

When Big Brother calls him to the Diary Room to hand in Juanita, he says 'You don't need to ask me twice.' He tells Big Brother that it wasn't too bad, apart from the 4 a.m. problem. 'I don't know what happened. Did I rough handle her? I couldn't stop her crying. I actually thought there was a fault with her... You can't relax. I'm a bag of nerves. Even though she didn't wake after 4 a.m., 5 a.m., you can't switch off. Every hour I was awake, looking at the clock. It's really hard. You've got to respect all those single mums out there looking after babies. It's really hard work.'

Anna is next in line for Juanita and she jokes that she will leave her in the boys' room for the night. But Craig is quick off the mark, moving the cot into the girls' room for her. Anna has a couple hours of peace before she has to deliver any serious maternal care and spends it sunbathing with cushions shielding the baby from the direct sunlight. Then it's feeding time and she talks baby talk to the doll and pats her gently on the back to burp her. Darren watches approvingly. His first child was born when he was seventeen but he knows that virtual babies like Juanita are used to teach teenagers the reality of coping with a tiny baby.

'You see how long it took her to do that? It's all about patience. They know teenagers don't have any patience. Just take your time and wait,' he says. Then he adds, 'But when your friends are laughing at you on national TV, you don't have any patience.'

Darren is worried that he'll be a killjoy on Friday evening. 'I'll be knackered and when I see my kids I may just want to talk to them, not Davina.' Anna, like all the girls who have left the house, is worried about what she will wear for her grand exit. She's not planning the sort of sparkly number the other girls have all chosen but she's asked Big Brother to pass a message to her partner not to wear all denim, because that's what she's planning to put on.

'I don't want us to look like a pair of lezzies,' she tells Darren.

He confesses that he is worried that his children won't recognize him. Then he asks Anna what she plans to do on Saturday. 'I'll probably do a press conference. You know, the usual,' she says.

While Juanita naps, he and Anna improvise another of their little songs, each singing alternate verses, with Darren starting them off:

Anna, Craig, Darren, Juanita
Our time in the house in Bow
Is coming to an end
Three more days and we are home
With our family and friends.

Anna:
I'll miss you all, like a hole in the head
I'll think about you all – never
I'll meet you all on the first
Then I'll tell you what I think of you.

Darren:
I know what you think anyway
I don't have to wait till the first
Just for you to know how I feel about you
You are getting on my nerves.

Anna:
But I might be in the Caribbean
Spending a few pounds
I'll send a postcard to that place on the first
And I shall buy you all a round.

There can be no further verses because Juanita gives a howl and Anna changes her nappy. Darren is being fairly relaxed about his physical tests, not bothering with the shorts and singlets the others have opted for, but wearing baggy white trousers and a white long-sleeved top. Customized clothes are all the rage in the house: after Anna's message on her T-shirt, Darren has written 'Happy Birthday Slim C' on the back of his with a date. Despite his apparently laid-back approach to the task, he finishes his press-ups and manages four nets in his third and final ten shots at the basketball goal. His basketball total is eight out of thirty.

As soon as he has finished they are given their scores for yesterday. Darren got 54 per cent for his abysmal Highway Code test, Anna got an amazing 92.5 per cent for her physical challenge and Craig got a very creditable 82 per cent for looking after the baby. 'Not bad, considering,' he says.

Wanting to look his best on Friday, Craig asks Anna to give his hair a trim. Without a comb and with only a tiny pair of scissors, Anna does her best and her client is pleased with the results. She also compliments on him on the smell of his aftershave, and tells him 'Davina won't be able to keep her hands off you.' Then she carefully plucks a few grey hairs from his head.

When it's his turn to do the Highway Code test Craig does better than Darren, scoring twenty-nine out of thirty-five – but it's still not quite enough to have got him through a real driving theory test, where thirty is the pass-mark.

Anna is called to the Diary Room at half past seven to talk about her new charge. She tells Big Brother she's pleased with her results in the other two sections of the task and as for Juanita, 'She's perfect, just like her mother.'

She says it's an advantage being the last of the three to have the baby, because she reckons she has worked out what the different cries mean. 'I could sing them for you but I might be out of tune. I think I've worked out her cries but saying that I'll probably be up for six hours tonight. You can watch and giggle.'

'The boys did very well. Craig was scared – by the look in his eyes of pure panic. He'll be a smashing Dad.' She says she's tired because of being kept awake by the baby crying when Craig was looking after her but that she's excited about Friday. Over the course of the evening, all three of them have a private session with a psychotherapist.

As Anna 'breastfeeds' Juanita, Darren watches and tells her: 'I'll be your Juanita when she goes, Anna. I'm the right colour – but I'm a bit too big.'

'Do I have to burp you?' says Anna.

She goes to bed early, before 9 p.m., to try to catch up with some of the sleep she lost last night and to cope with the disturbed night ahead of her.

Craig is called in to see Big Brother at quarter past nine and it's one of his typically short chats. He says there is a good atmosphere in the house and that the time is passing quickly. He will miss the good parts of the house, like having no responsibilities. He will also miss being able to chat in the Diary Room – in the final week all three of the remaining housemates tell Big Brother this.

At ten to ten it's Darren's turn to go to the Diary Room. When Mel was evicted she left behind her book, *Wild Swans*, because Darren was enjoying reading it. He might have done better on the Highway Code test if he'd put the book aside for an hour or two to mug up his driving skills.

'I'm really engrossed with my reading. I've enjoyed the task, and I know I did really badly on the theory test but I don't mind. I'm really proud of Anna getting 92 per cent in the physical test and Craig with the baby. It's good that we've kept the meals going; it keeps us together.

'I'm not nervous about Friday, just overexcited, totally chuffed that I have done the full BB thing, it has been a wicked experience. I think the baby device is a good idea. I know they use it in America but it's good to show you how impatient you are when looking after a baby. Now I just want to read my book and go to bed and dream about Friday.'

He asks about the procedures for Friday night: will all three of them be leaving the house at the same time and what time are the TV shows? Big Brother says he cannot give any of this information. Darren then cheekily invites Big Brother to Thursday night's party.

Mel not only left her book for Darren, she also left a present for Anna: her feather boa. Anna sleeps with it draped around the top of her bed. Not that she gets much sleep. Despite going to bed early, she's up again before midnight and doesn't get back to bed until 3 a.m., then there's a 6- and 8- a.m. call from Juanita. An hour and a half later, she has another go at getting some sleep, but Juanita does not give her more than forty minutes' peace.

Craig has also had a restless and disturbed night and tells Anna that if he'd realized she was up he'd have joined her. He says his head was revolving around thoughts of his family, friends and the staff at his building company.

They all say tender goodbyes to Juanita when she goes back to the Diary Room at noon but they're relieved to see her go. 'I coped fine, but I'm very tired. She's a hungry little minx.' Anna tells Big Brother.

When the results of their last tests come through, Anna has scored 94 per cent in the Soul section, Craig has scored 83 per cent for Mind, and Darren has attained 81.75 per cent for Body. Their final scores are Darren: 76 per cent, Craig: 82 per cent with Anna coming top with 92 per cent: this means Anna can choose the theme for the final night party. The boys congratulate her and they have a group hug. She invites them both to the party and decides it will have a Spanish theme – she hopes that Big Brother can find takeaway tapas. She says she also wants a straw donkey filled with sweets. The album of music they all agree should be played at the party is Madonna's *Immaculate Collection*.

As a reward for doing so well in the Mind, Body and Soul task, Big Brother tells the housemates that they can each hear one song of their choice and they have an hour in which to make up their minds. It's not easy – they're all missing music madly and to have to confine themselves to one track is difficult.

In musical mode, Darren and Anna improvise another of their songs, this one is about the final few hours in the house. Anna's chorus is 'It makes me feel sick.'

Anna and Craig both have afternoon naps to make up for their disturbed night's sleep. Darren, who slept undisturbed, spends the time that they are asleep thinking up games for the party. Using a combination of soy sauce and coffee, he draws a donkey on the wall for pin the tail on the donkey, then he improvises a bow and arrows from sticks and twine from the garden. He draws a target on the wall, but instead of shooting at it wakes Craig, who is asleep on the sofa, by firing at him. When Anna gets up she aims her arrow at the portrait of Nick, trying to hit him on the nose.

Darren's on a roll, dreaming up more games for the party. With a can of spray paint leftover from the task, he paints a grid of four large squares on the grass in the garden for a ballgame, then they have a practice. Soon afterwards at six o'clock Darren is called to the Diary Room. He tells Big Brother that the three of them are getting on really well; their silences are comfortable now that they know each other so well.

'It's a cool friendship, they are brilliant people. When we started there were ten people and you didn't get a chance to know everyone individually... We are now so close that whoever wins we will be happy for them. We've been telling ourselves we are all winners...

'I'm coping brilliantly. Last week after being nominated, my kids were brought down and I saw them after missing them for eight weeks and I can't stop thinking about them. Now I know I'll see them in two days I'm worried that they might not recognize me when I come out. But it's good to be so close because now I don't have to repress my thoughts about them any more.'

He says that being in the house has taught him how much he values being around his children. He knows that they will have changed in the two months he has been away. He says he is proud to have lasted the duration and if he did it again the only thing he would change would be to bring more clothes – because he hates washing them – and more after-shave.

Just after eight o'clock they each hear their chosen track. Big Brother asks them each to tell the others why they have chosen this particular song and to introduce it in the style of a radio DJ. They all feel that this last-minute instruction takes the icing off the cake and spoils the treat of the music. None of them makes much effort to sound like a DJ but they do tell the others why they chose the tracks.

Anna goes first having chosen 'Together in Electric Dreams' by Phil Oakley and Giorgio Morder. She introduces it by saying: 'I chose it because it reminds me of Edinburgh where I used to live and my friends up there and the friend I have in London. And I like to play this song when I am out of an evening... No, I don't like to play it when I'm out because I can't!'

She cracks up laughing, and Craig reminds her there are millions of people watching. 'I mean, it reminds me of a club in Edinburgh and I like it,' she says. As the Eighties classic kicks in, Craig shouts to Big Brother to crank up the volume.

'It sounds very corny now and I'm just going to sit here and go red...' says Anna.

Darren isn't impressed by her choice and admits he's never heard the song before. Anna says he probably wasn't even born when it came out and she assures them both that she does have other musical tastes.

Craig's choice is a Rod Stewart track, 'I Was Only Joking' – only Craig isn't sure if that's the title of the song he really wants: 'I've got the right song in my head but I think I put the wrong title to it. It's one of my favourite songs from when I was at school because it reminds me of the rare occasions I was at school. Hopefully I picked the right song. I hope to God it is. And that's about it really. We'll have to sit and wait to see if it is the right one.'

When the first couple of chords are played he erupts with joy: it is the right one. He accompanies Rod Stewart all the way; word perfect and Darren and Anna join in, waving cushions in time to the music.

Darren's choice is 'Good Life (Buena Vida)' by Inner City. 'The reason I chose this song to be played is because it is the song that my children performed a dance routine to for Michael Barrymore's *My Kind of Music*. And we kept pushing them and pushing them to get the routine right and they got fed up of it so many times and we gave them so many treats. We were really proud of them when they got up on stage and did it. It was wicked.'

He, like Anna, is embarrassed that the song does not sound so good out of context. Craig tells him to enjoy it: 'Close your eyes and visualize that day. Forget us, forget everyone else.'

Darren tells them that his son and daughter wore Chinese suits and that their dance routine, which involved martial arts movements, was perfected by his brother. Anna tries to persuade him to do the dance routine, but he won't.

At the end of their three songs, they beg Big Brother for more. Craig offers to stand on the table and do a striptease, but Big Brother does not relent and the house is quiet again.

They are all going to bed much earlier, partly because of the havoc Juanita has played with their sleeping patterns and partly because they are willing the hours away until Friday. As the final day gets closer, they spend more and more time thinking about life outside the house. Darren, who did not have an afternoon nap, goes to bed at quarter past nine. Anna and Craig stay up, she plays patience and he reads a well-thumbed magazine. They agree that this has been a long, horrible day.

'It's been the worst, the boringest day, nothing to do. I don't know what to do with myself,' says Craig.

Anna says she'd like to soak in a bath for an hour and Craig expands the fantasy: 'That would be nice... with nice music in another room... a few candles... Baileys... and a nice bird playing with your toes... I want to be on holiday, chilled out, sitting around while the sun goes down, sitting with someone between your legs, touching you, leaning on you. I can't wait to get out.'

He says 'Two more sleeps' and Anna repeats it like a mantra. Later on in bed, she goes through her photo album, her mind on the people outside the *Big Brother* house.

With only one full day left ahead of them, the three housemates are grateful to Big Brother for providing the Spanish party to divert them. It's a tense time, and they are all trying to find ways of getting through the final hours. When they get up on Friday morning, Craig reminds Anna that they have 'only one more sleep' to go and he tells her she will miss the place.

'I'll be secretly visiting every week, dressed in a hooded cloak.' she says.

She and Darren, the two smokers, are trying to make their tobacco last by not smoking until the party but they're both desperate so at quarter to two they roll a thin cigarette and smoke it between them.

Anna goes to visit Big Brother in the Diary Room. She says she's bored.

'We've got nothing to say to each other. We know we've only got another thirty hours to go. We're not talking because we make each other nervous. We can't have a conversation about nature or life. We want to stay relaxed. I'm nervous of saying hello to Davina, saying hello to friends, asking them if I looked stupid on television. Seeing people again will be so mad. The three of us will probably just walk around together, go to the bar...

'We're all readjusting our minds to going. It's completely different to other weeks, there's no stay-or-go aspect, you're just going... I just want Friday night to be here now with none of this fucking faffing around. Yesterday and today have been the worst for boredom, I couldn't be bothered to get off my arse. Tomorrow I'll be run off my feet.'

She says she chose the Spanish theme simply because she wanted some good food.

'I was going to have an Irish theme but then I thought: Irish stew and Guinness? And then I thought tapas.'

She says she'll miss Big Brother telling her what to do, and will have to get her flatmate to take over. And she warns Big Brother not to call her into the Diary Room tomorrow 'because I'll be hyper, la-la, lu-lu, talking rubbish.'

Darren takes a cushion cover into the Diary Room and asks Big Brother to fill it with surprises for their party – presents for winning pin the tail on the Spanish donkey.

Anna's boredom is so acute that she has taken to writing bizarre messages in matches. 'Help. We are being brainwashed. Anna, Craig and Darren left weeks ago. We are body doubles brought in from Lapland. We want to go home. Help us please,' she writes before shuffling the matches again, resisting – despite her boredom – the urge to count them.

They all join in with the preparations for the party, blowing up balloons and decorating the table. Big Brother calls Craig in and tells him how to arrange the crepe paper like a Spanish flag. At Darren's suggestion, Anna goes to the Diary Room to invite the Task Master and any of the others from the production team who would like to come to the party. Unsurprisingly, Big Brother does not take up her invitation.

There's great excitement when the costumes arrive. The boys both have mata-dor outfits encrusted with sequins. Darren describes the tight trousers as 'dick squeezers'. He and Craig fence around the kitchen wielding two cardboard tubes for swords. Anna has a beautiful red and white flamenco dress.

They make sangria and drink a toast to all the past residents of the *Big Brother* house. Then they enjoy the music with Craig and Darren both vying to dance with Anna to 'Like a Virgin'.

Craig's enjoying himself so much that he admits to the others, 'I'm trying to control me hard-on.' And when 'Erotica' was being played, they all agree it makes difficult listening for a group as sexually frustrated as they are. Despite this, they all beg Big Brother to play the album again but to no avail. The party ends with Darren and Craig painting on the walls. Craig paints a large star on the Diary Room door and Darren adds a face to the artwork on the walls.

At half past nine Craig goes into the Diary Room and thanks Big Brother for the party. He says that although yesterday was slow and awful, the party has really brightened up today.

'In all honesty, when I first got here I thought I had no chance of winning. Now I've got a one in three chance. Fingers crossed for tomorrow. I don't know how it's going to turn out. Just got to hold out until tomorrow,' he says.

Just over an hour later, Anna goes to talk to Big Brother. She tells him how she's looking forward to a bath and reading the newspapers. She says she felt sad when 'Like A Prayer' was playing, knowing that she'll miss some aspects of the house.

'The hardest thing has been biting my tongue to keep quiet when people have wound me up.' She says she is irritated by people, 'who are too forthcoming about the good deeds they do'. She makes a reference to Craig who has been lecturing her and Darren on the importance of carrying donor cards. She agrees with him but wonders why he was going on about it so much and she wanted to tell him to shut up. She says she goes off people who are constantly talking about the good deeds they do; she prefers modest, humble people who don't talk about their hardships.

She says she thinks they've all been lonely and because she doesn't find it easy to chat to people, it has been more difficult.

'If I win I will be so happy but it will be the biggest surprise in my life. Deep down I know I'm not going to win... It will be a surprise if I do, because I am protecting myself, convincing myself that I'm not going to win. If you presume you will lose, then everything else is a bonus. If you presume you are going to win, you can be very disappointed.'

While Anna and Craig play basketball, Darren takes his turn talking to Big Brother about how much he is looking forward to going home. When he comes out, the other two are talking about Frank Skinner and David Baddiel, prompted by Anna singing 'Three Lions'. Darren impresses Craig enormously by telling him that he met them while he was working at the Dome. Anna is less impressed: 'I never really liked their show.' she says. Darren then goes into the Diary Room to talk to Big Brother:

'I wanna see my family, my friends, my kids, everything. I look forward to life beyond the perimeter fence. I'm looking forward to a Jack Daniels and Coke.

'This is the biggest thing I've ever done and I've gone the duration... I'm going to hug my kids to death. I just want to have conversations with other people.'

He says the great thing about winning would not be the money, but thinking about how people had chosen him, but he feels he's already won just by being there.

'I'd be happy for Craig or Anna to win because we're so close. It's cool. It so doesn't matter, because I've done it... I'm privileged and proud to have been here for two months and one week. Yesterday was boring but I made myself do something to get over it. Now the thought of leaving tomorrow is a big incentive. I'm so chuffed and excited about it.'

He thanks *Big Brother* for choosing him.

At ten to midnight Anna decides to go to bed. She kisses both the boys and tells them she is going to bed for the last time in the house. They shout 'See you on Friday!' to her.

'We're going home. Can you believe it?' says Craig to Darren.

Their final day dawns dark and miserable: it is pouring with rain. Anna whistles 'Rain Drops Keep Falling on My Head' and then starts a discussion with the others about whether they would stay an extra night or two in order to leave in good weather. Darren, ever conscious of his clothes and his image says he would stay even though he's desperate to leave.

'Tonight is the biggest thing I have ever done and I might slip and break my neck... I dread seeing Davina in a mac.'

Anna says she would leave, 'If there was flooding, no show and if I was offered more money to stay.' Craig agrees with her.

'It's a good job I don't have a lovely eviction outfit. It's the worst day of the whole nine weeks, love it,' says Anna, who then imagines opening the door to find a boat waiting for them.

There's none of the anxiety of previous Fridays because they all know they are going to leave and they all have to pack. It doesn't take long.

There's no sign of a break in the weather and by quarter past three they are amused to see a cameraman on a crane, looking down over their garden. Both the man and the camera are muffled in waterproofs. They wave from the window to him, and eventually he waves back. It's a rare contact with the world that within a few hours will come crashing in on them.

Regardless of the weather, Darren is determined to have one last session in the hot tub. He spends ten minutes in there, the rain splashing down around him.

Anna has a final session in the Diary Room. Despite telling Big Brother yesterday that she will be in no condition to talk today, she's in a reflective mood.

'I've learnt to control my moods and I think of the little things now. I've relaxed in here. It's been hard. It's been easy. The whole thing has been a bizarre experience which I'm very glad I did.

'It's brilliant to be here in the last three... Everyone's in the same sort of mood, we're not letting ourselves get too anxious because we don't want to use up all our adrenalin and be exhausted before eight o'clock. We're keeping it nice and calm. When I have a moment to myself afterwards – when it's all died down – I'll probably have a nervous breakdown and sob uncontrollably. No, I'm only joking, I'll just have a swift g 'n' t and be fine.'

She jokes that she's going to leave wearing 'a sequinned boob tube, leather hot pants, stilettoes and a headband'. Then she says she will go for the other option: a pair of jeans, a black vest, trainers and a denim jacket.

After she leaves the Diary Room Darren reminds her that she was going to ask Big Brother for cigarettes. She goes back in and pleads in typical Anna fashion: 'If someone could just peg it down to Tesco I'll pay you back later. A few Marlboro Lights would be brilliant.' Twenty minutes later she is called back to the Diary Room: for once, Big Brother has relented and their request for cigarettes is granted.

The last few residents in the house have shared a joke that there aren't crowds of fans gathered outside on Fridays, just tape recordings of crowd noise played by the production team to keep their spirits up. Darren now adds to the artwork by drawing some tape recorders with umbrellas over them on the wall of the washroom. Anna is very amused and says it is her favourite piece of art from the whole house.

At 5.25 p.m. they are all called to the Diary Room together to hear a run-through of the plans for the evening shows. One of them – the one with the least votes – will leave during the early programme between 8.30 p.m. and 9.30 p.m. The other two will have to wait until the second show: 10.30 p.m. to 11.30 p.m., to find out who the winner is. Big Brother then speaks to each of them individually about their families and friends who will be there. There is good news for Anna: her partner will be there to greet her at the gate. When she walked into the house, Anna knew she had to be very careful not to mention her partner's name as her family and colleagues did not all know that she is a lesbian. But since *Big Brother* has been on the air she has told everyone and is dying to be reunited with Anna.

Anna tells the others quietly. Darren says he's keen to meet her.

'Stop it, she's MY girlfriend!' says Anna.

At quarter past six they open their last bottle of wine and drink a toast to each other. Anna plays 'It's Been a Hard Day's Night' on the guitar. The last couple of hours seem to drag and tension is beginning to mount by a quarter to nine – there is only fifteen minutes until the announcement that will tell them who will be the first of the three to leave the *Big Brother* house.

WEEK NINE FACT FILE

**MAIN TASK
PASS ☑ FAIL ■**
Mind, Body and Soul. The housemates must each do three different challenges individually: learning the Highway Code in seven hours; doing press-ups, running and basketball hoops to test strength, speed and stamina; and looking after a virtual baby, a sophisticated doll with a microchip which records how much attention they lavish on it.

MINI-TASK
Completing the newspaper they started last week. They pass and are rewarded with Chinese takeaway and a video, *The Bone Collector*.

PARTIES
Anna opts for a Spanish party for the last night. They get tapas, paella, flamenco and matador costumes, castanets, sangria and a Madonna album.

TREATS
Their favourite songs are played for them on Wednesday evening as a reward for completing the Mind, Body and Soul task successfully.

WHAT THE EXPERTS SAY

Although there are no nominations in the last week, it's interesting to look back at the way different members of the group tackle the business of naming two of their housemates each week. Dr Peter Collett and his colleague Tina Cook have come up with eight different categories of nomination reasoning:

1 *Difficulty* Several contestants talk about how difficult the nomination procedure is. Mel uses this method the most with phrases like: 'I hate to say this' and 'I'm really struggling with this.' She implies that nominations are unpleasant and that she'd rather not be doing them.

2 *No reason* This is used by housemates who want to suggest that they hold no grudges. Nick has used this method, implying again that he only nominates because he has to.

3 *Negative reasons* Craig excels at these: for example, he says Caroline 'has an annoying laugh' and Sada 'is selfish and extremely boring'.

4 *Positive features* This is another technique employed by Nick. He nominates but then says something good, like saying Sada and Caroline 'are both really nice people with hearts of gold'.

5 *Incompatibility* This is Anna's favourite reason: 'I get on with others better' she says several times, suggesting there is nothing wrong with the nominee, but she's been forced to make a choice.

6 *The team* Andy and Nick both use this, implying that they have the greater good of the whole group at heart by nominating those who don't pull their weight.

7 *Favours* This is Darren's method. He suggests he is being kind to the nominee: 'She's missing her mum' or: 'So he can see how his business is going,' or: 'So he can see his little brother race.'

8 *Qualifiers* Both Anna and Mel use phrases like 'I think' and 'I feel' which soften the blow. It sounds better to say 'I feel he's not pulling his weight,' than 'He's not pulling his weight.'

THE RESULT

Outside, the rain has been unremitting all day but the spirits of the 2,000 people who have turned up to watch the last three contestants leave the house are not dampened. They cheer, shout, clap and stamp when Davina appears. Over five million people have taken part in the telephone vote by the time the first of the three leaves and by the end of the evening, 7.7 million will have voted. For the early programme, screened between 8.30 p.m. and 9.30 p.m., there are 7.5 million viewers – more than 30 per cent of the total watching television at that time. At its peak, the programme attracts 8.2 million viewers – a 33.4 per cent share of the audience. The second show later in the evening, pulls in a phenomenal average of 9 million viewers, 46.5 per cent of the total audience and peaks at 10 million, which at 56.5 per cent is comfortably more than half of the total viewing public.

The three survivors sit together on one of the blue sofas, waiting for Davina to make the announcement. She pauses for what seems like hours before saying Darren's name. A look of delight spreads across his face. The others hug him hard, Anna whispering, 'I love you, I love you.' Unlike all the previous evictions, he has very little time to prepare: he has to leave the house in sixty seconds time. Knowing this, all three of them have their bags packed and ready.

As the door opens there are more hugs. For the first time all day, the rain has stopped, luckily for Darren who has chosen to leave dressed in white. Anna and Craig stand and wave but without the frenzy of previous weeks: they know that in the space of a couple of hours they too will be crossing the bridge to join their families and friends. Craig has made use of the paints to write a message: 'Kelly, Lauren, Bev, Mum, Robbie, Won't Be Long Now, Love Craig' on the door.

For the final night, a stage has been built outside the studio and Darren is whisked along by Davina, greeting his family, signing a few autographs, posing for a battery of cameras and then on to the stage, where he is received with wild cheers by the crowd. Then in a whirlwind Davina takes him into the studio where he sees a very touching video of his children welcoming him home. He's been told by Big Brother that the children will not be at the studio. But then Davina admits she's been 'doing a Nick', because his three children are there. There is an emotional reunion and Darren cannot hold back his tears.

In the time between Darren leaving and the final announcement of the winner, Anna withdraws into herself, becoming very quiet and thoughtful. She and Craig hug and when Anna says she thinks she will cry, he tells her to hold on and be strong. Craig busies himself cleaning up the kitchen and makes a cup of tea for them both. Just before the big moment, Craig dashes to the loo for a pee. Big Brother calls him back to the living area and he and Anna are clutching each other's hands, side by side on the sofa, when Davina's voice comes through. When Craig's name is announced as the winner he immediately says 'Anna's a winner as well.' Altogether 3,539,683 voted for Craig.

Then it's Anna's turn to be whisked away and Craig is left alone for ten minutes in the house. The ten have finally been reduced to one. The voting has been very close: Craig is only 2 per cent ahead of Anna. For Anna there is an ecstatic reunion with her partner, as well as other friends and family. Then it's into the studio to hear Davina tell her that George Michael wants to take her out for dinner and to discover that Kathy Burke, one of Anna's favourite actresses, has written her a letter that describes her as 'a top woman' and concludes with an invitation 'to come over for a cup of tea'.

On his own now, Craig paces around the empty house which has been his home for so long and in which he has never been alone before. He clears up the mugs he and Anna used, gets himself a glass of water and gives a thumbs-up to the camera.

Then it's his turn. Davina breaks with the show's traditions and goes up to the door and into the house. After offering to make tea for the cameramen, Craig gives her a guided tour that ends with her interviewing him in Claire's old bed. Then the final *Big Brother* contestant, the winner of the whole show, walks out of the house to be greeted by a spectacular fireworks display. Like all the others, he breaks into a run when he sees his close family and friends waiting at the gate to the *Big Brother* compound. But within seconds, Davina is dragging him away, to flash his familiar cheeky grin to the bank of press photographers and meet his cheering fans. It's on his way to the stage where he'll receive his £70,000 prize money that Craig sees Joanne Harris – she's a very special person to Craig, an eighteen-year-old with Down's syndrome. For the first time, viewers are told that Craig is donating all his prize money to a fund to take Joanne to the US for a heart and lung transplant. Because she has Down's syndrome she is not eligible for a transplant on the NHS and the total fund needed is £250,000. Craig's own donation will, he hopes, encourage others to raise the rest. It is a heart-stoppingly moving moment and tears well in the eyes of millions of viewers across the land: but there's no time to savour the emotion. There is only time for a quick hug for Joanne from Craig and then he's rushed to the stage.

After a few moments of solitary acclaim Craig is joined by all the other *Big Brother* housemates. All of them that is, except one: flanked by bodyguards, Nick arrives to make the presentation to Craig – the climax of nine weeks of *Big Brother*. And then it's over, the cameras stop rolling, the internet has nothing more to show and the house stands deserted.

The contestants, who have not been together since Sada's eviction have an end-of-show party afterwards. It is a strange and emotional experience for all of them, but particularly for the last three who have been cooped up in the house until Day Sixty-four. It's not quite over for them – they face a huge press conference the next day, with forty journalists and six television cameras focused on them.

Darren is first to speak after the press conference and graphically describes the events of the last twenty-four hours.

'All three of us were very calm. Normally on a Friday evening there would be a massive adrenalin rush, as big for the ones who were not up for nomination as for those facing eviction – just a huge surge of excitement. But we knew we were all going and we were all winners.

'When I heard my name all I could think was, 'Now I'm going out. This is it.' Then there was only sixty seconds and Craig and I hugged so hard with all our strength and we didn't say anything – but we didn't need to – then I grabbed Anna. I can't explain the feeling, you've been with these guys all this time and, yes, you want to go but you also want to say goodbye. With these people you've found a way to exist, they're important.

'Davina makes it all worthwhile, she's been my high every Friday evening. At ten to nine every Friday her voice came into the house and that was when you knew it was all real; it was all happening. We knew there were cameras staring at us all the time but they didn't seem real. Davina's a major celebrity so just hearing her voice was a big high every week.

'Meeting her was something else. She's got gorgeous eyes, she's so tactile, warm, on my level, just there. Seventy days ago I would have been star-struck meeting her but after being in the house and that reception from the crowd, I didn't feel at all nervous. And she makes it easy – I just worked off her.

'It was brilliant to see my family, they were wearing T-shirts with my name on and all grabbing me and rubbing my head. But I only got a minute with them; I had to put them to one side until later. There were so many press cameras to smile at and then the crowd – that was unbelievable. The highlight of the whole sixty-four days was standing on that stage and looking at all those people who came out in the pouring rain to see Anna, Craig and me. I loved it and I didn't feel nervous – I just gave it to them. Apart from seeing my daughter's birthday on video, this was the best moment in my *Big Brother* life.

'I wasn't nervous in the studio, although it was a strange moment when I saw myself on the screen. I looked away at first; I didn't want to see it.

'I've grown stronger in the house. Before I went in, the video of my kids would have made me cry. But I was able to hold it. But when they came on, I couldn't hold it. It was so good to see them. I whispered to them because I wanted this to be an occasion for them and me, forget the rest of you. I said, 'Let me see how much you've grown. Did you miss Daddy?' I told them I'd talk to them properly later on.

'Missing them was the toughest thing I had to handle in the house and I didn't take any pictures of them with me. I would have a little cry thinking about them and I talked about them to Big Brother a lot. But the best was being able to talk to a psychotherapist. He really helped me handle it. He told me I didn't need photos because I've got them in my head. He asked me if I could see them in my head and told me to use that ability to see them. I went to bed that night with a big smile on my face because all I could see was them. I learned to make it a joyful experience, missing them.

'That's why I was able to be joyful when I saw the video of them. And even though I cried, I made the meeting with them joyful, too.'

It was not only his children Darren was reunited with. He also met the other contestants.

'I was very excited, I couldn't wait to see them but it was a lot for me to handle. When I met them they were getting ready to go on stage, having their makeup done, and they were very into this celebrity lifestyle. They've adapted to it. Certain characters have changed and I looked at them and wondered whether that was because we were in a strange environment before or has celebrity changed them. I had to stand back and watch. Then I thought: 'OK, give me a week or two, then I'll be able to do this.' I told myself: 'Darren, you can't just come out and be like this, these people have had time to adapt.'

'Mel was brilliant because she only left the house a week before. She said, 'Are you OK? It's mad, isn't it?' I kind of clung to her; I was walking around with her. I'd walked out of a house only minutes before where we shared one KitKat Chunky between three of us, into this.'

Darren managed to break through the security cordon round the contestants to get to his children and family for twenty minutes and he kissed the children goodbye before they were taken home to bed. He arrived at the party with 'Welcome Home, Daddy' balloons stuck to his back.

'At the party there were so many people I've never seen before coming up and talking to me. Normally I love that sort of thing and I can handle it. Working at the Dome, I know all about greeting people. But I needed some space. I found an alcove to sit in, then I made my way across the room to see Tom but it took so long with so many people talking to me. In the end I went to the toilet and sat there for ten minutes, just to breathe. I looked in a mirror – a mirror without a cameraman behind it! I wanted to see who this Darren was that everyone was saying hello to, because I felt I was seeing everyone but myself. Then I took some good deep breaths, went back to the party for a couple of drinks and then said goodbye.'

All the contestants spend their first night of freedom in a hotel. Darren persuaded the driver who was taking him there to make a detour to his mum's home, where his children were sleeping.

'I wanted to see my mum. I rang her and she sounded so cool and laid-back – then I realized she thought she was talking to my brother! When I got to the house I just opened the bedroom doors a crack to see the children asleep. That was all I needed. I didn't kiss them or disturb them, just looked at them. Then I grabbed a leg of chicken – there's always food at my mum's – and jumped back in the car.'

Darren has no regrets about his time on *Big Brother* and feels 'very proud' of himself for going the whole distance. Before he went in, he prepared his children for his absence by writing little messages on the calendar for the whole nine weeks. On 15 September, the final night, he wrote 'Daddy's not coming out this day – because he's already out much earlier.' He even drew up a rota for the Gameboy and the camp bed to stop them squabbling.

'I concentrated on coaching them, I didn't coach myself enough. So I'm proud that I managed for two months and one week without even speaking to them on the telephone. I knew they would be well looked after. The mother of my children is the best mother in the world. But I so wanted to see them.'

Darren always refers to his ex-girlfriend as 'the mother of my children' rather than mentioning her by name as he wants to protect her from any undue attention. He feels it was his choice to go on *Big Brother* and that he alone should take any consequences that should arise from it.

'If it had worked out as a bad show with a lot of criticism I didn't want it to reflect on other people just because they know me. I'm a private person, I don't want to share the details of my private life with other people in the house or with millions of viewers.'

When he first went into the house he was surprised by its size, although the garden was smaller than he expected. Because of his height, he could see over the fence by standing on a chair.

'But all I could see was the second fence, and that made me realize we really were cut off from the world.'

When Davina asked him in the studio which one of the females in the house he fancied, she was expecting him to say Marjorie, the chicken. But instead he said Sada.

'I really liked Sada. We connected. She was missing her boyfriend badly and I was missing my children. She knew what I was going through. She'd just put a hand on my shoulder and say: 'How are you doing?' I was happy for her to go because she so wanted it, but I missed her.' He then went on to talk about the other housemates.

'Andrew left after Sada but I remember her much more clearly than him. I only spoke to him when we were in a group. He was very dedicated to the tasks and I didn't really connect. But he's cool.

'When I first met Caroline I did not find her funny but then one day her humour just clicked with me. She was making up funny words to the song Sada sang about the earth goddess. From then on I found her hilarious. The boys didn't really get her humour but I would hold my hand up and admit I thought she was really funny.'

Darren perhaps felt more strongly about the Nick saga than any of the group: 'I was angry because other people had been shown these names and they didn't do anything about it. He didn't show me names but he'd drop little phrases in, like poison. But I took no notice. I told him he was full of crap, bullshit, but in a friendly way, then we'd start play fighting.

'After we found the names I was still angry the next morning but Mel told me she had spoken to Big Brother about it and Tom said he had finally done something about it and Craig blew it open. So I was still really upset that they hadn't said anything earlier but I could accept what they were telling me.

'The second reason I was angry was because I was worried about there being enough money for the mother of my children. I never expected to be in the house so long and although the children would be fed and clothed, I wanted them to have extras for the summer. So I gave Caggie a note with the details of my Visa account. I wrote it in lipliner. But Big Brother saw me and called me in and took the note. I was told that if I used the girls' makeup again to write with, it would be confiscated.

'So I was really angry to find he'd been writing notes and getting away with it, and he had a pen or pencil which I needed. And I couldn't believe he came on a game show, surrounded by cameras and cheated.

'After the confrontation everyone was feeling sorry for him and saying he should stay. I was outraged. I didn't see how they could be saying that when he had shown their names, he had written my name on the blackboard for Craig. And Craig and Nicky were facing eviction, and he'd written their names. How could they all be feeling sorry for him?

'I went into the boys' room and he started crying. I didn't want his crocodile tears. I told him not to give me that crap. He stopped crying and became the old Nick, told me I was selfish. I thought, 'Right, this is strangling time,' and I started to walk towards him and Big Brother called me, just in time.

'Then when he was leaving, I was the last person he hugged and I was still angry. But I saw sorrow in his eyes. I hugged him and said I was sorry, but he's brought it on himself. Afterwards, we all missed him.

'When I saw him last night I said to him, "You're a fucking wanker, I'm so going to get you. I know you've been writing for a newspaper and if you've said anything nasty about me I'm coming for you." I said it in a jokey way, but he got the message.'

Darren did not know how much Nichola adored him until he left the house.

'She's brilliant. I fell in love with her beautiful eyes as soon as I saw her. I joined in with her art because I loved it. I didn't join in with the clay painting, that was only two days after we arrived and I wasn't stripping off – later on I wouldn't have given a monkey's. I wish we hadn't had that row, but we were always friends.

'Claire was a breath of fresh air, just what we needed to cheer us up and get us going. I got on really well with her; we like the same music, the same food.

'Tom was cool but I never really got close. At first he was very quiet and then he opened up and everything came out. Conversations with him were always very personal and that's not what I wanted, so I limited my contact with him to a group thing.

'Melanie leaving was one of my saddest days. She's just brilliant. I know she's been seen as a tease and a flirt, but it didn't seem like that at all in the house. She always had time for a chat, for fun. It sounds strange but we had fun making bread and biscuits. She was my Spice Girl, Feisty Spice.'

Of course it was Anna and Craig he ended up spending the most time with.

'Anna is the one I think I will still be in touch with in ten years' time. She kept me going, big-time. She's got a wicked sense of humour. But we could be silent together. I adored her. She's really beautiful to look at, too.

'I'm not too happy about Craig's practical jokes. When I heard he'd wiped his bum on my pillow I was furious. My whole family were outraged – they phoned in and complained and apparently my pillow was changed. I can't believe Craig did that or hiding the lighter and the cigarettes.

'But I've got to commend him for giving the money to Joanne. On the last day he said to me, "Just remember this name: Jo." I asked if it was a girlfriend and he said no. All he said was: "That's what I'm doing it for." Well done, Craig, it's a wicked thing to do.'

Just as Darren's biggest moment on coming out of the house is being reunited with his children, for Anna it is seeing her partner again. At the press conference she is asked questions about how it feels to be Britain's most famous lesbian and whether she sees herself as a role model for gay girls. She answers that she wasn't expecting this kind of attention.

'I went in as myself. I'm not very political... I'm not going to preach about it. But if people look at me in the way I live my life and take from that, good.'

Afterwards she says she is surprised and pleased that the general public who voted for her are obviously very tolerant of her sexuality.

'It's not an issue for me that I'm a lesbian and I never want it to be an issue. It's dawned on me in the hours since I've been out just how much support I've been getting and I'm so happy about it.'

She says that her girlfriend was very supportive of her decision to go in but also very wary: 'She thought the whole show was bizarre and that it could go really pear-shaped for me as a gay woman. Also, because her family did not know, we discussed it before I went in and decided I would not mention her name or anything about our life. It was horrible that I could not even say her name out loud. But in the end I did speak to Mel about her a bit.

'It may have been a good thing that I couldn't mention her, couldn't fall back on talking about my partner. In a group situation if someone does refer to their partner all the time it is adding another person to the group. Sada did it, and it worked against her.'

When Anna was nominated in week six she caught a glimpse of her partner cheering and waving when she crowded around the door as Tom was evicted.

'I cried after seeing her but I realized then that she was happy to come forward; it wasn't a secret anymore. But I thought she could be there just as my flatmate, not as my partner. I cried after that, I so wanted to be with her. But it was also lovely because I was really wanting to see her properly but also wanting to keep going in the house.

'On our anniversary I wore my special T-shirt but Tanya was outside with a loud hailer yelling my name and I never heard her. She tried so many ways of getting in touch with me.'

Anna says it is too early to make plans for her future but one thing that is certain is that she and her partner want to have children.

'I would really like to have a child. There are lots of options open to us, through sperm donation. We could have the father involved, or not involved. Tanya and I differ on that: I want the father involved, she doesn't. I think the child should have a choice of finding their father if they hate me after about twenty years.'

She has no regrets about her time in the house, even though it was more difficult than she anticipated.

'I didn't think I would be as lonely as I was, or as depressed, or that my emotions would have been so up and down. Because they were strangers I felt I couldn't really relate to them, not until the end. It takes me a while to fit into groups. By the sixth or seventh week I was comfortable being myself. I find it hard to be forthcoming with people I am not really close to. When I wanted to leave, Big Brother told me to speak to the group, which I would not have done otherwise. Even though I felt an idiot and hated myself for crying in front of people, I'm glad I did it.'

She, like Darren, deliberately held a lot of herself back.

'It was a form of self-protection. I wasn't going to open myself up to friendships or bond with people because I knew it was all temporary, it was only a game show. I did get very close to Mel but not until the last few weeks. In the beginning I was in the girlies' camp and I suppose it was envy more than anything that we resented how well Mel was getting on with the boys. We thought she was a flirt but she was just getting on with them.

'I can't believe she has had a bad press for teasing and flirting: she didn't realize she was being seen like that and neither did I. I would so defend her against those accusations. Everyone fell for Mel. Those boys would run over each other to get to her. Not just Andy and Tom, but Darren and Nick and Craig, too. She'd chat to them all exactly the same.

'Mel is very well balanced, very mature, very sorted. Of all the people in the house, she's the one I would most like to stay in contact with.'

She didn't have time to get to know Sada well and she believes she found the *Big Brother* experience the most difficult: 'It changed the dynamic of the group for the better when she went.'

'Andrew, I didn't click with. I was surprised when he was evicted but glad it was him, not Caroline. He was very sure of himself. Perhaps his sleazy talk upset the voters. He always seemed very comfortable with what he was saying.

'Caroline cracked me up. She's a real in-yer-face lady – whatever thought is in her head she says it. A lot of people couldn't handle it but I loved it. I'm not like that myself but I love up-front people like her. And she was so funny. She told us stories about her life, and it hasn't been easy, but she deals with it by making the stories funny, but they're also very touching.'

Anna wasn't impressed by Nick's humour.

'It was like him: very arrogant, very condescending, picking on people's flaws and weaknesses in a clever way. He'd just say one sentence and it would make you laugh, but the thought would stay in your mind. I have absolutely no desire to ever see him again. I was so upset by the stories he told, the lies. And his attitude. When he was asked why he cheated he shrugged and said, "A lot of athletes these days take drugs."'

She describes Nichola as 'full-on twenty-four hours emotional'.

'She would express how she was feeling with screaming, language we couldn't understand. When she's wound up she can never finish a sentence and it ends 'veuva, veuva, veuva.' That's how she got the nickname. We'd be calling for the veuva interpreter every time she lost it. I never got close to her; she's very defensive. Everything about her is intense. She's even intense when she's meditating: her meditation is not a calming experience. It's electric meditation.'

Anna found Tom difficult to talk to, 'I never had a proper conversation with him. He made statements rather than discussing things.' But she did get on with Claire.

'She's lovely, a little star. We couldn't have asked for anybody better to come into the group. She portrays herself as ditzy but that's not her. But I think it works to her advantage, because people are pleasantly surprised to find she is an intelligent woman, as well as having this cute image.

'Craig was delighted with her and I think her two weeks in there saved his sanity. They were the two biggest chatterboxes, Craig could tell all his anecdotes all over again to her. She probably thought me and Mel were the most boring girls in the world but we were all very settled and slowed down by the time she came in.'

Darren and Anna got on extremely well, and were very in tune with each other's humour and music. 'Darren's a fun guy with a great sense of humour. I didn't get close to him personally because he stayed closed off about his private life, which I think is a quality. I had no need to know about his personal life. He talked about himself, he was very able to express his feelings and he could contribute to any discussion. He just kept private information private and I respect him for that.

'He has a great sense of humour and I love his quirks. He's a control freak; everything has to be in its place and he likes routines. On Friday evenings we always opened our bottle of wine at 8 p.m. On the evening of Craig and Claire's nomination, Claire suggested we open the wine at 5 p.m. I told her to watch for Darren's reaction: he couldn't understand why we had broken the routine.'

Anna was not at all surprised by Craig's victory.

'I chose him to win in the first week. He has all the qualities. He's good-natured, hunky, likes a laugh, cheeky. He survived because the public loved him, because he came up for eviction so often and they voted him in. I was the opposite: I survived because I didn't come up for the vote except once. I was more of a house person: Craig was more of a public person.

'You can't have a deep conversation with Craig, he just exchanges information with you or tells you another anecdote. He doesn't have much depth. But he's very likeable. What he has done with the money is sound, marvellous.'

Craig's plan to give the money to Joanne's appeal fund was hatched long before he went into the *Big Brother* house but he was forbidden to mention it in there. The production team felt it might distort the voting, as people would see a vote for Craig as a vote to help Jo. News of his intention was published in his local paper and after it was announced on the show every newspaper in the land carried details of the appeal.

'Thinking about Jo gave me a determination to win,' he says, 'although I was really surprised when I did. I hoped I'd stay in the house long enough for people to know my name, so I could do charity events to raise money for her. But now I can do those as well as handing over the prize money, which is just great.'

Jo is cousin to Craig's best friend, Lee McCarthy, who has been one of his closest mates since they were at junior school together in Liverpool. Jo's family have known Craig's family 'for longer than I can remember' he says and he's come to know her very well.

'She's unique, a very special person. She does everything normal – she went to a normal school and she joined the Brownies and she likes music and dancing. But she's got a heart condition that means she's now ill a lot of the time and needs oxygen. That's why I didn't really expect her to be there when I came out. I hoped she would be, but I wasn't expecting it. It was great seeing her there.'

Craig was never tempted to walk out of the house – partly because of his determination to do well for Jo and partly because 'when I filled in my application form I apologized for my spelling and I wrote, "I won't let you down. I'll do my best." And that's what I did.'

'When the show was halfway through, I changed my focus from staying in for a few weeks to getting through to the end but I still didn't expect to win.'

He found the *Big Brother* house bigger, cleaner and better equipped than he imagined it would be: 'It didn't stay clean – although I did my best on that score. It was weird being in there. At first you are very aware of the cameras, you hear them buzzing and you see them following you around, but then you get more relaxed, but you never completely forget. Sometimes you are more off guard than others.'

True to his straightforward nature, he won't discuss the personality traits of his other housemates, insisting that they all got on well.

'I liked them all but in different ways. They brought different things to the group. Some liked to train with me, some liked to cook, to chat. There were all different reasons for liking them.'

Even his row with Caroline was, he says, only a 'mild disagreement'.

'I don't think people outside can realize how little things become very irritating in there, when you can't walk away. You are in such a confined space, denied so much – your friends, family, television. You become irritable and so do the people around you.

'I can deal with problems and stress in normal life and I dealt with them in there, but it was harder.

'I didn't agree with Nick's methods and I told him what I thought at the time. But I met him again when I came out and we shook hands and I don't have any hard feelings. I'll be happy to see him again, have a drink. Hopefully we can smooth everything out.'

He says he did think about Claire after she had gone and admits that he sent signals to her by pulling his ear.

'I'm very flattered and feel very privileged that she's fond of me, that's a nice feeling. She's a lovely girl, and I do want to see her – I want to see all of them.'

He says that although both Darren and Anna found the last week long and quite difficult, for him all the problems were in the early weeks.

'There were people who were thinking of walking out and I played a part in talking them out of it, which gave me a bit more strength to cope myself. When you are trying to help or advise someone else, you are also convincing yourself. I gave Anna a packet of chocolate biscuits and a Snickers bar to cheer her up when she wanted to go.'

He enjoyed all the tasks and challenges, especially the physical ones. Although he started the bike challenge thirty hours after the others, he put in extra shifts and made up the hours he missed.

'I even did half an hour for Caroline and then she attacked me for being lazy.'

Now he's planning to do a real-life cycle ride from John o' Groats to Lands End, 'I wasn't a cyclist, but doing the task has shown me that I quite enjoy it and I'd be happy to have a go. Doing physical things helped me to become mentally stronger.'

He says he thought about home every day and the time he had to think about his life has helped him put things into perspective.

'I've looked at what I have done and what I am doing with my life in a way I've never had chance to do before. I've looked at what I've achieved, who's closest to me, who's helping me, supporting me. It's made me realize how I don't give enough time to the people I love. I can easily work 100 hours a week, with no time to remember what I ate the day before or what materials I ordered. Now I've realized that what I want out of life is more than work. I've been too wrapped up in work, missed out on family birthdays, other events. I fell into the trap of putting things off because of work pressures and in the end you never do them.

'Now I'm aware of how fast life is going and I've told myself I'm going to take more time out to appreciate the important things.'

The most important thing is his family: his mother, his stepfather Robbie, his sister Bev and her two daughters, ten-year-old Kelly and eight-year-old Lauren.

When Claire left the house he gave her a message to pass on to his mother, to tell her that he loved her and was sorry he didn't say it to her more often.

Another person he is very fond of is Shelley, the girlfriend he told Big Brother about on the tenth anniversary of them first becoming close. When they split up they agreed that one day they would get back together again and marry.

'That was just our fantasy, I don't know whether it will happen. But it was great to see her when I came out of the house and I can't wait to have a good talk with her. She's one of my very best friends, a brilliant friend.'

Whether it is to Shelley or not, he wants to get married one day and have children.

'I won't be calling my daughter Juanita! Juanita turned me grey. But at least I've now got some experience of holding the baby, thanks to *Big Brother*.

'There's lots of things I can thank *Big Brother* for. Most of all, for choosing me and letting me have this experience. And I want to thank the public for voting me the winner. It's great. Whatever happens now, I'm going to enjoy it.'

IT'S OVER

It's over. The three surviving contestants have spent sixty-four days – the whole of the summer – in the *Big Brother* house. Millions more feel they have spent their summer in there too: logged on and switched on to every bit of action, every hint of romance, every nuance in the relationships between the eleven people who carried their suitcases over the threshold. We've had high drama, tension, rows, tender moments, depressions and exaltations. By the end of it, we know the people in there as well – perhaps better – than we know our own families.

For the *Big Brother* production team, it's been a marathon that started months before the show went on air. They've worked round the clock seven days a week, to bring more than forty hours of television to the nation plus a twenty-four-hour live webcast. In terms of the technical and editorial systems needed to produce it, there has never been another programme like it. But also, there has never been another programme like it in the way it has caught the popular imagination. Whole forests of newsprint have been dedicated to it; it has been the main talking point in pubs, restaurants, shops and offices; it has caused nightmares for employers who have had to close down their internet connections to stop the staff logging on when they should be working. Teenagers have staggered bleary-eyed and pale back to school at the end of a summer holiday spent watching *Big Brother*. It has sparked serious debates on radio and television, as well as hours of spin-off fun as the stars of the show have guested on other programmes.

E-mails for the contestants have flooded into *Big Brother* at a rate of 1,500 per day. There have been loads of unofficial websites carrying news, gossip and fan material. There have been sophisticated attempts by outsiders to rig the voting and downright bribery, such as the gym that offered a free session to anyone who phoned the Claire eviction line (thereby keeping Craig in the house). The website team has been overwhelmed with poems about the contestants, suggestions for tasks for them to do, jokes about them and stories from old school friends and workmates.

Although everyone connected with the programme knew that it was a good formula and it has worked well in other countries, nobody predicted the enormity of its success. Peter Bazalgette, creative director of the production company, Bazal, sums up its appeal as 'a riveting, revealing personality contest with the added spice for everyone of being able to take part.'

Executive producer, Ruth Wrigley shares his feelings: 'In twenty years in telly, I've never experienced anything like it,' she says. 'It's a brilliant format. It's about people-watching, which is something we all love to do. It has elements of a soap opera, of a game show, of a documentary. The nominations procedure means there have always been highs and lows because basically we were saying to them, you can love these other people and you've got to live with them and pull together to complete tasks, but at the end of the day you've got to nominate them to be kicked out.'

It is the rhythm of the nominations that has given highs and lows to every week in the house, with the air-punching delight of the survivor providing a contrast to the shock (and sometimes relief) of the contestant who was given their marching orders on Friday evening. Afterwards, came the slump of all the housemates, as another empty bed appeared in one of the bedrooms, followed by the relative calm of Sunday when the task and the shopping dominated the day. Then there was tension on Monday, when names had to be named, and more stress on Tuesday until the results were announced. Wednesday and Thursday were relatively quiet days, although at least two of the residents knew that their fate was being decided by the viewers' votes. Friday was the most difficult day of all; with the high emotions of saying farewell and the excitement of the crowd and the outside world spilling into the house as the surviving contestants got glimpses of family and friends cheering from a hundred yards away. This was then followed by the realization that they were, for another week at least, back in the *Big Brother* loop.

However, despite the strains that life in the house put on them, the contestants unanimously agree that it was a great experience and if they had their time over they would do it again. 'Fabulous', 'brilliant', 'amazing', 'fantastic' are the words they use about it. Even Nick, who left the house under a cloud, feels it was 'a great idea and fun to be part of'. They went in unknown and came out with the kind of fame and celebrity it takes showbiz hopefuls years to achieve. For all of them, it has offered the chance to change the direction of their lives, if they choose to.

They were all, with the exception of Claire, hugely surprised to find out just how big the programme became, how well-known they were, and how half the nation was talking at bus stops and in trains, often to complete strangers, about the goings-on in the *Big Brother* house. They knew they were going into a television show but had no idea that the minutiae of their lives would be the biggest talking point of the whole summer.

Everyone has their favourite moments, some of them funny, some dramatic, some romantic. Perhaps the images that will be remembered most vividly are the discovery of Nick's notes by Darren, followed by the confrontation in which Craig starred as chief prosecutor; Nick's tears in the bedroom or the shots of him walking away from the house and going out through the back door instead of across the bridge to the cheers of the crowd and a hug from Davina. However, there are plenty of others: the kiss between Mel and Andy, Mel being massaged by Tom – and his erection; her final tender goodbye to him, with a kiss. There are more touchingly close moments, such as those between Craig and his soulmate, Claire, who spent hours together in the hot tub. There's the naked clay painting, so early in their time in the house and with so many of them romping around without clothes. There's the songs, including those made up by Darren and Anna, Sada's goddess song, the 'Only a Game Show' reprise during nominations and their own masterwork, 'D, C and G'. Another moment of high drama apart from the unmasking of Nick, is perhaps the first real row in the house which takes place between Caroline and Craig and continues for two days. There's the shock of Darren's nominations being heard and his changing the names on the re-run. And who will ever forget Caroline's raucous, ear-shattering laugh? And Darren's magic moments with Marjorie, the most famous chicken in Britain (she's even got a website devoted to her)?

At the beginning of the programme, the press rushed to condemn it as voyeuristic and made much of the fact that people were switching on their TVs or logging on to the net in the hope of seeing the residents in the shower, on the loo or in bed with each other. But the show was never about these elements. There was a camera in the lavatory not because there was ever any intention to broadcast the film but simply to stop the toilet being used as a refuge away from the all-seeing eye of Big

Brother. Glimpses from the shower were used, but they were shot from above and always discreet – there was no vicarious nudity. As for bed scenes, if they had happened the cameras would have been there to record them. However, there was nothing more dramatic than Claire and Craig having an under-the-duvet cuddle.

What the programme is about is all human life – the day-to-day interaction of people with each other. It is like every office you have ever worked in, every team you have ever played in, every club you have ever belonged to, every class-room you have ever been in. The fascination is watching the characters relate and react to each other, seeing them develop, seeing them play each other off, watch-ing cliques and schisms develop. And because you can see it from all perspectives, it is even more compelling.

Ruth Wrigley believes that the show has worked beyond all expectation because of the people who went into the house. It would always have worked but without their combination of personalities, it would not have achieved the same addictive watchability.

'The one thing that hurt me was some of the early press coverage, which suggested we could have chosen better people. We were criticized for choosing them because of the way they looked and because they were seen as wannabes, trying to kickstart their own show-business careers.

'In fact, we chose them all because we liked them. They are all different and that was important but, essentially, what won them a place in the house was if we liked them. I don't think if they had been plastic showbiz wannabes they would have intrigued and enthralled the public they way they have.

'I think it was at the time of the Nick debacle that their characters came through. We saw how strong and essentially nice they were. I think if they had been one-dimensional, people would not still be talking about them after nine weeks.'

For Ruth and the rest of the team, there was a feeling of relief when the first few programmes had gone out.

'The hardest work was setting everything up. My toughest months were March and April. But until it started running there was always this "Will it work, will it work?" question at the back of my brain. I felt huge relief when we did the trial run with stand-ins inside the house because I realized that the technical systems were working, but also because I found myself compelled to watch whatever they were doing in there – and these were people I wasn't especially interested in.

'Once we were on air, it was a matter of being able to churn it out. The team was superb. It must be a first to bring together such a big team and find that they all grow into their roles. It was a near vertical learning curve for all of us. But everyone handled it superbly and I only had one 3 a.m. phone call.'

That call was, of course, the night that Darren found Nick's notes in his suit-case. Ruth told the producer on duty to tell them in Big Brother's voice that they should sleep on the affair and talk about it in the morning. That's what they did, giving everyone a chance to prepare for what turned out to be one of the most dramatic events of the whole year on television, not just the *Big Brother* run.

'Nick was the biggest surprise of the whole thing. He was chosen to balance the group, as a slightly older, middle-class, educated male. Out of all of them, I thought he would be the first to be voted out. I thought that he would be very underwhelming and not at all popular in the house or outside the house. I got that one wrong!' says Ruth.

But she doesn't reckon the production team got any of the contestants wrong. The final three in the house were, she thinks, a fantastic combination. She is full of praise for the winner, Craig:

'Craig is a great winner. He didn't shine out in the first few weeks but I always knew he had great strength. He came to the fore during the Nick debacle when he took control. He was a hero, the way he acted round the table when they confronted Nick. He didn't humiliate him but he was firm and fair. That's when he won the heart of the nation.

'Then the fun side of him came out when Claire joined, even if it left him a little bit down after she left. He's a super person, a very straightforward man of great honesty and integrity and those are the qualities the public recognizes in him. He said to us from the beginning that he wanted the money for charity and I feel sure he'll use his fame to do more work for others. And I expect he'll be the most popular builder in the north west!'

Ruth also believes both of the runners up would have made a worthy winner:

'Anna is just a great person. She's bright, talented and she's got a wicked sense of humour. She got more into my head – into *Big Brother*'s head – than any of the others. She really knows what she is doing. The only thing I can't answer about Anna is why she did it in the first place: she and Tom were the two least likely members of the household.

'She has a very real musical talent and I hope she'll now go on to a great future in the music business. Perhaps a single with George Michael?'

'Darren is Mr Charisma. He's funny, gorgeous and he's absolutely devoted to his children. Some of the others in the house have accused him of being selfish and vain – but show me a man who isn't. He brought a lot of fun to the house because he's really just a big kid and all the girls in there loved him and got on well with him. Just looking at him cheered me up every morning. I think he will go on to a great career – modelling, presenting television shows – or even becoming a celebrity cook. After all, it's Darren's meals which have kept the others going.'

One of the amazing things about *Big Brother* is that it has not simply been a television sensation but it has truly been a multimedia package, with the website becoming Britain's biggest site just over a week after it was launched, soon overtaking all European sites. It received between 3 and 3.5 million hits every day, and on the day of the Nick drama it received 7.5 million, an enormous number of hits for an individual site. Not only were more people using it, but they were staying on-line for longer, averaging fourteen and a half minutes, compared to between thirty and sixty seconds average for other sites. At any given moment of the sixty-four days, 8,000 on-line video streams were being watched around the world.

It also pushed the frontiers of telephone voting, with the final contest between Darren, Craig and Anna more than doubling the record set by the vote for Mel the previous week. The appeal of the series was universal: research shows that viewers from across the social spectrum have been tuning in, although there is a marked bias towards younger people, with seventy-five per cent of all the sixteen to thirty-four year-olds in the country tuning in at the same time. Viewing figures were so healthy that Channel 4 achieved its highest share of the weekly television market in its entire eighteen-year history.

'Big Brother's real significance is that it is a paradigm for content in the twenty-first century because it works across at least four media,' says Peter Bazalgette. 'It drives viewers to free-to-air television, it drives viewers to the web, it was the second most popular service on Orange WAP phones (which provided an update service) and it was a massive event for the press. The hunt is now on for more big ideas that can create a dominant event in television schedules, dramatically increase ratings and exploit all the media in one go.'

Channel 4 is already planning a follow-up programme to see how the eleven *Big Brother* survivors get on in the outside world, especially after the first frenzied rush of publicity is over. Will Tom settle back to life on the farm? Will Caggie and Nicky enjoy sharing a flat – and will Caggie land a recording contract? Will Sada break into movies? Will Craig and Claire ever get it together away from the eyes of the cameras? Will Mel enjoy a snog with either Andy or Tom? Will Darren miss Marjorie? Will Anna find a home for her talents in the music industry? Will they all remain friends with each other? Will they keep in touch with Nick?

After taking them into our homes for so long, these are the questions that everyone wants to know the answers to. The *Big Brother* contestants have been part of our lives for the whole of the summer of 2000. The weather may not have been brilliant, but the telly was!

BIG BROTHER

THE ORIGINAL SOUNDTRACK

FEATURING
LEFTFIELD
UNDERWORLD
ORBITAL
GROOVE ARMADA
MOBY

& THE THEME
TRACK TO THE TV
SERIES PRODUCED BY
PAUL OAKENFOLD
& ANDY GRAY

DOUBLE CD
SINGLE CD/CASSETTE
OUT NOW